International Finance
and
Global Macroeconomics

International Finance
and
Global Macroeconomics

Sukumar Nandi, Ph.D.
Professor of Economics
Indian Institute of Management
Lucknow

Saṁskriti

SAMSKRITI
C-9020, Vasant Kunj, New Delhi-110070

© Author 2003

ISBN: 81-87374-24-1

Typeset by Vaibhav Graphics, New Delhi
Printed at Shivam Offset Press, New Delhi
Published by M. Sengupta for Samskriti, New Delhi

CONTENTS

Preface

"Many such autumns faded in haze of time
The harvested crop
Time and again,
Instead of being sent home,
Gone away to foreign shores
Neat and clean"

["The Sailing" in *The Seven Stars Nights*, by
Jibanananda Das, translated from Bengali]

The world's economy has undergone fundamental changes during the last two decades. The volume of international trade in commodities and services has increased manifold. The participation of the developing countries has increased impressively. Trade as a vehicle of economic growth has been adopted as the dominant paradigm and developing countries have been pursuing it with all seriousness. The dissolution of the USSR has resulted in the emergence of a number of countries who are busy in transforming themselves to market economies. In the milieu of these changes several important trends have emerged which are as follows:

First, the seriousness of the attitude of the developing countries to capture a share of export markets has resulted in keen competition that is revealed in prices and quality of the products. Since exchange rate is a component in international prices, many developing countries have tried to keep their currencies undervalued. Often a competitive devaluation of the currencies of such economies is also noticed.

Second, the global financial markets have been characterized by chronic instability. This has been the result of two forces – the flexible exchange rate regime after the breakdown of the Bretton Woods Agreement in 1971 and the emergence of fund managers on the international platform. This has created immense problems for the small developing countries regarding the stability of their exchange rates and the world is experiencing one crisis after another.

Third, many developing countries including the so-called transition economies have adopted US dollar as a second medium of exchange in their domestic transaction. This dollarization has posed a new challenge to the economists and they are busy to analyzing its implications.

Fourth, since the middle of 1980s international capital flow has become a dominant force and many countries are using foreign capital to supplement their meager capital base in the effort to accelerate economic growth. Thus foreign direct investment has been a critical component in the strategy of economic development.

The above analysis shows the areas of economic discussion that are the recognized domain of open-economy macroeconomics. This is termed as international finance. The importance of this subject has increased, thanks to the new developments in the world capitalist development. The discussions in the classes of business schools and university departments are based on books written mostly in the context of the country to which the author belongs to. And India is not there. This void is to be bridged and the present book is an attempt towards this end.

The problems of international finance emanate from the domestic economic disequilibrium of the country concerned at the micro level. This is important as the external problems of the country are the spill-over of the domestic problems. Because of this the problems of the open economy have been discussed with adequate rigour. Though this book is written with the text book model in mind, some of the topics are the results of the research carried out by the author. For example, the chapter on *Foreign Direct Investment* that is based on research carried out by the author with two young colleagues

– Dr. Biswajit Nag and Dr. Soma Mukhopadhayay, Assistant Professors of Indian Institute of Foreign Trade, New Delhi.

This book is written for the students who take International Finance as an elective course, and the students of the economics departments of the universities who are specializing in international economics. The core chapters of the book can be covered in one-semester course. The students should have an exposure of elementary economic theories for better understanding of the topics covered in the book. Some of the topics will be of interest to the researchers and professionals who want to specialize in International Economics.

There has been a continuous request from the students to get the lecture notes published for its wider dissemination and a reluctance on my part for lack of time and other priorities. Finally, for the students I have added a few chapters to the notes I used in my classes. Because of this, the present book is dedicated to my students.

As an author I owe intellectual debt to the leading economists in the area of international economics whose ideas have nurtured me for the last three decades. Also I owe intellectual debt to my teachers of the Economics Departments of Calcutta University and Utah State University. I would like to thank all of them. I would also like to thank my colleagues at Vidyasagar University, West Bengal, National Institute of Bank Management, Pune, Indian Institute of Foreign Trade, New Delhi, Indian Institute of Management, Lucknow, for their cooperation and support. I would also like to thank my students whose inquisitive queries induced me to think more.

Finally, I thank my wife, Karabi, for her moral support. My daughters — Susmita and Nabanita, continuously urged me to finish the manuscript through phone and writings while remaining busy in their own studies at a distant place. I thank them too. My sincere thanks are due to my publisher, Samskriti, and specially Shri M. Sengupta for his professional efficiency and seriousness to bring out the book in its present form.

Despite my best efforts some errors may remain for which the usual caveat applies.

July, 2003

Sukumar Nandi
Indian Institute of Management
Lucknow

Dedication

To all my students — past, present and future

One

Introduction

"....the problem of rational economic order is determined precisely by the fact that knowledge of the circumstances of which we must make use never exist in concentrated or integrated form, but solely as dispersed bits of incomplete and frequently contradictory knowledge which all the separate individuals possess. The economic problem of society is thus a problem of the utilization of knowledge not given to anyone in its totality".

[Friedrich Hayek, 1945; p. 519]

The volume of international trade all over the world has increased significantly in recent times as the spate of globalization increases. Indian economy has also undergone reforms and the government has initiated conscious efforts to increase the share of India in world trade. Along with the expansion of international trade in merchandise, there have been significant changes in the nature and structure of merchandise trade, in the trade of services and in the world financial market. The combined effects of all these changes have initiated strong waves in the international financial system, and that is reflected in severe financial crises in some countries during the last two decades. Even now some countries like Argentina and Russia are struggling hard to come out of the financial crises that have strong external connections.

The world financial system has become very complex. Last two decades have also seen the successful formation of trade blocs like European Union (EU), North America Free Trade Area (NAFTA), and ASEAN. Some other blocs are also in the process of formation. World has also seen the disappearance of a dozen currencies that are replaced by the new entry of Euro, the sole currency of European Union. Impact of these changes on the world economy as a whole is yet to be ascertained.

1.1 International Linkages in Financial Markets and Contagion

During the last five years the world economy has experienced financial contagion. One may trace the financial turbulence through a chain of financial events that include the collapse of a speculative real estate bubble in Bangkok. The latter surfaced in the guise of the default of the Somprasong Land Euro-convertible in January 1997. That this default can create shock waves that will rock the currencies of countries like South Korea, Indonesia, Estonia and as far as Brazil could not be imagined even a decade ago. The velocity of this contagion shows the degree of integration of the leading financial markets of the world.

The term 'contagion' means transmission of disease from one body to another. Sometimes it refers moral corruption. In recent times the question of contagion is better addressed at two levels. First, contagion can be addressed at the cross-market level, or, how volatility in one market transmits to other market. Second, contagion can be explained at cross-country level, i.e., contagion crosses political boundaries through the linkages of markets.

Regarding the cross-market level, speculative pressure in the currency market sometimes becomes so severe that the central bank of the country is compelled to impose restrictions on swap transactions. But this inadvertently translates the demand for domestic currency to selling pressure in the equity market. This happens because currency speculators use the equity market to raise funds required to cover the short positions in domestic currency. Thus volatility is transmitted from currency market to equity market and this exactly happened in the case of south Asian currency crisis.

Regarding the cross-country contagion one opinion is that the transmission channels of contagion had been super active through the dynamics of devaluation in an effort of maintaining competitiveness in international trade. The initial depreciation of the Thai baht and some other currencies within Asia resulted in the depreciation of the real exchange rates of these economies. This caused an increase in the relative competitiveness of these economies *vis-à-vis* other emerging market economies. Now the chain effects started. The currencies of the emerging market economies became over-valued *vis-à-vis* the currencies of the first group of countries and as a consequence these countries came under pressure for the depreciation of currencies. The cross-country contagion had its full impact.

The understanding of the implications of the world financial system requires a good command over the subject called open economy macro-economics. This can be treated as the basics for international finance. The starting point has been the domestic money market and then analysis has progressed to explain the links to international markets. Open economy macroeconomics is a subject in itself and this chapter presents the basic principles that piece together the important parameters influencing the different series of events in international markets.

Foreign exchange markets are the place where the pulse of the external sector of the economy is felt, and perhaps for this reason the book on international finance starts with the analysis of this market. It is said that sun never sets in the foreign exchange markets of the world. Monday morning trade starts in Sydney and by the time Monday closes at the foreign exchange markets of SanFransisco, Sydney prepares for Tuesday trade. Different types of trade including spot and forward have been discussed in the book.

Once the reader becomes familiar with the functioning of the foreign exchange markets, knowledge of the dynamics of the movements of the exchange rates becomes an imperative.

The theories of the exchange rate movements have also been discussed here. There are two principal schools of thought in the literature regarding exchange rate determination — the monetarist school and the Keynesian school. But exchange rate is one area where successful synthesis of the two strands of thought is seen in some famous models. The principal models have been analyzed in lucid detail without sacrificing the rigour.

In the area of international payments process banks have a very important role. The functioning of international banks and the structure of the world financial markets have also been elaborated. Offshore banks have assumed significant importance in today's world of financial intermediation. Three important issues — determinants of international banking, international debt crisis with some Latin American experiences, and the new phenomenon 'dollarization' have been explained in detail. The reader with some background in macro-economics will find the discussion interesting.

Exchange rate is also a price and its fluctuations should influence the bottom lines of any firms who have exposures to international transactions. This aspects of risks, known as currency risks, is taken care of with the help of hedging instruments like forward cover and the like. These are also known as derivatives.

Central banks on behalf of their governments issue currencies against limited backing and these fiduciary issues are the liability of the central banks. But central banks gain income as the liability has zero interest and this is known as seignorage in the literature. This aspect has assumed importance in the literature in recent time in the perspective of dollarization in many countries and also US dollar is a second currency in many developing countries. This issue has become important in view of the emergence of Euro as the single currency of European Union consisting of twelve members in the beginning and the members except United Kingdom have adopted Euro as the currency replacing their earlier currencies. But the countries are sovereign and there is no political union.

The operations of multinational corporations have changed in view of recent globalization. There has been a debate whether the activities of the multinational firms impinge on the sovereignty of the nation.

Along with US dollar being adopted in many countries as the official currency, the issues has come in the literature as to what extent US monetary policy influences the policies of other countries and whether interest rates of the countries converge to the US interest rate. With the convergence of the interest rates of different countries with the US one is related to the world capital mobility and the maintenance of a particular interest rate is part of an overall policy constraint every country faces.

Recently, there has been a large body of literature in open economy macro-economics that has extended its horizon. This literature has been placed lucidly in this book. The models have been explained without the mathematical explanations, and the inter-relations of different models have been explained.

Foreign direct investment is an important area of international finance at present and many developing countries are eager to get foreign capital to supplement their meager investment base at home. The Government of India has been active recently to attract foreign capital with the liberalization of the domestic economy.

In the Appendix things like the LTCM story, Asian currency crisis have been discussed.

1.2 Why International Finance

During the last two decades the financial integration of the world economy has been rapid on an unprecedented scale. International trade and commerce has increased, but much beyond the growth of financial markets across the globe. The 1992 survey of *The Economist* magazine revealed the following information about the globalization of the world economy[1]:

In 1980 the stock of international bank lending, i.e., cross-border lending plus domestic lending in foreign currency, was equivalent to US $324 billion. In 1991 it had increased to US $7500 billion. The combined GDP of the 24 OECD countries in 1980 was US $7.6 trillion[2]. In 1991 the GDP was US $17.1 trillion. So during the period 1980-1991 the stock of international bank lending has increased from 4 per cent of the GDP of OECD to 44 per cent of the same.

Between 1986 and 1990 the volume of worldwide cross-border transaction in equities alone grew at a compound rate of 28 per cent a year. During the same period outflows of foreign direct investment from Japan, Germany, France, Britain and the United States increased from US $61 billion per year to US $ 156 billion, an annual growth of 27 per cent.

Another decade has passed meanwhile and the integration of the global economy has accelerated since 1992. In 2001 the cross-border flow of foreign direct investment became US $270 billion per year and the stock of FDI had been US $ 3 trillion. In the same year the daily turnover in the foreign exchange market had been US $1.7 trillion equivalent. Only 1 per cent of this amount was meant for covering merchandise trade and 99 per cent was the sales and purchase of currencies only.

The technological innovation has helped the process. In the developed industrial economy there is nothing like domestic financial market, the latter has been global. In this perspective, the study of international finance has become very important for the understanding of the finer nuances of different financial phenomena.

1.3 The Approach

International finance is taught in universities and business schools mainly from two angles — open economy macro-economics and finance side. In the former case international

---

1. Source: *World Economy*, a supplement of *The Economist*, September 19, 1992.
2. 1 trillion = 1000 billion

macro-economics and the world financial system get more space in discussion, while in the latter case the economics side is relatively suppressed. Perhaps economics does better justice to the subject compared to finance as a discipline, and following this logic the new subject Financial Economics has emerged that has treated the subject in a rigorous way. Regarding the debate and methodology this book has adopted the middle path. We hope that this book will be a good introduction for those who want deep and rigorous understanding of modern financial economics.

Two

World Financial Architecture and Recent Development[1]

Weariness descends on the core of human civilization,
Big cities stand with their heart full of sorrows
And they lose priceless clarity of all efforts,
Determination and dreams.

[Jibanananda Das, *translation from Bengali*]

The evolution of the world financial system to come to its present form has been a long journey it had passed through five principal types of financial systems that the world had experienced: the gold bullion standard, paper gold standard, Bretton Woods standard, flexible exchange rates and very recent cooperative joint intervention. Each system evolved depending on the need of the time and the will of the leading nations of the world who were able to carry the 'burden' of the world currency. But the major characteristics of the financial system determine the dynamics of the money supply of the countries who are the partners of trade and the common world system. We need to know about the different financial system that prevailed in the world to understand the evolution of world money. A better understanding of the world monetary system would help understand how the domestic money supply in member countries was affected by the change in the world financial system. Though we are aware today that the domestic financial system cannot be fully insulated from the

---

1. This chapter is partly based on chapter 3 of my book "*International Money and Finance*" (Nandi, 2001).

global phenomenon, the situation in the immediate post-war period was not much different in the Group-of-ten countries[2] The level of économic integration among these countries made them inter-dependent.

2.1 The Gold Standard

The classical gold standard emerged as a true international standard by 1880 when majority of independent countries agreed to switch from bimetallism, silver monometallism and paper to the gold as the basis of their currencies. The key rule was maintenance of gold convertibility at the established par. When the countries adhered to the fixed price of gold *vis-á-vis* their currencies and maintained it, it amounted to a fixed exchange rate. According to recent evidence, the exchange rates throughout the period 1880-1914 were characterized by high degree of fixity of the main countries, and violations of gold-parity points and devaluation was rare. The stability in the price of gold and the ease of the supply of gold compared to world demand did facilitate this situation. The period was an ideal example of classical full-employment equilibrium situation in the industrial world with real income changing very little and so the increase in the demand for monetary gold was small enough to be met by available production and supply.

According to the established literature, a time-consistent credible commitment mechanism is necessary for an international monetary arrangement to be effective among the countries. The adherence to the gold convertibility rule provided such a mechanism. Also, apart from the reputation of the domestic gold standard and the constitutional provisions regarding the same, some other mechanism like improved access to international capital market, the operation of the rules of the game, and the hegemonic power of England might have enforced the countries to adhere to the international gold standard rules.

---

2. The group of ten were Belgium, Canada, France, West Germany, Italy, Japan, Netherlands, Sweden, United Kingdom and the United States.

The main countries at that time realized that gold standard did provide the improved access to the international capital markets and for this the support for the regime increased. Also countries believed that gold convertibility would be a signal to creditors of sound government finance. Again this had been the case for both developing and developed countries seeking access to long-term capital, such as Austria-Hungary and Latin America. Also Japan used short-term loans to finance Russo-Japanese war during 1905-06. The example of England being on the gold standard was an added attraction for other countries to be on the same standard. In fact, England had been the centre of the world monetary system because of her economic might and political influence. The fixed relation of British pound with gold assured the countries to stick to the gold standard.

The success of the gold standard had been largely due to the commitment mechanism the participating countries used to follow regarding the internal adjustment of policies faced with external shocks. Since rules were followed sincerely and adjustment facilitated, the commitment to the convertibility of gold was strengthened and there was less chance of leaving the gold standard. Further, the hegemonic power of England acted as an anchor. The literature mentions that the classical gold standard of 1880-1914 was a British-managed standard. There were several reasons for this. At that time London was the centre for the world's gold, commodities and capital markets. Second, many countries substituted sterling for gold as an international reserve currency. Third, there had been extensive outstanding sterling-denominated asset outside Britain. Fourth, the Bank of England could attract whatever gold it needed by the manipulation of its bank rate and other central banks would adjust their discount rates accordingly. In this way, the Bank of England did exert a strong influence on the money supply and price level of the member countries. The central banks of other countries accepted the leadership of the Bank of England because they benefited from using sterling as a reserve asset, even though they might have been constrained from following independent discretionary policies that might have hurt the cause of gold standard.

Gold standard was an asymmetric system (Giovannini, 1989). England was the centre country and the Bank of England used the bank rate to maintain gold convertibility. While Britain could follow an independent monetary policy, other countries like France, Germany etc., accepted the dictates of fixed parities and allowed their money supply to adjust passively. England, as the leader, had been benefited in multiple ways. It enjoyed the seigniorage earned on foreign-held sterling balances. Also financial institutions in London used to earn handsome returns for the central location and easy access to international capital markets.

In an influential study Professor Nurkse (1944) has argued that in crucial times the principal member countries did not behave properly in the sense that they partially sterilized their gold inflows, and the results had been that domestic and foreign assets of these countries moved in opposite directions during this period of gold standard. The rules of the game dictated that they should not interfere with the influence of gold flows on the money supply. Perhaps they became concerned about the potential inflation and thus became pro-active in the control of money supply.

2.2 The Demise of Classical Gold Standard

World War I created a massive shock that the financial system could not endure and the classical gold standard ended. The war reduced the economic strength of the main European countries in general, and England in particular. The anchor role England used to provide for the stability of the system ended as the United States pushed England back from the leadership role. A reformed system — gold exchange standard — prevailed for a short period 1920-1929; it was an attempt to restore the salient positive features of the classical gold standard while allowing a significant role of domestic stabilization policy in response to specific needs. But frictions emerged as the conflict between adherence to gold standard rule and discretion of policy for domestic compulsion could not always be resolved. Also there was an attempt to economize the use of gold as reserve by restricting its use to central banks and also by encouraging the use of foreign exchange as a substitute for gold.

The gold exchange standard was destined to be a failure as it suffered from a number of defects. First, the use of two reserve currencies — sterling and US dollar — was creating problems as there was an absence of leadership as a hegemonic power unlike the earlier period when Britain shouldered the role. Second, there was little cooperation among the key members — Britain, France and United States. Two strong members, i.e., France and the United States, were reluctant to follow the rules of the game. They created deflationary pressures in the world by persistent sterilization of their balance-of-payments surpluses. The system could not bear it and ultimately it collapsed with the Great Depression. But by that time it had transmitted deflation and depression across the world (Eichengreen,1989; Friedman and Schwartz,1963; Temin, 1989).

2.3 The Bretton Woods International Monetary System

With the end of the World War II, the victors assembled at Bretton Woods, New Hampshire, USA to build up the World Monetary System, which came to be known as Bretton Woods International Monetary System (BWIMS). The principal objectives were to remove the ills from the financial system and to create a stable world monetary order. For this several measures were adopted. First, the floating exchange rate system was stopped. Second, the gold exchange standard was scrapped as it was thought to be responsible for the international transmission of deflation in the early 1930s due to its vulnerability to the problems of adjustment, liquidity and confidence. Third, the new system sought to stop the "beggar-thy-neighbour" devaluation, trade restrictions, exchange controls and bilateralism prevalent after 1933.

A group of economists led by J. M. Keynes, E.N. White and Ragnar Nurkse argued for an adjustable peg system, which had been expected to combine the good features of stability of the exchange rate under the fixed exchange rate gold standard, on the one hand, and the monetary and fiscal independence under the flexible exchange rate standard, on the other. Also the coordination role of an international monetary agency was planned. The latter was supposed to have considerable control over domestic financial policy of the members. But the two sides had differences over minor details. The Keynes plan contained more domestic policy autonomy than the White plan, and the latter put more emphasis on exchange rate stability. While both the teams — the British and the American — were not in favour of a rule-based system, the British team was primarily interested to prevent the deflation of the 1930s, and it attributed that partly to the deflationary monetary policies of the United States and partly to the constraints of the gold standard rules. Thus the British team was in favour of an expansionary system.

But the American team led by the US Assistant Secretary of the Treasury, Harry Dexter White presented a system which was closer to the gold standard as it put emphasis on the fixity of the exchange rates. The salient feature of the proposed system were as follows. Though the importance of rules as a credible commitment mechanism was not formally mentioned but they proposed strict regulations on the linkages between *unitas* (the proposed international measure account) and gold. In case any member country did face fundamental disequilibrium in the external sector, it could change the exchange rate parity with approval from three quarter majority of all the members of the new institution.

Ultimately, the prescription of both the teams prevailed as the Articles of Agreements of the International Monetary Fund incorporated the elements of both the Keynes plan and the White plan, with an emphasis on the latter. The acceptance of the Plan became in conformity with the ground reality that it was the United States who was going to shape the international financial system.

Two institutions emerged out of the Bretton Woods Agreement — the International Monetary Fund (IMF) and the

International Bank for Reconstruction and Development (IBRD). The latter was planned to take care of the long run growth of the war ravaged economies of the world and the IMF was assigned the role of maintaining the world monetary order and stability of the exchange rate system. With these objectives in mind the articles of the IMF were written. The main points of articles were:

- The creation of par value system
- Multilateral payments
- The use of Fund's resources
- The powers of IMF
- The nature of the organization

The Par Value System

Article IV of IMF defines the numeraire of the international monetary system as either US dollar or gold of the weight and fineness on July 1, 1944. All the members of the Fund were asked to declare a par value of their currencies and maintain it within 1 per cent margin on both sides. If any country faces fundamental disequilibrium, it can exchange the parity after consultation with other members. If the change of parity is within 10 per cent, the decision of the members will not be rejected. However, if the change is more than 10 per cent, the country concerned needs to have approval of the IMF. In case a decision is made for a uniform change in par value of all currencies in terms of gold, it is to be done by the approval by a majority of all voting members of the Fund and by each member separately with voting quota more than 10 per cent. The Article IV, Section I (a) of the Agreement reads as

Expression of par values. The par value of the currency of each member country shall be expressed in term of gold as a common denominator or in terms of the United States dollar of the weight and fineness in effect on July 1, 1944.

The importance of gold as the numeraire was obscured mostly when most of the countries excluding the USA had chosen to define their par values in terms of US dollar.

John Williamson suggested that the neutral gold numeraire had been chosen to give the United States the symmetrical option to change its exchange rate of dollar along with other countries. Gold was chosen as a conveniently neutral numeraire for defining par values of the exchange rates of the currencies, but gold was not perceived as the fundamental asset which would act as a brake on the issue of currencies and help in the determination of the common price level of the commodities in the member countries the way it had been in the nineteenth century (Williamson, 1977). Even no single currency, nor even US dollar, had been recognized as the 'key' currency linking the principal currencies in the world in 1945.

2.4   Multilateral Payments Mechanism

Article VIII of the IMF states that members are supposed to make their currencies current account convertible though they can keep capital control as stated in Article VI(3). The members are to avoid discriminatory currency and multiple currency arrangements. Again Article XIV allows the countries to keep their currencies not convertible for a period of three years and, during this period, exchange control can be maintained. In fact, it had taken a long time for the developing countries to make their currencies convertible in current account transactions.

Countries would adjust their exchange rates depending on the domestic equilibrium for which the current account balance is one important parameter. Here, Professor Mundell raised an interesting issue when he stated the following:

Only (N-1) independent balance of payments instruments are needed in an N-country world because equilibrium in the balance of (N-1) countries implies equilibrium in the balance of Nth country. The redundancy problem is the problem of deciding how to utilize the extra degree of freedom.

(Mundell, 1968, p.195)

Because of the demonetization of gold in all private transactions, as well as its virtual demonetization in official transactions too, the redundancy problem as stated by Mundell had arisen in a very strong form after 1945. All currencies operating in the system were potentially independent national fiat monies. The amounts of these fiat monies were not related to their base of monetary gold, neither the exchange rates of these monies were tied to the traditional gold parity. As gold failed to act as the Nth currency, US dollar slowly took its place. This created the conditions for the Fixed-Rate Dollar Standard.

2.5 Resources of IMF

The size of the total fund of IMF, contributed by the members' quota in the form of 25 per cent in gold and 75 per cent in national currencies, was initially US $ 8.8 billion, and the amount could be increased every five years if the majority of the members wanted. Under the scheme of White plan, members could obtain resources from IMF to help finance short and medium term payments, disequilibrium in external transactions. IMF established a number of conditions on the use of its resources by the countries suffering from balance of payments deficits. It sets the requirements and conditions for the repurchase, i.e. the repayment of loan. All these are to facilitate the management of currencies which are of greater demand for the payments of international obligations. The conditions imposed on the member country seeking loans from IMF are derived from a monetarist model of Professor Polok, and in many cases this has been resisted by the countries.

2.6 The Structure of Organization

IMF is governed by a Board of Governors who are appointed on the voting strength of the members. The Board makes the policy decision regarding the actions of the members. Also a number of Executive Directors and one Managing Director are selected by the members. The power of the members is reflected in the voting rights, which are proportional to the members' quota (of contribution).

Under the agreement the USA had to maintain a fixed price of gold at US $35 per ounce, and when the members are maintaining fixed parity, the gold price used to be an anchor of the system, which converted the gold standard into a dollar standard.

The architects of the Bretton Woods Agreement were not very much specific about the system of the functioning of the system. The evolution of the system was partly based on subsequent interpretations of the economists who were engaged in research. Several important features were mentioned (Tew 1988; Williamson, 1985). One such feature is that all currencies were treated as equal in the articles of agreement, which implies that each country was required to maintain its par value by intervening in the currency of other countries. This position dictated by theory would not have been meaningful, as other countries can fix their parities in terms of US dollar as the United States was the only country that pegged her currency in terms of gold.

2.7 Historical Stages of the Bretton Woods Agreement: 1946-1960

The period of transition from the war to peace in the post World War II was very long and painful and the functioning of the Bretton Woods system had not been on the desired lines. The system started functioning normally by 1955 and till 1958 full convertibility of the currencies of the major industrial countries could not be achieved. Under the Article XIV of the Bretton Woods Agreement, the countries could continue to use exchange controls for an indefinite period of transition after the establishment of the IMF in March, 1947. The countries used exchange control to preserve their foreign exchange and also every country had negotiated a series of bilateral payments agreements with each of its trading partners. The countries in war ravaged Europe were in desperate need for the imports of raw materials and capital goods and thus the allocation of scarce foreign exchange had come under the control of the government.

Even before the start of the World War II, political uncertainty in Europe induced massive capital flight from Europe to the United States. In 1934, American administration resorted to the devaluation of dollar and the price of gold was raised from $20.67 per ounce to $35.00. These phenomena induced the flow of gold to the USA from rest of the world and when the War came to an end, the United States had become the holder of the two-thirds of the world's monetary gold stock. Simultaneously, Europe experienced depletion of the dollar and gold stock and the economy had been running well below capacity. The Organization for European Economic Cooperation (OEEC) experienced a huge trade deficit with its trade with the United States. OEEC was established in 1948 to coordinate the funding of the Marshall Plan, and the latter facilitated huge inflow of capital to the economies of Europe for reconstruction and development. In fact, huge amount of foreign capital, mainly from the United States, was invested in the countries of Europe to lead the economies towards reconstruction and development.

The period 1946-1960 saw some dynamic events which had significant effect on the international financial system.

In 1949, Great Britain devalued pound sterling by 30.5 per cent and after this 23 countries reduced their parities with US dollar by more or less similar magnitude. This spate of devaluation helped the European countries to adjust their external sector efficiently and, as a result, they could eliminate their large trade deficit. But large scale changes in the parity conditions by a number of countries created the impression that monetary authorities could perpetuate their disequilibrium situation for some time and that would create condition for speculation. As such, there were perceptible resistance from the monetary authorities to change their parity and slowly the Bretton Woods system had been reduced to a fixed exchange rate regime even though it was an adjustable peg system in the initial stage. It is interesting from academic point of view that the authorities preferred the spill over of domestic disequilibrium into the external sector in their adverse balance of payments rather than correcting their exchange rates.

Even before the British devaluation of pound, France devalued French franc in January 1948, and this created a multiple exchange rate system, which created problem in the form of broken cross rates between pound and dollar. The system was rectified with the devaluation of pound. In 1950,

Canada also floated its dollar and this situation continued till 1961.

There was another problem towards the end of 1950s and it was the inadequacy of the IMF's resources to meet the liquidity problem of the world, which the growth of the world's monetary gold stock could not meet. The gap was bridged by the holding of US dollar. The supply of the latter was due to the balance-of-payments deficits of the United States. During this period the latter used to have surplus in the current account, but owing to huge investment abroad and the outflow of capital in the capital account, the balance of payment became negative. The important thing was that dollar substituted gold in a significant way and the problem of the shortage of gold was taken care of.

2.8 The Period 1960-67

From the year 1960 the Bretton Woods system started functioning normally as the principal members started intervention in the foreign exchange market to buy or sell US dollars for the maintenance of parity of their currencies. Also the US Treasury started buying or selling gold with the central banks of other countries at the pegged price of $35 per ounce. The member countries on their part pegged their currencies with US dollar at fixed rate within a band of 2 per cent on either side of the parity. Thus each currency being anchored to US dollar had been indirectly pegged to gold.

The evolution of the system in the '60s turned out to be a bit different compared to the ideal situation the planners had visualized. Instead of the original system of equal currencies, the mechanism evolved into a variant of the gold exchange standard in a kind of gold-dollar system. The British pound lost its importance in the international field and US dollar became the single important international currency. The decline of pound was because of multiplicity of reasons, the principal reason being the relative decline of the British economy in the world. As it had been fully convertible, by the end of '60s, dollar was used as a currency of international reserve.

Further, while the intention of the Bretton Woods Agreement had been the adjustable peg system in the exchange rate mechanism, the system that evolved over time could be called a fixed rate system. The reason that monetary authorities became too conservative regarding the adjustment of the parities was perhaps they were unwilling to take the risks of changing the parities as that might lead to the possibility of speculative capital flows and follow up behaviour by others. Thus the resulting system took the shape of a fixed exchange rate dollar-gold standard. This evolution created some problems in the international financial systems which were not uncommon in the inter-war period also and these can be divided into two categories: liquidity and confidence.

2.9 The Liquidity Problem

Towards the end of sixties the United States started experiencing deficit in its balance of payments and this was mainly due to huge capital outflow in the capital account transactions. Since the USA is a reserve currency country, it did not have to adjust its domestic policies to the changes in the balance of payments. The dollar outflows had been sterilized by the federal reserve as a matter of routine. The outflows of dollar meant that other countries, particularly European countries, had been holding dollar reserve. This created different perception in some of the main European countries and there was resentment against the 'do-nothing' attitude of the US Federal Reserve on the deficit balance of payments situation. In 1965 France began to convert outstanding dollar liabilities into gold through the gold window. That created some pressure on the price of gold.

Meanwhile, US monetary authorities responded to the emerging world situation by initiating measures to improve the balance of trade, changing the fiscal-monetary policies, imposing curb on the export of capital and taking measures to prevent the conversion of outstanding dollars into gold. But these policies could not change the situation much and the liquidity problem continued.

The liquidity problem in the international scene was due to the maladjustment of the demand and supply of gold, as the short-fall of the latter began to be felt in the early 1960s. All through the forties, the price of gold had been declining, and this reduced the production and supply of gold. The stagnant price of gold also reduced its production in the mid-sixties and it was apparent that the supply of gold from the Soviet Union would not bridge the excess demand gap. Meanwhile, the demand for gold had been increasing. Apart from a significant increase of private demand, the demand was increasing also due to increased volume of trade and commerce among the countries. The prospect of the world monetary gold stock growing fast enough to finance the growing world real output and the value of international trade seemed to be impossible. Even during 1957-58, the gap between the two in the group of seven countries had been significant.

Professor Robert Triffin (1960) pointed out that the supply of dollars arising out of the negative balance of payments of the United States could not substitute monetary gold on a permanent basis as the US monetary gold reserve would decline significantly relative to the dollar liability held in foreign countries. The level of the world monetary gold stock held in Group of Ten countries did not grow in proportion to the growth of real gross domestic product and volumes of trade. The gap between the demand for monetary gold (to support the increasing money supply) and the available supply had been bridged by the dollar reserve. So long the dollar-gold convertibility at fixed rate had been there, dollar was considered as a substitute for gold. But everything has a limit and this was no exception, and some countries started having the apprehension of the USA not adhering to the gold-dollar convertibility.

2.10 Special Drawing Rights (SDR)

The discussion on the liquidity problem stated in the previous paragraph implies that there had been a feeling that the growth of international reserves had not been adequate enough to supply reasonable liquidity to the growing international trade and commerce. Though apparently no real strain was visible, however, there was a fear that the lack of liquidity might act as a constraint on the economic growth of the world. Moreover, the mechanism of increasing the international reserve was too much dependent on the running of deficit balance of payments on the part of the United States. This was unstable by design, as Professor Triffin had viewed. So the members of the IMF felt the need to create a supplementary reserve fund which would bolster international trade and commerce. The result had been the First Amendment of the IMF Articles of Agreement in 1967 and this empowered the IMF to create a Special Drawing Account to supplement its quota system that operates under its General Account. Under the new scheme a reserve asset was to be created by the IMF and that would be called Special Drawing Rights (SDR), and this will not be backed by the deposits of the members, but the value of SDR as a reserve asset will rest on it being regarded as an acceptable means of exchange between the IMF and the central banks of the member countries.

The value of SDR was initially set equivalent to $1 or set at $\frac{1}{35}$ th of an ounce of gold. Under the scheme each member was allocated a specified annual amount of SDR in proportion to their quota with the IMF, and the country could draw upon its SDR allocation if it experiences a balance of payments deficit. The member is required to consult the IMF in the case of drawing from the quota, but in drawing the SDR allocation the member need not consult the IMF. Further there is no condition-ality attached with SDR drawing and it is not subject to repayment. Thus SDR has increased the amount of international reserve.

The cumulative total holdings of SDR allocated to a country is known as the 'net cumulative allocation' of the country and over a 5-year period the member has to maintain its SDR balance at an average of 30 per cent of its net cumulative allocation. This percentage was reduced to 15 in 1979. The first allocation of SDR during the period 1970-72 was to the amount of US $9.5 billion. In July 1976, the value of SDR was changed from $1 to a weighted basket of 16 currencies. Later in January 1981, the value of SDR was redefined and pegged to a basket of 5 currencies and these currencies were Pound sterling, French franc, Japanese yen, US dollar and German mark.

A country upon drawing the SDR can exchange the same with other foreign currency and can increase its reserve. All members of the IMF are bound to accept the SDR in exchange for their currencies up to three times their net cumulative allocation. The country that draws its SDR allocation is to pay a rate of interest to the Fund and the country that exchanges the allocated SDR with its currency gets this rate of interest. Thus the SDR is an indirect loan mechanism through which international liquidity increases.

2.11 Market Price of Gold and Confidence Issues

Gold had been the anchor of the system and it was supposed to give stability to it. But the pegging of the official price of gold at $35 per ounce by the US Treasury attracted attention of the speculators, who pushed the free market price of gold in London market to $40 per ounce from the US Treasury buying price of $35.20. But gold served as backing to the US dollar with a 25 per cent gold reserve requirement against Federal Reserve notes. So, US monetary authority apprehended that the speculation in the gold market might spill over to the official demand for the conversion of dollar into gold. As a remedial measure, US Treasury supplied gold to the Bank of England to restore stability and requested the monetary authorities of Group of Ten countries not to buy gold at prices higher than $35.20 per ounce. In November 1961, the London Gold Pool was formed by the United States and seven other countries, and it could stabilize the price of gold. The central banks of the seven countries supplied 40 per cent of the gold stock in this pool.

The sixties witnessed two phenomena not conducive to the stability of the financial system. First, there had been a growing scarcity of the gold as the production of the yellow metal levelled off by 1965-66. Also the demand for gold increased mainly from the private sector. Second, there had been a perceptible increase in the US inflation rate as the money supply increased partly due to Vietnam War. Some economists think that the USA followed an inflationary policy at home this time because of domestic compulsion.

The two phenomena cited above created a crisis of confidence regarding US dollar and during 1967-68, the London Gold Pool became a net seller of gold, losing gold of about $3 billion equivalent at the pegged price. There was apprehension about the devaluation of dollar, though the scarcity of gold in the world was one reason (Gilbert, 1968, Johnson, 1968). The resulting situation had its consequences. In March 1968 the London Gold Pool was abolished and it was replaced by a *two-tier arrangement*. The monetary authorities of gold pool stopped buying and selling gold in the market, but instead they started transaction of gold only among themselves at fixed price $35 per ounce. This was an official tier in which central banks only could transact among them. But a private market was allowed in which gold as a commodity could be traded at free market prices. Along with that the United States removed the 25 per cent gold reserve requirement against Federal Reserve currency. Thus, the link between gold production and other market resources of gold and official reserves was severed. The result of these new arrangements was that gold had been demonetized at the margin. The system evolved into a *de facto* dollar standard, though gold convertibility remained.

By 1968 the system also reduced to a *de facto* fixed exchange rate system. The major industrial countries agreed not to convert their huge dollar reserve into gold. Meanwhile European countries and Japan became economic power blocs and they became increasingly reluctant to absorb more dollar liabilities. These countries also were not ready to readjust their exchange rate upwards as they expected the United States to make the readjustment. Faced with these contradictory pulls and pressures the International Monetary Fund found itself helpless as its resources were not enough to prevent devaluation by major industrial countries by providing them adequate assistance for adjustment (Dominguez, 1993).

2.12 Demonetization of Gold

The establishment of the two-tier system after the closure of the London Gold Pool could not maintain the stability of the gold-dollar parity for long and the United States was forced to close the gold window in August 1971. The closing of the gold window to foreign official holders marked the end of the gold exchange standard. The last functional link between dollar and monetary gold was severed. With this the Bretton Woods System collapsed, but the institutions created as a result of the agreement — IMF and IBRD — survived. IMF still had an important role as a clearing house for different views on monetary policies, as a centre of information, as the primary source of adjustment for the countries outside the Group of Ten and as a monitor of the world financial system. Particularly, the developing countries need the guidance and help of the IMF to standardize their financial system.

It took several years for the monetary authorities to formalize the demonetization of gold as an international reserve asset. On 1st January, 1975, the official price of gold was abolished as the unit of account for the international monetary system. Monetary authorities could enter into gold transactions at market determined prices and IMF terminated the use of gold. The United States ended the 41-year ban on gold ownership for US residents. Within a short time US Treasury started auctioning a portion of its gold stock. Thus gold became like any other commodity in the market.

2.13 Gresham's Law in International Level

In the 1960s the adverse price movements in the international level brought asymmetry in the intrinsic values of two principal assets — gold and US dollar. Under the Bretton Woods System, gold and US dollar parity was fixed at $35 per ounce of gold and at this rate US authorities were committed to buy and sell gold with foreign central banks. As the US economy experienced inflation by approximately 40 per cent during the 1960s, it was presumed that price of gold too had risen. There was persistent upward pressure in the gold market. The market perception of gold being officially undervalued, US authority secured an agreement from the foreign central banks not to convert their US dollar reserve into gold. But that could not save the situation and US President Nixon announced the suspension of dollar-gold convertibility in 1971. Thus US dollar had driven out gold from the market which was stated in a law by the economist Thomas Gresham in the sixteenth century. The law propounds the theory that whenever there exists a discrepancy in the prices of two assets by market perception, and if the nominal values are the same, the asset which is undervalued will disappear from the market and the asset which is over valued will remain. This is an explanation of the decline of the Bretton Woods System given by the renowned economists Jurg Niehans (1984) and Paul De Grauwe (1989).

2.14 Decline of the System

The Bretton Woods Agreement had the plan of making the United States the centre country so that it could perform the anchor role for the stability of the system. Unfortunately the United States could not perform that role because of a set of reasons. The United States was to fix the price of gold at $35 per ounce and also to maintain domestic price stability to safeguard the intrinsic value of dollar. Of course, the price of gold could be adjusted with the consent of the majority of the members having quotas in IMF of 10 per cent or more. But there was no enforcement mechanism for the USA and only the credibility of the country and a commitment to gold convertibility had assured the sustainability of the system. The rest of the world, the (n-1) countries, had to accept the price level set by the United States through their commitment to fixed parities of their currencies *vis-à-vis* US dollar. This had the implication that the (n-1) countries had to follow a definite set of fiscal and monetary policies which were consistent with the fixed parities. But the countries could change their parities because of the adjustable peg. In the process disequilibrium in the domestic economy might happen but this contingency was not spelled out in the sense that there had been no constraints placed on the member countries regarding the extent to which the domestic monetary and fiscal policy could deviate from the pattern set by the United States (Giovannini, 1993; Mundell, 1968).

The crisis of liquidity in the world financial system had not been properly addressed. The countries were to keep reserves against their currencies either in the form of gold, or in some principal currencies such as dollar. But in reality US dollar had been the main currency which was used as the reserve currency because of the gold convertibility. There had been the gold convertibility clause and a crisis of confidence too and these prevented the United States to supply the monetary reserve demanded by the (n-1) countries. In addition to it, the USA followed an inflationary policy in the late sixties, but was unwilling to devalue the dollar This reinforced the confidence problem regarding US dollar. So when some countries tried to liquidate their dollar liabilities and transform that into gold, the United States got panicky and closed the gold window in 1971, signalling the collapse of the system. Thus the American decision to suspend gold convertibility ended the important aspect of the Bretton Woods System. The second part of the system — adjustable peg — disappeared 19 months later.

The system collapsed for several reasons. First, there were two major flaws that undermined the system. One flaw was the gold exchange standard. This placed the United States under threat of a convertibility crisis and the country addressed this problem by the pursuit of policies that made adjustment more difficult. The second flaw was the adjustable peg. Since the cost of discrete changes in parities with dollar was high, the system evolved into a disinclined fixed rate system without an effective adjustment mechanism. This they had to do in face of growing capital mobility.

Finally, America adopted an expansionary monetary policy that was not appropriate for a key currency. The creeping inflation, though low in magnitude, was sufficient to initiate a speculative attack on the world's monetary gold stock in 1968. That led to the collapse of the Gold Pool. By that time the system evolved into a *de facto* US dollar standard. So the United States had the obligations to maintain price stability.

The country failed in it and this ultimately led to the collapse of the system.

2.15 Post Bretton Woods Era: Managed Floating Exchange Rate

The period between 1971 and 1973 had been one of shocks and adjustments for the major countries of the world and in March 1973 the world turned to a generalized floating exchange rate. In the new system the monetary authorities started extensive intervention to influence both the levels of volatility and the exchange rates of their currencies. By 1980, the dynamism of the system stabilized and members started intervening only to control the volatility of the system. The Group of Seven countries started a coordinated attempt of exchange market intervention to bring stability. The decade following 1980 witnessed enormous capital flows across political boundaries and a relative dis-intermediation of the international banking system. This had an impact on the world financial system, particularly on the viability of the international banking system. Some banks in Japan could mobilize enough capital and became very large in terms of the asset size. The countervailing power emerged and the Basle Committee introduced capital adequacy norms for all banks operating in the international market. The capital adequacy ratio (CAR) initially proposed as 8 per cent of the risk-weighted assets acted as a constraint on the expansion of credit portfolio of the banks. The latter had an important impact on the money supply of the member countries.

2.16 The Second Amendment of IMF Article

The Second Amendment of the IMF Articles came into effect on April 1978 and it formally gave the IMF members a large degree of discretion in the selection of their exchange rate arrangements. IMF had been urged to adopt a policy of 'firm surveillance' over the exchange rate policies of the members.

The Second Amendment Article IV defined the responsibility of the members. Each member was obliged to notify the IMF of its exchange rate arrangement. The members were free to select the exchange rate arrangement they would think right for their interest, but they were to supply information to the Fund. Also a member was to avoid manipulating exchange rates in order to prevent effective balance of payments adjustments or to gain an unfair competitive advantage over other member which might hurt the interest of the latter. In a way the Second Amendment reduced the power of the IMF in a big way.

2.17 Appreciation of US dollar

During the period 1980-1985, US dollar experienced substantial appreciation against major currencies. The nominal effective exchange rate appreciated by 50 per cent and the same happened with the real rate. This was the result of the divergent macroeconomic policies pursued by the United States, Japan and European countries. The US authorities followed a relaxed fiscal policy but a tight monetary policy, with the budget deficit skyrocketing from US$ 16 billion in 1979 to US$ 204 billion in 1986. As the US real interest rate increased relative to other countries, capital from other countries flowed to United States to finance the growing current account deficits and as such dollar appreciated. The US government argued that the dollar appreciation was the reflection of the growing strength of the domestic US economy.

The appreciation of dollar hurt the export and import competing industries of the USA and this increased the balance of payments problems. The public sentiments went in favour of protection and the trade partners of the United States were convinced that the negative balance of payments of the United States was the reflections of its growing budget deficits. But a parallel thinking also developed that US dollar should be allowed to have its true level.

2.18 The Plaza Accord

Finance Ministers of G-5 countries — France, West Germany, Japan, United States, United Kingdom — met at Plaza Hotel in September 1985 and after the deliberations on their respective view points, they issued a Communiqué which is known as

Plaza Accord. According to the Accord, the exchange rate of US dollar did not accurately reflect the changes in the economic fundamentals like the measures Japan was to take to stimulate domestic demand, or the US commitment to reduce budget deficits. There was also agreement for the depreciation of dollar and the countries agreed to cooperate on this issue. The dollar started to decline and the extent of the decline of dollar caused concern among the members.

In February 1987, the G-7 countries (Canada and Australia together with G-5 group) met in Paris to consider the situation of declining US dollar and reached an agreement known as Louvre Accord. In this, the G-7 countries agreed that further decline of dollar was not desirable and the then exchange rates were true reflections of the economic fundamentals. Implicit had been the agreement that the US dollar should be kept within a 5 per cent target band against the deutschmark and the yen. But the accord could not completely prevent the decline of dollar.

In October 1987, there had been a collapse in the stock markets around the world and as a consequence the dollar came under pressure as the crash in the stock market induced the fear of world recession. The governments of some industrialized countries started the loosening of their monetary policies and reducing the interest rates. In January 1988, the trade deficits of the United States showed the sign of improvements, and US dollar embarked on the recovery phase.

2.19 International Capital Flows

The flexible exchange rate system in the world had been associated with an increasing strength of the international money managers who were able to make large scale capital flight from one country to another within a very short time. The trans-border capital flows had been effected to make profit either from the possible fluctuations of the exchange rates due to the potential changes in the short-term interest rates or the potential changes in the prices of the stocks in well-integrated stock exchanges of different countries. The first reason had been man-made on some occasions leading to a pre-planned attack on a currency and this has led to a destabilization of the currency, when the concerned central bank failed to take care of its total liability denominated in the form of total currency in circulation with the banks and the public. This type of situation had been very common in the 1990s when several countries became victims of the international currency predators.

2.20 The Financial Architecture

The period of 1990s had been marked by a series of currency crises and the intervention of different governments in response to these crises first in the European Monetary System (EMS) countries and then in Mexico. The crisis then spread to South East Asia and it soon spread to other countries like Brazil and Russia. Though each country had its own unique features in the currency crisis, there were certain stylized facts in this phenomenon. The EMS crisis of 1992 was initiated by German reunification and the reluctance of other member states to pursue policies, which could have checked inflation. The Mexican crisis had resulted as a combination of several factors after Mexico experienced huge capital inflow till 1994 when the crisis occurred. The forces were as follows: First, interest rates increased in the United States making investment in Mexico less attractive. Second, a rebellion in the state of Chiapas increased doubts among the investors about the political stability. Along with that when one presidential candidate of a political party was assassinated, capital inflow to Mexico reduced drastically and Mexico had to use its depleted reserve to save the currency.

The Russian crisis in the aftermath of 1998 was a culmination of external shock like a decline in the prices of raw materials to an asymmetric expectations of the creditors. The decline in tax receipts of the government due to the fall in the price of oil led to an imbalance in the budget of the Russian government. The Parliament blocked the reform proposal of the government and the currency became weak due to capital flight. In this situation Russia sought help from the IMF and after some controversy got a loan of $11.4 billion. This created an upward expectation in the financial market and investors started buying short-term rouble debt to earn very high interest rates. Interestingly, no one understood that rouble might depreciate further because of high interest rates, and this precisely did happen. In August 1998, Russia allowed the rouble to float and suspended the redemption of rouble denominated debt. The depreciation of rouble initiated a 'run' on the bank, as depositors wanted to withdraw roubles to buy dollars. The banks were the holders of large debts which were 'frozen' and so they could not pay their depositors. The country had to suffer for the irrational decision of the investors first to put money with wrong expectations and then withdraw capital leading to the collapse.

Examining the evolution of the international monetary system one finds several important factors. First, the maintenance of the fixed exchange rate system in the beginning and the flexible exchange rate system since the early 1970s always had to face the n-country problems as the number of independent exchange rates would be always smaller than the number of currencies. Thus, it is impossible in theory for all the governments to pursue independent exchange rate policies. The history of the evolution of the system since 1950 has shown how the governments had to solve the n-country problem at different times. IMF had not been successful to control exchange rate policies, though it had been the source of balance of payments credit. The willingness of the United States to allow other countries adjust their exchange rates *vis-à-vis* US dollar solved the n-th country problem in the initial years till 1960. Later on the United States experienced deficit in the balance of payments and other countries accumulated dollar reserves and they substituted gold reserves by dollars. The United States tried to solve this problem by a realignment of the exchange rates by Smithsonian Agreement in 1971. But this arrangement fell apart in 1973 when the USA devalued the dollar unilaterally. This induced other governments to float their currencies.

The second lesson of the evolution of the international financial system is the market behaviour in the pegged exchange rate system. When the latter is firmly in order, investors are tempted to take advantage of the interest rate differences without covering their foreign exchange exposure. But the moment market suspects the stability of the pegged rate system, the investors rush for cover. The resulting conversion of currencies and the large amount of capital flows can produce the anticipated exchange rate fluctuation, which the investors apprehended. This has happened time and in again; this happened in Europe in 1992-93, in Mexico in 1995, Asia in 1997-98 and in Russia in 1998 (Goldstein, 1998; Adams *et al*, 1998). The repeated crises has reopened the debate about whether restrictions should be imposed on the international capital flows, what should be the appropriate exchange rate arrangement for the new market economies and whether IMF needs restructuring. Some economists are in favour of introducing some sort of a tax on the international capital flows as suggested by Tobin. This will make the transfer a bit costly but opinions differ on this issue. Again the enormity of the crisis as seen in Asia in 1997-98 has induced thinking along the line whether the IMF in its present form can take care this sort of problem in future.

2.21 Exchange Rate Arrangements

In recent times different countries have arranged different types of exchange rate arrangements and broadly these can be categorised as under :

— Currency pegged to another strong currency or SDR
— Currency pegged to a currency composite
— Flexible exchange rates of a single currency
— Flexible exchange rate under cooperative arrangement
— More flexible or managed floating exchange rate
— Independent floating exchange rate

Countries like Angola, Liberia, Iraq, Oman, Panama, Syria and Beliz have pegging arrangements with US dollar. Again countries like Benin, Cameroon, Congo, Mali and Senegal have a fixed peg system with French franc. The countries like Lybia and Myanmar have pegged their currency with SDR, while some countries have pegging arrangement with specific currency e.g., Bhutan with Indian rupee, Brunei with Singapore dollar, Estonia with German mark and San Marino with Italian Lira.

The countries who have a pegging arrangement with a currency composite are: Bangladesh, Burundi, Cyprus, Fiji, Iceland, Jordan, Malta, Slovak Republic, Tonga and Vanuatu.

The countries like Bahrain, Qatar, Saudi Arabia and UAE have currency which are quite flexible though not of the elite group. On the other hand the countries like Austria, Belgium, Denmark, Finland, France, Germany, Ireland, Italy, Luxembourg, Netherlands, Portugal and Spain have flexible and elite currencies which are also stable through cooperative arrangements. These countries belong to the elite OECD group. Some countries have currencies whose exchange rates are described as managed floating. Their list is quite long and the principal countries in this group are— Algeria, Brazil, Chile, China, Costa Rica, Egypt, Georgia, Hungary, Indonesia, Israel, Iran, Malaysia, Pakistan, Russia, Singapore, Sri Lanka, Thailand, Venezuela and Vietnam. This position was as on June 1997. Some countries have opted for an independent floating exchange rate regime and this list is very long. Some of these countries are: India, Albania, Australia, Canada, Ghana, Jamaica, Kenya, Lebanon, Mexico, Peru, Sweden, Switzerland, United States and Zambia.

The above shows that the exchange rate arrangements of the different members of the IMF are of various nature and this has made the system much more complex. Each country follows a course regarding its currency's exchange rate according to the strength of the economic fundamentals. In fact, the Second Amendment of IMF Articles in 1978 has empowered the members to choose their own exchange rate regime and supply information to the Fund accordingly.

2.22 The Tobin Tax Proposal on Capital Movement

Professor James Tobin argues that in a world of flexible exchange rates the dynamics of the short term capital flows has a destabilizing effects on the stability of the exchange rates and in fact, it can disrupt the whole process (Tobin, 1978):

> National economies and national governments are not capable of adjusting to massive movements of funds across the foreign exchanges, without the real hardship and without significant sacrifice of the objectives of national economic policy with respect to employment, output, and inflation (p.154).

Tobin argues that in the highly integrated world of today it is difficult for the national economies to pursue independent monetary policies. If domestic interest rate rises, this can induce a sharp appreciation of the currency in real sense. Again, a fall in the interest rate will lead to a real depreciation. This effect will have an adverse impact on the economic parameters of the economy and Tobin suggests that a tax can be imposed on all foreign exchange transactions so that the destabilizing effects are minimised. The proposed tax will reduce the incentive for the speculators to instigate huge capital inflow and outflow of the economy in response to a small interest rate change. Tobin suggests that this type of tax should be imposed on all types of foreign exchange transactions without exception and then only it will be effective. Though it may have a negative effect on the international trade, Tobin thinks that the trade-off is worthwhile as it will have a stabilizing effects on the exchange rate and through that on employment and income.

Many economists believe that Tobin's tax is a bit harsh measure as a flat tax on all foreign exchange movements can reduce the volume of trade of the markets and the consequent reduction in liquidity can increase the volatility of the market, and it is an adverse and unwelcome situation to what is desired. Also with today's innovative financial markets, it is highly probable that the tax will be circumvented as financial innovation will induce a replication of instruments that would remain unaffected by the tax.

2.23 The G-7 Study for World Monetary Reform

The Asian crisis in 1997 induced the G-7 countries (the 7 countries are — the USA, Canada, United Kingdom, France,

Germany, Italy and Japan) for a fresh study for revamping the world monetary system and the finance ministers of the seven countries bought out a Report entitled *"Strengthening the International Financial Architecture"* which was accepted in a summit in Cologne in June 1999. The Report identifies five main areas which are to look into for strengthening the world monetary system (G-7, 1999). The areas are:

— transparency and best practices
— strong financial regulation in industrial countries
— strong macroeconomic policies and financial system in emerging countries
— improving crisis management with private sector involvement
— promoting social policies to protect the poor

Regarding the *transparency* the Report emphasizes that transparency is needed to ensure that information about existing conditions, decisions and actions of the authority should be made accessible, and easily understood by the economic agents. When the latter get sufficient market information, they can efficiently allocate the resources to minimize risks. Transparency also promotes healthy market expectations of the agents that help maintain stability in the system.

Monetary authorities should publish information about their reserve position, the leverage position and external indebtedness. The countries are to be encouraged to apply uniform standards and sound practices to foster the development of sound financial system. International institutions should disclose their evaluations of the respective countries' financial system.

2.24 Stronger Financial Regulation

The Report emphasizes that inadequate and inefficient evaluation of the credit proposals are also responsible for the creation of bad assets. Excessive risk taking along with high degree of leverage can make the financial system fragile and spread negative expectations. The Report identifies three areas which are to be addressed by the industrial countries and these are:

- improving risk measurement and its management
- assessing the implications of the activity of the *highly leveraged institutions*, and,
- evaluation of the implications of the activities of the Offshore Financial Centres

The three areas are inter-connected as it is the offshore regions where the probability is very high that highly leveraged financial institutions are engaged in high risk business. The resultant loss, suffered, erodes the bottom line of the parent institutions.

2.25 Strong Macroeconomic Policy

The Report discusses the spectrum of macro-economic and financial policies the emerging countries should adopt in the current global scenario in sufficient detail. One important area is the exchange rate regime which should be supported by consistent macroeconomic and fiscal policies by the respective governments. The financial system should also work in an efficient manner by maintaining a proper leverage position.

The Report also asks the G-7 group for its firm commitment to work together with the important financial institutions of the world to improve the standard of supervision of banking and financial system. It also requests the governments of the emerging countries to narrow down the zone of the government guarantee for private sector loan so that the problem of *moral hazards* can be minimized.

The G-7 countries also caution the emerging countries (there are 11 in the group and they are—Argentina, Australia, Brazil, China, India, Mexico, Russia, Saudi Arabia, Korea, South Africa and Turkey) to proceed for capital account liberalization with proper sequencing of policies and creation of necessary infrastructure. The International Monetary Fund (IMF) and other similar institutions are asked to monitor closely the trans-border capital flows to minimize the potential destabilizing effects of the latter. It is accepted that the international capital market has an important role for the improvement of productivity in the emerging countries. The report also asks the emerging countries to adopt best practices regarding debt management with greater reliance on long term debt, if possible, denominated in domestic currency and removal of biases that encourage short term debts.

2.26 Crisis Prevention and Crisis Management

Regarding crisis prevention the G-7 report envisages a framework for preventing crisis without introducing moral hazards. The main element in this framework is the involvement of private creditors in all the aspects of debt management strategies. The Report recognizes that the official financial assistance in certain situations can play an important role in the prevention of crisis, and even when crisis occurs, in limiting the risk of contagion. The Report also urges the emerging countries to develop a mechanism for a more consistent and systematic interaction with the main creditors for the restructuring of loan and thus spreading the liability over a larger time horizon so that the risk of contagion remains limited.

The Report advises the debtor countries to establish sound and efficient bankruptcy procedures and strong judiciary to promote transparency and equity in the insolvency regime. The Report puts emphasis on both the commitment of countries to meet their obligations and market discipline.

2.27 Formation of a New Group: G-20

On the initiative of G-7 a new group has been created in the world scene and it is called G-20, which comprises 7 members of G-7, a Representative each of European Union and jointly of the International Monetary Fund and the World Bank, and 11 major emerging countries. On this, the G-7 is of the view that they propose to establish a new mechanism for informal dialogue in a framework of Bretton Woods institutional system, and to broaden the dialogue on key economic and financial issues among major emerging economies for the promotion of world growth and stability. Some sort of a *collective management of the world financial system* has been the motivating force behind the formation of G-20, as this group constitutes the largest chunk of the world economy on the basis of market size. Whether countries outside this grouping will cooperate with this idea is a question which only future will answer.

2.28 New Initiative of IMF and the Poor

The financial crisis of 1997 had proved that it were the poor in the affected countries who were hit the hardest and a realization dawned among the academics that there should be some safeguards for the protection of the people in the lower rung of economic ladder in case financial crisis erupts. The World Bank has taken the initiative in this field and it has developed a set of *Principles and Good Practices in Social Policy* in April 1999 with the objective of identifying and managing the social dimension of financial crisis. Also the IMF programme "Enhanced Structural Adjustment Facility" has been renamed as *Poverty Reduction and Growth Facility*. This exercise signals an important shift of emphasis toward the achievement of social objective in the programmes supported by the IMF.

Both the World Bank and the IMF are committed to achieve significant results and these twin institutions supported other measures which are consistent with the objective of poverty reduction. They also supported the G-7 initiative of debt reduction of heavily indebted poor countries. But the approach relies on the positive aspects of the market mechanism and they advise the poor countries to do the necessary reforms so that the fruits of the progress reach the real poor.

2.29 The New International Financial Architecture

In the last two decades the world financial system has undergone significant changes and there is a growing concern among the academic community about the stability of this system (Eichengreen, 1999; Blinder, 1999; Goldstein, 1999). There has been a broad consensus about what the emerging countries should do regarding external financial transactions and these are: adoption of a floating exchange rate regime, less reliance on foreign currency borrowing and extremely cautious approach regarding capital account liberalization. Along with these elements there has been an emphasis on the role of market in the new scheme of things.

There are still certain gray areas which are to be looked into. The stability of the world system depends on the interdependence between the macro-economic policies of the global financial powers, particularly the United States, European Union and Japan. But the present arrangement may not be considered as sufficient. As for example, the low interest rate policy as well as weak yen policy pursued by Bank of Japan since the middle of 1995 had been necessary to fight the domestic recession. But this policy led to a huge Japanese investment in the USA at a cheap cost and also huge Japanese loan to South Asia. In early 1999 there had been a sharp reversal of the yen decline *vis-à-vis* US dollar and the G-7 passively accepted that though it was not good for the recovery of Japan. The market took the signal that yen was going to appreciate further which was consistent with the American attempt to reduce the deficit in current account in its trade with Japan.

There is another issue which should be addressed properly and it is the liquidity of IMF, which obtains its resources through quota subscriptions from members. In return, IMF creates international liquidity. This is supplemented with the creation of the Special Drawing Rights (SDR). But in the present scenario of market-led world financial system what is feared is that IMF may create too much liquidity in the system which it may not endure. Being the international lender of last resort IMF should not create any moral hazard problem so far as the management of the current account of individual member is concerned. But the market perception should be clear that IMF has the means to prevent a crisis situation of a particular member from degenerating into a systemic instability.

2.30 A New International Economic Order

Since the breakdown of the Bretton Woods system in 1971, and despite increased trade and financial liberalization, the world economy has not performed particularly well. There have been two major oil shocks in 1973 and 1979; there was a major debt crisis in the developing countries throughout the 1980s. There have been over hundred episodes of systemic banking crises including the dramatic financial crisis in East Asia in 1997, and continued growing divisions in the world economy between rich and poor. According to the *World Development Report 2002* published by the World Bank, the average level of per capita income (PCY) in the rich developed countries, which constitute only 17 percent of the world's population, is nearly $28,000 per annum compared to a figure of about $500 in the poorest developing countries, that contains about 40 per cent of the world's population. The gap is wide enough, but even this understates the degree of income inequality because it compares only the average income for rich and poor countries. The gap becomes much wider if we consider the distribution of income within countries. For example, the ratio of the average income of the richest 5 per cent of the world's population to the average income of the poorest 5 per cent is over 100:1. There are nearly three billion people in the world living in primary poverty, and nearly one billion suffer various states of malnutrition because they live on the equivalent of less than $1 per day.

The situation has not improved. Meanwhile, population has increased and the absolute numbers in primary poverty have increased too. The world distribution of income shows little sign of equalizing. If we consider *international* inequality between countries measured by the Gini ratio, the Norwegian Institute of International Affairs (2000) calculates a figure of 0.59 (excluding China from the sample) compared with 0.6 in 1950. For the average developing country growing at 3 per cent per annum, it would take eighty years to catch up with the current living standards in developed countries, let alone narrow the absolute gap. Apart from the colossal income differences, there is huge discrepancies in other indices of welfare such as literacy, life expectancy, housing and other basic needs between the two group of countries.

Against this background, it is no wonder that there have been frequent periodic calls from international development agencies, international statesmen, professional economists and the developing countries themselves for a New International Economic Order (NIEO) to address the issue of global inequality, or what is sometimes called the 'North-South' divide. When this is a reality the issues that require urgent attention are:

- the nature of commodities produced by the developing countries,
- the terms of trade,
- the volatility of primary product prices,
- the deflationary bias in the world economy.

The last issue is related to the restructuring programme of the IMF when it is to bail out a member from chronic balance of payments crisis. The IMF is to recognize the structural characteristics of the particular developing country before suggesting measures.

The evolution of the world's financial system, and the description of the new financial architecture will not be complete without a discussion of the new experiment of the twentieth century, i.e., the formation of European Union and the new currency Euro. We discuss this in the next section.

2.31 European Union and Euro

The single currency of European Union Euro was launched on January 1, 1999 and it is a composite currency consisting of 12 currencies whose weights are proportionate to the importance of the economy. Here we discuss the systemic impact of the Euro on the global financial system.

At the time of launch, Euro 1 = US $ 1.17 and that was the theoretical value. But during the last two years Euro has lost heavily against US dollar and in December 2000, Euro was quoted around US $ 0.88, which means a depreciation of about 24 per cent.

Euro is in physical existence from January, 2002 as it has come in circulation as a medium of exchange, and the countries who have taken up the currency have a dual currency system for the period January to June, 2002. Euro presently is the only legal tender in the Euro zone. At present, twelve countries have accepted Euro as the currency and they are: Austria, Belgium, Finland, France, Germany, Ireland, Luxembourg, the Netherlands, Portugal, Spain and Greece (from January 1, 2001). Three other countries are the members of the European Union, but they have not adopted the Euro yet and they are: Denmark, Sweden, and the United Kingdom.

2.32 European Union as Optimum Currency Area

The success of the Euro becoming the single currency of the European Union (EU) depends on the EU becoming an optimum currency area. To fulfil the latter criterion EU should satisfy some conditions. First, the members of EU should possess similar economies in the sense that they should have compatible economic structures with same level of economic diversification. In that case the countries would get same type of external shocks and same type of exchange rate they can follow. In the absence of the similarity, same type of external shocks would create different type of effects and the countries would require different exchange rate policies.

Second, the economies of the countries under EU should be properly integrated so that they face the same phase of business cycles at the same time. This will facilitate adopting same interest rate policy and one monetary policy. This condition is tough but very important, because if interest rates deviate from one another, diverse capital movements will create problems for the single monetary policy. The latter is crucial for the credibility of Euro being the single currency in EU. It will be a difficult proposition for the European Central Bank (ECB) to fight inflation in one country with high interest rate and tackle recession in another country with lower rate of interest.

Third, the member states should have a common economy in the sense that the movement of capital, labour as well as commodities should face no restrictions across the political borders. This implies a single market condition and the industries in the concerned countries should be ready to face this competition.

The three conditions as outlined above are necessary for the establishment of the optimum currency areas. The fact is that EU member states are yet to achieve this stage. But the Maastricht Treaty tried to ensure that the eleven countries were similar by imposing four *convergence criteria* related to the exchange rate, inflation rate, interest rates and the public deficit (budget deficit) in relation to the gross domestic product. First, the exchange rate of the country must remain within the *normal fluctuation margin* of the Exchange Rate Mechanism (ERM) for 2 years. Second, the rate of inflation should be no more than 1.5 per cent above the average rate of the three best performing member states. Third, the long term interest rate should be in line with the best countries in term of performances. Fourth, the budget deficit should be not more than 3 per cent of the gross domestic product of the country.

On the surface the success of the convergence criteria in the case of 11 countries shows the success of the common currency. But ground reality may remain different. When all capital market instruments are converted to common currency, the interest rates will converge, but that will not ensure the similarity of the objective situations of the capital markets of the member states. Failure of this implies that capital will not move to the capital poor regions as expected initially. All these show the difficulties in the way of the member states under EU forming the optimum currency areas.

The literature explains the optimum currency areas as an ideal state and it defines whether a group of countries can enter into a monetary union without much negative externality. In a sense every country with its own currency is a monetary union, but that does not guarantee that the country presents an optimum currency area. Big countries like the United States, Russia, China and India are not optimum currency areas, as different states either in the United States or in India do not exhibit the similarity of the economic structures as described under the optimum currency areas.

But the monetary unions do function and this they do with relative success because of the functioning of some adjustment mechanism like flexibility of factor prices and mobility of labour and capital across the regions. Flexible wages and interest rates will clear the markets and that takes care of the unemployment and under employment of factors of production. Free and unrestricted mobility of capital and labour is very important in this adjustment mechanism without which sectoral unemployment will prevail.

What is the real situation in European Union? Different studies suggest that the cultural and linguistic differences among the countries in Europe form a significant barrier to labour mobility. It has to try hard to achieve the type of labour mobility as seen in the United States. But sociologists raise a more fundamental issue and that is whether the social friction that may result duo to labour mobility in the face of cultural differences are desirable from the stability aspect of the society. This is an apprehension and for this economics has no answer.

The success of the Euro will depend largely on the role of the European Central Bank (ECB), which is located in Frankfurt and which is controlled by a set of independent central bankers who are not vulnerable to the political opinion. The ECB will see rough days ahead as it tries to impose strict monetary and fiscal discipline on the weaker countries for the stability of Euro and its success will depend to what extent it can withstand the potential political pressure. The formation of European Union and its impact is discussed here from the perspective of the theory of optimum currency areas.

2.33 Euro and a Historical Introspection

Euro is a unique experience in recent times and many economists are inquisitive about the stability of the new currency. The stability of a currency depends on three factors – the credibility of the government that backs it, the breadth of its market and the constancy of its purchasing power. Since the currency is, in general, a fiat currency, the acceptability depends on the credibility of the issuer, and here the role of the government is important. The breadth of the market in space depends on the transaction domain of the currency and it is proportionate to the gross domestic product of the country. The constancy of the purchasing power of the currency depends on monetary policy that, again, depends on the political stability. This is linked to first one and stable currencies are protected by strong state power.

The British pound and US dollar have been the most important international currencies of the last two hundred years. The pound was the dominant international currency of the nineteenth century because of the following reasons: Britain's monetary policy tied to the gold standard had a history of stability. Again, British empire had become the greatest empire of its time and it was run from the financial centre of London. The pound faded with the end of World War I as British economy became weak and after World War II Britain's empire fell away and US dollar took over as the world's principal currency (Mundell, 1998).

The famous international currencies in history had been produced by strong political powers in their golden times. The story remains the same for the Persian daric, the Macedonian stater, the Byzantine bezant, the Arabian dinar, the Greek drachma, the Roman denarius, the Venetian ducat, the Spanish maravedi, the French livre, and of course of more recently the British pound and American dollar.

The great currencies of history had always been made of precious metals and the viability of the currency was not dependent entirely to the existence and security of the state. In the middle ages when Genoa, Florence, or Venice suffered military defeat, their currencies – sequins, florins, and ducats – still enjoyed a fall back value of about 3.5 grams of gold. But this is not applicable for paper currencies and Confederate paper currencies lost their value at the end of Civil war in the United States in 1864 (Mundell, 1998).

After the end of World War II, US dollar replaced pound sterling as the world currency and it was waiting in the wings since the end of World War I. In 1920s the gross domestic product of the United States was more than three times of its economic rival Great Britain. During this period dollar was anchored to gold standard and the economy had been enjoying ·high and stable rate of growth, low employment and price stability. So it was no accident that dollar replaced British pound as the world currency after the end of World War II.

The 1944 Bretton Woods meetings missed a great opportunity of the creation of a genuine multilateral world currency and that was a theoretically interesting option. But history reveals that international monetary reforms in the direction of a world currency had been blocked by the strong and presiding superpower. Great Britain did it in the nineteenth century and the US also blocked the international monetary reforms that would reduce the role of its currency in international financial system. In the Bretton Woods meetings both Keynes plan of Britain and White plan of the US put forward provisions for a world currency – *bancor* for the Keynes plan and *unitas* of the White plan. But United States rejected the idea of world currency. The Bretton Woods system finalized the agreement with a world financial system based ·on gold and US dollar and there was no provision for a separate world currency. Thus US dollar became the international currency through the commitment of gold window on the part of Federal Reserve of the United States.

Stability of Euro

Viewed from this perspective, Euro is a unique experiment in recent time. It is now the currency of European Union with the exception of United Kingdom. Several more countries are to join EU soon. The once famous currencies like French franc, German mark are all history now. Generally a question comes in the discussion i.e. how stable Euro will be? We have seen above that stability of a currency depends on the strength of the state, the size of the transaction domain and the backing for the currency. In this case Euro has some weaknesses. The

European Union cannot be considered a strong central state. Again Euro will have no formal gold or foreign exchange backing. But these weaknesses are offset by two important considerations.

First, the European System of Central Banks (ESCB) will have huge amount of gold and foreign exchange reserve. Second, though the EU is not a central state, it has the binding force of NATO backed by the US and it survives and becomes stronger with the inclusion of members who were former communist states. With eleven countries already having Euro as the currency of medium of exchange, the stage has been set for the core of a single currency area and it has all the potential to become worthy alternative to the US dollar. Even if that time is not near, the Euro-dollar exchange rate will be very important for the stability of the world financial system.

Role of the World Stock of Gold

The world stock of gold above ground is placed by some estimate as 110,000 tons and at current prices its value will be US$ 1.1 trillion (@ $300 an ounce). Financial authorities including central banks hold about 33 per cent of this stock (Mundell, 1998). Most of the monetary gold is held by the EU countries and they hold 366 million ounces. The United States hold 262 million ounces, Switzerland hold 83 million ounces and all other countries together hold 200 million ounces. Though gold is largely demonetized at present, there is a possibility that it may come back in future at the centre stage should any major instability occur due to lack of faith in any major currency of the world.

Three

Economics of the Open Economy

"The first panacea for a mismanaged nation is inflation of currency; the second is war. Both bring a temporary prosperity; both bring permanent ruin."

[Earnest Hemingway]

3.1 Introduction: Reality and Economics

Economics as a subject teaches how to see and analyze the reality around us with a vision that is distilled with economic tools of analysis. Students of economics are interested in the real world, in understanding what happens, more specifically, what is the effect of what, and what policy can do about the real world. But the observation of reality can better be explained if we compare an artist's canvas with a snap of a photographer. The latter shows reality much more than what a naked eye can see! But the former, i.e., the canvas, is a description of the same reality through the eyes of the artist. The latter is similar to a model that tries to describe reality for a better analysis what is not possible through the snap of the photographer.

Economics is about policy, especially how policy can be made better to disperse better justice to the environment. As Milton Friedman reminds us that even, not to have a policy is to have a policy. If economics is not about policy, what is it about? To explain what economics is all about, it is shown in a schematic way in the form of a diagram. It explains how economics confronts reality and at the same time influences it through different policy implementations.

Figure 1 pictures two different activities in economic research: (i) the collection of data, which attempts to capture the 'real world' of economic activity in quantifiable variables, and (ii) the construction of models, which attempts to represent the abstract world of economic theory in mathematical relations among a small number of variables.

Finally, Figure 1 shows us a third field of economic research, econometrics, which attempts to validate models with the variables made available from data collection.By far, economic theory, leading to new models, ranks highest in the pecking order of Economics research. Econometricians depend both on the models given to them by theorists, and on the data made available by data collection efforts. A very important function in economics is the sincere collection of data. The people who are engaged in data collection, and who wrestle with issues of how best to measure such variables as productivity, price changes, and technical progress do an invaluable service to economics.

Figure 1, by itself, is probably too simple an exposition of the division of labour as observed in the tradition of economic research. It is true that all empirical endeavours, including the work of data collection, are theory-laden, as the theoretical perspectives goad the economics for the selection of empirical evidences. Data collections are not ignorant of what goes on in the world of theory.

But good economic analysis is about the real world, history, events, policy-making, and it is also an abstract, formal process, involving logic. Finally, it is a programme which bears fruit in models, which confront data and stand-up to tests of econometric assessment. These models help us pinpoint what

Figure 1

Real World Economic Activity ➜ Data Collection ➜
➜ Observation and Economic Analysis ➜ Economic Theory ➜
Theoretical Models ➜ Analysis ➜ Conclusion and
Comparison with data

---

the important variables are, which cause other important variables to move, and what policies can do to make things better.

In the perspective of initial comments we build up the model of open economy macroeconomics starting with the classical analysis.

3.2 Monetary Economics - The Classical Tradition

David Hume and the Quantity Theory of Money

The Quantity Theory of Money (QTM) is the first attempt of the classical economists to give full theory of price level and it establishes the relation between price level and money stock of a country. The origin of the theory can be traced back to the writings of the *Three Essays* by David Hume (1754). Through his writings Hume proved the position of the mercantilist[1] belief wrong that countries could become rich by generating balance of payments surpluses and accumulating gold. Also Hume's book *Three Essays* is dominated by several interrelated causal mechanism in economics and Quantity Theory is one of these. Here QTM places the stock of money in relation to the stock of available goods and this relation determines the equilibrium price level. Given prices of commodities in foreign country, an increase in the domestic stock of money causes domestic prices to rise relative to foreign prices.

---

1. The doctrine of Mercantilism dominated both economic and political thinking for over a century from the publication of Machiavelli's *The Prince* in 1532 to Thomas Mun's *England's Treasure by Foreign Trade* published posthumously in 1664. The doctrine was associated with the concept of a strong State, with a positive balance of trade and the accumulation of foreign exchange (gold and other precious metals). The latter was seen as the means of acquiring political strength and national prosperity. Edward Misselden was perhaps the first writer to use the term 'balance of trade' in his book *The Centre of the Circle of Commerce* (1623). He argued that the policies of the State should be to secure a favourable balance of trade by promoting exports and discouraging imports, the country thereby receiving treasure and growing rich. The writers were not sure about the precise means by which the accumulation of treasure would make a country rich. Thomas Mun is taken as the typifying mercantilist thinking in the seventeenth century.

The second causal mechanism is the specie-flow mechanism, which shows that relative prices cause money (precious metals like gold) to vary inversely. The third relation is the loanable fund doctrine, which states that, the supply of and demand for loans together are the cause of the change in the interest rates. Hume also established the causal relation between the interest rates and profit rates. This is known as the arbitrage principle.

The issue of causality in macroeconomics has been debated extensively and part of that debate has attained philosophical undertones (Hoover, 2001). The causality aspect of the Quantity Theory of Money has been debated and researched in two parallel schools — one later on led by the University of Chicago and the other by the famous group of economists known as Keynesians based mostly in Cambridge at two sides of the Atlantic ocean. Some even suggest that it is the nature of the initial construction of QTM that creates controversy always (Laidler, 1991). With this brief note we turn to the QTM proper.

The classical tradition of money begins with the following identity:

$$PQ = MV \hspace{3cm} \textit{Equation 3.1}$$

where M is the quantity of money in the economy, V is the velocity of circulation of money, P is the price index, and Q is full employment output, a proxy for total economic activity.

This equation (3.1) as it stands is an identity. If the quantity of money is low, and there is a lot of activity in nominal terms, then money must be turning around fast, or velocity must be high. However, if the quantity of money is high, and velocity is high as well, but little real production taking place, then prices will be high. The government is expanding money, and people are trying to get rid of it to get the purchasing power, so that prices will be high.

What the classical economists implied was that if people have more real money, they will buy more goods and services. If their wealth increases in the form of possession of more money, they will increase their consumption. So a fall in prices keeping the level of money constant will increase the real money wealth and that will lead to more consumption. This was emphasized by A.C. Pigou and is known as real balance effects.

The first step in the evolution of the quantity theory from a mere tautology to a Theory came from the Cambridge, UK 'cash-balance' interpretation of Equation (3.1), and this interpretation came from the renowned economists Alfred Marshall and A.C. Pigou. The above equation was reformulated as a demand-for-money function:

$$M = k\,PQ, \qquad \text{where } k = 1/V \qquad\qquad Equation\ 3.2$$

The Cambridge school simply took the real quantity of money (M/P) as the endogenous variable, set Q as the exogenous variable, and assumed that V, the velocity of circulation, was constant. Once the level of output is determined, the amount of real quantity of money M/P becomes a solution value of money market equilibrium. This development is a classical rebuttal to the Keynesian position that an increase in quantity of money can ensure full employment. But Keynes at one place attributes unemployment to inadequate supply of money:

Unemployment develops, that is to say, because people want the moon; -- men cannot be employed when the objects of desire (i.e., money) is something which cannot be produced and the demand for which cannot be readily choked off. There is no remedy but to persuade the public that green cheese is practically the same thing and to have a green cheese factory (i.e., a central bank) under public control.

[*General Theory*, p.235]

One may wonder how Mr. Keynes did reconcile this 'green cheese' statement with the rest of his book *General Theory*, where he forcefully advanced the argument that economy might reach an equilibrium at less than full employment!

This approach is a well-defined hypothesis: it states that demand for money depends in a proportional way, or with unitary elasticity, on real output. It is thus a transactions-based demand for money. It also tells us that interest rates do not matter for the demand for money. It is a clear and simple theory, which can in principle be rebutted by the evidence. In this sense, it is not trivial.

The second approach to understanding Equation (3.1) as a theory comes from Irving Fisher. His approach is not a theory of demand for money, but a theory of price adjustment. The relation becomes the following model of prices:

$$P = (V^* / Q^*)\, M$$

$$P = q.\, M, \qquad \text{with } q = V^*/Q^* \qquad\qquad Equation\ 3.3$$

Fisher assumes that both output and velocity are constant in the long run. Thus, prices are proportional to money stocks. Thus, the quantity theory of money is a theory of price-level determination. Fisher affirms that this theory is a long-run theory and he is careful to point out that things may be different in the short run. This led to the debate regarding the neutrality of money in later years.

3.3 Quantity Theory as Theory of Output

Fisher argues that the adjustment of prices and output may be sluggish and asymmetrical. Thus while money is doubled, prices may not double immediately, but it increases slowly, while output may initially decline, then increases from the present level and ultimately come down to initial level. This is a long run process and it leaves ultimately prices proportional to money supply. Most economists today accept the Fisher interpretation of the quantity theory of price adjustment. It is a long-run theory of price adjustment, *ceteris paribus*. Prices will double if money doubles. In the short-run, other factors, such as oil shocks, and supply shortfalls will affect the behaviour of the overall price index.

Fisher's theory holds good only in the absence of nominal government bonds in the economy. Because if there are nominal bonds, an increase in the quantity of the money supply will put upward pressures on the price level. This reduces real value of bonds, and thus lower interest rates. The latter may have effects on saving, investment, and production and this makes the relation between money supply and price level less than proportional. Fisher's approach assumes money as the only issue of the government.

Again the Fisher approach is only valid when money is 'fiat money', the paper issued by the government. In a commodity money standard, when gold or silver serve as the media of exchange, or when these are used as 100 per cent backing for the paper currency, neutrality does not hold. An increase in the quantity of gold, for example, has direct effects on the price of gold, on employment and investment in the mining sector, and thus has relative price effects as well as 'real effects'. Thus, a monetary expansion in the form of an increase in gold is far from being neutral.

The debate between monetarists, Keynesians, and new classical economists (arising from rational expectations) centres on the adjustment process of output. Is the output 'hump' following a monetary expansion a tidal wave or merely a ripple? Should monetary authorities attempt to fine tune the behaviour of aggregate output through money stock changes? In this perspective economists in the Keynesian tradition believe that there is scope for the monetary authority to help the economy move out of recessions by appropriate expansionary policies. On the other hand, the monetarist tradition argued forcefully by Milton Friedman and Anna Schwartz in *A Monetary History of the United States*, establishes the position that money stock changes have long, variable, and unpredictable lagged effects on output. Thus, the economists in the monetarist tradition believe that any attempt to fine tune output by monetary policy may backfire: expansion policies during a time of slackness may kick in just when the economy is in an expansion, and could stimulate inflation. The monetarist approach argues in favour of a policy of constant, smooth monetary growth, which, they believe, would lead to stable prices, and this is the famous *x-per cent rule* of constant money supply.

The rational expectation approach (REA) (that is also known as New Classical Approach) is a new twist on the monetarist tradition. This approach holds that the monetary authority can affect output temporarily, but only if the policy change is unexpected. When people expect monetary policy to become expansionary, they will forecast high prices, and thus will not feel richer, and spend more, when the money stock increases. If people are caught off guard with a sudden increase in the money stock, then there may be temporary effects.

The rational expectations approach also raises the issue of time consistency in Central Bank behaviour. The Central Bank may find it optimal to say one thing (no expansion in the money stock) and do another (expand the money stock), in order to finesse an increase in output. One of the key contributions of this approach has been its focus on the credibility of government policy. While the Central Bank may find it optimal to dissemble once or twice, it cannot do so forever as people will understand the model behaviour of the Central Bank and neutralize it. Whatever the opinions about the short-run adjustment, and the 'real' effects of monetary policy on output, the message of the Fisher model is clear and straightforward: In the long run, monetary expansion means higher prices, or continued higher rates of monetary growth mean higher rates of inflation.

3.4 Purchasing Power Parity

The Purchasing Power Parity (PPP) theory states that prices of traded goods will be same everywhere in the world whether one buys these at New Delhi or New York if we neglect tariffs and transport costs. The (PPP) is a natural open-economy extension of the quantity theory of money. Like the quantity theory, it starts with the tautology:

$$P = E\,Pf \qquad\qquad \textit{Equation 3.4}$$

where P is the price index for tradable goods in the domestic economy, expressed in domestic currency, Pf is the price index of tradable goods in the world market, expressed in foreign money, and E is the exchange rate, the price of one unit of foreign money in terms of domestic money.

Equation (3.4), as it stands, is trivial. Excluding tariffs and transportation costs, it states that the domestic cost of traded goods is simply equal to the foreign price, quoted in foreign money, multiplied by the exchange rate. For highly mobile traded goods, assuming no transport cost, simple goods arbitrage would see that Equation (3.4) is true.

Equation (3.4) becomes a causal monetary theory of exchange-rate determination when we couple it with Fisher's monetary theory of prices, for the domestic and foreign economies. Rewriting Equation (3.4), and making use of the information in Equation (3.1), the following expression emerges:

$$E = P / P f \qquad \text{\textit{Equation 3.5}}$$

And $\quad P = q\, M\, d$

$\quad P_f = qf\, Mf \qquad$ we get from Equation (3.3)

This gives the following

$$E = (q / q^f)\, M^d / M^f \qquad \text{\textit{Equation 3.5 (a)}}$$

Or, if the first term is taken as a constant, it implies that exchange rate between two countries becomes proportional to the ratio of the two countries' money stock, provided it is true that if domestic and foreign price levels are proportional to the money supplies in two countries.

Purchasing Power Parity is one building block of monetary theory of exchange rate determination. Like Fisher's theory, it is a long-run theory: we are talking about long-run relations between money and prices in each country, and thus long-run relations between relative money supplies and the exchange rate. In the short run, events like oil shocks, supply shortages, or technological changes can and do affect the exchange rate as well as price level of the countries.

It is important to see that the tautology of Equation (3.4) becomes a causal theory of exchange-rate determination in Equation (3.5). Money determines prices in different countries, and relative money supplies determine the exchange rate. Both price levels and the exchange rate are endogenously determined by the money supplies.

If one interprets Equation (3.4) as a causal theory of

domestic-price determination, it may lead to misguided policy decision. If one believes that all goods in the economy are tradable, and that foreign prices are more or less stable, then one way to stop inflation, and keep domestic prices constant, is to simply freeze the exchange rate, or at least slow down its rate of change.

3.5. Purchasing Power Parity: an Elaboration

The Purchasing Power Parity theory is about the long-run, and leaves open the question of short-run adjustment, or dynamics like Fisher's quantity theory. Many papers are published on the deviations from PPP in academic journals, but still it is very popular. For a given monetary expansion in the home country, given a constant money supply in the foreign country, if the home country increases its money supply, prices adjust sluggishly, or 'crawl' to their long-run level, while the exchange rates jump more than double, and then comes down, and may move to its long-run level either from above or below. The PPP theory gives broad hints about the exchange rate movement. It is monetary policy that drives both prices and exchange rate in the long run. Failure to come to terms with control of the money supply will only lead to upward movements in both the exchange rate and the price level.

3.6 The Monetarist Arithmetic

The classical tradition focuses on the quantity of money and its effects on the aggregate price level and the exchange rate. Why do governments bother to issue money? The question, of course, comes down to alternative means of financing government deficits. Governments have two options: (1) print money or (2) issue bonds. The following expression represents the government budget deficit:

$$\frac{G}{P} + \frac{iB}{P} - \frac{T}{P} = \frac{\Delta M}{P} + \frac{\Delta B}{P} \qquad \text{Equation 3.6}$$

where G is nominal government spending, B is the stock of bonds, i is the interest rate, T is tax revenue, M is money supply, P is the price level, and Δ is the first-difference operator. Government spending and interest payments on existing debt in excess of tax revenue must be financed either by printing money or by issuing more bonds.

Regarding the financing of fiscal deficit Sargent (1987) raises an interesting and provocative question. He points out that sooner or later, a government following a policy of bond-financed deficits will be forced to default on its debt. As the amount of outstanding bonds increases, so do the debt-service payments of the government with the amount of outstanding bonds. Sooner or later the government will have to 'destroy' its outstanding debt, if its own deficit is to be brought under control. One way to destroy its debt is to print money, increase the price level, and wipe away the real value of outstanding government bonds. In this way, inflation becomes an instrument of government policy, rather than an objective of economic policy.

Sargent points out that without a fiscal correction (an increase in T or a decrease in G), increased bond expansion sooner or later becomes unsustainable. The government will have to run an inflation, to get the deficit under control. What the author points out is that the corrective inflation at the end after a period of bond financing of deficits, will result in a higher rate of inflation, than if the government had simply financed its deficits from the beginning by printing money.

Because if the government prints money to finance its deficits, from the start, inflation will show up. But the government does not have to pay interest on past issues of money that remain in circulation. Period-by-period, the government prints money to pay for the excess of G over T, but the government does not owe any interest of past issues. When following the bond-financing scheme, however, inflation does not show up, but the government has to issue new bonds at each period, not only to cover the excess of G over T, but also the interest payments on the outstanding bonds held by the public. As bond issues mount, so do the interest payments. When the crisis point finally arrives, there is a large stock of bonds to be paid. To liquidate that higher inflation is necessary compared to printing of money for financing deficit period wise.

The 'unpleasant' aspect of the Sargent's monetarist arithmetic is that bond financing does not negate the quantity theory, but brings it back with a vengeance, in the absence of a fiscal reform. The use of bond instruments for financing deficits can defer inflation for a time, but sooner or later bonds will lose their worth, if the government does not put its fiscal house in order. This is an important lesson for many developing countries.

3.7 Balance of Payments Adjustment

In 1931 gold standard was abandoned. Since the automatic adjustment mechanism of balance of payment (BoP) was no longer possible, different explanations were given to explain the BoP disequilibrium and these are:

(i) it is a problem of distorted relative prices in international trade,

(ii) it is a problem of excessive expenditure of the country relative to output, and

(iii) it is a problem emanating from the domestic monetary disequilibrium.

The above three ways of viewing the BoP difficulties correspond to the so-called elasticity approach, absorption approach and monetarist approach.

The Elasticity Approach

The elasticity approach to balance of payments adjustment focuses on the current account of the balance of payments. On the assumption that there may be distortion in relative prices in the international market, it explores the question: what conditions must prevail in the foreign exchange market for a devaluation or depreciation of the currency to improve the balance of payments starting from equilibrium, with the balance of payments measured either in foreign or domestic currency? It is basically a partial equilibrium analysis - holding constant everything else that may affect the supply of and demand for foreign or domestic currency, except the change in the relative price of foreign and domestic goods arising from the change in the exchange rate itself. It also assumes that the supply elasticity of all goods are infinite. It implies that the domestic price of exports, the foreign price of imports, and the prices of import and export substitutes are constant. Also autonomous expenditure in money terms is held constant.

Under these assumptions, the condition for a devaluation to improve the balance of payments is known as the Marshall-Lerner condition, which states that devaluation will improve the balance of payments on current account if the sum of the price elasticity of demand for exports (η) and imports (ψ) exceeds unity in absolute value i.e. if:

$$| \eta + \Psi | > 1 \qquad\qquad\qquad Equation\ 3.7$$

The intuitive explanation of the condition is as follows: Consider a small x percent devaluation which leads to a x percent fall in the foreign price of domestic exports. If the demand for exports rises by less than x percent, foreign exchange earnings will fall; if demand rises by more than x percent foreign exchange earnings will rise, and if demand rises by exactly x percent, foreign exchange earnings will remain the same. In this last case of unitary elasticity of demand, it would then only require a minute cutback in import demand (an elasticity of demand for imports slightly above zero; $\Psi > 0$) for foreign exchange earnings to improve in total. Any combination of price elasticity of demand for exports and imports will improve foreign exchange earnings provided they sum to greater than unity.

A seemingly contrary result was derived by Harberger (1950), and is repeated by Stern (1973). They suggest that the income effects of devaluation alter the Marshall-Lerner condition, making it more stringent. The explanation is that these models hold real expenditure constant implying a rise in autonomous expenditure in money terms, so that in a two-country model, *money* expenditure rises in the devaluing country and falls in the appreciating country. This raises imports and reduces exports for the devaluing country, and the condition for balance of payments improvement becomes:

$$|\eta + \Psi| > 1 + m_1 + m_2 \qquad \textit{Equation 3.8}$$

where m_1 is the marginal propensity to import of the devaluing country and m_2 is the marginal propensity to import of the other countries. Of the two specifications which one should be preferred depends on whether a successful devaluation is interpreted to mean one which improves the balance of payments *with* real income falling or without real income falling.

The Absorption Model of the Balance of Trade

The Keynesian tradition, like the classical tradition, starts with the following identity in an open economy situation:

$$Y = C + I + G - T + EX - IM \qquad \textit{Equation 3.9}$$

where Y is national product, C consumption, I investment, T tax payments, EX exports, and IM imports. As it appears, equation (3.9) is trivial: it must be true.

However, the absorption approach, assumes that the trade balance (EX-IM), is the dependent variable:

$$(EX - IM) = Y - (C + I) + (T - G) = (Y - A) + (T - G),$$

$$\text{Where } A = C + I \qquad \textit{Equation 3.10}$$

Equation (3.10) tells us that the trade balance depends on how much an economy produces in excess of its domestic absorption (consumption and investment), and how much its government saves. Thus, this relation would predict chronic trade deficits for countries which have (1)chronic fiscal deficits, with T < G, and for countries which have (2)low private saving or high investment relative to domestic production, with Y < A. Equation (3.10) offers a simple and striking explanation of chronic trade deficits. It tells us that chronic fiscal deficits are mirrored in trade deficits. It also predicts that countries that keep their fiscal house in order and that have high saving rates (low C relative to Y) will have chronic trade surpluses.

The correct policy for correcting a trade deficit, then, is fiscal stabilization, and in the longer-term, a policy of increasing domestic production relative to domestic absorption, through increasing productivity and personal savings.

In a functional macroeconomic sense the absorption approach to the balance of payments may be regarded as superior to the partial equilibrium elasticity approach. But it unfortunately gives the impression that it *plans* to spend in excess of *plans* to produce that is causal in the explanation of balance of payments deficits. In practice this may not be the case. Equations (3.9) and (3.10) which portray the balance of payments as the difference between income and expenditure, or savings and investment, are derived from the national income *identities*, and causation must never be inferred from identities. A deficit in the first instance may be caused by an autonomous fall in exports; by an autonomous rise in imports, or by an autonomous deterioration in the real terms of trade. This may be quite independent of decisions to spend more than output, because real income has been depressed. For the simultaneous achievement of macroeconomic goals, the diagnosis of the true *initial* source of the deficit is important if the correct policy is to be adopted.

Suppose the deficit is not caused by excess demand at full employment, but is due to an exogenous fall in real income. In this case dampening demand to cure the deficit will simply lead to an even lower level of real income. This confusion is similar to the IMF adjustment programmes in developing countries that is taken as stemming from *ex ante* excess demand whereas the real root of the problem may be poor export performance, import penetration, or a cyclical worsening of the terms of trade.

In an important paper Johnson (1958) establishes the impression that balance of payments deficits are not simply associated with excess monetary demand for goods. The latter may cause the former. He distinguishes between what he calls a stock deficit and a flow deficit. The former is self correcting through a rise in interest rates caused by a once-for-all switch out of domestic assets. The latter is not self-correcting and the monetary authorities accommodate the deficit by expanding the money supply. In either case, the deficit is *caused* by an excess supply of money, with equilibrium in the money market being restored by a loss of international (foreign exchange) reserves. This interpretation of the absorption approach led to the emergence of the monetarist approach to BOP.

The Monetary Approach

The essence of the monetary approach to the balance of payments is that it takes the balance of payments as a whole, that is, the current and capital account together. It assumes that changes in international reserves are a function of disequilibrium between the supply of, and demand for, money. An excess supply of money leads to a loss of international reserves and an excess demand for money leads to a gain in international reserves. Again, the changes in the level of reserves are the mechanism by which the balance between the supply and demand for money is restored. A currency depreciation can only be successful if it increases the nominal demand for money relative to the supply, as the price level rises. This is achieved by reducing the real supply of money in relation to the real demand. Johnson (1977) once asserted that 'all balance of payments disequilibria are monetary in essence'.

3.8 Further Implications

The trade balance is simply exports less imports, evaluated in domestic currency, thus we can write trade balance (BOT) as,

$$BOT = EX - e.p^* IM \qquad \text{Equation 3.11}$$

where e is the exchange rate, p^* the foreign price level, EX exports and IM imports. The current account is simply the balance of trade, BOT, plus the net interest receipts of the home country — interest income on foreign capital owned by domestic residents, Kf,d, less interest payments on domestic capital owned by foreign residents, Kd,f:

$$\text{Current Account} = BOT + e.i^* K_{f,d} - i K_{d,f} \qquad \text{Equation 3.12}$$

where i* is the foreign interest rate and i is th domestic rate.

The capital account is simply net car al inflows, or changes in domestic capital owned by for gners, less the changes in foreign capital owned by domestic residents, and this can be written as,

Capital Account = $\Delta K_{d,f} - e \Delta K_{f,d}$ Equation 3.13

Finally, the net foreign asset position of a country is simply the amount of foreign capital owned by domestic residents less the amount of domestic capital owned by foreign residents. The net foreign asset position of a country tells us if a country is a net creditor or a net debtor, and this can be written as,

$$NFA = e. K_{f,d} - K_{d,f}$$ Equation 3.14

With these definitions, one can easily understand that the persistent trade deficit, financed by capital inflows, sooner or later, will change the net foreign asset position of a country from the status of a net creditor to that of a net debtor. The result shows in the changes of the international reserve of the country. Sometimes international reserve may increase even though balance of trade is adverse. This happens through the capital inflow in capital account.

3.9 Classical and Keynesian Models: A Comparison

On the surface, there does not seem to be any consistency and similarity between the classical models of the quantity theory of price adjustment and purchasing power parity with the Keynesian absorption model of trade. The classical models take stocks as the exogenous policy variables, while the absorption model concentrates on flow variables (fiscal balance, income, consumption, and investment). The classical models concentrate on the adjustment of price indices, either the aggregate price level or the exchange rate, while the Keynesian model looks at the adjustment of a flow, the trade balance. Finally, the classical models speak of the long-run effects of policy changes, while the absorption model is interested in the short-run adjustment of flow variables.

The key difference is that economists in the classical tradition believe that the economy is inherently stable and will adjust to long-run equilibrium without need of government intervention. The classical economists believe that government intervention is usually a part of the problem, not the solution. Keynesians, however, believe that the economy can get stuck in the short-run disequilibrium of a persistent trade deficit, with high unemployment, and that corrective government intervention may be called for in order to help the economy move smoothly from short-run adjustment of trade-flows to balance, and to long-run adjustment of prices and exchange rates.

The discussion of market failure, of course, admits the need for government intervention like the standard case of public goods with externality. Whether this case can be extended to the macro economy is still a debate that goes on in different planes.

3.10. Appendix

India's Balance of Payments

India is one of the three large economies in the process of transition (apart from Russia and China). It is important to observe how the external sector of India has been changing after the economic reforms in 1990. This can be discerned by seeing the actual data of India's balance of payments. The data are in millions of US dollars.

India's Balance of Payments in US Dollars: Selected Years

(US $ million)

Items	1990-91 PR			1997-98 PR			1998-99			1999-2000		
	Credit	Debit	Net	Credit	Debit	Net	Credit	Debit	Net	Credit	Debit	Net
1	2	3	4	5	6	7	8	9	10	11	12	13
A. CURRENT ACCOUNT												
I. **MERCHANDISE**	**18477**	**27915**	**-9438**	**35680**	**51187**	**-15507**	**34298**	**47544**	**-13246**	**38285**	**55383**	**-17098**
II. **INVISIBLES (a+b+c)**	7464	7706	-242	23244	13237	10007	25770	16562	9208	30324	17389	12935
a) **Services**	4551	3571	980	9429	8110	1319	13186	11021	2165	15721	11865	3856
i) Travel	1456	392	1064	2914	1437	1477	2993	1743	1250	3036	2139	897
ii) Transportation	983	1093	-110	1836	2522	-686	1925	2680	-755	1745	2410	-665
iii) Insurance	111	88	23	240	183	57	224	112	112	236	122	114
iv) G.n.i.e.	15	173	-158	276	160	116	597	325	272	582	270	312
v) Miscellaneous	1986	1825	161	4163	3808	355	7447	6161	1286	10122	6924	3198
b) **Transfers**	2545	15	2530	12254	45	12209	10649	62	10587	12672	34	12638
vi) Official	462	1	461	379	-	379	308	1	307	382	-	382
vii) Private	2083	14	2069	11875	45	11830	10341	61	10280	12290	34	12256
c) **Income**	368	4120	-3752	1561	5082	-3521	1935	5479	-3544	1931	5490	-3559
i) Investment Income	368	4120	-3752	1561	5020	-3459	1893	5462	-3569	1783	5478	-3695
ii) Compensation to Employees	-	-	-	-	62	-62	42	17	25	148	12	136
Total Current Account (I+II)	**25941**	**35621**	**-9680**	**58924**	**64424**	**-5500**	**60068**	**64106**	**-4038**	**68609**	**72772**	**-4163**

(Contd.)

India's Balance of Payments in US Dollars: Selected Years (Contd.)

(US $ million)

Items	1990-91 PR			1997-98 PR			1998-99			1999-2000		
	Credit	Debit	Net	Credit	Debit	Net	Credit	Debit	Net	Credit	Debit	Net
1	2	3	4	5	6	7	8	9	10	11	12	13
B. CAPITAL ACCOUNT												
1. Foreign Investment (a+b)	**113**	**10**	**103**	**9266**	**3913**	**5353**	**5892**	**3580**	**2312**	**12240**	**7123**	**5117**
a) In India	113	10	103	9169	3779	5390	5743	3331	2412	12121	6930	5191
i. Direct	107	10	97	3596	34	3562	2518	38	2480	2170	3	2167
ii. Portfolio	6	-	6	5573	3745	1828	3225	3293	-68	9951	6927	3024
b) Abroad	-	-	-	97	134	-37	149	249	-100	119	193	-74
2. Loans (a+b+c)	**9432**	**3899**	**5533**	**17301**	**12502**	**4799**	**14771**	**10353**	**4418**	**13060**	**11459**	**1601**
a) External Assistance	3397	1193	2204	2885	2000	885	2726	1927	799	3074	2183	891
i) By India	-	6	-6	-	22	-22	-	21	-21	-	10	-10
ii) To India	3397	1187	2210	2885	1978	907	2726	1906	820	3074	2173	901
b) Commercial Borrowings (MT & LT)	4282	2028	2254	7382	3372	4010	7231	2864	4367	3207	2874	333
i) By India	30	24	6	11	-	11	5	-	5	20	-	20
ii) To India	4252	2004	2248	7371	3372	3999	7226	2864	4362	3187	2874	313
c) Short Term to India	1753	678	1075	7034	7130	-96	4814	5562	-748	6779	6402	377
3. Banking Capital (a+b)	**10106**	**9424**	**682**	**8910**	**9803**	**-893**	**8197**	**6717**	**1480**	**11259**	**8532**	**2727**
a) Commercial Banks	7960	7056	904	8164	9424	-1260	6768	6434	334	10859	7955	2904
i) Assets	425	789	-364	580	2775	-2195	1344	2741	-1397	2653	1863	790

(Contd.)

India's Balance of Payments in US Dollars: Selected Years (Contd.)

(US $ million)

Items	1990-91 PR			1997-98 PR			1998-99			1999-2000		
	Credit	Debit	Net	Credit	Debit	Net	Credit	Debit	Net	Credit	Debit	Net
1	2	3	4	5	6	7	8	9	10	11	12	13
ii) Liabilities	187	456	-269	52	242	-190	124	135	-11	201	227	-26
iii) Non-Resident Deposits	7348	5811	1537	7532	6407	1125	5300	3558	1742	8005	5865	2140
b) Others	2146	2368	-222	746	379	367	1429	283	1146	400	577	-177
4. Rupee Debt Service	-	1193	-1193	-	767	-767	-	802	-802	-	711	-711
5. Other Capital	3117	1186	1931	3815	2463	1352	3958	2801	1157	4018	2510	1508
Total Capital Account (1 to 5)	22768	15712	7056	39292	29448	9844	32813	24253	8565	40577	30335	10242
C. Errors & Omissions	132	-	132	167	-	167	-	305	-305	323	-	323
D. Overall Balance (Total Capital Account, Current Account and Errors & Omissions (A+B+C))	48841	51333	-2492	98383	93872	4511	92886	88664	4222	109509	103107	6402
E. Monetary Movements (i+ii)	2492	-	2492	-	4511	-4511	-	4222	-4222	591	6993	-6402
i) I.M.F.	1214	-	1214	-	618	-618	-	393	-393	-	260	-260
iii) Foreign Exchange Reserves (Increase - / Decrease +)	1278	-	1278	-	3893	-3893	-	3829	-3829	591	6733	-6142

(Contd.)

India's Balance of Payments in US Dollars : Selected Years (Contd.)

(US $ million)

Items	Apr.- Jun. 1999 PR			Jul.- Sep. 1999			Oct.- Dec. 1999			Jan.- Mar. 2000		
	Credit	Debit	Net	Credit	Debit	Net	Credit	Debit	Net	Credit	Debit	Net
1	14	15	16	17	18	19	20	21	22	23	24	25
A. CURRENT ACCOUNT												
I. MERCHANDISE	**8148**	**12305**	**-4157**	**9660**	**13053**	**-3393**	**10172**	**13976**	**-3804**	**10305**	**16049**	**-5744**
II. INVISIBLES (a+b+c)	**6461**	**4059**	**2402**	**6977**	**4696**	**2281**	**7736**	**4159**	**3577**	**9150**	**4475**	**4675**
a) Services	3194	2782	412	3403	3186	217	3956	2896	1060	5168	3001	2167
i) Travel	671	556	115	662	520	142	809	530	279	894	533	361
ii) Transportation	361	522	-161	475	716	-241	430	642	-212	479	530	-51
iii) Insurance	48	27	21	62	18	44	70	41	29	56	36	20
iv) G.n.i.e.	154	71	83	105	69	36	162	61	101	161	69	92
v) Miscellaneous	1960	1606	354	2099	1863	236	2485	1622	863	3578	1833	1745
b) Transfers	2808	7	2801	3095	11	3084	3315	8	3307	3454	8	3446
vi) Official	57	-	57	66	-	66	126	-	126	133	-	133
vii) Private	2751	7	2744	3029	11	3018	3189	8	3181	3321	8	3313
c) Income	459	1270	-811	479	1499	-1020	465	1255	-790	528	1466	-938
i) Investment Income	442	1267	-825	426	1493	-1067	429	1255	-826	486	1463	-977
ii) Compensation to Employees	17	3	14	53	6	47	36	-	36	42	3	39
Total Current Account (I+II)	**14609**	**16364**	**-1755**	**16637**	**17749**	**-1112**	**17908**	**18135**	**-227**	**19455**	**20524**	**-1069**

(Contd.)

India's Balance of Payments in US Dollars : Selected Years (Contd.)

(US $ million)

Items	Apr.- Jun. 1999 PR			Jul.- Sep. 1999			Oct.- Dec. 1999			Jan. Mar. 2000		
	Credit	Debit	Net	Credit	Debit	Net	Credit	Debit	Net	Credit	Debit	Net
1	14	15	16	17	18	19	20	21	22	23	24	25
B. CAPITAL ACCOUNT												
1. Foreign Investment (a+b)	**2004**	**664**	**1340**	**2915**	**1849**	**1066**	**2542**	**1803**	**739**	**4779**	**2807**	**1972**
a) In India	1996	645	1351	2904	1806	1098	2468	1722	746	4753	2757	1996
i. Direct	454	2	452	649	1	648	400	-	400	667	-	667
ii. Portfolio	1542	643	899	2255	1805	450	2068	1722	346	4086	2757	1329
b) Abroad	8	19	-11	11	43	-32	74	81	-7	26	50	-24
2. Loans (a+b+c)	**2636**	**2416**	**220**	**3092**	**2878**	**214**	**2913**	**2678**	**235**	**4419**	**3487**	**932**
a) External Assistance	448	459	-11	718	591	127	929	577	352	979	556	423
i) By India	-	2	-2	-	3	-3	-	4	-4	-	1	-1
ii) To India	448	457	-9	718	588	130	929	573	356	979	555	424
b) Commercial Borrow-ings (MT & LT)	627	560	67	766	747	19	601	735	-134	1213	832	381
i) By India	6	-	6	-	-	-	14	-	14	-	-	-
ii) To India	621	560	61	766	747	19	587	735	-148	1213	832	381
c) Short Term to India	1561	1397	164	1608	1540	68	1383	1366	17	2227	2099	128
3. Banking Capital (a+b)	**3107**	**1852**	**1255**	**2256**	**2099**	**157**	**3397**	**2132**	**1265**	**2499**	**2449**	**50**
a) Commercial Banks	2714	1849	865	2255	1896	359	3394	1841	1553	2496	2369	127
i) Assets	708	404	304	558	573	-15	1256	320	936	131	566	-435

(Contd.)

India's Balance of Payments in US Dollars : Selected Years (Contd.)

(US $ million)

Items	Apr.- Jun. 1999 PR			Jul.- Sep. 1999			Oct.- Dec. 1999			Jan.- Mar. 2000		
	Credit	Debit	Net	Credit	Debit	Net	Credit	Debit	Net	Credit	Debit	Net
1	14	15	16	17	18	19	20	21	22	23	24	25
ii) Liabilities	14	64	-50	58	5	53	84	25	59	45	133	-88
iii) Non-Resident Deposits	1992	1381	611	1639	1318	321	2054	1496	558	2320	1670	650
b) Others	393	3	390	1	203	-202	3	291	-288	3	80	-77
4. Rupee Debt Service	-	518	-518	-	3	-3	-	49	-49	-	141	-141
5. Other Capital	1024	542	482	711	634	77	557	839	-282	1726	495	1231
Total Capital Account (1 to 5)	8771	5992	2779	8974	7463	1511	9409	7501	1908	13423	9379	4044
C. Errors & Omissions	466	-	466	-	912	-912	421	-	421	348	-	348
D. Overall Balance (Total Capital Account, Current Account and Errors & Omissions (A+B+C))	23846	22356	1490	25611	26124	-513	27738	25636	2102	33226	29903	3323
E. Monetary Movements (i+ii+iii)	-	1490	-1490	591	78	513	-	2102	-2102	-	3323	-3323
i) I.M.F.	-	78	-78	-	78	-78	-	78	-78	-	26	-26
iii) Foreign Exchange Reserves (Increase -/Decrease +)	-	1412	-1412	591	-	591	-	2024	-2024	-	3297	-3297

Four

Exchange Rates, Interest Rate and Foreign Exchange Market

"Paper money is beginning to act more like paper and less like money."

[Jerome Smith]

"The actual rate of exchange is largely governed by the expected behaviour of the country's monetary authority."

[Dennis H. Robertson]

Like any other market in economic theory, foreign exchange market is also a commodity relationship market, and it is defined as the relation between buyers and sellers for the purchase and disposal of the currencies of different denomination. A student desiring to send some amount of US dollars to New York as an application fee is to approach a local bank for the purchase of the required dollars. He is asked to submit a specified amount of Indian rupees to the bank and he obtains a demand draft of US dollars drawn on a New York bank. The relationship between the amount of the Indian rupee and US dollars is determined by the price of one unit of US dollar in terms of Indian rupee, and this price is the exchange rate of the Indian currency.

Exchange rate is the price of one unit of foreign currency in terms of the domestic currency.

There is a *two-ness* in the transactions in the foreign exchange. Any transaction is between two currencies. Each person involved in the transaction is simultaneously a buyer and a seller of currencies. The bank in the above example is buying Indian rupees and selling US dollars. The student is also doing just the opposite, selling Indian rupees and buying US dollars. Each transaction again involves two banks as the Indian bank is using its dollar balances when it issues the draft to the student. Lastly the Indian bank by selling US dollars making itself short of it, and it is to purchase equal amount of dollars to square its position. This aspect is unique in foreign exchange transaction and it makes it a bit complicated process.

4.1 The Players

By its nature foreign exchange market (FEM) is a global market. The principal players are the governments, the central banks, commercial banks, other financial institutions, brokers, business corporates and individuals. The major transactions are between the commercial banks, which are authorized dealers in foreign exchange.

The central bank is an important player as it has the primary responsibility of maintaining the stability of exchange rate of domestic currency. The stock of the latter is issued by the central bank for circulation in the domestic economy. Part of this may be floating in the international market. It is the responsibility of the central bank to preserve the intrinsic value of its liability. This gives credibility to the domestic currency in the international market. It is not without reason that people are reluctant to hold Italian lira or Indonesian rupiah.

Commercial banks are the providers of liquidity to the economic system and this they do by facilitating the cash flow of currencies of multiple denominations. They hold foreign currency for this and the portfolio of commercial bank has the important element in the form of foreign currency either in the form of cash or short-term monetary instruments. Trading in foreign exchange is an important source of revenue to the banks.

Corporate houses enter into FEM to convert their asset or liability in foreign currency into the domestic currency. The latter being the currency of the balance sheet, the corporate are to insulate the balance sheet position from the fluctuation of the exchange rate. Firms doing international business should pay the suppliers in the local currency in each country in which they operate. They also receive payments in different currencies from their customers. These foreign currency cash flows are converted into domestic currency.

The brokers and individuals, though small players, have their important role in FEM. The brokers provide some crucial services to the banks when the market behaves in an erratic manner.

Two more players have become active in the area of international finance now-a-days and they are investors and speculators.

Many corporate businesses own property and acquire business abroad. The capital flow both ways and the repatriation of earnings are of foreign currency. This they surrender to the central bank of the country and get the domestic currency. In case of portfolio investment in bonds, shares abroad larger sums are involved and the investors are to enter into the FEM for regular conversion of domestic currency into foreign one and vice versa.

The large-scale presence of speculators in FEM has been a dominant phenomenon since the middle of 1980s. Their role in FEM is to buy and sell foreign currencies for a margin. The transactions are not backed by any genuine demand for trade of merchandise. It is trading in currencies only.

The dynamism and depth of FEM depend on the behaviour pattern of these agencies. Modern technology has provided the full information to players and it is how they decipher the market information and use for their response it determines the course of market movement.

4.2 Trading Location

The currency market is truly global and it has no single physical location. Most trading in currency occurs in the inter-bank markets, among financial institutions located in different countries. Trading in FEM typically occurs through telephonic conversations and also through computer network around the globe. International markets remain always open during the weekdays. It opens first in Sydney, then Tokyo, Singapore, Hong Kong, Mumbai, Bahrain, Frankfurt, London, New York and Chicago. Thus when Europe is opening, Sydney is closed and markets remain open as the globe gets the sunshine during the day.

Most banks do their spot-market currency trading in the same centres though they have the technological capability to do trading with the distant corner of the globe. Still some centres have gained importance in the volume of trading. London is one such centre and New York is second. The importance of principal centres of the world is shown in the following Table.

In 2001 the amount of daily turnover in FEM all over the world was approximately US $1210 bn and only 1 per cent of the sum was accounted for the merchandise trade. Rest is pure speculation. The markets also deal with some financial products known as derivatives. These are hedge tools customers and/or financial institutions buy to safeguard against future potential risk due to adverse fluctuations in the exchange rate of the domestic currency. The typical products

Table 4a: Geographic Distribution of Global Currency Trading: Some Principal Centres [as on April 1998]

Country/ Location	Average daily turnover (US $ bn.)	Percentage share
London (UK)	637.3	32
New York & Chicago (USA)	350.9	18
Tokyo (Japan)	148.6	8
Singapore	139.0	7
Germany	94.3	5
Switzerland	81.7	4
Hong Kong	78.6	4
France	71.9	4

Source: Bank for International Settlements.

are currency futures, currency forwards, currency swaps and options.

The nature of trading in currency futures is different and it started first in Chicago Mercantile Exchange. Even today it is the predominant exchange for currency futures in the world. The exchange at Sao Paolo, Brazil comes next in terms of volume of trading. Trading in currency futures at other exchanges is minimum, as the customers prefer other forms of derivatives.

4.3 Favourite Currencies

The demand for a currency depends on the demand for the commodities to be imported from the country. If India wants to import machinery from Italy, India needs reserves in Italian lira, and India can buy that currency from FEM in exchange for some other currency or US dollar. The latter is international currency by the Bretton Woods Agreement. But in global markets, several currencies are traded most and that can be seen from Table 4b.

The US dollar is more dominant in spot markets trading compared to derivative trading. Also it has the predominant position in the foreign currency reserves of the member countries of the International Monetary Fund (IMF). Again, in

Table 4b: Foreign Exchange Trading by Currencies, 2001

Currency	Percentage of turnover
US dollar	42.5
Euro	18.8
Japanese Yen	11.4
British Pound	6.6
Swiss franc	3.5
Canadian dollar	2.3
Other currencies	12.2

Source: Banks for International Settlements.

1990s, many transition economies had adopted US dollar as their *de facto* medium of exchange and that had increased the demand for dollar in a large way.[1]

German D-mark and Japanese Yen are two strong currencies and many countries keep these two currencies as a part of their international reserves. Japan encourages trade in Yen in case of countries in south and Southeast Asia. Other currencies including British pound are not much favourite, though Euro is coming up fast. With the introduction of Euro in eleven countries of European Union, a significant realignment in the international currency holding is expected. Currencies like French franc, deutschmark, lira, escudo etc., have been replaced by Euro in the respective countries.

4.4 Quotations in Foreign Exchange Transactions

In FEM the price quotations of any currency becomes a two-way quote, like for INR/USD, the quotation is like

$1= Rs. 48.90/97

The above is an inter-bank rate, and bank is willing to buy at the rate of $1= Rs. 48.90 and sell @ 48.97. This is said as bid/ask rate and the difference between the two is known as spread.

Again, a dollar/D-mark quotation will read like 1.5000/10. The bank which quotes this rate reveals that it will buy mark (sell dollars) at 1.5010 and sell mark (buy dollar) at 1.5000. It means that it buys cheaper and sells dearer a particular currency in exchange for the other one. The opposite is true for the person who has asked for a quote. The difference between the purchase and sell rates is called "spread". Spreads

---

1. In the transition economies like the so-called CIS countries, e.g., Tajikistan, Ujbekistan, and east European countries like Hungary, Poland etc., people started using US dollar as medium of exchange. This happened mainly for two reasons: the countries were in the process of introducing their own currencies, and/or, the people were waiting for the stability of the home currency. In the intervening period they were using US dollar. In fact, in many countries dual currency systems are in operation, US dollar being the second currency.

change according to market volatility.[2]

A foreign exchange rate consists of an integer part and 4 decimal points (sometime 2 decimal points). Thus the decimals are expressed either at 10th thousands or hundreds. Each such 0.0001 is called *basis points* or *pips*. For example, a 40 pips change in the dollar/rupee exchange rate $1= 48.0000/10 means $1= 48.0040, or, $1=47.9960.

4.5 Direct and Indirect Quote

The above prices showing a unit dollar in terms of rupees as 48.0000 is known as direct quote. This is the prevailing system and Reuter screen shows rates in this fashion except some currencies like British pound. In this case the dollar/pound rate is shown as pound/dollar rate.

If we take the reciprocal of the direct quote, we get the indirect quote and in case of the above dollar/ rupee rate this will be Re 1= $ 0.02128, that is reciprocal of 48.0000. The indirect quote has one advantage. In this format an increase in value means the currency is moving up. But in direct quote, an increase in value means the currency is moving down. In 1992, dollar/rupee rate was 31.3700 and compared to that rate in 2001 is 48.0000. It implies that Indian rupee has gone down about 50 per cent during last 9 years.

4.6 Direction in the Market

In FEM the exchange rate is a relative price. So when one currency goes up, it implies that other currency is going down. In case dollar/rupee rate changes from 48.0000 to 48.0005, market signals that rupee is going down, and it also means that dollar is going up. Thus unlike in the markets for stocks,*there is no directions for the market.* But there is direction of movement for the currencies. In the case of stock markets, the index of the

---

2. Spread is an important variable in FEM. This denotes the fraction **p**(ask) - **p**(bid). Sometimes spread is expressed in logarithm form

    $$S = \log p\,(ask) - \log p\,(bid).$$

    In the direct quote, spread is positive. Economists have used the change in spreads to predict the future behaviour of some macro variables like inflation and interest rates.

market gives an average direction and that reveals the aggregate movement of the stock prices.

4.7 Inter-banking

In the domestic or international transaction mechanism inter-banking occurs when a customer doing banking with Bank AA wants to pay a customer doing banking with Bank MM. Thus the system of inter-banking is important and the process of setting up of inter-banking involves the following steps:

i. Each bank is to create a vostro account
ii. Each bank is to ask other bank in foreign country to open nostro account for itself
iii. Each bank is to send the list of nostro and vostro accounts to the clearing centre [like EuroPEN in Europe]

The EuroPEN system is a bilateral clearing system. It uses nostro and vostro accounts to settle inter-bank transactions. It does not act as a clearing house but as a distribution hub. This makes the system easier as the transactions of all banks come to a single point for settlement among the participating banks.

4.8 Foreign Exchange Account

When an Indian company approaches a bank for the payments of French franc to a French company in France for the imports, the Indian company pays Indian rupee to the bank at a rate offered by the bank. The bank gives a demand draft drawn on a bank in France. That French bank may be a branch of the Indian bank, or may be a representative bank of the Indian bank. In either case the Indian bank is maintaining a French franc account with the French counterpart. This is known as a nostro account. This is an important accounting system in the international payment process.

A nostro account is opened and maintained in foreign countries to settle foreign currency transactions like exports, imports, remittances and other similar things. Nostro accounts are currency specific, that is, an Indian bank can open US dollar account in USA only, though a bank can maintain more than one nostro account in dollar in different cities of the USA.

All dollar deposits in the bank will be added to the nostro account that gives the liquidity to the bank so that it can meet the demand for dollars of the potential importers.

Parallel to the nostro account when the foreign bank opens a rupee account in India with an Indian bank, it is known as vostro account. Thus the Citi Bank in New York can open a vostro account with State Bank in Delhi and make all rupee payments in India on behalf of the American importers of Indian commodities.

4.9 Reimbursement Claim Solution (RCS)

For a large bank with a vast network and connection with a large number of correspondent banks, it becomes difficult to monitor all the transactions in multiple currencies. To address this problem some software are developed. Reimbursement Claim Solution (RCS) is a commercially available fully integrated solution designed for large network bank that offer a collection service to downstream correspondent banks for all export collection items, reimbursement authorizations and check collections. RCS is a fully scalable solution. It offers comprehensive functionality for the collection item transaction flow from the network of the downstream correspondents to the clearing centre of the correspondent service provider. This integrated approach provides an operating advantage to a network bank competing for correspondent banking services.

For a correspondent branch operation, RCS improves the operation by tracking and tracing payments on behalf of the customers of the branches. At the head office level of the correspondent, RCS automatically consolidate all claims by its branches and it provides the bank a wide view of all outstanding claim items. Thus at a point of time the bank can have an overall picture regarding the claims in a consolidated form.

In total there are many types of transactions in the foreign exchange market. What has been most apparent in the last fifteen years is that the majority of transactions in this market are not the ordinary exporters and importers settling their international accounts. The market is driven by the speculators and interest arbitrageurs, trying to take advantage of expectations about future exchange rates and international interest-rate differentials. This means, one's domestic currency can appreciate not because foreigners are trying to buy the products of the country, but because they are taking advantage of higher interest rates or expectations of an appreciation. Ordinary exporters, facing competitive international markets, may suddenly find their products 'price out' of competition, unless they pass-through the exchange-rate effect, by cutting the prices of their exports in domestic currency, so that the international prices remain the same after the appreciation. This was the Japanese trick. However, the pass-through means lower profit margins in domestic currency, and exporters can not do this just for so long. So large capital inflows can cause problems for exporters and export production, and thus for employment.

4.10 Export and Import Transactions

The first use of foreign exchange is for the settling of international export and import transactions, accounts receivable and accounts payable. An importer in India ultimately pays a foreign supplier in the foreign currency. An Indian taking a trip abroad will need foreign currency for day-to-day expenses.

The foreign exchange market determines the spot rate for demand and supply of foreign currency. This exchange rate is not the same as the rate for bank notes one finds at Railway stations and airports. This tourist rate may be slightly above the quoted spot rate, since tourist exchanges have the added risks of keeping currency in hand and currency dealers at work. The quoted spot rate is the inter-bank rate for switching local currency from an account in a domestic bank to foreign currency in an account in a foreign bank.

The combination policy of devaluation and a fiscal austerity program is the traditional IMF recipe for countries in a chronic balance-of-payments deficit. This is what the international 'money doctors' prescribe, after their missions and diagnoses. It should be remembered that devaluation involves a cut in the standard of living. A devaluation means higher costs for imported goods, which could include food and medicine, as well as intermediate goods for production of manufactured goods. Fiscal austerity also means hardship. This is certain that the cure for a chronic balance-of-payments deficit is often harsh.

The question is to what extent should policy-makers rely on fiscal contraction, and to what extent should policy-makers opt for exchange rate adjustment?

For many countries, the exchange rate has become the anchor of expectations. Changes in the exchange rate signal further inflation, so that devaluation simply passes through to upward adjustment in prices. In Argentina, the sentiment was that it is Christmas time, so it is time for devaluation. So let's raise our prices in anticipation. Of course, the government would announce that this year's devaluation could be the very last. The Cavallo stabilization plan of 1991 fixed the exchange rate of the peso at a one-for-one parity with the US dollar, with full convertibility. The central bank would function as a 'currency board': domestic monetary expansion would be linked on a one-for-one basis with reserve changes. The central bank could neither monetize fiscal deficits nor act as a lender of last resort, to private banks facing liquidity problems.

The fixing of the exchange rate had an immediate effect on price expectations: inflation had come down, and stayed down, after many years. However, there had been a chronic trade deficit. The government was faced with a dilemma: it could devalue, and re-ignite inflationary expectations, or it could live with the trade deficit, loose reserves, and leave itself open to a speculative attack, or it could opt for further fiscal contraction. There was no question that the continuing trade deficit in Argentina was a 'warning signal' of an overvalued exchange rate, and that fiscal contraction was called for.

The position of Mexico is a bit different. It also faced a large trade deficit and slow growth, just at the time when the country should be hitting the ground running after the ratification of the North American Free Trade Agreement (NAFTA). Unlike Argentina, however, Mexico has not had a recent history of hyperinflation. The exchange rate is not the anchor of expectations for price setting. There is thus room for a significant devaluation to restore competitiveness and growth, and to reduce the trade deficit. Mexico, unlike Argentina, can make use of the exchange rate instrument for domestic adjustment.

It should be clear that the advisability of using the exchange rate instrument or the fiscal instrument depends on the 'initial conditions' of a particular country, on its recent history of inflation, on how inflationary expectations are linked to the exchange rate, and on government credibility.

4.11 Marshall-Lerner Conditions

The effectiveness of the devaluation (in a fixed system) or depreciation (in a flexible system) of the currency for reducing a trade deficit depends on 'well-behaved' demand and supply curves for foreign exchange. The precise conditions that guarantee that devaluations 'work' are the Marshall-Lerner (ML) conditions. These conditions simply state that the sum of the absolute values of the elasticities of home demand for foreign goods and foreign demand for home goods must be greater than one. The Marshall-Lerner conditions link the effectiveness of a monetary instrument with analysis of the demands for home and foreign goods in the 'real sector'.

The basic idea behind the Marshall-Lerner conditions is that the exchange rate affects the terms of trade between two countries. Terms of trade are defined as the ratio of export prices, Px, over import prices, Pm. In domestic currency units, the price of imports Pm is equal to the exchange rate E multiplied by the world price level P^*m.

Thus,

$$Pm = E.P^*m.$$

A devaluation or deprecation thus implies a fall in the terms of trade, in domestic currency units. Similarly, in foreign currency units, a devaluation of the home currency raises the terms of trade of the foreign country. The ML condition states that a depreciation or devaluation of a country's currency will improve its current balance if the total of the price elasticities of demand for exports and imports is larger than unity.

The effects of devaluation on trade balance can be decomposed into three factors:

(i)   A devaluation will reduce the real quantity of imports, and that will reduce the foreign exchange spent on imports,

(ii) The devaluation will increase the real quantity of exports, and

(iii) Since export price is denominated in domestic currency, export will bring more revenue in foreign exchange if the increase in real exports is much higher compared to reduction in prices.

But the elasticity approach needs another condition and this is:

(iv) We assume that the economy is initially in a position of balanced trade. Given this, the necessary and sufficient condition for the devaluation to improve the trade balance is that the sum of the elasticities of demand for exports and imports is greater than unity, or,

$$\varepsilon_x + \varepsilon_M > 1$$

where ε_X and ε_M are elasticities of demand for exports and imports respectively. This is also known as a stability condition in balance of payments.

4.12 The J-Curve

Even when the Marshall-Lerner conditions hold, and the demand and supply curves are well-behaved, there is still the possibility that the devaluation, initially, will make the trade balance worse, before making it better. The J-curve is a well-observed phenomenon. The emergence of J-Curve can be explained in the following manner. After the devaluation of the domestic currency, the value of imports in domestic currency increases and the volume does not decline because of lag effects of prices and contract obligations. On the other hand, the volume of exports does not increase immediately, as price effects takes time to be effective. Meanwhile, the value of exports in foreign currency shall decline if invoices of exports are in domestic currency. The net results are a worsening of the balance of trade situation in the short run. In the long run the price effects become stronger, export increases and imports decline and balance of trade improves. This happens if the elasticities of demand for imports and supply of exports are smaller in the short run than in the long run. The course of movements of the balance of trade first falling and then moving up gives a shape like J and hence the name of the curve.

4.13 Contractionary Devaluations

In an exceptional situation devaluations may lead to a contraction of domestic output if the import intensity of domestic production is high. Further, if the imports are of intermediate goods, such as capital equipment, then the devaluation may result in a shrink in industrial production. Also export goods, which use imported capital goods, will become less competitive as a result of devaluation. Both these effects will lead to a decline in exports and domestic output.

Figure A: J-Curve: Movement of Balance of Trade over time

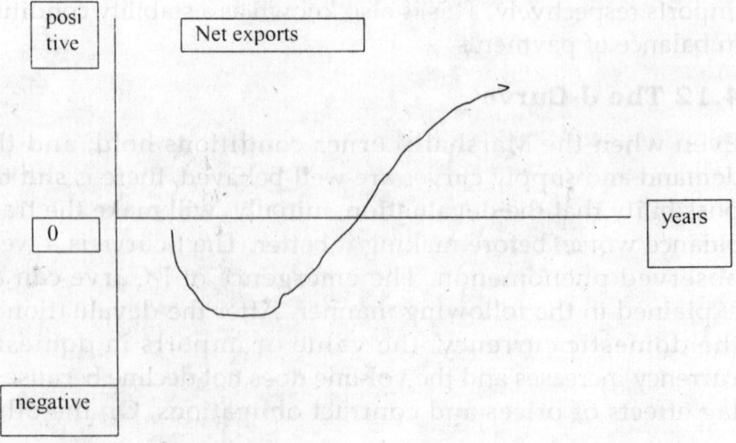

This has recently happened in case of some south Asian countries and also for some Latin American countries.

4.14 Forward Speculation

The participants in forward markets resort to speculation for gain and they generally follow two rules:

    (i) if depreciation is expected, buy forward, sell spot;

    (ii) if an appreciation is expected, sell forward, buy spot.

There are forward markets as well as spot markets. The forward markets exist to diminish risk in foreign currency contracts. If one knows one is to make payments in US dollars in three months, one can negotiate a forward contract to purchase US dollar now, at an agreed forward price. One then delivers the rupees in three months, and receives the dollar at the agreed price. There is usually a small margin requirement (about five percent, say) at the time the forward contract is signed. But for the risk covered, the margin is negligible.

The advantage of the forward contract is that it eliminates risk of exchange rate fluctuations. But it eliminates the possibility of gains from exchange rate changes also.

4.15 Market Efficiency

The forward speculation process is a good test of the efficiency of the foreign exchange market. If traders have expectations of an appreciation or depreciation, there will be actions in the forward markets. If there is a rush to buy or sell forward, the traders will adjust their prices for the forward contracts. After all, for every winner in the forward speculation gain, there is a loser. It is a zero-sum game in this particular sense. But in an efficient market, there should be no persistent speculative profit opportunities, though there can be random profits, with gains and losses distributed randomly. But if people are making persistent profits, then forward dealers are suffering persistent losses.

It is expected that the forward rate should reflect expectations of next period's spot rate, and it means that the current forward rate should be the best statistical predictor of next period's spot rate. This hypothesis has been verified for the major currency markets.

4.16 Hedging and Interest Arbitrage

Hedging is simple insurance against risk of any kind and exchange risk is one of these. If one makes a foreign investment, putting $1000 into £500 today in order to invest in a Guilt-edge security in the UK at an interest rate of 7 per cent, maturing in one year, one will have a gross return of £535. However, it is still not clear what your return will be in dollars: it may be more or less than $1070 assuming that the exchange rate may not stay at the initial one £ 1= $ 2. One can remove the risk of exchange rate loss (due to a depreciation of sterling against the dollar) by purchasing forward cover. At the foreign investment in guilt-edge securities in the UK is made, one can sell forward £535 for $1070 if the forward rate remains same as spot.

4.17 Covered Interest Parity and Forward Premium

Hedging does apply to any type of expected return denominated in a foreign currency. The covered interest parity is closely related to the use of forward cover as a hedge against exchange-rate risk in foreign investment. Let K be the initial amount of US dollars set aside for investment, r is the rate of return in the US, r* is the rate of return in India, S is the dollar-rupee spot rate, and F is the dollar-rupee forward rate. One can simply deposit the K dollars in the US at an annual interest rate of r, and after one year, receive a gross return of K(1+r). Alternatively, one can convert the dollar capital into rupee K/S, and after one year, receive a gross rupee return of (K/S)(1+r*). By selling the gross returns forward, one can guarantee a certain return in dollars,

$$(K/S) (1+r^*) F$$

The main insight of covered interest parity is that it should not make any difference where you put your money, in dollar deposits paying a net return r, or in rupee deposits, paying a return r*. Staying in dollars, or round-tripping, going into rupee, and then converting into dollars through forward sales, will not make any difference. Because if people could get a better return going into rupee, with no exchange rate risk, they would simply borrow in dollars, and invest in rupee, and pocket the difference. If mobility of capital is perfect and if the dollar-denominated and rupee-denominated assets are of equal risk, then we should have the following equality:

$$K(1+r) = (K/S)(1+r^*)F \qquad \text{Equation 4.1}$$

This relation simplifies to:

$$S(1+r)/(1+r^*) = F \qquad \text{Equation 4.2}$$

Subtracting S from both sides, we have:

$$S(1+r)/(1+r^*) - [(1+r^*)/(1+r^*)]S = F - S \qquad \text{Equation 4.3}$$

This simplifies to:

$$(r - r^*)/(1+r^*) = (F - S)/S \qquad \text{Equation 4.4}$$

Equation (4.4) is the exact covered interest parity relation. The right-hand side represents the forward premium (when $F > S$) or discount ($F < S$). In most cases, $(1+r^*) \cong 1$, so the approximate covered interest parity (CIP) relation becomes:

$$(r - r^*) = (F - S)/S \qquad \text{Equation 4.5}$$

Since the forward rate F is the expected spot rate, $E(S_{t+1})$, covered interest parity is a relation between interest rate differentials and exchange-rate expectations:

$$(r - r^*) = [E(S_{t+1}) - S]/S \qquad \text{Equation 4.6}$$

where the right-hand side of equation (4.6) is the expected rate of depreciation of the home currency.

The implication of the covered interest-parity theory for countries having fixed exchange rates is that they must coordinate their interest rates if they wish to maintain fixed (zero) expectations of exchange-rate changes. The Central Bank should have an interest rate target along with other parameters in the context of the management of monetary policies.

Uncovered Interest Parity

Uncovered Interest Parity (UIP) assumes that lenders and borrowers in the international markets treat domestic and ·foreign securities as perfect substitutes. This establishes a relation such as

$$r_t = r^*_t + (S_{t+1} - S_t) \qquad \text{Equation 4.7}$$

where the second bracketed term is the expected rate of depreciation of the domestic currency. The equation implies that portfolio managers always seek the compensation of the expected depreciation of the domestic currency in case of their investment. When the expected depreciation seems to be high so as to make the nominal interest rate inadequate to compensate the loss due to depreciation, foreign investors withdraw from the market. This creates a crisis like situation.

Further from the Purchasing Power Parity (PPP) condition we get

$$P = S. P^*, \qquad \text{Equation 4.8}$$

·Or, in logarithmic form

$$\log P = \log S + \log P^* \qquad \text{Equation 4.9}$$

after differentiating with respect to time t, we can write

$$(1/P). (dP/dt) = (1/S). (dS/dt) + (1/P^*). (dP^*/dt)$$

$$\text{Equation 4.10}$$

or, $\quad \Pi_t = \Delta S_t + \Pi^*_t$

or, $\quad \Delta S_t = \Pi_t - \Pi^*_t \qquad \text{Equation 4.11}$

From Equation (4.11) and equation (4.7) we get by substitution

$$r_t = r^*_t + \Pi_t - \Pi^*_t$$

or,

$$r_t = (r^* - \Pi^*_t) + \Pi_t$$

or, $r_t = R^*_t + \Pi_t$ *Equation 4.12*

or, nominal interest rate is the sum of real interest rate R* and the expected inflation rate Π, that is known as open economy Fisher equation.

4.18 Measuring Capital Mobility

The covered interest parity relation has another important function. It is the most widely quoted measure of capital mobility. One can use this measure to evaluate the degree of capital mobility between two countries. Most measures of capital mobility using the covered interest parity relation in the literature show near perfect capital mobility among the industrialized countries.

An alternative measure of capital mobility is uncovered interest parity. Similar to covered interest parity, it simply replaces the expected future exchange rate with the actual exchange rate at time t+1:

$(r - r^*) = [St+1 - S]/S$ *Equation 4.13*

The uncovered interest parity assumes perfect myopic foresight: expectations from time t to t+1 are perfectly realized, without error. It is said that uncovered interest parity is a stronger and more restrictive test of capital mobility, as it is a test of capital mobility with perfect, not just rational, expectations.

There is another test of capital mobility, and it is real interest parity: one would expect convergence in real returns for capital among countries where there are few restrictions to the mobility of capital. The real interest rate for any country is simply its nominal interest rate less the expected rate of inflation, p. Hence, we have the following real interest parity relation:

$$r - \pi = r^* - \pi^*$$ *Equation 4.14*

But this test, like uncovered interest parity, is more difficult than covered interest parity.

It assumes that the returns adjusted for inflation should be equal across countries. To put it other way, it tells us that nominal interest differentials should be reflected in inflation differentials, not just expected or actual percentage changes in the nominal exchange rate E:

$$r - r^* = \Pi - \Pi^*$$ Equation 4.15

This relation imposes Purchasing Power Parity as a short-run relation. Expected exchange rate changes, or actual exchange rate changes, linked to interest differentials, are equal to expected inflation differentials.

Feldstein and Horioka Approach

Another measure of capital mobility is the correlation of national saving with national investment, following the work of Feldstein and Horioka (F-H). Given the national income identity:

$$(S - I) + (T - G) = (X - M)$$ Equation 4.16

One sees that there is a link between aggregate savings/investment and the trade balance. Under perfect capital mobility, persistent savings-investment imbalances can be sustained, as capital inflows finance the trade deficits. This is seen in many developing countries including India.

F-H argues that in a world of capital mobility country's savings are free to flow to their productive uses anywhere in the world. So for perfect capital mobility there should be no relation between a country's domestic savings and its domestic rate of investment. This is placed in the model form that can be estimated using time series data and the equation is:

$$(I / Y)_t = a + b \, (S / Y)_t + u_t$$ Equation 4.17

where

I/Y =   ratio of gross domestic investment to national income

S/Y =   ratio of aggregate savings to national income

u   =   random error term with a normal distribution

The Null Hypothesis to be tested from the estimation is:

Ho:b = 0

The F-H relation has been estimated by many economists and the results have been a mixed one. Some even tried to measure the correlation between (I/Y) and (S/Y) across countries (Obstfeld, 1995; Nandi,1999).

4.19 The Real Exchange Rate

In the discussion regarding the exchange rate link to the real world and to the relative prices, it is observed that the exchange rate works through its effect on the terms of trade, or the relative price of a country's exports to its imports, in domestic currency terms. However, a more important link is through the 'real exchange rate', defined as the relative price of tradable goods to non-tradable goods.

Figure B pictures the production possibility frontier of an economy, as a division of traded and non-traded goods. The relative price of traded/non-traded goods is the equilibrium relative price, which determines the allocation of production between these sectors. The tradable goods sector of the economy is the growth-producing and employment generating sector of the economy. Countless studies have documented that countries that allocate more of their resources in the tradable goods sector have higher long-term growth rates, higher employment rates, and higher living standards, than countries, which do not. The reason is simple and straightforward: the tradable goods sector is the outward-looking sector of the economy, with a higher learning-curve. Goods that are produced in this sector must be competitive with goods produced internationally. Thus, this sector must respond and adjust to innovations more rapidly than other sectors of the economy. It is also the sector of producers whose market is not limited by the size of the domestic economy.

By contrast, the non-tradable sector is primarily the service sector, whose goods serve the local economy, with little or no competition from abroad. The need for a fairly high and stable

Figure B: Production Possibility Frontier

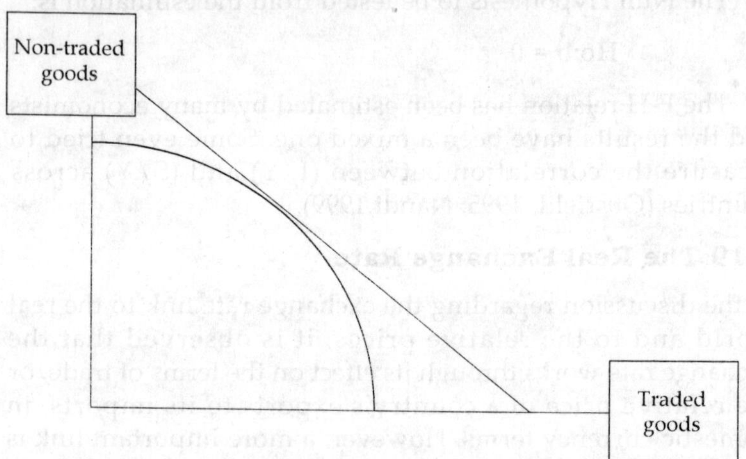

real exchange rate is obvious. With a high and stable real exchange rate there are strong and credible incentives for the allocation of resources to this sector. Unstable real exchange rates, by contrast, obstruct development of this sector.

What is the real exchange rate, in operational terms? Since we do not observe price series of tradable and non-tradable goods, one may approximate it with following relation:

$$\text{REXR} = \frac{P(\text{traded})}{P(\text{nontraded})} \approx \frac{S\,P^*}{P(\text{cpi})} \qquad \textit{Equation 4.18}$$

where P^* is the world price (in foreign currency) of tradable (or manufactured) goods, and S is the exchange rate. Given that the world price of tradable goods changes very slowly, one can normalize this relation, by assuming that the world price index $P^* = 1$, so that the real exchange rate is approximated by the ratio of the nominal exchange rate to the consumer price index, P_{cpi}. The consumer price index serves as the proxy for the non-tradable goods price index, since this index incorporates the prices of services and other non-tradable goods. Thus, the ratio of the nominal exchange rate to the CPI price index often serves as the proxy for the real exchange rate, *ceteris paribus*:

$$\text{REXR} \approx S/P_{cpi} \hspace{2cm} \textit{Equation 4.19}$$

However, the above definition can give misleading results. For example, a trade liberalization programme reduces the price of tradable goods, and thus lowers the real exchange rate (or causes a real appreciation). This would not be picked up by the ratio of the nominal exchange rate to the consumer price index. One can thus make use of an alternative measure, the ratio of the wholesale price index to the consumer price index:

$$\text{REXR} \approx P_{wpi}/P_{cpi} \hspace{2cm} \textit{Equation 4.20}$$

In the alternative scenario the above ratio gives a measure of real exchange rate, though this is used in a special situation as described.

4.20 Monetary and Fiscal Policy in Open Economies

An economy is 'open' to interaction with the rest of the world through two channels: through international trade, and through capital flows. Analysis of monetary and fiscal policy is at once richer, and more interesting, and more complicated in the open-economy context: the relative effectiveness of these two policy instruments depend on two other policy parameters: the choice of exchange-rate regime, and the degree of capital mobility, inflows and outflows, permitted by the government. Complexities apart, the relative effectiveness of monetary and fiscal policy is perhaps the single most important question facing policy makers whose national economies are subject to a myriad of expected and unexpected shocks.

The traditional analysis of monetary and fiscal policy is the IS-LM model of Hicks and Hansen, based on their diagrammatic illustration of the Keynesian system. Their analysis was of a closed economy: no trade, no capital flows, no balance-of-payments constraint, no exchange-rate decision. The two models that we will examine are built on the classical foundations of monetary theory and on the micro-economic analysis of the foreign exchange market. Both models tackle the problem of the appropriate use of monetary and fiscal policy under fixed and flexible exchange rates, and also the way these results depend on the degree of capital mobility.

The analysis creates the backdrop of the Mundell-Fleming and Dornbusch models under full or near-perfect capital mobility. Under fixed rates, monetary policy is weak, and fiscal policy becomes the policy-instrument for intervention. By contrast, under flexible rates, fiscal policy looses much of its effectiveness, and monetary policy comes into its own. The reasons why this policy-effectiveness 'switch' takes place, as the economy moves from one exchange-rate system to another, will become clear in the analysis of these two models. Later we will discuss the classical 'policy trilemma' where this problem is focused more sharply.

Both the Mundell-Fleming and Dornbusch models show the usefulness of good economic theory in analyzing real world situation. Both models use clear, easy to accept, and reasonable assumptions. The basic insights about monetary and fiscal policy in the open economy come from the two models.

4.21 Mundell-Fleming Model of Fixed Exchange Rates

The model dealing with balance of payments has also initiated discussion on the role of international capital flow in the determination of the exchange rate. Modern macroeconomics has adopted this approach to analyze exchange rate determination that originated with the papers of Mundell (1968) and Fleming (1962). Their theory known as Mundell–Fleming approach [MF] states that exchange rate enters the macroeconomic framework of output determination because change in the exchange rate affects the competitiveness of the country in the external front. The depreciation of the domestic currency has the same effects as the fiscal policy regarding its influence on the domestic demand for goods that is associated with each level of output and interest rate. The depreciation of the domestic currency shifts world demand for domestic goods and works in an expansionary manner.

The Mundell-Fleming model rests on the following three-equation set-up:

IS Curve : I(r) = S(y),   I′ < 0, S′ >0   *Equation 4.21a*

LM Curve: M/P = L(y, r),   Ly >0, Lr <0   *Equation 4.21b*

FF Curve: BOP = EX - IM(y) + NKI(r),   *Equation 4.21c*

IM′ >0, NKI′ >0

Here I′ means first derivative of I(r) with respect to the variable r, and same is the meaning of others. Similarly, L_y is the first derivative of L(y,r) with respect to variable y and the same meaning is applicable to others. The balance of payments (BOP) is defined as net exports (exports minus imports) plus net capital inflow NKI, the latter is a positive function of rate of interest. Since exports are autonomous, imports depend on domestic income and net capital inflow is a function of rate of interest, BOP depends on two variables, domestic income and rate of interest.

The IS (Investment-Saving) curve summarizes equilibrium in the goods market, in which investment I must be equal to aggregate saving S. Investment is negatively related to the domestic interest rate r, while aggregate saving positively responds to increases in domestic income y. Hence we see I′ <0 and S′ >0.

In Figure C the shift of the IS and LM curves are shown on the right, the three markets are in equilibrium at E. The LM (for

Figure C: Mundell-Fleming Model

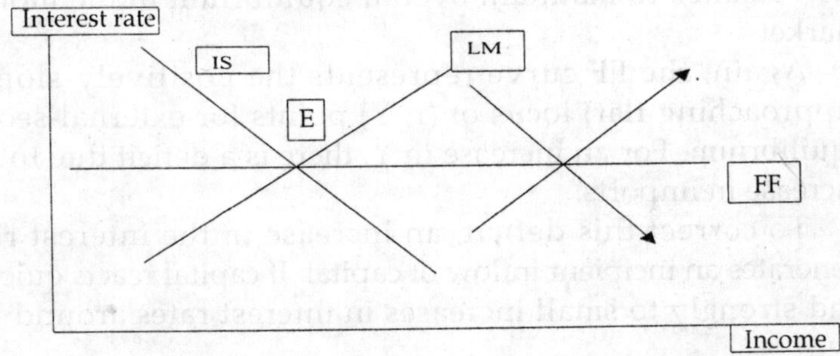

Liquidity-Money Demand) curve summarizes equilibrium in the money market. Exogenous supply of real balances M/P must be equal to demand L, which is positively related to income (based on transactions demand) and negatively related to the level of interest rates. The latter is based on an inventory-theoretic cash-management approach. Hence we get $L_y > 0$ and $L_r < 0$.

The FF curve is the foreign sector or external constraint. The balance of payments definition includes exogenous exports EX, less imports IM which depend positively on domestic income, and net capital inflows. The latter depends positively on the level of domestic interest rates, relative to a fixed level of foreign interest rates.

The adjustment of the bond market is implicit in the analysis and that is through Walras' Law. The latter states that if there are N markets in the economy, and (N-1) markets are in equilibrium, then the Nth market is in equilibrium. Once we have equilibrium conditions for goods, money, and the foreign sector, bond market is automatically taken care of. When people are happy holding their money, goods, and foreign assets in equilibrium sense, they have to be happy with the domestic interest-bearing assets they are holding.

The IS curve represents the negatively-sloped locus of (r, Y) points which clear the commodity market. A rise in Y increases savings S; thus, r must fall to induce more investment to match the increase in S. The LM curve gives the positively-sloped locus of (r,Y) points which clear the money market. An increase in Y increases demand for money; with a fixed real supply (M/P), only an increase in r will decrease demand for cash balance to maintain overall equilibrium in the money market.

Again, the FF curve represents the positively-sloped (approaching flat) locus of (r, Y) points for external-sector equilibrium. For an increase in Y, there is a deficit due to the increase in imports.

To correct this deficit, an increase in the interest rate generates an incipient inflow of capital. If capital reacts quickly and strongly to small increases in interest rates around the world, only a small increase in the domestic interest rate would be needed to restore external-sector equilibrium after the increase in Y. Thus, the higher the degree of capital mobility, the flatter the FF curve. The horizontal curve shown in the diagram implies perfect capital mobility.

The MF framework has an important implication for monetary theory. We see that under condition of perfect capital mobility and with given interest rate of the world, monetary policy works by generating a depreciation and through that a current account surplus, and not through the interest rate channel. It draws attention to the important role of exports in the generation of aggregate demand. It also explains the relation between interest rate and exchange rate.

The MF framework implies an equilibrium exchange rate that can be obtained as the condition of goods market equilibrium or, as the equilibrium condition of the whole system. The model does not allow any role of exchange rate expectation, neither the depreciation has any effects on the domestic price system.

The overall equilibrium of the system is at E. At this point, all three markets are clear. How can we be sure that all three markets will clear at the same point? The assumption of convertibility of the money supply under fixed exchange rate guarantees that the LM curve will pass through the intersection of the IS and FF curves. Under full convertibility, the change in the money supply is linked to the reserve (R) changes induced by the balance of payments:

$$\Delta M = \Delta R = BOP\,(Y, r)\,,$$

$$BOP_Y < 0, \quad BOP\,r > 0 \hspace{3cm} Equation\ 4.22$$

Thus, a displacement of the interest rate above the FF (along the IS curve) will cause a surplus in the balance of payments, an increase in reserves, an increase in the money supply, and a rightward shift of the LM curve. Further, a rightward shift of the LM curve depresses domestic interest rates below world levels, and causes an outflow of capital. The loss of reserves generates a contraction in the money supply, forcing interest rates back up, until the initial equilibrium is restored at E. Under perfect capital mobility the change in the level of international reserve and the money stock move in tandem. This induces interest rate adjustment, and the latter causes capital movement to stabilize both   exchange rate and balance of payments.

4.22 Recent Advances in Open Economy Macro-economics

Following the publication of the paper by Obstfeld and Rogoff [1995] there have been lot of discussion regarding the applicability of the traditional doctrines of international economic theory for the explanation of modern day problems of both developed and developing countries.

Five

Theory of Exchange Rate Determination

"We have indeed in many fields learnt enough to know that we cannot know all that we would have to know for a full explanation of the phenomenon".

[F. A. Hayek]

Introduction

There has been a tremendous growth of the literature on exchange rate in the past two decades. The success or failure of an open economy depends crucially on the management of its exchange rate. Given this importance it is no wonder that exchange rate is one of the heavily researched areas in the economics literature. In case of an open economy the exchange rate of the domestic currency is the crucial link between the domestic economy and the world. When the country is having a flexible exchange rate regime, the domestic economy is expected to adjust whenever exchange rate changes. This makes the exchange rate change very important. There are several theories that explain the movement of the exchange rate both in the short run and the long run.

The exchange rate reflects the bilateral quantitative relation between two sovereign currencies, which themselves are the numeraire in their domestic markets for the determination of the nominal prices of the commodities. This aspect brings the exchange rate into the central place of the open economy macroeconomics. Further, since it reflects the external price of the sovereign currency, the authorities attach importance to the stability of this rate. Thus, many governments give much weightage to the stability of the exchange rate. Moreover, the stability of the exchange rate is important to safeguard the economic interests of the country and this aspect will be made clearer a little later.

The exchange rate as defined above is the indirect quotation of the same in the foreign exchange market (popularly known as forex market). But the direct quotation (which is more popular) defines the exchange rate of a currency as the price of foreign currency in terms of the domestic currency.

5.1 Determination of Exchange Rate

The existing theories explain the movement of the exchange rate rather than the determination of the rate initially. The initial determination of the exchange rate is done by the gold content of the currency as announced by the sovereign government. In the olden days of the bullion standard, the intrinsic value (metal value) of the coin had been more or less synonymous with the face value. Thus the metal content of the respective coin could determine the exchange rate. This system worked smoothly till the first decade of the 20th century. Subsequently, paper gold standard replaced the gold bullion standard and paper currency came into circulation to meet the historical needs of the time. The evolution of money in its present form and its intrinsic nature can be discerned from the following passage:

"Currency differs from other things in that an increase in its quantity exerts no direct influence on the amount of the service it renders. Inconvertible paper currencies.

The exceptional character of this 'quantity' statement in regard to the value of currency has been described in many ways. But the central fact in the account now submitted is that an increase in the amount of money in a country does not increase the total services which it performs. This statement is not inconsistent with the fact that an increase in the amount of gold in a country's currency increases her means of obtaining goods by exporting gold, and also gives her the power of converting some of her currency into articles of ornament. It merely means that the purpose needs to be clearly defined and generally acceptable. Next, it needs to command a stable purchasing power; such stability can be attained by an inconvertible paper currency, so long as the government (a) can prevent forged notes from getting into circulation, and (b) can make the people absolutely certain that currency will not be issued in excess. Gold coins may indeed be regarded as currency based on the belief that their nature will not countenance a violent increase in the currency drawn from her stores. If we were to discover (in spite of the opinion of geologists and mineralogists that no such thing is physically possible) a mine of gold ore with contents as large in volume as those of a vast coal mine, then gold coin would cease to serve any good purpose."

(Marshall, 1924; pp. 91-92)

This rather long quote explains in detail the nature of money and how the stability of its price depends on some economic circumstances. From the value of money in general we look for the determination of the exchange rate. But the process can be further explained by studying the history of the gold standard.

5.2 Gold Standard: A Brief History

The international gold standard dates from 1870, though the oldest known gold coins date from the sixth century B.C. The system lasted until 1914, when the first World War started, and then had a brief revival in the 1920s. But Britain was on a full legal gold standard from 1816, and on a *de facto* gold standard since 1717. Until the late 19th century most countries were on a bimetallic standard. Some countries, particularly China and Mexico, were on silver alone and remained so into the 20th century. When gold was discovered in California in 1848, Holland and Belgium switched from bi-metallism to silver alone in 1850 as gold was considered to be too unstable to provide the basis for the currency. After the Civil War, the United States too adopted a *de facto* gold standard with the resumption of the specie payment on the Civil War greenbacks in 1879. Two decades later it moved formally into the system with the Gold Standard Act of 1900.

The initial exchange rate system had been nearly a fixed exchange rate, between the currencies of the countries on the gold standard. Further, the system remained assured by the possibility of profitable gold arbitrage whenever exchange rates reached the gold export or import points, determined by the mint charges and the cost of shipping gold. The fluctuations in the exchange rates had been influenced by the changes in the production costs in the mint, by the gradual decline in the shipping costs and also by the interest rate changes.

The system of gold standard which remained functional in the 19th and early 20th century had been typified by three broad features. First, the nineteenth century gold standard was a gold coinage standard in which gold coins remained in domestic circulation and these were interchangeable with notes at the central bank and the latter maintained a gold reserve to maintain and safeguard interchangeability.

Second, within the gold standard of the 19th century, British sterling operated as an international currency on equal terms with gold. According to Professor Tew (1948) the sterling was even stronger compared to gold and the latter derived its value as a monetary asset from its convertibility into sterling. In the case of the settlement of the international transactions, both gold and sterling were used as overseas banks of many countries held working balances in sterling.

Third, it is interesting to compare the gold standard of the period 1870-1914, based on gold and the internationally acceptable sterling with the gold exchange standard of the post-1918 period. The crucial difference between the two periods had been the much weaker position of sterling and many other currencies were established in countries on the basis of gold standard. Thus the structure of the gold exchange standard in the post-1918 period had been weak and before the full realization of its weakness another World War broke out in the late thirties, putting an end to the system.

The gold standard had evolved basically into a system of international balance-of-payments adjustment as theoretically developed by the classical economists. The classicists contended that the movement of goods at the international level was the result of the differences of the relative price levels, and the dimension of the movement of goods would be determined by the laws of the comparative advantage. While the changes in the relative price level would depend on the supply of money and natural advantages, the surplus and deficits in international transactions were taken care of through the shipment of gold and/or through the accounts in British sterling. Thus the quantity theory of money as developed by Hume and the comparative cost doctrine as developed by Ricardo supplied the theoretical building blocks of the gold standard (Meade, 1951).

The brief description of the system of gold standard helps in the understanding of the exchange rate mechanism in the world. The essential points which are important can be written as: the cost of production of gold and the stability in the price of it, the system of money supply as in practice in the principal countries, the operation of the law of comparative advantage, the movement of the relative price levels and the cooperation among the central banks of the countries. These factors used to influence the exchange rate of the principal currencies.

5.3 Models of Exchange Rate Determination

A large number of models have been developed in literature to explain the fluctuation of the exchange rate and a systematic grouping in some schematic form is difficult, though not impossible. Broadly, we can put all the models into two categories—the monetary and the non-monetary models. Later on various subgroups of models have been developed within each group. The aim of this brief survey is to give a broad synoptic view of the whole literature.

The Purchasing Power Parity Theory (PPP)

The Purchasing Power Parity (PPP) theory was developed first by Cassel (1918) and since then it has been one principal building block in the monetarist literature. In its simple and absolute form it states the following equation:

$$E = P/P^*$$

Equation 5.1

Where P and P* are domestic and foreign price levels and E is the exchange rate or the price of foreign currency in terms of the domestic currency.

Expressed as in equation (5.1), the exchange rate between any two currencies is equal to the ratio of their price indices. Thus the exchange rate is a nominal magnitude on prices. Further, equation (5.1) can be rewritten as:

$$P = E \cdot P^* \qquad\qquad \text{Equation 5.2}$$

Or the exchange rate converts the foreign price into the domestic price. In other words, equation (5.2) implies the law of one price, i.e. a tradable commodity like HMT watch should cost the same whether it is purchased at Mumbai or New York, when we ignore the transport cost. The PPP doctrine is often used to explain the long run movement of the exchange rate. From equation (5.1), after logarithmic transformation, we have:

$$\text{Log } E = \log P - \log P^* \qquad\qquad \text{Equation 5.3}$$

Differentiating equation (5.3) with respect to t (time), we get:

$$(1/E) \times (dE/dt) = 1/p \cdot (dp/dt) - (1/p^*)(dp^*/dt)$$

or, we can write using symbols

$$g_E = g_P - g^*_P \qquad\qquad \text{Equation 5.4}$$

where, g stands for rate of growth of the concerned variables.

Thus equation (5.4) explains that the rate of fluctuation of the exchange rate (here direct quote) is the difference between the rate of inflation of domestic economy and foreign country. Thus if India experiences inflation at the rate of 10 per cent, while the USA has an inflation rate of 5 per cent, then the Indian rupee is expected to depreciate by 5 per cent over the year.

As mentioned above, the PPP explains the long run movement of the price level and the empirical test of the doctrine has been conducted on many occasions by different researchers. A good survey of that can be had in Officer (1976) and Dornbusch (1987).

Empirical evidences on PPP based on studies for the last three decades are a mixed one. The studies on time series PPP relationship for aggregate price indices show evidence of persistent deviations. Once relative prices are not strictly constant; PPP is seen to perform differently depending on the type of index chosen for empirical analysis. But the studies of high inflation situation generally lend support to the PPP as in these situations close cumulative movements of internal prices and exchange rate are seen. When an inflationary process is on, wages, prices and the exchange rate fluctuate with different frequencies and intensity. But if hyper-inflation takes over, the variability of different prices converges to the movement of the exchange rate. Such tests are carried out in Isard (1977) and Kravis and Lipsey (1978). The common experience is that deviations from PPP become the least under the hyper-inflation situations.

PPP and Price Level in Poor Countries

There has been an interesting statistical observation in international scene and that is the positive relation of country's price level to the level of per capita real income. To put it differently it means that the intrinsic value of one US dollar when converted to Indian rupee increases much more than what it can buy at the United States. The discrepancy in the price level in between rich and poor countries is explained in terms of the prices of nontradables. It is observed that nontradables are far more expensive in the rich countries.

Bela Balassa (1964) and Paul Samuelson (1964) have explained the relative lower prices of nontradables in poor countries. The Balassa – Samuelson (B–S) theory assumes that the labour in poorer countries are less productive in the traded sector, but the international productivity differences in the nontradable sectors are negligible. PPP ensures equality of prices of tradable goods in all countries. The lower productivity of labour in poorer countries will lead to lower wages of labour. This reduces the cost of production of nontradables in poorer countries and so the prices of nontradables will be lower. Thus rich countries with higher productivity in tradable sector will have higher wages and higher prices for nontradables. This means that their price levels will also be higher compared to poor countries. The B–S productivity differential postulate has statistical support as observed in some studies.

5.4 PPP and Real Interest Parity

Under the assumption of perfect international mobility of capital and risk neutral speculation, a link can be established between the nominal interest rate and the expected rate of depreciation of the currency in the following way:

$$i = i^* + x \hspace{3cm} \textit{Equation 5.5}$$

Where i and i* are the nominal interest rates of the home country and abroad and x is the expected rate of depreciation. Equation (5.5) is also known as open economy Fisher equation. Also the relation of nominal interest rate and the real interest rate is shown by:

$$i = r + \Pi \hspace{3cm} \textit{Equation 5.6}$$

Where Π is the expected rate of inflation and r is the real interest rate. Combining equations (5.5) and (5.6) we get the relation of real interest parity (Dornbusch, 1987):

$$r^* = r + [(\pi - \pi^*) - x] \hspace{2cm} \textit{Equation 5.7}$$

Where second terms is the expected rate of real appreciation. Thus real interest parity prevails when the difference of the two real interest rates equals the expected real appreciation. The implication of this is clear. Under exact PPP, real exchange rate is constant. This gives a simple but robust policy guide to the authority who remains cautious about the competitive strength of the country's exports. It is the real exchange rate which is important for the latter.

5.5 Monetary Approach to Exchange Rate

Since an exchange rate is the price of one country's money in terms of that of another country, it makes sense in theory to analyze the determinants of that price in terms of the outstanding stocks of and demand for the monies of two countries. This is the basic rationale of monetarist approach.

The monetary approach to the balance of payments and the exchange rate emphasizes that payments surpluses and deficits reflect the imbalances between the demand for money in each country and the supply of reserves that result from the monetization of domestic assets. When the demand for money increases at a greater rate than supply based on domestic assets, the supply of commodities will exceed the demand and the country will realize a trade surplus in international transactions. The latter induces more inflow of foreign assets resulting in an increase in domestic money supply and possibly higher price level also.

The monetary approach places the problem in a general equilibrium framework. The model in a two-country case can be put as follows following Frankel (1983):

$$M - p = b_1 y - b_2 i \qquad \text{Equation 5.8a}$$

$$M^* - p^* = b_1 y^* - b_2 i^* \qquad \text{Equation 5.8b}$$

$$i - i^* = E(e) + b_3 k \qquad \text{Equation 5.8c}$$

$$E(\Delta e) = E(\Delta p - \Delta p^*) - b_4 (e - \bar{e}) \qquad \text{Equation 5.8d}$$

$$e = (p - p^*) \qquad \text{Equation 5.8e}$$

Here, p, m and y refer to the logarithm of exchange rate, price level, money supply and real income respectively and i is the interest rate, k is the cumulative balance on the external private capital account. The definition of the exchange rate is direct (i.e. value of foreign currency in terms of domestic currency). Further, bars indicate long run equilibrium value, asterisks indicate foreign country, D indicates first difference and E the expected value in the sense of mathematical expectation.

Equations (5.8a) and (5.8b) are money demand function of two countries, where prices are set at long run values and come as a solution of these. Equation (5.8c) states that interest rate differential is explained by the expected change in the exchange rate and/or in response to accumulation of international credit (K< 0) or indebtedness (K > 0). Equation (5.8d) states that the expected change in the exchange rate is due to the expected inflation differential and/or deviation of the exchange rate from the equilibrium value. Equation (5.8e) expresses the PPP doctrine straight away.

The solution of the equations (5.8a) to (5.8e) in terms of the exchange rate gives the following expressions in the reduced form:

$$E = (m-m^*) - b_1 (y-y^*) + b_2 E (\Delta p - \Delta p^*) - (1/b_4 - b_2) (r-r^*) +$$

$$(b_3/b_4)k \qquad \qquad \textit{Equation 5.9}$$

Here, r is the real interest rate {that means, $r = i - E (\Delta p)$ }

The estimation of equation (5.9) means a joint test of a set of hypothesis, and all of these hypotheses are not central to the validity of monetary approach. The latter can be tested by examining the validity and stability of the coefficients in equation (5.9) and by testing when $b_3 = 0$ (which means whether uncovered interest parity holds).

5.6 Overshooting Exchange Rate

Exchange rate exhibits much more volatility compared to other prices. Some analysts argue that in the short run, following a disequilibrium in the money market, prices will adjust slowly to the new equilibrium level, but interest rate and exchange rate adjust quickly. This non-uniform speed of adjustment to the equilibrium level allows some interesting behaviour in the movement of the exchange rate.

Suppose the interest rate parity condition holds like the following:

$$i = i^* + (F - S)/S \qquad \qquad \textit{Equation 5.10}$$

Where S and F are spot and forward exchange rates respectively. Now, given the foreign interest rate i*, if domestic rate i declines, the second term in the RHS, i.e. (F-S)/S, which is the expected depreciation of the domestic currency, must decline to maintain parity. When domestic money supply increases leading to the increase in prices, this higher price level should induce depreciation of the currency by PPP, because

$$S = P / P^*$$ *Equation 5.11*

This higher expected future spot rate (a higher value of S means depreciation in this case) will be reflected in a higher forward rate (F) now. But if F rises, while at the same time (F-S) must fall to maintain the interest rate parity, S will have to increase more than the forward rate F. But once prices start rising, it reduces real money balances leading to an increase in the interest rate. Over time as interest rate increase, the exchange rate (S) has to decline to maintain parity. This shows that the initial increase in S will be much higher than its long run value, or the exchange rate will overshoot its long run value. This non-uniform speed of adjustment of different prices gives an overshooting exchange rate which is the important feature of the model of Dornbusch (1976). Later on, this model has been extended by incorporating PPP into it in Driskell (1981).

5.7 Dornbusch Model of Flexible Exchange Rates

The Dornbusch model was published in 1976, after the start of the post-Bretton Woods system of floating exchange rates. The Dornbusch model shows what good theory can do to clear up some very widespread misunderstandings. The volatility of the major exchange rates after switch over from a fixed to floating system was quite pronounced. No one ever expected the exchange-rate swings to be so pronounced and so prolonged. The feeling among the policy-makers at the Smithsonian Accords in 1971 and 1973, which destroyed the Bretton Woods system, was that floating would quickly restore exchange rates to sustainable stable equilibrium rates, in which trade would be balanced. The feeling was that markets could do the job better than finance ministers and central bank governors in smoke-filled rooms could. If the market was efficient, and doing its job, then exchange rates would quickly settle down to correct levels, trade would be balanced, and uncertainty would diminish.

Of course, as data show, nothing like that happened. Exchange rates went wild; trade imbalances persisted, and actually deteriorated in the 1980's. One reaction was that somehow the market was inefficient, or expectations irrational — that the exchange rate was following a speculative bubble, or was subject to a 'herd instinct', based on expectations not grounded on fundamentals. The contribution of the Dornbusch model is in showing that wild exchange rate fluctuations, far from being a rare occurrence in an efficient market with 'rational' or 'consistent' expectations, based on market fundamentals, should be what we should expect. High volatility in the exchange market is a natural consequence of a high degree of international asset arbitrage coupled with a relatively slow speed of adjustment by price setters in domestic goods markets.

The basic set-up of the Dornbusch model is in three equations:

DD (Demand)Equation : $\qquad\qquad y = -y^* + d(e-p),\ \ d > 0$

LM (Liquidity-money) Equation: $\ \ m/p = L(y, r),\ Ly > 0,\ Lr < 0$

AA (Asset Arbitrage) Equation: $\Delta e = r - r^*$

Equation 5.12

The DD equation represents goods market equilibrium. Output demand y is equal to its long run normal level-y when the real exchange rate is constant, with $e = p$. When the real exchange rate is above its equilibrium level, in the case of a real depreciation, with $e > p$, demand is above the long-run level, and there is excess demand. For the case of a real appreciation, with $e < p$, there is excess supply. This DD block simply integrates into a macroeconomic setting with the idea of the real exchange rate as the key variable for determining resource allocation and equilibrium levels of demand in the real sector of the economy.

The second equation, the monetary sector, is expressed in logarithmic terms. Demand for money L is a positive function of output and a negative function of the domestic interest rate.

The AA (asset arbitrage block) simply states the uncovered interest parity relation. The expected and actual rate of change in the exchange rate is equal to the interest differential, r - r*.

The diagrammatic exposition of the Dornbusch model appears in the Figure 5a.

The DD curve summarizes the equilibrium (e,p) pairs for equilibrium in the goods market. We see that the DD curve is simply a straight line through the origin. As long as e and p change uniformly, equilibrium is maintained in this market.

The AA curve integrates the asset-market equilibrium conditions from the money demand-supply relation and the asset arbitrage conditions. It is a downward-sloping curve. Why? An increase in the price level p lowers the real money stock, which in turn forces interest rates to rise.

The rise in interest rate generates an incipient capital inflow, which causes an appreciation of the exchange rate, so e falls. Thus, asset-market equilibrium relations imply a negative relation between p and e. The Dornbusch model makes one important assumption about dynamic speeds of adjustment. Note in the goods market or DD block that the parameter d > 0 is finite: the goods market does not clear instantaneously, but takes time to adjust, in order to ensure that y = - y*. However, Dornbusch assumes that exchange rate changes takes place instantaneously, in order to satisfy the asset-arbitrage condition. This operating assumption guarantees the overshooting of the exchange rate in response to a monetary expansion.

Zero capital mobility issues

There is one important implication of the Dornbusch model as shown in the above diagram. To evaluate the dynamics of the adjustment path under zero capital mobility, simply draw the AA curve as a flat horizontal line. Under zero capital mobility, a rise in price level p lowers real money, which raises domestic interest rates. But this interest rate increase generates no incipient capital inflow, so the exchange rate does not appreciate. The exchange rate stays the same for all levels of prices.

Figure 5a: Dornbusch Model: Monetary Expansion with Overshooting

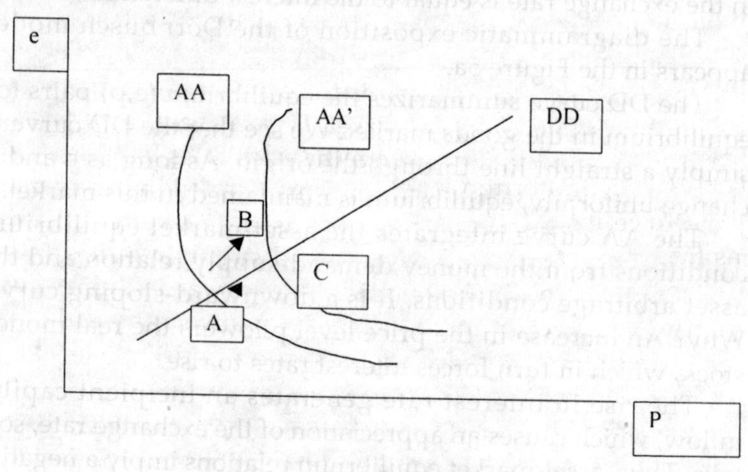

When AA curve is flat, the exchange rate jumps to a new long-run level, and stays there, as p gradually adjusts. Therefore, with zero capital mobility, overshooting vanishes. It follows then that capital mobility is the driving force behind overshooting exchange rates. When capital is mobile, and arbitrage opportunities appear, exchange rates will remain volatile and remain far away from long-run purchasing power levels. Thus under conditions of efficient markets and rational arbitrage, the exchange rates may remain out of equilibrium for a longer time.

5.8 The Portfolio-Balance Approach

The portfolio-balance approach (PBA) points to the links between the balance of payments flows and adjustments in the asset stocks. It emphasizes that the models of the capital account should be rooted in the behavioural models of the supplies of and demand for the portfolio of stocks. This aspect is same as the monetary approaches. Both the monetary approach and the PBA generally assume that each country's money balances are held entirely by the citizens of that country. But while the monetary approach regards home currency securities the PBA regards them as imperfect substitutes.

Following Dooley and Isard (1983) and Isard (1995) the basic features of PBA can be explained in the context of a two-country two-currency world which are having two composite private sectors with different sets of asset preferences. The net portfolio holdings of the two private sectors combined correspond to the liabilities of the official sectors of the two countries, and this is net of the liabilities of the official agencies to each other.

The symbols of the model are as follows :

- $\bar{M}$ and $\bar{M}^*$ are the stocks of non-interest bearing claims on the home and foreign governments respectively corresponding to the monetary bases.
- B and $\bar{F}$ are the privately held stocks of interest bearing claims on the home and foreign governments, referred to as bond and securities.

The assumptions are that M and B are denominated in the home currency unit and M^* and B^* are denominated in foreign currency. The net portfolio holding of home private residents, which are assumed to hold the entire stock of home base money, are denoted by M, B and F, and similarly, those of foreign private residents by M^*, B^* and F^*.

The model can be written as:

$$M = \bar{M} \qquad \qquad \text{Equation 5.13}$$

$$M = \bar{M}^* \qquad \qquad \text{Equation 5.14}$$

$$B + B^* = \bar{B} \qquad \qquad \text{Equation 5.15}$$

$$F + F^* = \bar{F} \qquad \qquad \text{Equation 5.16}$$

$$W = M + B + SF \qquad \qquad \text{Equation 5.17}$$

$$W^* = M^* + B^*/S + F^* \qquad \qquad \text{Equation 5.18}$$

Here (5.13) to (5.16) are the relevant market clearing conditions, and (5.17) and (5.18) define the nominal portfolio wealth (W and W*) of the two private sectors, and S is the exchange rate of the home currency (home currency value of one unit of foreign currency).

The size of the stocks of the four financial assets are determined by the interactions of the monetary policies, budget deficit, and official interventions in the foreign composition of private portfolios in each country is assumed to depend on the own-currency rates of return on domestic and foreign bonds, together with a set of other variables. One such variable is the scale of monetary transactions within the country. The rates of return are the own rates of interest on home and foreign bonds, denoted by r and r* respectively. Also the expected rate of appreciation of the home currency unit, π reflects the rate of return partly. Also Z and Z* denote the vectors of other variables that are meaningful to home and foreign nationals respectively. Further, there is no difference between the desired and actual compositions of financial portfolios. Thus the rest of the model can be written as :

$$M/W = m (r, r^* - \pi, Z) \qquad \text{Equation 5.19}$$

$$B/W = b (r, r^* - \pi, Z) \qquad \text{Equation 5.20}$$

$$SF/W = f (r, r^* - \pi, Z) \qquad \text{Equation 5.21}$$

$$M^*/W^* = m^* (r, r^* + \pi, Z^*) \qquad \text{Equation 5.22}$$

$$B^*/S = b^* (r, r^* + \pi, Z^*) \qquad \text{Equation 5.23}$$

Also by definition, portfolio shares must add to unity, or

$$m + b + f = 1 \qquad \text{Equation 5.24}$$

$$m^* + b^* + f^* = 1 \qquad \text{Equation 5.25}$$

It is assumed that private portfolio holders are risk averse and so they perceive home and foreign bonds as imperfect substitutes. Also for the convenience of analysis, we can focus on the case in which the asset stocks are determined exogenous by the policy authorities and the endogenous variables are the interest rate and the exchange rates. The latter adjust to clear the market.

5.9 News and Volatility in the Exchange Rate

The market for stocks has always been in the forefront in the use of the latest technology so that the market remains organized and economic agents are equipped with full information set. The efficient market hypothesis (EMH) describes the asset market as efficient if the asset price 'fully reflects' available information, some concept of equilibrium expected return or equilibrium prices are required.

In mathematical symbols, using the concept of equilibrium expected return, the excess market return on asset i (W_{it}) can be written as:

$$W_{i,t} = h_{i,t} - E\left(h_{i,t} / I_{t-1}\right) \qquad \text{Equation 5.26}$$

Where $h_{i,t}$ is one period percentage return, I_{t-1} is the information set, bar denotes the equilibrium value. If the market for asset i is efficient, then the sequence $W_{i,t}$ should be orthogonal to the information set, i.e.,

$$E\left(W_{i,t} / I_{t-1}\right) = 0, \qquad \text{Equation 5.27}$$

And also it is not serially correlated. Thus EMH implies two things simultaneously: it assumes that agents in forming their expectations in period (t-1) are rational in the sense that they cannot make systematic errors in their decisions and also they know the expected equilibrium prices.

The structure of stock market and foreign exchange market is more or less similar. One implication of EMH is that when EMH is operational, whether some agents can make abnormal profit or not. Also in the foreign exchange market EMH implies that the forward rate is the best predictor of the future spot rate. When agents on both the sides optimize through their decision, the forward risk premium (B_t) in the equilibrium should consist of two components: a constant risk premium term and a time-varying component of the risk premium.

Putting all the variables in natural logarithm to avoid Siegel paradox in this particular case (Siegel, 1972) we can write:

$$F_t = \Delta S_{t+1} + e_{t+1} + b_t \qquad \text{Equation 5.28}$$

When ΔS_{t+1} is the actual change in the exchange rate in logarithm, l_{t+1} is a random forecasting error and b_t is the risk premium.

In the forex market the role of news comes through in the equation and this explains why the forward market of the exchange rate is so much volatile.

Researchers have built models to capture the nature of the distribution of l_{t+1} so that a systematic pattern can be discerned about the volatility of the exchange rate. While historical volatility can be modelled with sufficient accuracy, but historical volatility is a poor guide to the prediction of future volatility. This is the essence of all types of uncertainty in the literature.

Another aspect of the forex market is about the role of expectations. Most models are based on the assumption of normality about the fluctuation of the exchange rate, though the empirical basis of this assumption is poor. It is not a surprise then that the predictive power of most models is very poor compared to the simple random-walk type model.

In the pursuit of a fair knowledge of the movement of the exchange rate, researchers have emphasized the non-linear dynamic system which can typically describe the movement of the exchange rate in the short run. One such theory is chaos model in which chaotic behaviour is defined as a non-linear deterministic system in which all time paths are bounded, though trajectories starting close together, diverge exponentially as time passes. In such a situation one can venture only a short run prediction, and a long run prediction would be hazardous.

5.10 The Foreign Exchange Market

The players in the foreign exchange market have to function with large stake in the form of exposure of their portfolio to the fluctuation in the prices. This makes them very sensitive to the slightest change in the market. News, vital economic information and even rumour can change the perceptions of the agents who then revise their expectations. This way the premium in the forward market may change though economic fundamentals remain fixed. In the very short run a sudden shift in demand will change the exchange rate as shown in the Figure 5b.

Here the vertical axis shows the rupee price of US dollar (direct exchange rate) and horizontal axis shows quantity of dollar. As the demand curve shifts up, the price increases, which means a depreciation of rupee.

One school believes in this line of approach for the explanation of the movement of the forward rate. This is the approach of the economists, who of course place due importance in the interest differential. There is another institutional view, known as Cambist view or dealing-room view, which claims that only interest rate differential matters in the determination of the forward rate. In other words, the Cambist approach predicts that the forward rate is determined by relative interest differential. But the two approaches give the same result under two different scenarios. In a world full of uncertainty, both the relationships will lead to the same result

Figure 5b : Demand and Supply of dollar changes the price: a shift of the demand curve

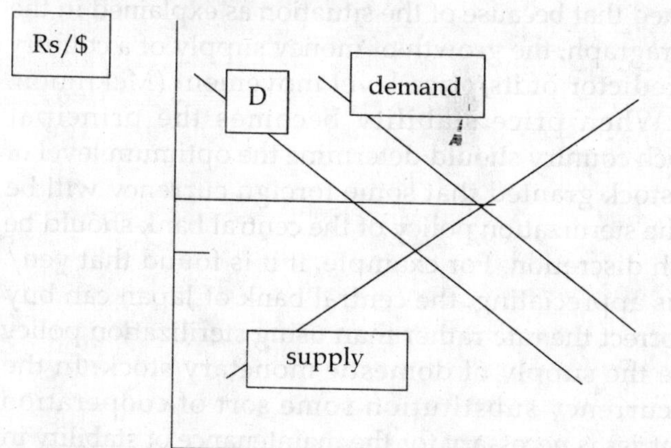

if the speculators are risk neutral, whereas in a completely certain world the same result would hold if Purchasing Power Parity holds and Fisher equation guides the determination of the nominal interest rate *vis-à-vis* the rate of inflation.

5.11 Currency Substitution and Exchange Rate

It is generally assumed that domestic residents do not hold foreign currency for its use as a medium of exchange. This assumption does not hold in countries which have fully convertible currencies and where multinational corporations (MNCs) have significant influence in the gross domestic product. Because of their involvement in the international trade, MNCs hold multiple currencies as a hedging device against potential loss due to the exchange rate depreciation. In this situation actual supply of money domestically is bound to be quite different from what the central bank supplies with the result that both the price level and the exchange rate of the domestic currency will be at variance with what the central bank predicts depending on its own estimate of monetary aggregates. The situation is much more prominent with the US dollar. Since the latter is an international currency, many central banks hold the dollar in their portfolios, as a result the US money supply has a limited bearing on the US inflation rate.

It is argued that because of the situation as explained in the previous paragraph, the growth of money supply of a country is a poor predictor of its price level movement (Mckinnon, 1982,1988).When price stability becomes the principal objective, each country should determine the optimum level of the money stock granted that some foreign currency will be held. Also the sterilization policy of the central bank should be applied with discretion. For example, if it is found that yen/dollar rate is appreciating, the central bank of Japan can buy dollars to correct the rate rather than using sterilization policy to influence the supply of domestic monetary stock. In the context of currency substitution some sort of cooperation among countries is necessary for the maintenance of stability in the exchange rate.

5.12 Disequilibrium Models

As noted earlier the instability in the foreign exchange market started in the middle of 1980s and volume of trading also increased rapidly. The currency trading assumed a nature of commodity trading with little link to the trade of merchandise trade where money is supposed to be used as a medium.

The market for foreign currencies now-a-days reveals turnover of more than a trillion US dollars per day. Only a tiny fraction of the volume of transactions is due to the international movement of commodities in the market. The market is more concerned about the small changes in the spot rate, and economic fundamentals are not able to predict such type of changes. Thus new types of models are developed which basically assume disequilibrium in the market. For example, some participants in the exchange market rely on 'follow-the-leader' approach and behaviour is guided by conventional wisdom; changes in the exchange market reflect a bandwagon effect. Further, there may be 'speculative bubble' in the exchange rate. As explained in MacDonald and Taylor (1989), if e_t is the spot rate and e^*_t is the equilibrium value, then the relation

$$e_t = e^*_t + b_t \qquad \text{\textit{Equation 5.29}}$$

shows how rational bubble (b) can make the important difference in the expectation of the agents in the market. Such a situation may emerge when the market exchange rate has deviated from the fundamental solution. It is argued in Dornbusch and Frankel (1988) that significant appreciation of the US dollar in the early 1980s was partly due to the operations of the bubble. An interesting aspect of this 'bubble hypothesis' is that once the nature of the distribution of the bubble, b_t is known or approximated, efficient forecast can be made about the spot rate. This type of approach has some problems. First, the success of the estimation depends on the assumed model of the exchange rate. The model specification may go wrong. Second, 'bubbles' may be generated within the system through a measurement error or through small sample bias.

5.13 Exchange Rate Systems and Policy

Over a long process of historical evolution and with innovative experiments of countries a set of exchange systems are seen in the literatures that are being practiced by the countries. In this section we will explain these systems briefly.

Which system a developing country chooses depends on its circumstances at the time and also on the long run goals of economic policy. A country may wish to pursue exchange rate stability because of the instability and perceived disadvantages of floating rates. In this case it will wish to choose some form of fixed exchange rate regime. Again, a country may wish to use its exchange rate to achieve various real objectives in the domestic economy, such as a faster rate of economic growth and full employment. In this case it can set a target for the*real* exchange rate. A real exchange rate target will require frequent changes in the nominal exchange rate faced with different price situation. Here the country will wish to choose some form of flexible exchange rate regime.

If a country has liberalized its capital markets and the capital account of the balance of payments, that makes capital freely mobile, it will be difficult for the country to pursue an exchange rate target and operate an independent monetary policy at the same time. When heavy capital outflows cause the possibility of currency depreciation, the only effective way to stop this is to raise domestic interest rates. The reverse dilemma occurs with capital inflows. The way opens to the economy to reconcile internal and external equilibrium is either to control capital movements, or to allow the exchange rate to float. Theoretically, free floating allows a country to pursue an independent monetary policy. But no country is completely indifferent to the value of its exchange rate.

Five main types of exchange rate regimes can be distinguished. Proposals for alternative exchange rate regimes fall within one or other of the five main categories.

The five main types of regime are:

(i) *rigidly fixed exchange rates*, including: the old gold

standard; currency boards; currency unions, and 'dollarization' (adopting the currency of another country e.g. the US $).

(ii) *pegged exchange rates* such as the old Bretton Woods adjustable peg system (or gold exchange standard), and pegging to a basket of currencies.

(iii) *managed exchange rate flexibility* including crawling pegs; exchange rate bands, and crawling bands.

(iv) *freely floating exchange rates.*

(v) *multiple exchange rates*, of which dual exchange rates are a special case.

5.14 Rigidly Fixed Exchange Rates

The Gold Standard

The old gold standard was in operation in its purest form between 1880 and 1914, and it collapsed in 1931. It was a fixed exchange rate system under which balance of payments adjustment was supposed to be achieved automatically through internal adjustment provided certain rules were adhered to. We have already discussed this system in Chapter 2.

5.15 Currency Boards

A Currency Board System (CBS) is an extreme form of fixed exchange rates. It requires each unit of a country's currency to be backed by an equal amount of a reserve currency, such as the US dollar. The CBS was widely practiced in Africa under British colonial rule before independence; and more recently, between 1991 and 2002, Argentina anchored its currency to the US dollar in this way. Linking a weak currency to a stronger currency can be a useful anti-inflation device to gain monetary credibility. The CBS has similarity with the old gold standard system, where the currency had to be backed by gold, is clear.

There are two major serious disadvantages of CBS. First, that credit for entrepreneurs to invest is not elastic to the needs of trade, because it depends on the availability of the reserve currency. Second, if the reserve currency appreciates in value, so too does the currency that it is linked to it. This can cause serious problems of competitiveness with other trading partners, and damage exports potential due to loss of competitiveness. Recent example is Argentina. It went into serious recession with the appreciation of the US dollar in 2000/01, and Argentina's Currency Board was disbanded in 2002.

5.16 Currency Union

Currency Union (CU) is another extreme form of hard peg. In this system countries decide to adopt a single currency, so that by definition exchange rates between member countries of the Union disappear. CU is the real life experiment of optimum currency area concept. The ideal conditions for an optimal currency area are:

(i)   economic cycles should be synchronized and economic shocks symmetrical so that a single monetary policy is suitable for all members;

(ii)   labour and capital are freely mobile so that the under-employment of factors of production is minimized;

(iii)   fiscal prudence is maintained by each member.

European Union is a successful story of currency. In this twelve countries initially have merged their currencies and they have a single currency Euro. It is expected that another set of countries is ready to join the Union soon.

Dollarization is a variant of the Currency Union. In this experiment the country simply adopts the currency of another country, say US dollar. As far as monetary and exchange rate policy is concerned, the country becomes an adjunct to the country issuing the currency. This seems to be the last resort for countries unable to manage their own affairs. In recent years, countries such as Ecuador and El Salvador have dollarized.

5.17 Pegged Exchange Rates

An exchange rate is said to be pegged if the central banks accept an obligation to prevent the market rate of exchange from deviating by more than a specified amount from the peg, also called a margin. Some multiple of the margin gives the band – or maximum range within which the exchange rate is allowed to move without a change in the peg. The Bretton Woods system was a pegged exchange rate system. In this each country's currency was pegged to the US dollar, so that bilateral rates of exchange between countries were also pegged, and each country was obliged to maintain rates within a margin of one percent either side of the central rate. The system was called the 'adjustable peg system'.

The problem of maintaining the pegged system is the problem of synchronization of monetary and fiscal policies with the country of the currency to which the currency is pegged. In South Asia some countries like Thailand and South Korea pegged their currencies with US dollar. Since the middle of 1990s these countries found difficulties to closely follow the fiscal and monetary policies of the United States because of system rigidities and other reasons. Soon their currencies went out of sync and became over-valued. Once that was revealed in market perception, crisis came. The rest is history.

Choice of a currency to which the domestic currency would be pegged is a major issue. This issue is called the 'Optimal Peg'. There are two broad choices of peg: (i) pegging to a single currency such as, for example, the dollar, pound or Euro; and (ii) pegging to an individually tailored basket of currencies reflecting the trade of the country concerned.

The choice of the peg will depend on what the country is trying to achieve, or its objective function. If the objective is macroeconomic stability, pegging against a single currency is unlikely to give the desired result since movements in a country's exchange rate will bear no relation to its own balance of payments, as the currency's exchange rate will move according to the currency to which it is pegged.

Pegging to a basket of currencies where the weights reflect the direction and elasticity of total trade (exports and imports) between the country and its trading partners is much more useful for the stability of the exchange rate and also the currency movement can be used for the promotion of trade and correction of balance of payments.

5.18 Managed Exchange Rates

With managed exchange rates there are no rigid pegs or fixed parities that the authorities are obliged to preserve. In this system the currency is free to vary, but the authorities intervene to avoid excessive appreciation or depreciation. A weak currency may lead to excessive depreciation which the authorities may wish to avoid because of its negative fall out on domestic front. Again, countries with a strong currency may wish to avoid appreciation if they want to accumulate reserves.

Sometimes a country may engineer the depreciation of its currency that would otherwise appreciate if the foreign exchange market were left to operate freely. Such behaviour is sometimes referred to as 'leaning against the wind'. This is done to achieve special object in the external sector, may be to change the term of trade *vis-à-vis* a particular trade partner.

One type of managed exchange rate system is the crawling peg. In this system a country maintains its pegged exchange rate within agreed margins at a level equal to the moving average of the market exchange rate over an agreed previous time period. Both appreciation and depreciation within a tolerable limit are allowed in such a way that it should have minimum impact on the balance of payments.

5.19 Freely Floating Exchange Rates

Only a handful of elite currencies have the free floating exchange rate system. In this the exchange rate is left to find its own level in the market without any official intervention. This implies that theoretically the country is completely indifferent to its exchange rate, though in reality no country can afford to remain aloof in this regard.

Leading currencies like US dollar, Canadian dollar, yen, Euro, Australian dollar and some others are free floating currencies. The fiscal and monetary policies of these concerned countries are always maintained at an efficient level in the sense that inflation is kept at a minimum. The economies are mature in the sense that the balance of payments of these countries can absorb the effects of exchange rate fluctuations without any significant fallout in the domestic economy.

The three currencies — US dollar, Euro and yen — have additional responsibilities of maintaining stability of the world financial system under the G-3 Agreement in which Japan, Germany and the United States are to synchronize their exchange rate policies so as to avoid unwarranted fluctuations of their currencies.

5.20 Multiple Exchange Rates

Multiple exchange rate systems imply different exchange rates for different transactions either on current or capital account. The official definition of a multiple exchange rate of the IMF is as follows:

It is 'an effective buying or selling rate which, as a result of official action, differs from parity by more than one percent'.

The IMF has traditionally been hostile to multiple exchange rate practices. It views them as an interference with a free market mechanism internationally. But IMF tolerates this system as they are to be preferred to more direct means of control which have typically been resorted to when multiple exchange rates have been abandoned.

Multiple exchange rates can be viewed both as a form of exchange control and as a rational response to the fact that different types of goods have different price elasticity in world trade. When foreign currency is scarce, the governments of the developing countries use multiple exchange rates as policy tools for the allocation of resources according to desired objectives. But the discretion used by the governments create distortion in the markets in the form of the operation of black market of foreign currency and capital flight.

5.21 The Relative Merits of Different Exchange Rate Regimes

The basic feature of fixed exchange rates is that they give stability and certainty to the nominal exchange rate and serve to anchor the national price level. But the flexibility exchange rate system has some advantages and these are:

First, it gives a country an extra degree of freedom in the pursuit of simultaneous internal and external balance. But under fixed rates, the domestic economy must be subordinated to the needs of preserving balance of payments equilibrium.

Second, it offers the possibility for the monetary authorities to pursue an independent monetary policy as money supply is no longer endogenous. It is subject to change through changes in the level of foreign currency reserves which occur under fixed rates.

Third, flexible exchange rates may help to insulate economies against external disturbances like price shocks that would otherwise affect the balance of payments, and feedback to the domestic economy. This is possible by suitable movements of the exchange rate to neutralize the effects.

For a small developing country the maintenance of a flexible exchange rate system may become a luxury as the cost of it in the form of an independent monetary and fiscal policies and the adoption of swift measures to insulate the domestic economy from external shocks may be high. Viewed from this angle many developing countries go for pegged exchange rate system.

Exchange rate is the important link with the foreign commodity and financial markets and the swings in this rate trigger movements of money and commodities across national borders. Many countries find it increasingly difficult to maintain stability in the exchange rate in the volatile world of flexible exchange rate regime. Because of this many countries have opted for dual currency system, the second currency being US dollar. Even in extreme cases some countries have adopted US dollar as the medium of exchange.

It is clear that trans-border movements of money and capital may be both the cause and the effects of exchange rate changes. An efficient combination of fiscal and monetary policies can maintain equilibrium and stability both in the domestic and foreign sector of the economy.

Six

Analysis of Banks and International Money Flows

"Money and currency are very strange things. They keep going up and down and no one knows why. You want to win but you lose no matter how hard you try".

[Abbot Gilles de Muises of Tourani]

6.1 Economic Role of Banks

Banking is like any other form of economic activity. Like other economic agents, banks are both dealers and producers. They are dealers, in the sense that they bring together lenders and borrowers, and they are producers as they transform raw base money or cash issued by the government into more convenient checks or demand deposits, which have greater security than cash, and also they transform short-term deposits into longer-term loans. In the process they do the financial intermediation and maintain liquidity in the system.

6.2 Risk Reduction

In their role as dealers, bankers help to reduce risk in the economy. There are two types of risk: the more familiar default risk and the less familiar withdrawal risk. In reducing these risks, banks make their profits. Let us consider default risk. A would-be supplier of credit, or lender-creditor, wishes to make a loan, in order to earn interest on excess cash-balances. The creditor may search out prospective borrowers from among the public. But the creditor must evaluate the individual risks of default. Further, to the normal costs of acquiring information, there is the higher risk of concentrating the loan with one or a few individuals. Because of this, the creditor would charge a high interest rate on this loan, in order to compensate for the risk. By going to a bank, with a long-standing reputation and a diversified portfolio of assets, the creditor markedly reduces the risk of any default on the loan. The rate of interest should be lower in this case.

6.3 Intermediation and Interest-Rate Expectations

Banks do financial intermediation as they transform short-term deposits into longer-term assets or loans. Typically, short-term deposits are less risky for depositors, and so they require a lower rate of interest. Longer-term loans, on the other hand, offer borrowers a lower risk of withdrawal, so borrowers will be willing to pay a higher interest rate to the bank. For this reason, banks usually transform short-term liabilities (deposits) into longer-term assets (loans).

The banks generally borrow short to finance long term assets and use this leverage to earn the spreads which accrue to them as income. They borrow short through a sequence of, say, one-period deposits, offering rates r1 now and expected rate r2 next period. Again, the banks can borrow long. On the lending side, the bank can offer a two-period loan at an interest rate i, or it can extend a sequence of two one-period loans at interest rates i1 now, and expected interest rate i2 next period.

The time management of both deposits and credit portfolio will depend on the difference between the short term interest and long term ones. The business of the banks is the quantum of spreads that is defined as the difference between the average returns from the created assets and average costs of deposits.

6.4 International Banking Operations

International banking operations are essentially to facilitate the movement of goods across the political boundary of countries. Banking system came along with the development of money as an institution. As civilization narrowed down the social distances and mankind learned about the benefits of exchanging commodities across political boundaries, the present-day international trade developed. The transaction of commodities across countries required financial intermediation in the international level and thus international banking business was born. What started with movement of gold and silver across country-borders became ultimately an efficient institution of international transfer of not only yellow metal but the currencies of sovereign countries. In this way the emergence and growth of international banking is closely interwoven with the development of international trade and international capital movement.

This gives the general perspective of the growth of international banking. But there are many aspects of this development. From a historical standpoint, the recent growth of international banking can be regarded as a reversion to the situation before World War I when European banks dominated the world capital market During the period 1940-1960 regulatory control on capital flow and convertibility of the currencies reduced the importance of international banking. From 1960 onwards globalization of capital market started and the emergence of surplus in petro-dollars in the seventies gave the much needed liquidity to the international banking business. The latter has been characterized by an increasing turnover in international trade, a phenomenal increase in the international flow of capital and also an increasing flow of funds from the banks to non-bank sectors. To understand the causative factors properly the literature has attempted to identify the factors supporting the internationalization of banking business. Thus factors like non-financial multinational corporations, the proximity to customers abroad, the competitive advantage with better information technology and the benefits due to international diversification have been mentioned in the literature in the contexts when these become relevant (Nandi, 1996). These factors along with other forces of globalization have established the huge international financial architecture which rule the international financial market today. The theoretical studies mentioning the factors helping the expansion of international banking are important, but in today's scenario the major business of international banks is based on international trade, international transfer of capital and money and derivatives.

The literature abounds in the exploration of the causative link in the development of international banking, but not many studies are found testing the theory empirically. There have been several studies which attempt to measure empirically the role of the different factors behind the growth of the US banks in the international field (Nandi, 1996).

6.5 Determinants of International Banking Activity

In today's world no country can afford to be autarkic either in the field of international trade or in international banking. But the latter is subject to much more restrictions in almost all the countries compared to the former. What determines the growth of international banks in the domestic banking sector of a particular country? Analytically we can proceed as follows:

Since international trade is closely related to international banking, volume of international trade (imports and exports together) is a determinant of the growth of international banking and the relationship is direct. Assuming that no specific restrictions are imposed on the operation of foreign banks so far as their operations are concerned in international banking *vis-à-vis* the practice of international banking done by home country's banks, it can be said that an increase in the turnover of international trade should have positive impact on the growth of international banking. Alternatively, the ratio of export to gross domestic product can be taken as the explanatory variable. This alternative formulation can be tested.

Foreign direct investment has been cited as an important determinant for the expansion of international banking. In fact, the presence of international banks facilitates the inflow of foreign capital and it is expected that the increase in foreign direct investment should have a positive impact on the growth of international banking.

Banking service as a commodity is supposed to have positive income elasticity. As national income is growing, demand for banking service should increase. To what extent the increase in income will help the growth of foreign banking activity in domestic soil depends on the preference of the consumers and also the participation of the foreign banks in the trade, both domestic and international, of the host country. If we take per capita income as the explanatory variable for the growth of international banking activity, then the growth of per capita income may facilitate the growth of international banking in the host country on the assumption that foreign banks have complementary role in the domestic banking structure.

The growth of domestic deposit should have influence on the activity of foreign banks. But in many countries the foreign banks are not allowed to create a domestic deposit base, though this facility is crucial for the increase in business. Foreign banks often face difficulties in the creation of domestic deposit base even when it is allowed, as the cost of the maintenance of deposits may be too high compared to business. Many foreign branches of Indian banks operating abroad have not created the domestic deposit base for this reason.

An increase in domestic deposit is supposed to have positive influence on the deposit mobilization of all banks including the foreign banks. That helps the building up of the asset portfolio. To what extent deposit mobilization will affect the activities of foreign banks depends on the competition between domestic banks and the foreign banks in the host country. Foreign banks prefer the creation of a domestic deposit base in the domestic currency as this helps in the expansion of business. Many countries do not allow the foreign banks to create a domestic base, as the latter is perceived to help the foreign bank to mount an attack on the domestic currency.

Again, the exchange rate changes affect the activities of the foreign banks. An increased volatility of the exchange rate increases the risk factor in international banking, and unless this aspect is properly taken care of, this acts negatively so far as the growth of international banking is concerned. We need to understand that the balance-sheet of the foreign banks in the head office is in their mother currency. If Indian rupee appreciates *vis-à-vis* their mother currency, that would show good results in their foreign operations.

An index of activity of foreign banks may be their aggregate asset structure, though the number of branches may be another indicator. Some studies take both In our case we take the aggregate asset structure as the index of the activities of foreign banks. This is the dependent variable the behaviour of which is supposed to be explained by the independent variables like domestic deposit base, exchange rate changes and others as explained earlier.

We thus find that the expansion of international banking in a country depends on several factors like importance of trade in GDP, the dynamism of the exchange rates, the deposit base and some others as explained earlier. The literature also examines the quantitative strength of different variables using an econometric model. We will rather pursue here another type of international banking activity which is conducted in offshore areas and specially tax haven locations.

6.6 Offshore Banking and Tax-Haven Centres

Offshore banking initially started in offshore regions but in its current form it has nothing to do with its geographical indications. It is more as a type of banking sharply different from traditional type and it is operational even from some important centres like New York and London, though jurisdiction varies in offshore operations. Also it is a fact that major businesses in offshore type of banking are done from offshore areas like Hong Kong, Singapore, Bahamas etc. Offshore banking comes under the category of external and Eurocurrency banking when we find the following:

Currency ≠ location of the bank ≠ residence of the borrower/depositor

The above characterizes the international banking practice when an Indian citizen deals with Korean won in a bank at Hong Kong. Offshore banking is conducted out of primary financial centres such as London, New York, Chicago, Tokyo and also secondary centres such as the centres in the Caribbean and the Asia-pacific region. The primary financial centres benefit from a strong industrial base on which the money requirements of the customers depends, while the secondary sectors derive their importance from the proximity of the economies which are either the source of a large financial resources or have substantial independent requirements for financial services.

6.7 Why Offshore Finance Centre a Preferred Destination

In some situations very small nations with good infrastructures and strategic locations create offshore financial centres (OFC) as a matter of policy to attract foreign capital so as to invest the same for the growth of domestic economy. These countries hardly known outside the region have escaped the agony of poverty through this process of foreign capital investment. In return to this facility, these centres (with support from the local government) offer a large number of services to the potential investors in their banking system and these are:

- excellent communication links with the outside world,
- absence of any tax burden (or even when tax exists, it is bare minimum)
- non-existence of any treaty to exchange tax information with other countries,
- predominant use of major world currencies
- no exchange control,
- the facility to disguise the ownership of corporate vehicles through the use of nominee directors and bearer shares,
- no reporting requirements for companies like annual reports,
- no system of supervision of companies such as Annual General Meetings,
- Maintenance of secrecy and confidentiality.

The list is long and the main idea is to give all facilities to the foreign investors so that OFC can earn money by selling confidentiality.

A small sub-category of offshore banks exists in the tax-haven areas like Cayman Island, Nassau, Bahamas, Bahrain, Monaco, Andorra etc. All offshore centres have the common denominators of customer confidentiality, very low taxes on offshore business and an absence of foreign exchange control. However, the activities in the centres vary depending on location, convenience to other financial markets, legal and accounting matters and communications. Some of the specialized services are the following: company formation and management, administrative services for 'paper' branch and subsidiary banks, portfolio management for trusts, Euro-bond underwriting and placement, incorporation and management of captive insurance companies, ship registration, storage and transshipment of merchandise etc. Thus in today's world of globalization the offshore centres have assumed great significance.

One should be clear about the difference between a tax haven and offshore centres. A tax haven is a jurisdiction with a high level of banking and commercial secrecy through which businesses or individuals can hold assets and earnings and move the same to other places and different jurisdictions with little or no tax impact. While many offshore financial centers are tax havens, many are not. These two are different and this should not be confused. Perhaps the governments in the countries creating the offshore financial centers would like to state that these centres operate in tax efficient zones and these are created to derive benefits of large scale movement of finance capital.

Capital flight and so-called money laundering are two phenomena from which the developing countries suffer most. The offshore financial centres in tax haven regions are often the conduit for the large scale transfer of funds. The mechanism of transfer and volumes have been studied in the literature (Nandi, 1999).

6.8 Panama: an Offshore Centre

Panama is an independent republic with no exchange control and a very liberal tax laws. It is bilingual, as both English and

Spanish languages are used here. It has a very good infrastructure both in air transport and telecommunications. There are a large number of local and foreign financial institutions and also a large spectrum of legal and accounting expertise. The banking secrecy is protected by various laws. There is no tax on offshore business and its legal system is well established. Panama has a long tradition in commercial banking and offshore business. The legal system is liberal in the incorporation of companies, Eurocurrency business, banking secrecy and private banking. The huge amount of capital deposited in the banks here is often used in the domestic investment. Also the fees generated in the business and the small level of taxes facilitate the generation of income and employment. Of course, a large amount of cash of doubtful origin pass through the OFCs like Panama and this is part of international money laundering nexus.

6.9 The Isle of Man: Offshore Financial Centre

The Isle of Man is outside the sovereign jurisdiction of United Kingdom. It is in the centre of Irish Sea and eighty miles away from Manchester. This tiny territory has its own government for the last 1200 years and it has obtained the status of an offshore centre. This island takes pride in its numerous attractions along with its ability of providing a safe tax-free environment for the investors. The well established company laws of the island allow a variety of corporate vehicles including companies limited by guarantee and hybrid companies, and also companies limited by share capital.

Companies that are not owned by the residents of the Isle of Man (IM) and those that conduct their business completely outside the IM, even if they may have an office there, are granted exemption from all IM income taxes. Non-resident companies from other jurisdictions like Panama or Irish non-resident can maintain their base at IM and can apply for IM residency under Part F of Isle of Man Companies Act, and they are eligible for income tax exemption. The ownership of the companies need not be a matter of public record, and this way complete secrecy can be maintained. The companies can carry on lawful business in any country and in any currency that they desire according to their convenience.

The island has an excellent financial infrastructure, and most banks, accountants and insurance companies are represented there. For example, Ulster Bank (Isle of Man) Limited is a wholly owned subsidiary of Ulster Bank Limited, and the latter is a member of Nat West Group, which is one of the world's largest banking organization. Under the rule of the Financial Supervision Commission responsible for the Depositors Compensation Scheme, deposits are protected up to 75 per cent of the first GBP 20,000 per depositor. The investors are offered several options regarding the opening of account, the variations in minimum amount, minimum withdrawal and interest rate structure. For example, an investor can keep money in fixed deposits, the time may vary from one week to five years at an interest rate which is known in the beginning.

The list is not exhaustive, and some centres within well-established countries are providing the same level of services. Some OFCs are now targets of the Russia's organized crime like Nauru, and the Russian syndicate has evolved an ingenious way of using front organizations to cover Russian connections. The crime branches of many countries in OECD group are trying to identify the Russian connections because of their potential of wrong-doing. The role of these OFCs in the illegal transfer of money across the globe has been explained in detail in Chapter 14 where money laundering has been explained.

6.10 The Fixed-Coefficient Model of the Banking System

The economic position of the banks in the society and their roles in shaping the monetary policy can better be understood with the help of a model. An early model of the banking system, based on a fixed coefficient approach, explains how banks engage in monetary expansion. The model rests on three equations:

$$R = r\,D \qquad\qquad\qquad\qquad \textit{Equation 6.1a}$$

$$C = k D \qquad \textit{Equation 6.1b}$$

$$MB = R + C \qquad \textit{Equation 6.1c}$$

where, R represents the reserves of the banking system, C the currency in circulation, D demand deposits, and MB, monetary base, equal to the sum of reserves and currency in circulation. The coefficient r represents the required reserve ratio of bank, with respect to deposits, while k is the ratio of cash to deposits, a ratio determined more by the state of communications and financial technology, as well as custom. For example, the less financially developed an economy is, the greater the need for cash for ordinary payments rather than cheques. Substituting the reserve and cash equations in the monetary base definition, one can obtain the following deposit multiplier:

$$MB = rD + kD$$

And, from this we get

$$\Delta D / \Delta MB = 1 / (r + k) \qquad \textit{Equation 6.2}$$

·With a required reserve ratio of 0.15 and a cash/deposit ratio of .05, for example, the deposit multiplier is 1/.20, or 5. For every one dollar of monetary base that the government injects into the economy, deposits expand by a factor of 5. This model shows the role that the banking system plays in the money supply process. The government can reduce the money supply either by reducing monetary base, or by changing reserve requirement, since a higher reserve ratio r will lower the multiplier, and reduce the amount of deposits offered by the banking system.

There is no role of interest rate in the model. Particularly deposit and lending rates can be accommodated in the model as these are important in the functioning of the banking system.

In an expanded model, let us assume that the reserve ratio would depend on the lending rates i, and the discount rate i_{disc}, the rate at which banks can borrow to supplement reserves. Thus the interest rate r would become a function like the following:

$$R = r\,(i, i_{disc}), \text{ with } r_1 < 0,\ r_2 > 0 \qquad \text{Equation 6.3}$$

The first negativity implies that higher lending rates would lead banks to keep less reserves. Again, the second positive sign implies that higher discount rates would force banks to hold more reserves so they would not have to borrow from the Central Bank.

Similarly, the cash-deposit ratio k would depend on the deposit rate r, or we can write,

$$k = k(r), \text{ with } k' < 0, \qquad \text{Equation 6.4}$$

Since higher deposit rates would provide incentives to put more cash in the banking system.

6.11 The Euro-dollar System

The Euro-dollar system evolved through a complex process of history. Some countries in east Europe preferred to deposit dollars in non-American banks in Europe. Also some American banks were eager to do banking outside the legal arms of the Federal Reserve of the USA. Again, there is a surplus of dollar depositors relative to dollar borrowers in USA, and the opposite has been the case in Europe with a surplus of dollar borrowers, relative to dollar depositors.

Euro-dollar system developed as an inter-bank market. Given the assumptions of regional imbalances in dollar deposits, differences in legislative requirements, differences in transactions costs, it made sense for US banks to shuffle funds from surplus US banks to London branch banks, for later distribution to European banks. In the process the Euro-dollar system grew, in its early development, from the mid-60's up through the early 1970's, as an inter-bank market for dollars. The interest rate in the Eurodollar markets is known as the LIBOR rate or London Inter-bank Offered Rate.

Since rouble was not fully convertible, the Russians wanted to store the proceeds of their gold sale in a hard currency. However, Russia could hardly deposit the money in Chase Manhattan for fear of siege. The London banks accommodated the Russians, and started taking deposits, and making loans in dollars. It is important to see the Eurodollar bank facilitating the development of the dollar as the vehicle currency or key currency, in world business. Bilateral payments imbalances were settled in dollars, or in gold, under the Bretton Woods fixed exchange-rate system. Again, multinational firms kept their consolidated accounts, across several countries, in dollars. There were obvious savings, in terms of information and accounting costs, in doing business in dollars.

The American banks doing the Euro-dollar business outside the jurisdiction of the Federal Reserve System, could offer deposit rates that were not regulated at zero (the famous Regulation Q), and could charge borrowers rates without ceilings set by state usury laws in the United States. The result was that borrowing and lending in dollars in the Euro-dollar markets was much more a 'market oriented phenomena', or a much less distorted market, compared to the internal US market.

The market grew and stabilized through the mid-70. Many thought that the Euro–dollar market had peaked. Then came the OPEC crisis and that paved the way for rapid expansion of the Euro-dollar markets.

6.12 Capital Inflows and Financial Opening

In Dornbusch model under a flexible exchange rate system, a capital inflow will lead to a nominal appreciation of the exchange rate, and in the short-run, a real appreciation. We see from the Mundell-Fleming model that a capital inflow will lead to an increase in reserves and an increase in the money stock. This will lead to a drop in interest rates, and lead either to inflationary pressures, or to an ensuing capital outflow. However, the inflationary pressures are hard to avoid in a fixed exchange rate system if the capital inflows are sustained and exogenous. Then some other measures become necessary.

If there is a sudden wave of massive capital inflows, it creates danger in the form of either a strong exchange rate appreciation, or a strong inflationary pressure in a fixed exchange rate system. The latter creates a real exchange rate problem, and the ensuing speculation against the currency for a probable devaluation. Capital inflows may pose acute challenges for countries beginning or in the midst of a stabilization effort.

6.13 Asian and Latin American Experiences of 1990s

There had been a marked pattern in the capital inflows to Asia and Latin America in the 1990's with some regular features: a marked increase in international reserves in the recipient countries and a surge in stock prices. However, there is one important difference between Asia and Latin America: in Latin America the inflows have been accompanied by a real exchange rate appreciation, while Asia, an appreciation has been less common.

In Asia, before July 1997, the capital inflows have gone hand-in-hand with large increases in investment as a percentage of GDP, usually an increase of 3 percentage points or more. In Latin America, by contrast, the inflows have been associated with a decline in private savings. Another key difference is sterilization. Singapore was probably the most successful in limiting the expansion of credit and monetary aggregates. The literature shows that Asian countries could use foreign capital more efficiently compared to Latin America. Also the latter experienced a decline in the savings-GDP ratio.

Capital inflow into the newly emerging market economies has another implication when the latter go for financial opening. Recent research has revealed that financial sector reforms and opening that sector to international competition has increased the risk of financial crisis in such countries. But again the financial sector opening has the potential of higher long term growth of GDP. Clearly there is a trade off between short term crisis and higher long term growth. In this perspective the countries should undertake financial sector reforms with caution. The monetary policy has an important role in making the inflow of capital smooth and building up a hedge at macro level in the face of potential fragility of the financial system.

6.14 Dollarization

Dollarization of a country currently means replacement of its currency completely by US dollar so that the latter becomes the legal tender. In a milder sense, it also means allowing US dollar to be used as a medium of exchange side by side the domestic currency. The first, i.e., full dollarization ensures a way of avoiding a currency and balance of payments crisis as there is no domestic currency and so no fear of sudden depreciation and capital flight from the country.

Full dollarization has some sacrifices. Currency is a sovereign symbol of the country. As the issuer of the national currency, which are mostly fiduciary issues now-a-days (which means less than 100 per cent backing by gold and foreign exchange reserve), the Central bank earns the seigniorage revenue and this is passed on to the government as profit. This is lost to the government.

Further, a country adopting dollar as the currency is to relinquish any possibility of having an autonomous policy regarding monetary and foreign exchange issues, and also refrain from the use of Central Bank credit to provide liquidity support to the banking system.

6.15 Currency Board and Dollarization: a comparison

Currency Board (CB) is the nearest competitor of the full dollarization system. Under Currency Board system (CBS), the authority commit to trade foreign exchange for domestic currency at a fixed rate on demand. Through this mechanism the Central Bank can increase the base money supply because this is the only mechanism. There is no extension of domestic credit to the government or banks. So the domestic currency is fully backed by a corresponding stock of foreign exchange and the domestic currency remains fully convertible.

Under CBS the monetary authority loses much of the independence of monetary policy, but it can capture the seigniorage of issuing the domestic currency. At this stage a comparison with the dollarization is important. A dollarization means the country loses the seigniorage and more important fact is that it would be permanent.

The loss of seigniorage is sometimes significant. One estimate puts the domestic currency in circulation in Argentina as equivalent to USD 15 billion and the annual increase in demand for currency is USD 1 billion (at a rate of 0.3 per cent of GDP). The foregone interest earning on the stock of money is estimated to be USD 0.7 billion, and that is about 0.2 per cent of GDP of Argentina.

What are the benefits of dollarization? It is an extreme step for a country suffering from chronic instability in currency and this saves the economy from currency instability. It is argued also that it helps integration to the economies of the US dollar area and Europe.

6.16 Dollarization and the Function of Money

Non-US residents having dollars in their portfolio is not really dollarization. These dollars simply serve as a store of value, much like gold. Neither it means that countries prices are quoted in dollars, especially in times of high inflation. It occurs when US currency becomes a medium of exchange. This is the decisive function of money. Dollars can serve as a parallel medium of exchange, or they can serve as the only medium of exchange.

It is easy to understand why dollars may become a parallel currency in times of high and unstable inflation rates. Domestic residents avoid the inflation tax on their domestic money holdings, and at the same time have the convenience of using dollars as a medium of exchange.

Of course, it is a flight from the domestic money. But it also reduces the inflation tax base of the domestic monetary authority. If the need for inflation tax revenue does not abate, then a higher inflation rate will be needed to wring out the same inflation tax revenue, from the diminished tax base.

This problem, of forcing a higher inflation tax on those who are unable to acquire dollars, has regressive distributional effects. While the upper and upper-middle classes acquire dollars, and protect themselves from the inflation tax, the middle and poorer classes get stuck with an increasing share of the inflation tax burden. Inflation becomes decidedly regressive once dollarization takes place, and ultimately can lead to increased social and political instability.

6.17 Dollar Deposits in Foreign Banks

In several countries in Latin America, dollar deposits were permitted, in domestic banks. The use of dollar deposits in foreign banks is similar to the Eurodollar phenomenon. The governments recognize that their citizens keep dollars as a store of value, and often use dollars as a medium of exchange. So instead of trying to de-dollarize, and forcing these citizens to put the deposits in Miami banks, why not simply permit dollar deposits in domestic banks? The country would avoid capital flight (legal or illegal), the banks would get the additional business, and finally, the government would gain additional reserves, which could be invested in US Treasury bills, and thus produce much needed revenue for the government.

6.18 Seignorage and Dollarization: Multiple Equilibrium Points

Mode of financing the annual budget is the prime areas of fiscal policies and the government of any country is reluctant to sacrifice that power. In many developing countries the government tries to part finance the budget deficit by printing money. This is done by rationalization taking recourse to economic theories one way or the other. The government budget deficit, financed by money creation, is written as follows:

$$g - t = \Delta M / P = (\Delta M / M)(M / P) \qquad \text{Equation 6.5}$$

$$g - t = \Pi (M / P), \text{ when } \Pi = \Delta M/M \qquad \text{Equation 6.5a}$$

where g represents real government spending, t real non-inflation tax revenue, M the money supply, P the price level, Δ the first difference operator, π the long-run inflation rate, equal to the rate of monetary growth, $\Delta M/M$. This second relation expresses the deficit as a tax on real balances held by the public, with $(g-t)$ equal to $\pi (M/P)$. The term $\pi (M/P)$ thus expresses the inflation tax needs of the government, for financing its deficit. The demand for money, especially during times of high and unstable inflation rates, is simply a function of the long-run inflation rates.

Philip Cagan introduced the following non-linear exponential form, linear in logarithms, in his influential study of hyperinflation:

$$M/P = A \exp(-\eta)$$

$$\text{Log } M - \log P = \log A - \eta$$

Or, $m - p = a - \eta$ *Equation 6.6*

The deficit or inflation tax need of the government is a straight line, whatever the inflation rate; the government needs fixed revenue from inflation, $\pi (M/P)$. The vertical line is thus a demand for seignorage or tax revenue from inflation. The non-linear curve captures the demand for money effect on the private-sector supply of inflation tax revenue to the government. At low rates of inflation, inflation tax revenue increases, but at a certain point, when the parabola bends, higher inflation actually decreases the demand for money to such an extent, that the inflation tax revenue falls. As Professor Phillip Cagan notes:

> *The desire to subdue inflation is obviously not enough and must be confirmed by performance. The conclusion appears inescapable, therefore, that the reduction of inflation requires the maintenance of slack demand.*

[Phillip Cagan, *Persistent Inflation*, 1979, Columbia
University Press, p. 249]

The implication of this analysis is that for a given deficit of the government, and a given deficit-financing need for inflation tax revenue, there can be two equilibrium inflation rates, which

Figure 6a: Inflation Laffer curve

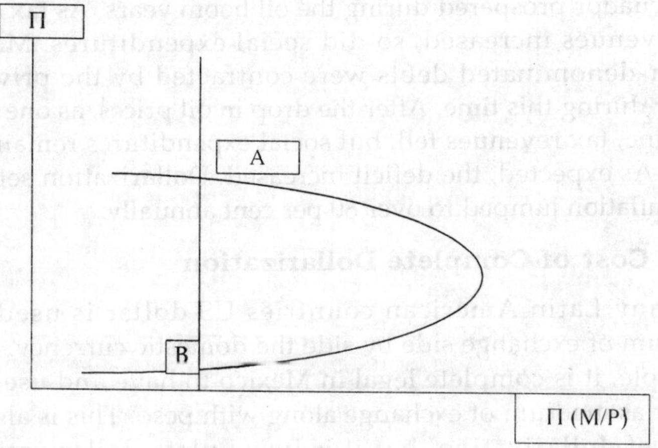

equate the supply and demand for inflation-tax revenue. As seen in the diagram, at B, the low-inflation equilibrium, a given deficit can be financed with a relatively high demand for domestic money and a relatively low inflation rate. However, at A, the high inflation trap, the same deficit is financed under conditions of a low demand for domestic money and a relatively high inflation rate.

The lesson from this analysis is that dollarization, by decreasing the demand for domestic money, can lead to a jump in the equilibrium inflation rate from B to A. Fiscal deficits do not have to change—they can actually fall somewhat—but inflation rates can explode, when dollarization triggers a flight from domestic money.

Such inflationary explosions have been rather common in Argentina and Brazil, before their last stabilization plans. This analysis shows quite clearly that a continuing fiscal deficit, however moderate, can lead to both inflation and inflationary instability, once dollarization takes hold.

Of course, once a country is at the high-inflation equilibrium, there is no reason why it cannot fall back to the low-inflation equilibrium, if there is a positive shift in demand for domestic money. This is what happened in Ecuador in the early 1980's, with its securitizations plan.

Ecuador prospered during the oil boom years. As tax and oil revenues increased, so did social expenditures. Many dollar-denominated debts were contracted by the private sector during this time. After the drop in oil prices, as one can imagine, tax revenues fell, but social expenditures remained high. As expected, the deficit increased. Dollarization set in, and inflation jumped to over 80 per cent annually.

6.19 Cost of Complete Dollarization

In many Latin American countries US dollar is used as medium of exchange side by side the domestic currency. For example, it is complete legal in Mexico to have and use US dollar as medium of exchange along with peso. This is also a form of dollarization, but it is incomplete dollarization. Complete dollarization happens when the country abandons the use of its own currency issue, except perhaps for small coins, and uses dollars as the media of exchange? This is what Panama has done, and what Liberia did for several decades.

The issue of complete dollarization is akin to the issue of the Euro as the medium of exchange for members of the European Monetary System. The argument for a country giving up its own currency, in favour of a currency beyond its direct control, is that it imposes a harder budget constraint on the fiscal authority. The result is that the fiscal authority no longer has the option of printing money to finance its deficits. It must either tax or borrow in the bond market. Long-awaited tax and expenditure reform may finally come when a country has no other option, other than facing the discipline of international bond markets.

The problems of dollarization are many. How can a country get the dollars to serve as the currency and monetary base? The only way, of course, is to run a surplus with the United States. This once-over cost, a trade surplus equivalent of about 5 percent of GDP, is a high price to pay for a currency system.

The second cost is a continuing cost. What if the United States runs an inflation of five percent, or ten percent? By adopting the currency of the United States as legal tender, and rejecting any sort of domestic inflation tax, the citizens of this country, in effect, agree to pay an inflation tax to the United States government. Thus, complete dollarization appears to be a very drastic policy move, for a country in need of fiscal discipline.

6.20 Dollarization in Latin America

In Latin America several countries have been dollarized officially. Ecuador was dollarized in September 2000, and El Salvador was dollarized in January 2001. Unofficial or partial dollarization is widespread in Latin America; it refers to a process when individuals substitute domestic money with US dollar in order to conduct transactions and also to protect the intrinsic value of their savings by keeping money in dollar deposits. The degree of dollarization in these countries is calculated by taking bank deposits in foreign currency as a percentage of total liquidity. The following Table shows this.

Table: Deposits in Foreign Currency as a Percentage of Money Supply

Country	1990	1995	2001
Argentina	33.7	45.1	62.8
Bolivia	66.2	67.3	84.8
Honduras	1.4	17.0	27.6
Mexico	10.0	17.5	5.5
Nicaragua	27.3	57.6	70.4
Peru	38.6	57.1	55.0
Uruguay	80.1	73.7	82.2

Source: Federal Reserve Bank of Atlanta, Economic Review, and IMF reports.

We have discussed different aspects of dollarization in the above paragraphs. A dollarized economy will become dependent on a continuous flow of international reserve to maintain liquidity and thus the conditions of international markets become important. Such an economy should be competitive internationally so that it can attract capital flows either as foreign investment or net borrowing. All these depend on how successfully the government can implement the fiscal discipline and maintain it.

Seven

Management of Exposure and Risk: The Derivatives

"Every man, as long as he does not violate the laws of justice, is left perfectly free to pursue his interest his own way, and to bring both his industry and capital into competition with those of any other man, or order of men."

[Adam Smith in An Inquiry into the nature
and causes of the Wealth of Nations]

"It is the difference of opinion that makes horse races."

[Mark Twain]

7.1 Introduction

Derivatives are defined as *financial instruments, the value of which is determined by, or derived from some underlying financial instrument or asset.* Generally, derivatives are agreements between two or more parties whereby payments between or among the parties are determined by some pre-existing index or other agreed upon valuation. The term derivative indicates that it has no independent value i.e. its value is entirely derived from the underlying asset. A derivative contract or a derivative is to be distinguished from the underlying asset.

Usual derivative instruments in financial world are currency forward, currency future or option contract of predetermined fixed duration, linked for the purpose of fulfilment to a value of specified real or financial asset. Derivatives are meant essentially to facilitate temporarily hedging of price risk of inventory holding or a financial/commercial transaction over a certain period. In practice every contract has a fixed expiry date, in the range of three to twelve months from the date of the commencement of the contract.

7.2 History of Derivatives

Derivatives have probably been around for as long as people have been trading with one another. Forward contracting dates back at least to the 12th century, and may well have been around before that period. Merchants entered into contracts with one another for future delivery of specified amount of commodities at specified price. A primary motivation for prearranging a buyer or seller for a stock of commodities in early forward contracts was to lessen the possibility that large price swings would inhibit marketing the commodity after the harvest.

Although early forward contracts in the US addressed merchants' concerns about ensuring that there were buyers and sellers for commodities, 'Credit risk' remained a serious problem. To deal with this problem, a group of Chicago businessmen formed the **Chicago Board of Trade** (CBOT) in 1848. The primary intention of the CBOT was to provide a tool known in advance for buyers and sellers to negotiate forward contracts. The CBOT went one step further in 1865, and listed the first 'exchange traded' derivatives contracts in the US. These contracts were called 'future contracts'. In 1919 Chicago Butter and Egg Board, a spin off of CBOT, was reorganized to allow futures trading. Its name was changed to **Chicago Mercantile Exchange** (CME). The CBOT and CME remain the two largest organized futures exchanges — indeed, the two largest 'financial' exchanges of any kind — in the world today.

The first stock index futures were traded in **Kansas City Board of Trade.** Currently the most popular futures contract in the world is based on **S&P 500** index, trade on Chicago Mercantile Exchange. During the mid 1980s the financial futures became the most active derivatives instruments generating volumes many times more than the commodity futures. Index futures, futures on T-Bills and Euro-Dollar future are the top three most popular futures contracts traded today. In India, the commodity derivatives existed till three decades back when they were discontinued, but have now been re-introduced in certain commodities, such as Non-ferrous metals, jaggery, castor oil, pepper, etc.

Most derivatives were developed to manage, offset, or hedge against risk; some were developed primarily to provide the potential for high returns. Derivatives may also be classified as exchange-traded or over-the-counter (OTC). Exchange-traded derivatives are more standardized and offer greater liquidity than OTC contracts, which are tailor-made to meet the needs of buyers and sellers.

7.3 The Nature of Foreign Exchange Risk

Foreign Exchange Risk Management begins with the identification of what items and amounts the firm has exposed to risk associated with changes in exchange rates. The asset, liability, profit or any other expected future cash flow stream is said to be exposed to exchange risk when a currency movement induces a change in the home currency value of the cash flow. The term exposure used in the context of foreign exchange means that a firm has assets, liabilities, profits or expected future cash flow streams such that the home currency value of assets or other cash flow changes as exchange rate change. Since the value in home currency changes can effect the bottom lines of the balance sheets, the risk emerges out of foreign exchange movement.

All cash flows present or future, denominated in foreign currencies are exposed to foreign exchange risk. But some expected future cash flows denominated in home currency term may also be exposed. For example, the Indian company selling in the domestic market may be competing with firms based in Japan. In such circumstances changes in the yen/ rupee exchange rate will certainly influence the present value of the Indian companies expected future cash flow and also will alter the competitive position. This shows that foreign exchange exposure can change the competitiveness of firms in the domestic market also.

Foreign Exchange Exposure is of three types:
1.   Transaction exposure

2.   Translation exposure (Accounting exposure)
3.   Economic exposure

Transaction exposure arises because the receivable is denominated in a foreign currency. Translation exposure arises on the consolidation of foreign currency denominated assets and liabilities in the process of preparing consolidated accounts. This concept is also concerned with what might be called accounting exposure. Economic exposure emerges because the present value of a stream of expected future operating cash flows denominated in the home currency or in a foreign currency may fluctuate with the changes in the exchange rates. Transaction and economic exposure are both cash flow exposures. Transaction exposure is a comparatively straightforward concept by translation and the economic exposure is more complex.

7.4 Transaction Exposure

The cost of proceeds in home currency of settlement of a future payment or receipt denominated in a currency other than the home currency may fluctuate due to changes in the exchange rates. This is transaction exposure, which is by nature, a cash flow exposure. It may be associated with trading flows, dividend flows or capital flows. When foreign subsidiary of Indian companies sends dividend abroad, it is denominated in foreign currency and if the domestic currency depreciates, either the burden of higher outflow in domestic currency is to be born by the subsidiary, or the amount in foreign currency will be reduced and the burden will go to the parent firm. The consolidation of the accounts and the resultant transactions have a Time Space in between and the exchange rate changes can alter the intrinsic value of the cash flow. This is the nature of the transaction exposure.

7.5 Translation Exposure

Consolidation of financial statements involves assets and liabilities denominated in foreign currency. This process gives rise to translation exposure or accounting exposure. Consolidation of the accounts for the foreign subsidiaries into group financial statements denominated in home currency requires the application of a rate or rates of exchange to the accounts of foreign subsidiaries, so that all can be translated into the currency of the parent company. Both balance sheets and income statements must be consolidated, and this gives rise to translation exposure. Translating foreign currency profit and loss accounts at either the average exchange rate during the accounting year or at the end of the year will imply that the expected consolidated profit will vary as the different rates change. So, the whole amount of profit earned in foreign currency is exposed to translation risk in the sense that the consolidated profit in home currency is subject to change.

Balance sheet exposure is also related to the translation exposure. Some items in the balance sheet of the foreign subsidiary may be translated at the historical exchange rates *vis à vis* rupee. Thus the home currency translated value cannot change as exchange rates of rupee change and thus the exposure is not there in the accounting sense. Other items maybe translated at the closing exchange rate and thus the translated value in Indian currency is subject to change if exchange rate changes. Therefore, all foreign currency items which are consolidated at current rates are exposed in the accounting sense.

There are four basic translation methods. They are:
1. The current/non-current method (all working capital method)
2. The closing rate method
3. The monetary/non-monitory method
4. The temporal method

The first one uses the traditional accounting distinction between current and long-term items and translates the former at the closing rate and the latter at the historical rate. The closing rate method translates all foreign currency denominated items at the closing rate of exchange. The third method distinguishes monetary items as assets, liabilities or capital as monetary items and their amounts are fixed by contract in terms of the number of currency units related to the changes in the value of money. The non-monetary items are translated at their historical rates. The temporal method of translation uses the closing rate method for all items stated at replacement cost, realizable value, market value or expected future value and uses the historical rate for all items stated at historical cost.

7.6 Economic Exposure

The present values of future operating cash flows to be generated by the activities of the company are subject to change in terms of home currency when exchange rate movement takes place. Some experts classify transaction exposure as a subset of economic exposure. They argue that the present value of an uncovered foreign currency denominated receivable will change as exchange rates change. There is some merit in this argument, but separate terminologies are maintained because the multi-national companies face difficulties at different levels while they monitor and control external transactions.

The three types of exposures as explained above analyze the nature of foreign exchange risk. The treasury manager of a firm is to calculate the extent of the risk so that proper action can be taken to hedge the risk. The nature of risk in the foreign exchange transaction is dynamic in nature and the elimination of total risk is not possible most of the times. But efficient behaviour implies that risk is to be minimized. The financial instruments available in the foreign exchange market are called derivatives, which ensure some sort of insurance against specific risk.

7.7 Derivatives and Risks

Derivatives are used to minimize risks or hedge investment exposure, though sometimes used as investment vehicles by themselves. Derivatives shift risk from one party to another who is willing to bear such a risk. Often, revenues from sales in foreign lands are generated in foreign currencies. As a result, companies generating such revenues are subject to risk such as those of fluctuation in the foreign currency markets and increasingly use financial derivatives in order to minimize their exposure to risks.

7.8 Steps Involved in Problem Identification

Companies considering utilizing derivatives as a risk shifting vehicle must be selective and cautious. The first step is the identification of the risk that the company wishes to be protected against, such as fluctuations in exchange rate and interest rate. For example, an Indian software company with foreign sales in the United States payable in US dollar is exposed to exchange rate risk. The risk is that the value of the dollar may fall relative to the Indian rupee during the period between the order of the software and the payment. A decline in the value of dollar will affect the bottom line of the company.

The next step is to determine the amount and length of exposure to the risk. Focusing only on this one foreign sale, the measure of the risk to the Indian software company is the rupee value of the order. Again, the length of exposure is the period from the order to the receipt of payment for the software.

The third and final step is the determination of the type of derivative to be used. This depends on many factors like the nature of the company's assets and liabilities etc.

7.9 Derivative Strategy: An Example

Consider the following scenario. An Indian investor with a UK pound position desires some protection against downside risk, i.e., against a possible depreciation of pound sterling. He is sure that he needs that protection as pound is to depreciate heavily in next few months. Since financial markets may turn his expectations about pound wrong, he approaches a financial engineer. The latter is not only to provide him with the desired protection, but with a product that will pay off if his expectation is fulfilled. Also the investor wants the product to be zero cost and even to bring him in a premium, if possible.

Faced with a client like our investor, the financial engineer comes up with a product like the following. The vertical axis

Figure 7a: Example of a Complex Strategy

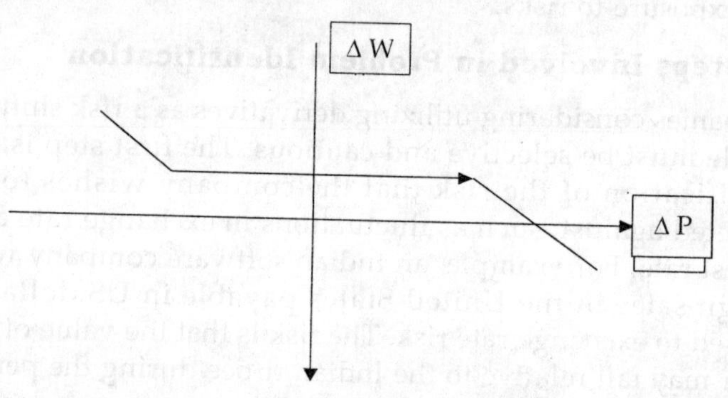

represents a change in the value of wealth representing in rupees (Δ W) and the horizontal axis represents a change in the price of the underlying financial instrument, the price of pound (ΔP). A positive change means a profit and a negative a loss. From the payoff profile of the curve we see that if the price of pound declines, i.e., the expectation is fulfilled, the investor makes a profit. Also, if there is a small change in the exchange rate in either direction (the horizontal part of the payoff curve), the investor will still get the premium. But when pound appreciates, he loses right hand side). It is a complex structure of derivative.

7.10 The Players in the Market

Hedgers

Hedgers are the persons who are interested in reducing a risk they already face. Suppose that an Indian company knows that it is due to pay $ 10 million to one of its US suppliers in 90 days. It is faced with a significant foreign exchange risk. The cost, in Indian Rupees (INR), of making the payment depends on the dollar exchange rate in 90 days. If the 90 day forward rate is at Rs. 50 per USD, the company can choose to hedge by entering into a long forward contract to buy USD 1 mn in 90 days for Rs. 50 mn. The effect is to lock the exchange rate that will apply to the dollar (USD) it requires.

This hedge using forward exchange rates requires no initial payment. In some circumstances it saves the company a significant amount of money. This example emphasizes that the purpose of hedging is not to eliminate risks but to make the outcome more certain and fix the value of the liability.

Speculators

The hedgers want to eliminate an exposure to movements in the price of an asset, speculators wish to take a position in the market. Either they are betting that a price will go down or they are betting that it will go up.

Futures contracts can be used for speculation. An investor who thinks that the USD will increase in value relative to INR can speculate by taking a long position in futures contract on the dollar. Suppose that an investor enters into a long position in a 180-day futures contract on the dollar at Rs.50 and if the actual spot dollar exchange rate in 180 days proves to be Rs. 50.50 then he would realize a gain of Rs. 0.50 per dollar.

There is an important difference between speculating using futures markets and speculating by buying the underlying asset in the spot market. Buying a certain amount of the underlying asset in the spot market requires an initial cash payment equal to the total value of what is bought. Entering into a futures contract on the same amount of the asset does not require complete initial cash payment. Speculating using futures markets therefore provides an investor with a much higher level of leverage than speculating using spot market. This happens because the requirements of liquidity are much lower in the former.

Arbitrageurs

People who do arbitrage are a third important group of participants in derivatives markets. Arbitrage involves locking in a risk less profit by entering simultaneously into transactions in two or more markets. Generally, it is risk free. Consider a stock that is traded on both the NSE and the BSE stock exchanges. Suppose that the price is Rs.372 on NSE and Rs.378 on BSE, an arbitrageur could simultaneously buy 100 shares of the stock on the NSE and sell them on the BSE to obtain a risk-free profit of

$$(378 - 372) \times 100 = 600$$

or Rs. 600 in the absence of transaction costs. Transaction costs would probably reduce the profit for a small investor. However, the large investment houses face very low transaction costs in both the stock market and foreign exchange market. They would find this arbitrage opportunity very attractive and would try to take as much advantage of it as possible.

Arbitrage makes the market more efficient by shifting excess demand/supply from one market to another. But such arbitrage opportunities do not last very long as the forces of demand and supply will make the prices nearer so that with transaction cost positive, the scope of arbitrage vanishes.

7.11 Types of Derivatives

Derivatives can be broadly classified into two categories: (i) Exchange Traded, and (ii) Over-The-Counter (OTC).

Financial instrument is exchange-traded if it is traded on a formal exchange. For example, most highly-capitalized stock is exchange traded as are futures and standardized options. Such instruments traded are on the floor exchange. These are transferable by virtue of the fact that the counter party to each exchange trade is the exchange itself. Alternatively, a financial instrument is traded over-the-counter (OTC) if it is not traded on a formal exchange. Most debt instruments are traded OTC with large brokerages making markets in specific issues. Forwards, Swaps and customized options are also traded OTC. Purchases and sales of securities executed otherwise than the standard lot size for the type of security. These are individually tailored non-transferable agreements between counter parties.

We describe briefly some of the derivative instruments below and these are: Options, Futures, Forward contracts etc. In a generic sense an option is a standardized contract giving the buyer the right, but not the obligation, to buy or sell an asset at a specified time at a pre-determined price. Options come in two varieties: calls and puts. One call gives you the right to buy x number of shares of a particular stock at the strike price before a specified expiration date; one put conveys the right to sell y number of shares of a stock at the strike price before the put expires.

Futures are standardized exchange-traded contracts to buy or sell securities, commodities, or other assets on a specified date at a preset price. Among the most common are interest rate futures, which derive their prices from fixed income securities such as Treasury bonds. Other major types include foreign exchange futures and Standard & Poor's 500 Stock Index futures.

Forward contracts are similar to futures, except that these are nontransferable agreements, as opposed to standardized contracts, between two parties to buy or sell an underlying asset at a future date at a set price. Forward contracts are used primarily for hedging foreign currency risk, although they are also used in commodities and interest rate transactions.

7.12 Forward Contracts

A forward contract consists of a commitment to buy or sell a specific and pre-determined amount of foreign currency at a later date and at an exchange rate fixed at the time transaction is completed. The delivery of the currency takes place on the agreed upon value date. The contract is usually between two financial institutions or between a financial institution and one of its clients. Forward contracts are not traded on any exchange. In contrast to spot transaction, the commitment of a forward transaction and the fulfilment are clearly separate in terms of time.

One of the parties to a forward contract agrees to buy the underlying asset on a certain specified future date for a certain specified price and therefore assumes a long position. The other party assumes a short position and agrees to sell the asset on the same date for the same price.

A forward transaction cannot be cancelled. But it can be closed out at any time by the repurchase or sale of the foreign currency amount on the value date originally agreed upon. Possible gains or losses are adjusted on this date.

The forward price and the spot price of a currency differ in normal circumstances. If the forward price is higher than the spot price, we speak of a forward premium. If the forward price is lower, we say a forward discount. The price differences reflect the interest rate differentials between the currencies in the foreign exchange markets.

The calculations of forward rate are done as follows:

Forward rate = spot rate +/- (premium/discount)

The forward premium/discount are calculated by the following formula:

$$(i) \text{ premium/discount} = \frac{\text{Spot rate} \times \text{interest rate differential} \times \text{term in days}}{360 \times 100}$$

And to take into account the currency risk coupled with the interest rate of the traded currency the formula is modified as

$$(ii) \text{ premium/discount} = \frac{\text{spot rate} \times \text{interest rate differential} \times \text{term in days}}{(360 \times 100) + (\text{foreign currency interest rate} \times \text{term})}$$

The formulas have the following implications:

(a) The size of the discount or premium is in direct proportion to the term, i.e., a longer term means a larger premium.

(b) The level of the interest rates of the currencies are not important but their differences determine the value of premium or discounts.

(c) The forward rates are calculated mathematically and no estimates are involved in it.

Example

A corporate has a USD 1 million payable in three months. The current spot price is say Rs.48.80. It will enter into a forward contract with a banker, at a pre-fixed price say Rs.50.15 at a maturity date of three months hence, when the corporate is due for payment. At maturity, after three months, the corporate will pay the banker Rs.50.15 million after adjusting with the margin money and take the dollar delivery.

Here the corporate takes the long position as he has committed to buy the requisite amount, whereas the banker has taken the short position as he will sell these dollars to the corporate.

The specified price in the contract is referred to as the delivery price. At the time the contract is entered into, the delivery price is chosen so that the value of the forward contract to both parties is zero. This means that it costs nothing to take either a long or a short position. As in the above example the corporate does not pay anything extra other than the strike price and the banker receives only the rupees with respect to the strike price agreed, which implies that it does not cost anything to take a long or a short position, thus, we say that the value of the contract at the time of initiation is zero.

7.13 Forward Pricing

The forward price for a certain contract is defined as the delivery price which would make that contract have zero value. It follows that the forward price and the delivery price are equal at the time the contract is entered into. As time passes, the forward price, i.e. spot rate of the underlying asset is liable to change, as it depends on the market forces of demand and supply, whereas the delivery price remains the same. The two are therefore not equal, except by chance, at any time after the start of the contract. Generally, the forward price at any given time varies with the maturity of the contract being considered, e.g. the forward price for a contract to buy or sell in three months is typically different from that for a contract to buy or sell in six months.

7.14 Benefits of Forward Contract

Forward contracting is very valuable in hedging and speculation. A simple hedging application would be that of a commodity-producer forward-selling his commodity at a known price in order to eliminate his price risk. Conversely a manufacturer may want to buy the commodity forward in order to assist production planning without the risk of fluctuation.

If a speculator has information or analysis which forecast an upturn in price, then he can go long on the forward market instead of the cash market. The speculator would go long on the forward, wait for the price to rise, and then take a reverse transaction. The use of the forward markets provides the scope for leverage to the speculator.

7.15 Forward Rate Agreement [FRA]

The forward rate agreement (FRA) makes it possible to fix in advance the interest rates of future interest periods. But there is no standardization as the agreements are traded in the inter-bank markets and not on exchanges. An FRA is an interest rate hedging instrument which can be tailor–made regarding the amount, the currency and the interest period. The special features of FRA are the fact that there is never any transfer of the principal amount but that only the interest differentials are paid out calculated on the settlement date. The London Inter-bank Offer Rate (LIBOR) is generally used for the agreements.

The typical quotation of an FRA can be like the following: an FRA 6 against 9 months, this means that the interest rate for a 3-month financing period starting in 6 month is specified in this case. Similarly, an FRA 5 against 11 months implies that the interest rate for a 6–month financing period starting in the 5 month.

The interest rates for the FRA are calculated according to the principle that the interest load for the entire period must be the same as for the two short time periods together. This means that in FRA 6 against 9 months case the total interest amount for 9 months is to be equal to that for the 6 months prior to the agreement and for period of FRA.

The formula of pricing an FRA is:

$$IR = \frac{[(IL \times DL) - (IS \times DS)] \times 36000}{[36000 + (IS \times DS)] \times DF}$$

and the notations are:

IR = FRA interest rate
IL = interest with long maturity
IS = interest with short maturity
DL = number of days – long maturity
DS = number of days- short maturity
DF = number of days – FRA

Example

Determine the price of an FRA in US dollar, 6 against 9 months if rates of 7.00 – 7.25 per annum are quoted for 6 months and 7.125 - 7.375 p.a. are quoted for 9 months.

In actual practice the FRA interest rate is taken as the middle rate of the relevant period. Following the formula, we have

$$IR = \frac{[(7.25 \times 270) - (7.125 \times 180)] \times 360 \times 100}{[360 \times 100 + (7.125 \times 180)] \times 90} = 7.242$$

Therefore, the FRA interest rate is 7.242 per cent p.a.

7.16 Currency Swaps

Swap is an OTC derivative instrument in which two parties agree to exchange streams of payments, or cash flows, over time. While the two main types are interest rate swaps and currency swaps, more esoteric mechanisms like commodity swaps or even tax rate swaps are also being introduced. These in a way are an extension of the conventional swaps in the foreign exchange market in which simultaneous sale and purchase of one currency takes place for another, for different maturities.

The foreign exchange swap consists of either A or B ,

A.   The combination of a spot transaction with a forward transaction
                    Spot purchase + forward sale
Or,   *Spot sale + forward purchase*

B.   The combination of two forward transactions with different terms

Forward purchase + forward sale
Forward sale + forward purchase

In currency swap both transactions must be concluded at the same time. Otherwise the foreign exchange risk cannot be excluded. A currency swap often complements a forward transaction as in the latter case it is not always possible to determine the maturity date at the time of the deal. The currency swap offers the opportunity to change the maturity to the desired date and still remain against the risk. Also the length of an existing forward transaction can be adjusted (shortened or otherwise) by means of a swap.

Forms of Swap

The most common form of swap is a 'vanilla' interest rate swap. With that structure, one party pays interest at a fixed rate while the other pays according to a floating rate such as LIBOR. Payments are based upon a specified notional principal and are netted against each other. Payments can be made quarterly with the life of the swap. Such a swap gives a party the ability to convert a floating rate asset or liability to fixed rate.

Various forms of Currency Swaps

1.   Cross currency Floating-to-fixed Swap: Suppose a European bank has medium-term floating assets denominated in US dollars. The bank requires to fund its medium-term floating dollar assets with medium-term floating liabilities. But it can raise funds cheaply on a fixed-rate basis in its domestic currency. A swap is a way to solve this problem.

2.   Basis Swap: This type of swap involves an exchange of floating-rate payments calculated on a different basis. The structure of a basis swap is the same as the simple interest rate swap, with an exception that the floating interest rate calculated on one basis is exchanged for floating interest rate calculated on a different basis.

3. **Amortizing Swaps:** Amortizing swaps are very popular for lease based transaction where the principal reduces annually or in smaller time period. For example, Company A has borrowed INR 90 million to buy a building. They have agreed with their bankers to pay back loan, principal plus interest at 11% fixed, over three years. Company A believes that interest rates are going to fall over the period and thus would prefer to pay a floating rate rather than the fixed rate. Company A can enter into a swap with the bank in which the notional principal decreases on each of the amortization dates.

4. **Zero-coupon Swaps:** In this type of swap the players will make only one fixed payment on maturity. The ultimate fixed payment is a single forward rate based on the compounding of the immediate cash flows at the contractual swap rate. This type of swap structure is most commonly used in conjunction with zero coupon bond issues, as in this case the issuer's net cash flow is almost identical to what it would have been if it had issued a low cost coupon floating rate instrument.

7.17 Currency Futures

Currency futures are forward transactions in foreign exchange with designated maturities and standardized contract amount. The latter are traded in exchanges. The markets were designed to solve the problems that exist in forward markets. The exchange-traded futures eliminate counterparty risk and offer more liquidity. This is an improvement over the forward contracts.

A futures contract is an agreement between two parties to buy or sell an asset at a certain time in the future at a certain price. Unlike forward contracts the futures contracts are standardized and exchange traded contracts.

Futures are actively traded for such assets as commodities, Euro-dollar deposits, baskets of stocks and Treasury bonds. For cash-settled derivatives, the underlying asset is any market variable such as a stock price, interest rate or commodity price upon which the future payments of the instrument are based.

Futures contracts may require actual delivery of the underlying asset upon the maturity of the contract. Otherwise, they can allow for cash settlement with the arrangement that, when the contract matures, the spot price of the underlying asset is compared to the contract price. A cash settlement is then made for the difference.

Currency futures are traded on the exchanges like Singapore International Monetary Exchange (SIMEX), London International Financial Futures Exchange (LIFFE), International Monetary Exchange (IMM) at Chicago etc. The typical settlement dates are the third Wednesday of March, June, September and December. Unlike forward transactions only a few currencies can be hedged with currency futures. In the LIFFE the currencies available for futures are Swiss franc, yen, sterling and Euro against US dollar. The buyer and seller of a currency futures contract do not deal with the bank, but with the clearing house of the exchanges as counterparty. The clearing house acts as an intermediary between the buyers and sellers for the smooth processing of the deals. An initial margin is to be paid to the clearing house as a guarantee. The deposit of the margin is mandatory for the participants. The daily price movement causes change in the value of the open position. To maintain the stipulated margin with the clearing house a variation margin is to be adjusted daily if any loss emerges. Again profits, if any, are credited to the margin of the counterparty.

The standard minimum units of different currencies are as follows as on December 2001:

Australian Dollars	1,00,000
Canadian Dollars	1,00,000
British Pounds	62,500
French Franc	2,50,000
Japanese Yen	12,500,000
Swiss Franc	125,000

7.18 The Role of Exchange

If risk is to be transferred efficiently for the macro management, there must be a large group of individuals ready to buy or sell. When a hedger wants to sell futures contracts to protect his business position, he cannot afford to wait around for a long time for a buyer, he needs to know he can effect the transaction quickly. The futures exchange brings together a large number of speculators. This makes quick transactions possible. Moreover, the exchange allows contracts to be bought and sold rapidly by quick clearing operations.

The exchange does the standardization. The exchange writes the specifications for each contract, setting standards of grading, measurement, methods of transfer, and times of delivery. By making the standardization in this way, the exchange opens the futures market up to almost anyone willing to hedge risk. In the pits, then, the auction process is facilitated because only price must be negotiated.

7.19 Nature of Operations

The nature of functioning of the futures exchanges is typified by the following properties:

1. Trading is done in a specified area in the exchange according to an established set of rules. This area is known as pit. Trading is done within specified hours. No trading may occur outside these scheduled trading times, though different commodities will have different trading hours.

2. Trading is done by open outcry. Therefore, all participants know all bids and offers, and all transactions are public knowledge.

3. All trading is done in contracts that are standardized for quality, delivery date, location, procedure, and contract size. Negotiation in the pit is limited to price only (bid/ask).

4. The exchange clearinghouse assumes the opposite side of all trades or contracts. The buyer and seller negotiate price, after which each has an obligation with the clearinghouse, and not with each other. This is important when the positions are later liquidated.

5. All futures contracts can legally be cancelled by taking an offsetting position. The exchange clearinghouse guarantees all contracts. This is possible because of the margin deposits of the members.

7.20 Interest Rate Futures

Interest rate futures (IRF) have become well established products in the world exchanges like SIMEX, LIFFE, IMM and Chicago Board of Trade (CBOT) and it offers an alternative to classical money market instruments. IRF are forward contracts for short term investments, money and capital market instruments with pre-determined maturities. These have standardized contract size and these are traded in exchanges. Thus IRF can be used to settle interest rates in advance.

The interest rates derived from the prices of IRF contracts are not the same as current interest rates for the relevant instrument, but these represent expected interest rates for the future periods. Purchase and sale of IRF are settled through the exchanges clearing houses like the case of currency futures. Same are the roles of initial margin and variation in margin.

Eight

Seignorage, Money Supply and Inflation

"A monetary system is like some internal organ; it should not be allowed to take up very much of one's thought when it goes right, but it needs a great deal of attention when it goes wrong".

[D. H. Robertson]

Since the beginning of 1990s many developing countries had experienced extreme instability in the exchange rate of their domestic currency. Though some could have come out with stability of their currency regime, many suffered for a long time. This instability in the financial sector has a profound effect on the growth and stability of the real sector of the economy. Money in the modern world is a fiat paper currency as its intrinsic value depends on the legal guarantee of the sovereign government. By issuing paper currency the government earns income that is known as seignorage in the monetary theory. Seignorage (SNG) is defined in the literature as:

.... a duty levied on the coinage of money for the purpose of covering the expenses of minting, and as a source of revenue to the crown, claimed by the sovereign by virtue of his prerogative.

[McKinnon, 1979: p. 283]

According to Professor S. Black (1998), seignorage is the excess of the face value over the cost of production of the fiat money. The rationale why the issuer should get the seignorage is that the minting of money makes its supply limited and for the resulting limited supply money yields a rent that should go to *seigneur*.

One interesting aspect of SNG is that it remained more or less absent during the era when money meant metallic coins, either silver or gold. The reason was obvious as the difference between the face value of the coin and the cost of production including the cost of the metal was not significant. This prevented the rulers to issue reserve money for the sake of reaping the SNG. The invention of paper money facilitated the process as such type of money could be released in the economy with a minimum cost.

During the period of metallic currency, principal gain from SNG was the premium or the commission charged when the coins were first released to the economy. Once the money was released, coins were to be maintained at a cost for its storage and transport. Even coins used to lose its weight through wear and tear leading to the situation that face value of the coin became less than the metal value.

During the regime of metallic coin, excess supply of money leading to inflation was a rare phenomenon as that would necessitate a large supply of the metal at a relatively less cost. Inflation in a commodity money situation may happen only when the commodity used in the minting of coins becomes excess in supply and also cost of minting of coins becomes less. Both are unlikely events and so there had been a long period of price stability during this phase of history. But once paper money came into circulation, these commodities, like gold and silver, were released for other social use. In a sense the introduction of paper money brought huge amount of social savings in the society.

But the introduction of paper brought huge advantage to the governments as they found in it larger scope of marshalling resources from the economy by giving paper money, which is very cheap to produce. This is the disadvantage of fiat money as a system. The intrinsic value of paper money depends on strict control on its supply and the legal backing of the government. But its being cheaper leads to its abuse by the issuer and then it loses its credibility. In this perspective J.M. Keynes observed:

> *There is no subtler, no surer means of overturning the existing basis of Society than to debauch the currency. The process engages all the hidden forces of economic law on the side of destruction.....*
>
> [Keynes, 1923; p. 80]

We have observed that paper money, also called fiat money, has no intrinsic value. Fiat money can retain its market perceived value if asset-holders remain confident that its rate of supply to the economy will remain strictly controlled. This remains true because the demand for paper money is derived from how readily it is accepted rather than how fully it is backed. This has been proved many a time through historical events and more recently it is revealed in the events of Thailand, Indonesia, South Korea, Russia, Brazil and Argentina. The governments of these countries fully backed their currencies. In spite of that the individuals and institutions that were holding monetary instruments denominated in these currencies lost confidence in the credibility of the governments and remained away from these financial instruments. The public perception was found true when it was revealed that the central banks of these countries were unable to purchase the domestic currencies at prices fixed by them. That led to large scale devaluation of these currencies as were seen in cases of Thai baht, Indonesian rupiah, Russian rouble, and Brazilian real etc.

One important element common in all the cases as stated above is that the governments of these countries tried to finance their budget deficits by the seignorage reaped through the increase in the supply of money. This makes SNG inter-related to budget deficit and inflation.

8.1 Measurement of Seignorage

The common measure of SNG is the real rent from issuing reserve money, and it is defined as currency in circulation plus reserve of the bank held by the Central Bank. The real rent is computed as the change in the reserve money divided by the price level. This we can write:

$$SNG = d\,M\,/\,P$$

Equation 8.1

Here d denotes change in the sense of differential calculus, M the reserve money as defined and P the price level. Since the differential d (M/P) can be expanded as;

$$d(M/P) = [P.\,dM - M\,.\,dP]\,/\,P^2 = dM/P - (M/P).dP/P,$$

therefore,

$$dM/P = d\,(M/P) + (M/P)\,.\,\Pi$$

Equation 8.2

where

$$\Pi = dP/P \quad \text{i.e., rate of inflation.}$$

Combining Equations (8. 1) and (8. 2) , we can write,

$$SNG = d\,(M/P) + \Pi\,.\,(M/P)$$

Equation 8.3

The SNG has two components. The first term on the right is the change in the real reserve money. It measures the increasing command over the commodities available to the government through the release of additional reserve money. The second term is the inflation tax that the authority collects from the holders of fiat money as the extent to which inflation erodes the intrinsic value (purchasing power) of the fiat money held by the public. It measures the capital loss suffered by the holders of paper money as price level changes. One interesting aspect of fiat money is that once the asset holders start thinking that the supply of fiat money is far in excess than what is warranted, the newly issued money debases the existing money in circulation. This is equivalent to the capital loss of the holders of the fiat money, and the first term is a measure of that as it indicates the change in the real reserve money.

8.2 Broader Measure of Seignorage

A rapid expansion of reserve money and hence money supply can lead to a gain to the government in the form of inflation tax and seignorage, and it may lead to a cost as the holders of existing money stock think it as a form of capital loss. This capital gains or losses induced by a rapid expansion of money supply can be measured by making the concept of seignorage a bit broader. This can be pursued by using the stylized set of accounts for the monetary authority that McKinnon used. According to McKinnon (1979), total assets consists of money reserves and investment denoted by I and total liabilities consists of deposits, say D. From this SNG is computed as

$$SNG = r.\ I - r^*\ D - C \qquad\qquad Equation\ 8.4$$

Where, r = open market rate of interest on investment
  r^* = deposit rate of interest on holding of international currency
  C = cost of servicing the existing stock of money

One implication of this McKinnon identity is that if the government has large external liability (that makes a negative I, or I < 0), it will lose seignorage. This is an interesting result as extended money creation by the government leads to loss of revenue on account of SNG.

Professor M.J.M. Neumann (1992) has deduced a formula of 'extended seignorage' (ESN) by using a similar format. His identity is:

$$ESN = SNG + (iD + i^*\ F + GR\ )/P \qquad\qquad Equation\ 8.5$$

Where, **ESN = extended seignorage**

  SNG = seignorage as defined above

  i = interest rate on the stock of private debt (D) held by the monetary authority

  i^* = interest rate on official foreign loan made by the monetary authority

  F = amount of foreign loan of the authority

  P = consumer price level

  GR= unrealized capital gains on assets

These equations put together a system that links inflation, seignorage, exchange rate movements, interest rate, fiscal deficit and some other macro variables. We can show the link between seignorage and exchange rate movements through a simplified version of monetary authority's accounts. Whenever there are changes in the balance sheet of the monetary authority, reserve money changes. Put in symbols, change in the reserve money (dM) is the sum of the changes in the net foreign assets (dF), changes in the net domestic credit (dD) and change in other items (dZ). We can write,

$$dM = d F + d D + dZ \qquad \text{Equation 8.6}$$

where Z = proxy for other items, or parameters that influence macro variables in the economy.
Dividing through by the price level P, we write

$$dM/P = dF/P + dD/P + dZ/P \qquad \text{Equation 8.7}$$

Similar to Equation (8.2), we can manipulate

$$d(F/P) = dF /P - (F/ P). dP /P, \text{ or,}$$

$$dF/ P = d(F/P) + \Pi . (F/ P) \qquad \text{Equation 8.8}$$

Similarly,

$$dD / P = d(D / P) + \Pi .(D /P) \qquad \text{Equation 8.9}$$

and, $$\quad dZ /P = d(Z /P) + \Pi .(Z /P) \qquad \text{Equation 8.10}$$

Combining Equation (8.7) to (8.10) we can write,

$$dM /P = d(F /P) + \Pi. (F /P) + d(D /P) + \Pi . (D/P) + d(Z/P) +$$

$$\Pi.(Z /P) \qquad \text{Equation 8.11}$$

As we interpret equation (8.11) we see that the generation of SNG depends on factors that change net foreign assets, net domestic assets and net change of other items (Z) being a proxy of some macro variables, along with rate of inflation and the extent the latter affects the parameters as mentioned.

8.3 Seignorage and Exchange Rate

Net foreign asset F can be written as

$$F = e . F^*,$$ *Equation 8.12*

When, F^* = dollar value of foreign assets, and

  e = exchange rate of domestic currency.

Expanding the expression we can write,

$$dF = de. F^* + e. dF^*,$$

or after a little manipulation , we get

$$dF/P = [de/e + dF^*/F^*]. F/P$$ *Equation 8.13*

When money supply is increasing rapidly, both the exchange rate (e) and the dollar value of foreign liabilities will increase. This means both de and dF^* will be positive. For a highly indebted country, net foreign asset (F/P) will be negative and that makes the value of the right hand side of [8.13] negative.

When net foreign liabilities of the monetary authority are large, the effects of exchange rate changes [as measured by dF/P in equation 8.13] subtract in a major way from the generation of SNG as in Equation 8.11. So a country with huge foreign liability and high inflation is caught in a bind as further money creation leads to a negative seignorage and more money creation is needed to compensate the latter. This aspect will be clear if we analyze the cases of two highly indebted

Table: Seignorage and its Components (year 1997)

Country	dM/P	dF/P	dD/P	F*	a**	b**
1	2	3	4	5	6	7
Russia	1.76	0.49	1.27	1.85	0.10	0.36
Zambia	1.22	- 0.15	1.36	- 28.6	- 2.27	1.92

Note: a^{**} = (de/e). F/P, b^{**} = (df/f). F /P

Source: *International Financial Statistics, IMF, March, 1999.*

countries, Russia and Zambia:

Column 4 shows direct gains from seignorage to GDP. Its value becomes low when the growth of reserve money becomes fast. In case of Zambia, growth of money supply became very high, that reduces the value of the gains from seignorage to GDP.

In column 3, the value shows the effects of exchange rate changes. When net foreign assets of monetary authority are large and negative (liability), the effects of exchange rate changes subtract in a major way from the generation of seignorage. Here the data of Zambia are striking as the figure is negative.

8.4 Dynamic Effects

Some economists prefer the study of the dynamic effects of reserve money changes. In the developed countries the growth of reserve money is stable and budget deficit does not lead to money creation. That leads to the discussion of seignorage in terms of a 'steady state' equilibrium. But critics point out that in the developing countries the growth of the reserve money is volatile and rapid. Even the economists have emphasized the existence of a Laffer Curve [named after Professor Laffer showing retrograde relation between rate of tax and tax revenue] relating seignorage to rate of inflation and growth of reserve money in the perspective of hyper-inflation. The idea boils down to the existence of an optimum seignorage point and whether a country makes a transition back to optimum point once it crosses the limit. Economists argue that this transition is very important for the highly indebted countries that have moved beyond their optimum international credit limits. They find themselves in a dilemma — they are caught in a spiral of accelerating inflation as they try to gain access to the increasing amount of foreign exchange needed to meet the debt service obligations. As the rate of reserve money creation increases, the task of meeting foreign obligations becomes increasingly difficult.

From this theoretical exercise we can write briefly the policy implications faced by the highly indebted countries today.

The countries that face twin problems of a large amount of foreign debt and its servicing obligations and a potential high inflation may have the temptation of servicing the foreign debt obligation by the creation of reserve money and appropriating the seignorage. But this boils down to the large scale debasement of the domestic currency and hyper inflation. In such a situation the country can better seek a rescheduling of debt obligation even if that means a default and adverse international repercussions.

8.5 Cost of Seignorage

Some developing countries are prone to maximize revenue from seignorage, and in the process these countries face trouble in unstable currency. There is also a cost of seignorage and that can be placed as follows.

The important cost of SNG is the resource cost of printing, issuing, storing and maintaining the stock of fiat money. Sometimes countries facing very high inflation are to import large stock of printed currency at a substantial cost.

Another cost of SNG is the *'inflation tax'* imposed on the economy as hyper-inflation sets in. The authority may collect resources through inflation tax, may even facilitate a desirable redistribution of income, but this also leads to currency substitution and a capital loss on fixed-income liabilities.

The literature has noted that through currency substitution and asset substitution the public can reduce their holdings of financial instruments denominated in domestic currency. The asset holders in unstable economies having track record of high inflation have become efficient in using this method and this way they insulate their assets from the negative effects of monetary disruptions. This situation is common in countries like Russia, Argentina, Peru, Bolivia, Serbia and some others.

A country with a large external debt faces capital loss when hyperinflation becomes chronic. A commitment to repay foreign liability is associated with several risks. International interest rates may increase, and that will increase the cost of debt. The country faces same effects when the domestic currency depreciates. While the first increases the cost in foreign exchange, the second increases the cost in domestic currency.

8.6 Conclusion

The monetary authority enjoys seignorage and inflation tax through the release of reserve money. So long the latter maintains an equilibrium relation with the country's GDP and other macro parameters, the economy faces no problem. Instead the society as a whole is benefited by the positive externality of the existence of money as an institution. Apart from that the control of reserve money gives several benefits to the authority and these are: (i) accrual of monopoly rents due to the difference of yields on official liabilities, and (ii) real gains to the issuers of financial instruments.

The authority gets the monopoly rents as the official financial instruments held by the private sector at rates below the market rates. One example is the reserve requirements of banks.

The authority issues fixed coupon bonds and when inflation continues due to rapid increase of reserve money, the real value of these bonds are deflated. The difference between the face value of the bond and the real value is the gain to the issuer.

Does sovereign money matter? Or, is it a desirable thing in the global scene that some 190 plus independent nations should have their own sovereign currencies? These are a bit complex questions. In the present chapter we get the theoretical backdrop about the cost and benefit of the issuance of reserve money, and now we are in a position to pursue this issue in the next chapter.

Nine

Government and Sovereign Currency

"For this reason the period under which the Bank of England did not pay gold for its notes – the period from 1797 to 1819 – is always called the period of the Bank restriction. As the Bank during that period did not perform, and was not compelled by law to perform, its conduct of paying its notes in cash, it might apparently have been well called the period of Bank license."

[Walter Bagehot in *Lombard Street*]

Money is an important institution ever invented in the forward march of human civilization for the smooth functioning of the exchange economy. Considering the fact that money has a positive externality in the economy every government finds it as its duty to provide a stable currency to its citizens.

One of the best documented histories of sovereign currency is of the dollar of the United States. The history records that Abraham Lincoln, in an 1839 speech before the Illinois legislature, spoke about the government's ability and obligation to provide a stable currency so that the exchange economy can function smoothly (Lincoln, 1839). The record of the successive governments in this field is not very encouraging though. One can establish convincing evidence in the somewhat dubious experience of the Greenback period, initiated in 1861 and lasting until 1879, when paper money issued by the government during the Civil War was made convertible into gold.

Even more than 150 years after Lincoln's remark, economists find themselves still wrestling with this same issue: *Is government the solution or the problem when it comes to protecting the purchasing power of money*? History is full with examples of what governments may do when their power of mintage is unlimited and the cost of it is not prohibitive. The hyperinflations of Germany in the 1920s and of Russia, Argentina, Bolivia and Brazil in the 1990s are sobering reminders of the effects of excessive money creation.

The important question today is:

What can be done to ensure that governments and their central banks deliver on their responsibility of protecting money's value?

In modern times money means fiat money, or currency released by the monetary authorities that are not backed by gold and/or other foreign currency assets fully. This fiat money is a monetary standard that are not supported by convertibility into intrinsically valued commodities like gold or silver. The combination of historical experience and the near-universal evolution of fiat money systems has created a widespread recognition that national monetary authorities will not deliver price stability unless careful attention is given to the incentive structures under which they operate.

Nobel Prize winning economist Friedrich von Hayek put it this way:

"History is largely a history of inflation, and usually of inflations engineered by governments and for the gain of governments."

[Hayek, 1976, p.27]

What is crucial is that the international financial system is to evolve a mechanism that will prevent such history from repeating itself. The challenge remains to devise sustainable institutional monetary arrangements that can protect the public from debasement of the value of its money.

In recent time, several nations have taken up this challenge by legislating price stability as the sole, or dominant, objective of their central banks. Such legislation with price stability as the principal objective of the central bank has already been passed in New Zealand, Canada, the United Kingdom and Sweden. While these new initiatives are laudable, it is too soon to tell whether they will be sufficient to ensure that governments and their central banks consistently deliver price stability. The stability of a currency and its credibility to the citizens depend on a set of macro-economic and social factors. Such legislation is but one of many environmental factors that may contribute to the protection of a nation's currency.

The history of money over the past two centuries shows nations groping for lasting institutional structures that provide incentives to limit their own governments' temptation to debase their currency in order to satisfy shortsighted political objectives. The approaches used in the past have stemmed directly from both the nature of money prevailing at the time and societies' views about the proper role of government.

In the perspective of the widespread temptation of the governments of the developing countries to debase their currencies to maximize the seignorage and inflation tax some economists have proposed a novel idea and this can be put as follows:

Perhaps the most innovative and lasting way countries can achieve stable purchasing power for their monetary assets is by competing against each other in the provision of money. Nations that excel at providing a superior standard of value may find citizens in other countries who prefer to import their currency. Facing such competition, the providers of domestic currencies will have to improve their own products.

9.1 The Gold Standard Implications

Since historical times governments have taken some role in providing money to the economy. In the beginning the role was limited to 'authentication' — verifying that coins contained the standard weight of metals as indicated. Even in this limited role, however, the authorities occasionally violated the public trust concerning the soundness of money. In the era of pure fiat monies, methods are devised to maintain the credibility of the money. The primary approach to keeping governments 'honest' and credible has been to remove the power to inflate from those with the most incentive to do so. This objective has been achieved by building in a high level of independence between the Central Bank — which has the power to inflate — and the Treasury — which has the incentive to inflate.

The central bank has been given independent responsibility for monetary policy, and this is meant to serve as a way for a government to commit to lower rates of inflation that would be realized without the existence of a separate monetary authority. Though this institutional structure is not a panacea, but this has proven especially useful: Studies have shown that countries with more independent central banks have lower rates of inflation. This is one important finding suggesting the importance of the independent central banks in the developing countries.

Despite central bank independence, the experiences of 1980s show that the central banks in some countries failed to maintain the stability of the currency. This has induced many countries to move toward more explicit central bank accountability for protecting the purchasing power of money.

Hayek was of the opinion that private agents (banks) may be given responsibility of supplying money subject to certain constraints imposed by the monetary authority. He contended that as long as private monies were allowed to circulate freely, competition would keep the value of these currencies constant over time. In case any issuer attempted to collect too much seigniorage by inflating away the value of its money, consumers would substitute into competing money. In the process currency issuers would have an incentive to remain honest. Hayek's proposal has historical precedent. So-called "free banking in some countries like Canada and Scotland tested the idea that money need not be provided by the central government. Under free banking arrangements, private banks competed against each other to provide the public with currency.

Critics of traditional private money systems have often used Gresham's law to argue that money must be provided by governments. This famous dictum states that bad money will always drive good money out of circulation. In other words it argues that only monies with the worst inflation rate would circulate. This led many to believe that a government monopoly on printing money is necessary.

Though there is a possibility that private companies and banks could compete in the provision of money, it is not clear that such private arrangements are sustainable as a practical matter, given the seigniorage opportunities inherent in government-controlled money or in any currency provided by a monopoly. Thus governments have powerful incentives to tax private money out of existence in order to become the sole provider of legal tender.

9.2 Competing Currencies: Competition among Governments

One aspect remains open in Hayek's proposal and that is what might make governments less inclined to intervene now than in the past. Furthermore, convertibility of private note issues into specie was taken as a given in all historical free-banking regimes. What incentives do governments have to forgo the seigniorage opportunities inherent in their provision of fiat money and return to the world of privately issued monies that are ultimately redeemable in specie?

Some economists argue that with the advent of flexible exchange rates, Hayek's vision of competition among currencies that can effectively regulate the quantity of notes may become a reality. Privately issued monies may not be allowed to compete as that may lead to a chaotic condition, but competition among different national currencies may serve the same purpose.

In today's world of close cooperation and integration in international currencies are increasingly competing to become the currency of choice. The dollarization in Eastern Europe, Russia and Latin America shows how a foreign currency can become a legitimate substitute for a domestic currency that has failed to maintain its value. Even in countries like Argentina having a currency board system, individuals' ability to hold dollar accounts encourages the government to maintain the integrity of its monetary system.

9.3 Some Barriers to International Competition in Money

Once the United States and the rest of the world broke away from the anchor provided by the gold standard, inflation rates almost universally trended upward and, in some cases, spun rapidly out of control. Effective demonetization of gold happened with the delinking of gold price to US dollar that came with the unilateral declaration of the USA in 1971 and with that Bretton Woods Agreement collapsed.

Though a price stability mandate would help to shift the focus of monetary policy away from short-term fine-tuning to long-term price stability, such legislation cannot be viewed as a panacea in the absence of clear incentive structures that remove the government's temptation to violate the mandate. However, in the light of the increasing integration of world markets, one suggestion can be made that the same competitive forces that have served market economies so well may ultimately constrain the excessive money creation that has been problematic for fiat money regimes in the past.

Why might competition among sovereign nations in the provision of money prove to be sustainable where private competition did not? The answer lies in the very same seigniorage possibilities that induce governments to undermine private competition in the first place. Unlike the case for the domestic economy, individual countries have no power to legislate their own monetary monopoly in the global economy. The US dollar will circulate as a medium of exchange in foreign countries only if it is considered superior in value to other national currencies. This means the United States, or any country, will enjoy the benefits of seigniorage outside its borders only if it wins the competitive battle in the monetary marketplace.

But the interesting question is: Why would a sovereign nation willingly give up its seigniorage to a 'competing' country? The answer comes from considering the mutual advantage of trade, wherein nations benefit from comparative advantage. A nation should be willing to import a competing currency when it needs a stable payments medium to strengthen a developing market economy with necessary liquidity. If a nation's monetary credibility is weak, importing a standard of value may enhance wealth within the country, and thus tax receipts, by more than the revenue gained from seigniorage.

This competitive mechanism for protecting the value of money can be enhanced by changing existing protectionist laws to foster more effective competition among currencies. We should heed Hayek's argument that countries around the world should abolish "any kind of exchange control or regulation of the movement of money between countries..." and provide "the full freedom to use any of the currencies for contracts and accounting."

Legislation requiring that the courts enforce "specific performance" would also increase the opportunity for currency competition. Currently, in most countries of the world, when there is a dispute involving a contract that is stated in terms of a currency or unit other than the national currency (such as gold), courts do not require performance in the stated unit, but only require an "equivalent payment" in the national currency, weakening the power of competition among national currencies.

9.4 A Market Approach to Currency Provision

Clearly, important goals are within reach. Inflation is low, and price stability is beginning to be recognized as the predominant long-term monetary policy objective of the central banks around the world. Flexible exchange rates, coupled with more-open capital markets, are enabling international currencies to compete with one another. Central banks cannot be complacent, however, because new challenges will surely arise. Just as fiat money replaced specie-backed paper currencies, electronically initiated debits and credits are likely to become the dominant payment modes in the future. The concept that money is like any other good and that competition among issuers can best guarantee its value should not be forgotten.

We will now see one of the best managed and controlled currencies in the world that is Indian rupee.

9.5 Indian Rupee in a Controlled Regime: An Empirical Approach in Historical Perspective[1]

The history of currency in each country is interesting and India is no exception. Indian rupee, the sovereign currency of India, has undergone a long process of evolution since 1950 before becoming a fully convertible currency in current account in March, 1993. The formal administrative systems of the rupee is as follows. The Reserve Bank of India, in accordance with policy formulated by the Government of India, administers the foreign exchange control system through its exchange control department. In this area a number of commercial banks assist the Reserve Bank in the implementation of its policies. The Controller of Imports and Exports issues the foreign trade license. India joined the International Monetary Fund in Washington on December 18, 1946. She became a member of the International Finance Corporation on April 18, 1956.

During the period 1973 to 1993 the exchange rates were computed from the value of rupee, which was determined on the basis of the relationship of rupee to a basket of currencies of India's major trading partners within margin of 5 per cent value adopted. The number of currencies and the value of weights attached remained a secret. Exchange rate of the rupee in terms of the pound sterling was accordingly fixed by the Reserve Bank of India. Exchange rates for spot and forward purchases of deutsche mark, Japanese yen and US dollars were based on latest available rates and Reserve Bank used to announce such rates every day. Exchange rates of other currencies were derived from the cross rates of the pound sterling with rupee. Reserve Bank stood ready to purchase currencies of some member countries of Asian Clearing Union

---

1.	This section is based on Chapter 2 of the book, S. Nandi, *Essays on International Finance*, National Institute of Bank Management, Pune, 1996.

(ACU), deutsche mark, Japanese Yen, pound sterling and US dollars, spot and forward, and to sell spot ACU currencies and pound sterling. The Reserve Bank started selling US dollar spot since February, 1987. The Reserve Bank permitted authorized dealers to fix the floor and ceiling rates for purchases and sale of US dollar and pound sterling on the basis of a formula furnished by it.

Authorized dealers were permitted to maintain balances and positions in 'permitted currencies', which are divided into two groups, Group A and Group B. The former consisted of 20 listed currencies (currencies like Australian dollars, Austrian shillings, Bahrain diners, Belgian francs, Canadian dollar, Danish kroner, deutsche mark, French francs, Hong Kong dollar, Italian lira, Japanese yen, Kuwait diners, Malaysian ringgit, Netherlands guilders, Norwegian Kroner, pound sterling, Singapore dollars, Swedish kronor, Swiss francs and US dollar). Authorised dealers are also permitted to buy and sell spot any permitted currency from and to banks in any currency outside the Bilateral Group (consisting former East Germany, Czechoslovakia, Poland, Rumania and former USSR).

9.6 The Arrangement of Currencies

All countries were divided into two groups for the prescription of the currency: the Bilateral Group of countries and the External Group of countries. Payments to and from the Bilateral Group must be settled in Indian rupees through the appropriate clearing account. Payments to the External Group of countries (countries outside the Bilateral Group) may be made in rupees to the account of a resident of any country in the group of any permitted currency. Regarding Asian Clearing Union (consisting of Bangladesh, Burma, Islamic Republic of Iran, Pakistan, Sri Lanka and also Nepal) countries, all payments on account of current international transactions between India and other members, except Nepal, are required to be settled through the ACU arrangement. The residents of Nepal obtain their foreign exchange requirements from the Nepal Rastra Bank.

9.7 Indian Rupee in Historical Perspective

Before 1947 Indian economy could maintain a set of separate policies for the stability of the external value of its currency, the Indian rupee, though the relation with the pound sterling was the primary concern. After independence the rupee was pegged to the pound sterling at a fixed parity of Re 1 = 1 s. 6 d. Since US dollar had a fixed parity with gold at $ 35 per ounce of fine gold, the rupee, through its relation with pound sterling, established a fixed parity with gold at Re 1 = 0.2686 gm of fine gold. The exchange rate of rupee for other currencies was determined on the basis of the cross-rates of these currencies against the sterling and the rupee-sterling rate. In 1949, the rupee was devalued against US dollar along with the devaluation of pound sterling and the gold content of the rupee was reduced to Re 1 = 0.1866 gm fine gold. This system continued until the mid-sixties. Meanwhile, the expansion of the money supply to finance the budget deficit created pressure on the price level. This disequilibrium in the domestic money market had a spill-over effect on the balance of payments and on the black market exchange rate of the rupee. A spurt in the activity of the black market occurred in the early sixties as the unofficial parallel economy began to flourish due to the complexities of official control and licensing policy.

In the sixties, the disequilibrium in the domestic money market had its effects on two fronts. First, sizeable black market activities flourished along with significant deviations of the black market exchange rate for the rupee from the official rate (Pick, 1960). Second, a mounting deficit in the balance of trade revealed that the rupee had become significantly over-valued leading to a loss of a competitive edge of Indian exports in the international market. This induced the devaluation of rupee in June, 1966 by 57.5 per cent against pound sterling. The corresponding devaluation of the rupee against the dollar brought the rate to US $ 1 = Rs.7.50. The gold parity of the rupee was reduced to Re 1 = 0.11888 gm.

In August 1971, the Bretton-Woods system broke down and an interim floating arrangement emerged for major currencies. The rupee was pegged to the US dollar at $ 1 =

Rs.7.50, but the pound sterling was continued as the intervention currency. The rupee-dollar parity was used for determining the rupee-sterling rate based on the market rate of pound sterling against the dollar. In December 1971, the Smithsonian realignment of currencies was made and the rupee was delinked from the dollar and relinked to the pound sterling at £ 1 = Rs.18.968. This led to an effective devaluation of the rupee against the pound by 5.38 per cent. Under the Smithsonian agreement, the dollar was devalued against gold, and the external value of the rupee against the dollar was adjusted accordingly at US $ 1 = Rs.7.279.

In September 1975, the rupee was delinked from the pound sterling and linked to a currency basket. The sterling continued to be the intervention currency and also the currency against which the components in the currency basket were valued regularly. But the identification of the currencies and their respective weights remained a secret. The system continued till the end of February 1993.

Since the middle of the seventies, there have been considerable uncertainties in the international money market. As a developing country, India had to peg its currency with any one major currency of the world. And when all the major currencies were floating, it meant unintended depreciation of the rupee. Thus the objective of the basket link was to prevent further depreciation of the rupee against other currencies which it had been undergoing since 1972 along with the floating pound. In the background of supply constraint of exportable goods, the government felt that the depreciation of the rupee, a result of a pegged currency in a floating world, would not help much in increased export earnings. On the contrary, it might lead to an increasing inflationary pressure via rising expenditure on imports. When the rupee was linked to the currency basket, the Reserve Bank of India announced that the currencies contained in the basket were for those countries who were important trade partners.

The discrepancy between the Indian stance on its currency (a basket-linked currency) and that of the International Monetary Fund (a managed-floating currency) was significant.

The IMF used to exercise surveillance over the exchange rate policies of member countries in order to discourage the manipulation of exchange rates. Again, member countries were required to intimate to the IMF the particular exchange rate arrangement adopted by them and also any change. In these situations the discrepancy in the respective position of India and the IMF leads to the conclusion that India had opted for an arrangement permitting discretionary management of the external value of its currency. The multi-currency basket was expected to provide a ready technique for managing the daily rate of the rupee against the intervention currency in order to stabilize the average level of the rupee while at the same time achieving a desirable market-related level for the US dollar.

9.8 Emergence of Dual Rates

Throughout the period from 1950 onwards the free market value of rupee *vis-à-vis* US dollar had always been lower compared to the official rate. The free-market rate (the so-called black market rate) deviated from the official rate time to time depending on the foreign exchange reserve position, the crisis in balance of payments, the level of exports over and above the unaccounted factors like illegal inflow of gold into the country. The deviations of the black market rate from the official rate is important in the sense that it is the black market premium which determined to a large extent the inflow of remittances through unofficial channels. The Reserve Bank of India adjusted the exchange rate of rupee consistently downward in the eighties leading to 8 to 9 per cent depreciation of the rupee every year on an average. A look at the data of official exchange rate and black market exchange rate of rupee indicates that rupee has been much more flexible downwards in the eighties, but the gap between the official rate and the black market rate had been wider compared to the earlier decade. The reasons for the fluctuation of the black market (read free market) exchange rate should be sought more outside the legal and organized sectors of economic activities.

In July 1991, the Reserve Bank of India announced the partial convertibility scheme of Indian rupee in the 60:40 ratio. Thus exporters could convert 60 per cent of their export earnings of foreign currency by free market rate, while they are to convert the remaining 40 per cent through official rate. Considering the fact that the prevailing free market rate had been approximately 15 per cent higher than the official rate (read the rupee value of US dollar), the exporters were getting some 12 per cent less value of their earnings in terms of rupees. That in the new system they were getting higher value of their export earnings compared to what they used to get during the fixed exchange rate regime was completely lost to them and their comparison with the potential free convertibility of US dollar by market rate convinced them that their export earnings were subjected to taxation. Ultimately, in March, 1993, the rupee was freely floated and thus abolishing the official rate.

Is Indian rupee a free currency now in the sense that Japanese Yen is one? The answer is no. Indian rupee is not freely convertible and trade in Indian rupee is practically banned. But the external value of rupee is now determined by the market forces and their rate is used now to convert export earnings of foreign currencies in terms of rupee. Thus Indian rupee has entered into a new era and the researcher requires some more time to understand the full implications.

9.9 International Transactions

Indian rupee is a restricted currency in the sense that the foreign exchange regime in India is a controlled one. Thus banks involved in international transactions are to function within well-defined parameters, which change too often by new circulars.

The accounts of banks are of two categories: resident accounts and non-resident accounts. The accounts of Indians and of Nepalese and Bhutanese nationals resident in these countries, and the accounts of offices of Indian, Bhutanese and Nepalese firms and companies in Nepal and Bhutan are treated as resident accounts. All other accounts in the banks related to foreign countries are non-resident accounts. Again, corresponding to the division of countries for prescription of currency purposes, the accounts of banks are directed into two groups: the accounts of banks in the Bilateral Group of countries and the accounts for the External Group of countries. Accounts of banks for the latter may be credited with payments for imports, interest, dividends etc., with authorized transfers from the non-resident accounts of persons and firms provided that both parties belong to same country or countries in the External Group. They may be debited for payments for exports and for other payments to residents of India. The balances in the accounts of banks in countries in the external group may be converted into any permitted currency. The prior approval of the Reserve Bank of India is required for all other entries on bank accounts. All these show the nature of the complex foreign exchange regime which maintains a large number of regulations for non-resident account holders. Since such economies are prone to capital flight, rules are made to prevent that, though one of the accepted fact is that in spite of all these regulations capital flight takes place on a regular basis.

From 1991, some relaxations have been made to attract foreign capital in non-resident accounts. Some concessions in the form of higher interest rates have also been provided. The result has been encouraging though inflow and outflow have become a common feature in these accounts. As a part of ongoing economic reforms exchange control rules are being made much more liberal and its impact on the inflow of foreign capital have become positive. There has been perceptible change in the interest structure of the country and the interest rate is expected to come down further. It is expected that domestic interest rate will converge with the world rate in the long run.

9.10 Price Level and Exchange Rate in India

Exchange rate of a currency is a price of the currency in terms of foreign currency. This leads to one implication that it determines the price of the exportable in foreign countries in terms of foreign currency. The price of tradable commodities in the foreign market is linked with the domestic price level through the exchange rate when the latter is fixed. In Indian case the movement of the price level in India is not compatible with the movement of foreign price level (read US price level). We find that relative inflation is much higher in India since the middle of 1984. Thus, following the large scale deviations of the domestic price level compared to world price level in case of a continuous inflation, if the exchange rate is not adjusted downward to compensate the price rise (to maintain the purchasing power parity), the foreign currency price of the exportable will be higher in foreign market and the operation of the law of demand will reduce the export of the country. This analysis leads to one additional responsibility of the monetary authority of the country following a fixed exchange rate regime, and that is, to adjust the exchange rate in face of inflation in the country so that the foreign currency prices of the exportable are not adversely affected. Technically speaking, two concepts are involved here and these are the Purchasing Power Parity doctrine (PPP) and the Real Exchange Rate (RER).

The Purchasing Power Parity (PPP) doctrine relates the price of a commodity in the home country, p, with its own-country price in another country e P* or

$$P = e\ P^* \hspace{4cm} \textit{Equation 9.1}$$

where e is the nominal exchange rate, and it represents the home-currency value of a unit of the foreign currency. The relationship is a 'strong form' of PPP, and it implies that, neglecting the transport cost, the price of an internationally traded good, say gold, should be same everywhere when expressed in some common currency. Thus an Indian, while buying his HMT watch, should pay same amount of money either in Mumbai or in London.

Though appealing, the empirical support of PPP has always been mixed in the literature. While Edison and Klovland (1987) finds some support for PPP in their studies based on long run time series data, Dornbusch (1985) and

Giovannetti (1992) have failed to find any evidence of support for PPP. In the later portion of this section we will see the empirical position of PPP in India.

The limited success of the PPP is sought to be explained in the literature in several ways. First, it is said that there are flows in the actual price level compared, because price indices in different countries include different goods, including non-traded goods, with different weights and thus PPP may fail when relative price changes. Thus the failure of the PPP is more apparent than real.

The second approach places a renewed emphasis on theories that postulate that there is no long-run and stable relationship between prices in different countries. These theories seek to explain the movement of the exchange rates by other factors including the price level.

The logarithmic transformation of (9.1) will be

$$\log e = \log P - \log P^*$$
Equation 9.2

and the estimable form of (9.2) is

$$\log e = a_0 + a_1 (\log P - \log P^*)$$
Equation 9.3

Thus equation (9.3) has been estimated using quarterly data of India for the period 1973 to 1991. Cochrane Orcutt method of estimation has been used to take care of autocorrelation. For official exchange rate the estimation is as under:

$$\log e = 1.554 + 0.056 (\log P - \log P^*) + u$$
$$t - \text{Statistic} \quad (0.912) \quad (0.673)$$

$$\text{Adjusted } R^2 = 0.987 \qquad \text{SEE} = 0.089$$
$$\text{D.W. Statistic} = 1.726 \qquad n = 73$$

Thus a look at the result shows that PPP does not hold in the case of India during the period 1973-1991 as the coefficient of the relative price level ($\log P - \log P^*$) is not significant.

9.11 Real Exchange Rate

A related concept of Purchasing Power Parity condition is the

Real Exchange Rate (RER), which can be derived by rewriting the strong form of PPP (equation 9.1). Thus we can write

$$RER = e\ \frac{P^*}{P}$$

Equation 9.1a

RER represents domestic currency price of foreign goods relative to home goods. The strong form of PPP indicates that real exchange rate should be a constant. Thus RER may deviate from the equilibrium value (some constant) in the short run, but in the long run it cannot go too far from the equilibrium value (some constant) as suggested by PPP.

When both the domestic and foreign price levels equilibrate in the long run, RER becomes one and then the test of the PPP in strong form becomes equivalent to the test of RER, i.e., whether RER hovers around unity or not.

Using the price levels of India and the United States (as a proxy of foreign price level) we have calculated the real exchange rate for India during the period 1973-1991. A look at the nominal and real exchange rates shows that the RER also depreciated overtime. Thus the adjustment of the nominal exchange rate following the currency-basket regime has over-compensated the price rise in India.

9.12 Exact Exchange Rate

We see that real exchange rate depends on the domestic price level. In India many prices are government administered and thus the government has power to influence the real exchange rate through the price level. In view of this another exchange rate is estimated. It is called Exact Exchange Rate (EER). Corresponding to a particular price level, EER is that exchange rate for which the real exchange rate will remain constant. If we take the 1973 price level, then we calculate EER as

$$EER = (\ RER\ of\ 1973.1\ ) \times \frac{CPI}{CPI^*}$$

The calculated values of both RER and EER are given in the following Table. The discrepancy between two rates shows actual deviations of the RER from the 1973 level.

One can interpret EER as the equilibrium exchange rate provided the anchor period (the rate that is taken for calculation) is assumed to have the equilibrium rate. The subsequent changes in the nominal rate are to compensate the relative inflation only. Since the concept of equilibrium exchange rate is hazardous and full of controversy, the information about the EER can be used as a good proxy for the equilibrium rate.

9.13 Exchange Rate of Indian Rupee and Current Account

The monetarist argue that the equilibrium in the domestic money market influences the changes in the exchange rate of the currency. Money is one important asset in the portfolio of individuals and some economists developed the asset-theory approach to the exchange rate determination. Along with this development another approach emerged in which the current account position of the country is considered as an important determinant for the changes in the exchange rate. By emphasizing the relationship between the current account and the exchange rate this approach developed a model of exchange rate determination that integrated the role of relative prices, expectations of the economic agents and the asset markets (Dornbusch and Fischer, 1980). This approach strikes a middle course, or some sort of a synthesis, between the two earlier approaches — the monetarist one suggesting the importance of monetary equilibrium and price level and the alternative one suggesting the importance of current account. But since trade flows out of changes in the current account are linked with the changes in the portfolio of international assets of the country at the macro level and since money is an important asset, the two approaches can be linked together. The intuitive explanation follows:

When deficits in the current account of a country are financed from the international reserve and the surplus in the current account augments the volume of the same international reserve, the changes in the current account position changes

Table 9a: Real Exchange Rate and Estimated Exact Exchange Rate in India (1973.1 - 1991.4)

Time/Year	Real Exchange Rate (RER)	Exact Exchange Rate (EER)
1973. 1	7.24	8.33
2	6.58	8.79
3	6.81	9.08
4	6.92	9.34
1974. 1	6.51	9.48
2	6.17	10.05
3	6.00	10.67
4	6.02	10.67
1975. 1	6.05	10.25
2	6.54	10.15
3	7.26	9.82
4	7.57	9.39
1976. 1	7.96	9.82
2	8.11	8.81
3	7.81	8.95
4	7.82	9.03
1977. 1	7.75	9.02
2	7.75	9.03
3	7.49	9.21
4	7.12	9.16
1978. 1	7.63	8.79
2	7.66	8.57
3	7.33	8.63
4	7.55	8.62
1979. 1	7.87	8.23
2	7.76	8.17
3	7.65	8.35
4	7.53	8.35

(Contd.)

Table 9a (Contd.) : Real Exchange Rate and Estimated Exact Exchange Rate in India (1973.1 - 1991.4)

Time/Year	Real Exchange Rate (RER)	Exact Exchange Rate (EER)
1980. 1	8.07	8.07
2	7.75	8.00
3	7.51	8.21
4	7.69	8.20
1981. 1	7.87	8.27
2	8.19	8.43
3	8.37	8.65
4	8.35	8.66
1982.1	8.99	8.26
2	9.20	8.25
3	9.08	8.47
4	8.90	8.61
1983. 1	9.12	8.69
2	8.94	8.96
3	8.70	9.32
4	8.85	9.43
1984. 1	9.10	9.35
2	12.67	7.02
3	9.88	9.56
4	10.33	9.58
1985. 1	10.10	9.78
2	10.36	9.54
3	9.78	9.75
4	9.84	9.83
1986. 1	9.88	9.89
2	9.79	10.18
3	9.67	10.43
4	9.81	10.63

(Contd.)

Table 9a (Contd.): Real Exchange Rate and Estimated Exact Exchange Rate in India (1973.1 - 1991.4)

Time/Year	Real Exchange Rate (RER)	Exact Exchange Rate (EER)
1987. 1	9.80	10.49
2	9.70	10.60
3	9.50	10.96
4	9.20	11.12
1988. 1	9.53	10.81
2	10.22	10.97
3	10.32	11.22
4	10.40	10.43
1989. 1	11.21	11.09
2	11.80	11.14
3	11.65	11.38
4	11.89	11.39
1990. 1	12.26	11.17
2	12.07	11.50
3	12.19	11.78
4	11.93	12.04
1991. 1	12.78	12.21
2	13.65	12.34
3	15.78	12.98
4	15.45	13.29

Note: RER = NER (CPI*/CPI), where CPI* is U.S. price level
Exact Exchange Rate (EER) = 7.24 (CPI/CPI*)
i.e., estimated exchange rate to keep the RER fixed
at 1973.1 level.

the holding of foreign currency position of the country. This also affects the supply of money at the domestic level. Seen from a different angle, a continuous surplus in current account will increase the supply of foreign currency leading to a relative decline of the price of that currency. Thus the exchange rate of the foreign currency valued in terms of the domestic currency declines or the exchange rate of the domestic currency appreciates. Thus present exchange rate (spot rate) is influenced by the realized trade flows. This argument also implies that the future spot rate will be influenced by the expected changes in the trade flows. If there is a sudden change in the perception of the traders engaged in the international trade that Indian economy is to import more petroleum in near future due to a surge in demand and a near stagnation in the domestic production, the expected demand for foreign currency, say US dollar, will go up and the future spot rate of rupee will decline. The expected depreciation of the domestic currency will induce the individuals to shift from domestic currency to foreign currency, where it is possible and thus further depreciation of the domestic currency becomes a possibility. Currency substitution is not possible in India, but traders can hedge the possible change in the expected trade flows due to exogenous shocks by withholding the stock of foreign currency. This may influence the free market exchange rate of Indian rupee in the recent situation.

The above analysis suggests that current spot exchange rate of rupee is influenced by changes in the expectations about the future position of current account, as well as the current position. Again, the short run effect of an exogenous shock affecting the current account can be different from its long run effect. If the country remains initially at equilibrium and an exogenous shock like Gulf War induces an expectation of a large trade deficit, exchange rate will fluctuate, though in the long run all prices and quantities adjust to the situation and equilibrium is restored in the current account. The new long run exchange rate will be a depreciated one which will equilibrate the trade flows and the current account. The short run spot rate approaches the long run rate over time. All these point to the fact that the position of current account may influence the exchange rate with lags and this consideration should be taken care of in formulating the model.

9.14 Empirical Estimation

Here figures of current account position in India since 1973 onwards are taken as the difference between exports and imports of the country. The equation for estimation is of the form:

$$E_t = b_o + b_1 CA_t + u_t \qquad\qquad Equation\ 9.4$$

The presumptive sign of the coefficient b_1 should be negative.

The estimation for the period 1971 to 1991 with quarterly data is as follows (using Cochrane-Orcutt method of estimation):

$$E_t = 8.296 - 0.018\ CA_t + e$$

t – statistics (9.41) (3.38)

   D.W. statistic = 1.87 SEE = 18.595

   Adjusted R^2 = 0.985 n = 73

   (ρ hat) = 0.015

And with one lag in current account the estimation is

$$E_t = 8.29 + 0.018\ CA_t - 0.0002\ CA_{t-1} + e$$

t – Statistic (9.44) (3.10)   (-0.024)

Adjusted R^2 = 0.980   SEE = 18.60

D.W. Statistic = 1.873   n = 73

(ρ hat) = 0.0135

The results of the two situations show that in both cases the coefficient of CA_t is of expected sign (negative) and significant when one lag of current account is introduced, the coefficient of CA_{t-1} is negative, but is not significant. The result shows the importance of current account in the exchange rate behaviour.

9.15 Black-market Premium and Price-ratio

The parallel movement of the official exchange rate and the black market rate all through the period 1973-1991 is an important characteristic of Indian economy. People used to sell foreign currency in unofficial market as that gave them a premium. The premium is calculated by using the formula.

$$\text{Premium} = \frac{\text{Black market rate}}{\text{Official rate}}$$

It is argued that the black market premium depends on the relative price level of the domestic economy. It means that if domestic inflation rate deviates too much from the world inflation rate (i.e. becomes much higher), the black market rate (read free market rate) will move away from the official rate. Thus the black market premium is related with the relative price ratio, or the ratio of domestic price level to world price level.

In search of an empirical relationship we have regressed the black market premium (PRM) or current account, the ratio of prices (that is CPI/CPI*), where CPI* is the U.S. price level and the rate of change of official exchange rate (DER) and the result of the estimation is placed below:

PRM = 1.08-0.0003 CA$_t$+0.223 (CPI/CPI*)-0.208 DER+e

t - Statistic (4.20) (-0.253) (+1.162)   (-0.75)

Adjusted R^2 = 0.736   SEE = 0.602
D.W. statistic = 2.22   n = 73

We find that the value of adjusted R^2 is significant. This suggests that the operation of black market premium can be explained by the normal explanatory variables like current account, the price ratio and the rate of change of official exchange rate. The sign of the coefficient of current account is satisfactory (negative), though it is not significant. The same is true of the coefficient of price ratio which is significant at 25% level. The coefficient of the exchange rate depreciation (DER) is of expected sign though not significant. The information on black market premium is available in Nandi (1996).

9.16 Currency-Basket and Indian Rupee - The SDR Approach

Since 1975 Indian rupee is linked with a basket of currencies of the countries who have been India's important trade partners. The numbers of currencies in the basket and the specific weights attached to these currencies have been kept a secret by the Reserve Bank of India to safeguard the exchange rate of rupee from speculation. In this context any discussion on India's currency-basket system can proceed on two lines. First, the system can be placed against the alternative systems of exchange rate management available for a country like India. This type of discussion can explain the pros and cons of the currency-basket system. Second, since rupee is supposed to be linked with the major currencies of the world, and these currencies are more or less floating, the SDR exchange rate of rupee can be compared with the same of some currencies, which are important for India's international trade.

With the collapse of the system of fixed exchange rate regime along with the Bretton Wood System in 1971, the weaker economies of the world faced the problem of instability of the exchange rate of their currencies. Strictly speaking, they could choose in between the two extremes: the exchange rate flexibility at the one end and the fixed exchange rate regime on the other. Which way the country should go depends optimally on the structural characteristics of the economy. If the economy is considerably open, a fixed exchange rate regime would ensure minimum external shocks. When the nominal exchange rate is fixed, the external shocks are absorbed through adjustment in domestic price structure and through a mobility of factors of production. Otherwise, some shocks can be absorbed by flexibility of nominal exchange rate.

When nominal exchange rate is made flexible, three courses are open to any country — full float of the currency, pegging to a single currency and linking the currency to a basket of currencies. These are broad categories and many countries use a combination to maintain stability of the exchange rate.

9.17 Choice Between a Peg and a Currency Basket

A single currency peg creates a small zone of stability with fortune of the pegging currency tied with the dominant one. It is easy to administer and in this context an adherence to the peg becomes also strong.

But the trade weight attached to the dominant currency may change over time and the fluctuation in the exchange rate of the dominant currency may create problem for the stability of the pegged currency. To provide a cushion for such an eventuality, the currency is pegged to a basket of currencies, and the negative effect of the wide fluctuation of a single currency remains to the value of its weight.

If the international trade is highly diversified both region and commodity-wise, and if a single trade partner does not have a good record of macro-economic stability, pegging to a currency basket is always preferable. Further, a single currency peg generally creates larger imbalances in the external sector, but again, in some situations it facilitates capital movement within the region.

9.18 The System of Currency Basket

A particular country, say country i, links up its currency (say rupee) to a basket of (n-1) other currencies in such a way that it selects a positive base exchange rate vector

$$e^*_i \text{ (where } e^*_i = e^*_{i1}, \ldots\ldots, e^*_{i,n-1})$$

and it attaches non-negative nominal weights w_{ij} to the currency of country j (sum of the weights or $\Sigma_j w_{ij} = 1$). The optimum number of the currencies and the value of the weights w_{ij} can be determined by an optimizing procedure, say, the minimization of its variance. The ith country adjusts the supply of its currency so that the observed current exchange rate vector e_i (that is $e_i = e_{i1}, \ldots, e_{in}$) satisfies the condition

$$\Sigma_j w_{ij} e_{ij} / e^*_{ij} = 1$$

Such a currency basket can be made consistent provided it satisfies some conditions specified in the literature (Williamson, 1982). Since we intend neither to measure the optimum value of the weights nor the number of currencies by any programming exercise, we are not pursuing this case here.

Assuming that the basket should contain the currencies of some important countries, and these currencies are floating, an attempt is made here to explore the quantitative relation between the SDR value of Indian rupee with the same of five currencies, which are US dollar, Japanese yen, German deutsche mark, French franc and Italian lira. The data used in this exercise are the monthly SDR exchange rate of six currencies (including Indian rupee) during the period 1984-89. The model can be written as:

Re/SDR = F (dollar/SDR, yen/SDR, mark/SDR, franc/SDR, lira/SDR)

The estimation of the model is as follows :
Re/SDR − 7.3444 + 0.332 (dollar/SDR) - 0.017 (yen/SDR)
T-stat.   (0.278) (2.30)   (-2.67)

- 0.036 (mark/SDR) + 0.274 (franc/SDR) - 0.005 (lira/SDR)
(-0.024)   (0.68)   (-2.53)

$$\text{Adjusted } R^2 = 0.996 \qquad \text{S.E.E.} = 2.693$$
$$\text{D.W. Statistic} = 2.003 \qquad n = 71$$

While the overall fit of the regression is good (evident in the value of R^2 and D.W. statistic), the coefficients of yen/SDR and mark/SDR are not significant. The sign of the coefficient of lira is negative and it is significant. The sign is puzzling and so is the sign of the coefficient of mark/SDR. Of course, this reflects the complex situation in the international currency world with near chaotic movement of some leading currencies.

One observation about the period of this quantitative exercise is important. The choice of the period 1984-1989, though inadvertent, coincides the period of liberalization initiated by late Rajeev Gandhi and it is characterized by at least two phenomena: more flexibility in the exchange rate at the official level and an increase in the foreign debt of the country. While the former helped the expansion of exports, liberalization increased imports too. The increasing gap between the imports and the exports had been filled up by increasing resort to international borrowing. The result has been an increasing volume of international debt though domestic industry registered phenomenal growth.

9.19 Official and Black Market Exchange Rate of Rupee: A Time Series Study

Black market or illegal market for a commodity emerges when legal barriers exist for the sale of the commodity or sale of the same for a maximum price for which adequate supply is not available. Thus it is the existence of excess demand for the commodity which acts as the origin of the black market. The nomenclature 'black' has been the synonym for the lack of sanction of the law. Since 1950 most of the developing countries had been practicing rigid control in the foreign exchange transactions to safeguard their limited foreign exchange reserve. But excess demand for foreign currency has led to a parallel market for foreign exchange where the latter becomes available at a premium. Thus black market for foreign exchange, particularly US dollar, has been operating in India since the independence of the country and the quotations for the black market price of US dollar are available in Pick's Currency yearbook (Pick, 1968). In fact, the latter has been publishing the black market quotations for all the currencies of the developing countries since 1950.

The theory of black market of currency is well established in the literature (Black, 1976; Bhagawati, 1978) The theoretical underpinning of the operation of the black market and the movement of the black market exchange rate can be summarized as follows:

The exchange rate of a currency is determined in the long run by the purchasing power of it and the latter is determined by the movement of the price levels of the two countries. The domestic price level depends on the excess money supply and the movement of the gross domestic product. If disequilibrium exists in the domestic money market and that creates a pressure on the price level, the spill over of this phenomenon on the international front of the country will be on two aspects

— the balance of payments of the country will worsen and the equilibrium value of the exchange rate will change. In the context of the fixed exchange rate regime, which had been the principal system under the Bretton Woods agreement, the official exchange rate cannot depreciate automatically. Thus the free market exchange rate will depreciate and it will move away from the official rate.

In the demand-supply framework, the above analysis implies that the demand for foreign exchange cannot be met by the inadequate supply of it. The latter is conditioned by inelastic exports of the country as the higher price structure of the domestic commodities makes these non-competitive in the international markets.

The common theoretical explanations hold for all countries, but the mode of operation varies from one country to another. Thus the excess demand for gold in India and Pakistan, the demand for luxury consumer goods in Bangladesh, the demand for western goods in former east European countries, the debasement of currencies in Latin American countries and present day Russia — all these have created the black market for foreign currency, and particularly US dollar.

9.20 Black Market Exchange Rate of Indian Rupee

All through the period 1950-1991, the parallel exchange rate of rupee has been deviating from the official exchange rate depending on factors which are partly economic in nature. There has been an attempt in the literature to explain the movement of the black market exchange rate. One such attempt in the monetarist tradition tries to explain the movement of the black market exchange rate by the disequilibrium analysis of the domestic money market. It is the failure of the official exchange rate to adjust properly in response to the changes in the relative price level which causes changes in the black market rate. Thus a model as given below is formulated in the literature to explain the movement of the black exchange rate (Blejer, 1978):

$$\log BMR = a_0 + a_1 (\log P - \log P^* - \log E) + a_2 (GP - GP^*) + u$$
$$\text{With sign } a_1 > 0, \ a_2 > 0$$

Where BMR   =   black market exchange rate
P =   domestic price level
P^* =   foreign price level
GP   =   domestic inflation rate
GP^* =   foreign inflation rate
E   =   nominal official exchange rate

The above model is based on Purchasing Power Parity theory. Using quarterly data of India during the period 1973-1991, the estimation of the model is as follows:

$\log BMR = 2.795 - 0.446(\log P - \log P^* - \log E) + 0.325 (GP - GP^*) + e$
t-statistics $=(1.33) (-2.04)$ (2.13)

$$\text{Adjusted } R^2 = 0.962 \qquad SEE = 0.39$$
$$\text{D.W. Statistic} = 2.13 \quad n = 73$$

The estimated value of the coefficient a_1 is negative contrary to expectation, though it is significant only at 5% level. The elasticity of the relative inflation rate $(GP - GP^*)$ is positive, and it is significant. Thus this model fails to explain the role of Purchasing Power Parity *vis-à-vis* official exchange rate in the movement of black market exchange rate in India, though the black market rate is explained by the relative inflation variable properly.

A slight different version of the model of black market exchange rate is as follows:

$\log BMR = b_0 + b_1 \log P + b_2 \log P^* + b_3 \log E + b_4 (GP - GP^*) + u$

With the presumptive sign as

$b_1 > 0, \; b_2 < 0, \; b_3 < 0, \; b_4 > 0$

The estimation of the model on the same data base (Nandi, 1996) is as follows:

$\log BMR = -1.770 + 0.103 \log P + 0.407 \log P^*$
       $(-2.33) \; (0.34) \quad (1.30)$

$$+ 0.699 \log E + 0.048 (GP - GP^*) + e$$
$$(3.117) \quad (0.26)$$

Adjusted R^2 = 0.96 $\qquad$ SEE = 0.31

D. W. Statistic = 2.05 $\qquad$ n = 70

(Figures in parentheses are t-statistics)

The sign of the estimated coefficient of log P is positive as expected but not significant. The coefficient of log P^* is positive but significant only at 20% level. The sign of the coefficients of log E is positive and significant contrary to expectation and estimated value of b_4 is positive but not significant. This shows that the variations of the official exchange rate have significant influence on the changes in black market rate and the elasticity is 0.699. This has important policy implications.

One common element we derive from the estimation of both the models and that is the elasticity of the relative inflation $(GP-GP^*)$ is positive in both the situations. While it is significant in the first case, it is not so in the second. Strictly speaking, theory gives poor explanation for the behaviour of the black market exchange rate in India.

Having explored the arena of traditional econometric fields, let us see the time series study of the black market rate. One possible explanation is the random-walk model

$$\mathbf{BMR_t = a_0 + a_1\ BMR_{t-1} + u_t} \qquad \textit{Equation 9.6}$$

The model is estimated using the same data base and also further estimation has been done by increasing the number of lags. The estimation of three other models increasing the number of lags only makes the position of the random walk model stronger as the estimated coefficients of the higher order lags are not statistically significant. Thus the economic agents in the market are guided by random walk philosophy in a strong way. When we read this result along with the earlier result of the effects of official rate on the BMR, we see that the movement of the two rates is not independent.

Table 9b: Estimation of Black Market Exchange Rate of Indian Rupee

Dependent Variables is BMR

Independent Variables	1	2	3	4
Constant	-0.684 (-2.03)	-0.025 (-0.37)	-0.025 (-0.357)	-0.019 (0.262)
BMR (t-1)	1.07 (50.78)	0.972 (8.25)	0.96 (8.01)	0.974 (8.06)
BMR (t-2)	-	0.44 (0.364)	0.013 (.077)	0.02 (0.12)
BMR (t-3)	-	-	0.042 (0.34)	0.138 (0.82)
BMR (t-4)				-0.118 (-0.948)
Other Statistics				
Adjusted R^2	0.97	0.96	0.96	0.96
D. W. Statistics	1.96	2.01	1.965	1.96
S.E.E.	79.18	0.414	0.412	0.402
n	75	74	73	72
S. E. of Regression	1.04	1.076	1.077	1.077

Note : Figures in parentheses are t-statistics

9.21 Relative Price Movement and Black Market Exchange Rate

One theoretical implication of the monetarist explanation of the movement of black market exchange rate (read free market rate as usual) is that the latter should reflect truly the movement of the relative price level. The idea is that if the domestic economy suffers from inflation and if the rate of inflation is higher compared to the world standard, the black market rate will be subjected to high degree of depreciation when official exchange rate is fixed or depreciating slowly than what it should be. We have seen earlier that the depreciation of the official exchange rate more than compensated the relative movement of the price level.

The position regarding the black market exchange rate is as follows. During the period 1954-1972, when India followed a fixed exchange rate regime, the movement of the black market rate more than compensated the movement of relative prices (Nandi, 1996).

The nature of the movement of the black market rate convinces the researcher that it is not always related to the movement of relative inflation. In fact, it has its own dynamic nature and a study of that requires the analysis of the structure of the economy along with its organizational aspects.

At present the black market of rupee is not a serious problem as the 'hawala' rate of dollar *vis-à-vis* rupee shows less than 5 per cent premium. That is a good indicator of the premium existing in the unofficial market. Also this is the expected outcome of the liberalization of the exchange rate of rupee and the latter has become a convertible currency in current account. We will see more about Indian rupee and other currencies in the Appendix.

Ten

Multinational Corporations and the Developing Countries

"Practical men, who believe themselves to be quite exempt from any intellectual influence, are usually the slaves of defunct economist. Madmen in authority, who hear voices in the air, are distilling their frenzy from some academic scribblers of a few years back."

[J. M. Keynes, *General Theory of Employment, Interest and Money*]

The degree of integration of the capital markets of different countries has increased in recent times with the tremendous surge of capital mobility across political boundaries. This phenomenon has also increased the role of multinational corporations in the economic development of the developing countries. Conceptually there are five ways in which a multinational corporation (MNC) can serve a foreign market:

(i)   invest directly by a Greenfield venture,

(ii)   invest directly by acquiring a local firm,

(iii)   invest directly by starting a joint venture with a local firm,

(iv)   enter into a strategic alliance with a local firm.

The 5th alternative is no direct investment in the host country, but the MNC can serve the host country market by exports or giving license to the local firm. The first four alternatives involve foreign direct investment (FDI) on the part of MNC. Whether the latter will go for FDI or the 5th

alternative depends on both the economic conditions of the host country and the business strategy of MNC. In the case of developed countries like OECD economies, the MNC has a free choice among the first four alternatives. But in case of developing countries and transition economies[1] there are restrictions and the choices are limited. This is because capital markets in most of the developing countries are not open and their currencies are not fully convertible. This places restraints on the behaviours of the MNCs who aspire to enter into such countries.

In developing countries with a developed capital market and large industrial sector, the acquisition of private firm is a realistic alternative to Greenfield entry[2]. Except in countries like south Korea with an advanced technology base, merger with local firms are troublesome because of huge gap in the level of technology, size and management philosophy. The same problem remains with strategic alliance with local firms of host country.

In the early phase of liberalization of the transition economies, the state owned firms are often put on sale and MNCs see it easy to acquire the state owned firms and thus they enter into the market of the host country. After that Greenfield entry becomes more feasible with merger and acquisition remaining for the future. The behaviour of the MNC regarding their entry and operations in the developing countries has attracted attention in the literature. The literature has identified three aspects regarding the MNC behaviours:
- target country characteristics
- investment characteristics, and
- industry characteristics

---

1. These are former command economies like Russia, Ukrain, Poland and other east European countries, CIS countries like Uzbekistan and others, China and Vietnam. The significant change of economic policies of these economies has changed the perception of foreign capital and FDI is welcome now.

2. Where the MNC start new enterprise with the import of both capital and technology. This is done to take advantage of cheap labour and/or source of raw materials.

The most common framework is the transaction cost analysis, that is, MNC chooses the mode of entry that involves minimum cost. The findings in the literature can be put in the following form:

First, larger MNCs are more prone to acquire than small ones. However, in recent times, smaller firms also have become more prone to acquire as the transaction cost of merger and acquisition (M&A) has reduced.

Second, MNCs with lower R&D intensity are more likely to buy technological capabilities abroad by acquisition, and firms with strong technological advantages are likely to set up Greenfield ventures.

Third, the greater the cultural and economic differences between the home and the host countries, the less the probability that MNC will go for acquisition. Generally, M&A concentrate in countries with similar cultural and business practices.

Fourth, acquisitions by MNC are encouraged by capital markets imperfections that lead to the undervaluation of the assets of firms. The same thing may happen in times of economic crisis like the Asian Currency Crisis of 1997.

Fifth, horizontal acquisitions are driven by the search for new markets, products and brand and seldom for cost rationalization. But such acquisitions may lead to "asset rationalization" of the acquired firm and this often damages the capabilities of the latter.

Sixth, Greenfield investments offer the MNC greater control and more ability to mould affiliate structure, system and culture than acquisition. Everything can be replicated from the investing country.

In sum, the entry of MNC in the developing countries induces certain important changes including technology transfer to the host country. But over the period of time there is more reciprocal process of technology transfer and sharing of intangibles like tacit knowledge (Bressman *et al*, 1999). From the investor perspective, M&A offer certain advantages over Greenfield investment of rapid entry and access to existing proprietary assets. In the case of developing countries, M&A

create advantage of rapid entry, access to local market knowledge and distribution system. It also creates contacts with the governments, suppliers and the consumers, and also it may be the only form of FDI where other opportunities are absent.

Sometimes established cultural and organizational inertia may create problem for MNC after acquisition of firms in host country and MNC may find it costly for the necessary assimilation process. Even valuation of assets of the firms in host country for acquisition may be difficult as the capital market is often imperfect and not developed. Such problems generally emerge in large developing countries that are opening to international competition for the first time. In such situations, Greenfield investment will be more suitable for the MNCs.

10.1 Greenfield Investment and M&A : A Comparison

Both the developing countries and the transition economies are rapidly integrating their economies to the world economic order. In the process the firms in such countries face intensifying competition, accelerating technological change and increasingly integrated world production. They seriously lack two things: capital and new technology. Here lies the importance of the entry of MNC. Now, a comparison of two principal modes of entry – FDI in Greenfield investment and M&A route – can be made from the perspective of the host country.

It is recognized that FDI inflow in the developing country help in upgrading competitiveness. It is a powerful tool in case of countries where domestic technological capabilities and skill are weak and that can not be raised at international level within a short period. Even when the country is strong in availability of skill, the pace of technical change at global level is so strong that without MNC participation it becomes difficult for the developing country to compete effectively (UNCTAD, 1999). In this case M&A as a mode of FDI inflow is an important way to restructure and upgrade competitive capability of the host country firm.

FDI investment in both the modes – M&A and Greenfield way – adds to financial resources of the host country as neither is financed by raising resources domestically. While Greenfield investment adds new productive facility which is an addition to existing production capacity of the economy, M&A transfer the ownership of existing asset into foreign hands. But money flows in both cases and the M&A transfer resources to the existing owners that can be invested in the economy. So the net financial effects are the same in normal times except in one situation, when the acquired company is broken up and different components are sold separately at a much higher price. This is known as *asset stripping* in the literature. This is a sign of imperfect capital market as the latter fails to assess the true value of the assets.

But in crisis situation (as in south Asia in 1997-98) many firms are sold at depressed prices and foreign capital acquires firms in host country through M&A cheaply. This involves a cost to the host country. The cost increases and becomes a net loss to the host country if the firm acquires through M&A is sold later when markets become normal and asset value increases. This can be prevented if the host country can manage extra liquidity in crisis time when FDI through Greenfield investment becomes rare.

10.2 Technology Issue

The inflow of FDI is associated with the inflow of new and frontier technology to the host country. The effects of technology transfer to the host country will be same in normal situation in either type of entry—Greenfield investment and M&A mode. A Greenfield investment involves the setting up of a new facility that brings new technology with new capital. The running of this new plant requires new and improved skill formation. This may not happen in case of M&A at least in the short run. For this Greenfield investment is preferred in the developing country.

In case of M&A, the acquired firm may need considerable technological upgrading to bring it to the world level. As a result, it may experience rapid change compared to the new facility under Greenfield mode that is already using frontier technology. The evidence for Asia and Latin America shows that M&A can lead to considerable technological upgrading and MNC can boost expenditure on R&D if the acquired firm already possesses research capabilities (WIR, 1999). Moreover, M&A may lead to the preservation and increase of technological capabilities in firms under competitive pressure in an open economy.

Sometimes FDI through M&A mode may lead to the downgrading of R&D activity and status of the acquired firm if the latter does not possess technological assets regarded as valuable by the foreign company. In this case M&A brings negative effects to technology of the host country. This is evidenced in East Europe and Latin America, where affiliates under simpler activity and put less emphasis on R&D.

In normal circumstances a MNC will tend to preserve the R&D base of a newly acquired firm and maintain links with local technological resources. Sometimes it goes further and tries to strengthen local technological efforts and linkages for the absorption of technology in host country. This is known as *asset seeking FDI,* and this type of FDI in the USA has been used by Mexico, South Korea and Taiwan to improve their domestic technological base. The results in term of defusing new and improved technology and knowledge locally depend on the strength and economic efficiency of the linkages established by the acquired firms. When these are positive, MNCs will retain and strengthen these, and in this case FDI through M&A mode will lead to better diffusion than the mode of Greenfield investment in the short run. But when the linkages are weak and inefficient, FDI through M&A will lead to less diffusion, and that makes little difference compared to the Greenfield mode.

The interaction between the existing domestic firms and the new foreign firms either through M&A mode or through Greenfield investment is complex and dynamic over time. Wang and Blomstrom (1992) isolate two channels for this interaction process. The interaction leads to the spill-over of superior technology across the firms having strong linkages.

The more disembodies aspects of superior technologies used by foreign firms can spread to domestic firms through the mobility of trained workers and managers, and through technical guidance provided to vertically-linked domestic suppliers. Thus, the mere presence of foreign firms exposes domestic firms to superior technologies: this is the demonstration effect. Two, competitive pressure exerted by foreign firms (in the form of lower prices or higher product quality) forces domestic firms to improve their technologies. Productivity gains materialize only if competition is effective — that is, it encourages domestic firms to catch up, and if domestic firms have the ability to innovate or imitate successfully. The latter requires that the technological gap should be small enough relative to learning capabilities of domestic firms. If it is not, isolated instances of foreign entry can degenerate into foreign monopoly. At the same time, the extent of spillovers may be limited by the tendency of multinational firms to concentrate their R&D activity in their developed country headquarters — the so-called 'headquarters effect'. The relative importance of these effects may explain why spillover effects have been stronger in some countries and for some sectors.

10.3 Indian Case

Did the foreign-controlled firms in India differ from domestic firms in terms of their conduct and performance? The literature reveals discriminating characteristics of domestic and foreign-controlled firms and it is found that as a proportion of sales, foreign-controlled firms spent less on R&D (presumably because they rely on technology imports) than domestic firms, but expenditure on advertising was broadly similar for the two groups of firms (Kumar, 1994). However, foreign-controlled firms were significantly more profitable in their operations, a result corroborated by other studies, Kumar (1994) concluded that the profitability of foreign-controlled firms was protected by entry-barriers: in knowledge - and skill-intensive industries, their technological strength, access to global marketing networks and brand names gave them a clear edge over domestic firms. He found that degree of seller concentration did not seem to affect profitability but there was market segmentation: foreign-controlled firms competed on the high value end of the market while domestic firms concentrated on the low-value end.

How did the multinationals defend these profit margins? Advertising intensity, measured as the ratio of advertising expenditure to net sales, was greater for foreign-controlled firms, but domestic firms relied more heavily on selling commissions. Of course, different industrial sectors differ in the advertising intensity: the overall difference in marketing strategies might reflect the difference in industrial concentration of foreign-controlled and domestic firms. Also it is seen that domestic firms have increased their expenditure on technology imports, especially in recent years, and have overtaken foreign firms in this respect. Unfortunately, we do not have comparable data for R&D expenditure, but these were typically quite small for all manufacturing firms in India. On the whole, the observable differences in conduct were not that large.

10.4 Market Structure and Competition

During the last two decades FDI has been a powerful instrument for the developing countries to exploit their existing comparative advantage and also create new competitive power in their effort to enhance their participation in world trade. This has been possible as long as the countries are able to create new skills and capabilities and attract the MNCs into higher value activities (WIR, 1999). In the process the entry of MNCs has certain effects on the domestic market structure of host country, though the effects are not clear. Usual measures like concentration ratios are misleading indicators, particularly when the country is open to import competition and MNCs concentrate in industries that are scale and technology intensive. Again, the entry of large MNC poses serious challenge to competition policy. Here the host country should be cautious with rules and regulation to maintain competitive conditions for the domestic firms.

Generally speaking, the relationship between openness to foreign investment and market structure is complex. Caves (1996) notes the positive relationship between the extent of foreign investment and the degree of market concentration found in empirical studies. In theory this could be due to rent-seeking foreign investment being especially attracted to sectors or countries with high concentration (and high profitability). Even so, the short-run effect of foreign entry, especially when it is Greenfield investment, is to increase the number of firms and reduce concentration. The long-run effects depend on the nature of competition between entrants and incumbents. If incumbent firms are moderately competent, there may well be virtuous cycles of technological competition. On the other hand, inefficient domestic firms with poor learning capabilities would lose market share to foreign firms. Insurmountable technological barriers and economies of scale may drive incumbent firms to the fringes. Foreign entry might thus increase market concentration through mergers and acquisitions, and occasionally, through predatory pricing.

The above discussion gives the perspective which the domestic firms should think seriously before the country opens up for foreign direct investment (FDI). Once the government is committed to economic liberalization, it can not discriminate between a domestic firm and a foreign firm. As a host country it should be policy neutral. It is now the financial strength and the grip over frontier technology that determines the hold of the original owner over the effective control on the firm.

Eleven

Global Transmission of Interest Rates and Monetary Independence

"All systems either of preference or of restraint, therefore, being thus completely taken away, the obvious and simple system of natural liberty establishes itself of its own accord. Every man, as long as he does not violate the laws of justice, is left perfectly free to pursue his own interest his own way, and to bring both his industry and capital into competition with those of any other man, or, order of man."

[Adam Smith in *An Inquiry into the Nature and Causes of the Wealth of Nations*]

The choice of exchange rate regime – fixed, floating, a combination of two or a pegged one – has been always a favourite question in international macro-economics. According to the prevalent view, there are two principal advantages in a fixed exchange rate regime and these are: (i) reduced transaction cost and exchange rate risk, and, (ii) a credible nominal anchor for monetary policy. The first facilitates international trade and investment of foreign capital. The second helps in the stability of the domestic currency.

The flexible exchange rate has the unique advantage that it allows the country to pursue independent monetary policy. There are other advantages also. In case of independent currency the government retains the seignorage and second, floating of currency can lead to a smooth adjustment to real external shocks even when price frictions exist in the economy. Of course the first one, i.e., monetary independence is very important and we take up this issue now.

Under flexible exchange rate the monetary independence is maintained and the monetary authority enjoys the advantage of discretion rather than the rules. Suppose the economy is hit by a disturbance in the form of a shift of worldwide demand away from the goods the country produces. In such a situation the government would like to respond so that the country can avoid a potential recession. The authority can go for a monetary expansion and depreciation of the domestic currency. This will stimulate the demand for domestic commodities and help the economy return to the desired level of output. This adjustment could not have been achieved under a fixed exchange rate regime when monetary policy would have been powerless.

Under a pegged exchange rate and unrestricted capital flows, the traditional literature argues that domestic interest rate cannot be set independently, as it should keep pace with the interest rate of the currency to which the domestic currency is pegged. But under a flexible exchange rate regime, domestic interest rate is less sensitive to changes in the foreign interest rates. Again the countries with intermediate exchange rate regimes should show less sensitivity to changes in international interest rates than countries with firm pegged rates.

Against the traditional views an alternative view stated by Calvo and Reinhart (2001, 2002) , and Hausmann, Panizza and Stein (2001) holds that there exists a "fear of floating" that prevents countries with *de jure* flexible regime from allowing their exchange rates to move freely. This view holds that factors like exchange rate pass through, lack of credibility and foreign–currency liability prevent countries from pursuing an independent monetary policy irrespective of the nature of exchange rate regime. The result is that many countries with floating exchange rate are following the monetary policies of major currency countries like the USA or some EU countries. It is also suggested that the interest rate may be more sensitive to the US interest rate in developing countries with flexible rates than in countries with fixed rates, as the flexible rate countries suffer from having to pay risk premium (for currency risk and default risk) and this premium is sensitive to international interest rates.

The main question is whether floating exchange rate regime do facilitate to follow an independent monetary policy in the sense that domestic interest rates in such countries are less sensitive to the changes in international interest rates. The empirical evidence on this issue is scarce and not decisive. It is also observed that the developing countries do not stick to a particular exchange rate regime and they often change the nature of the regime in response to both internal and external shocks.

There are several factors that determine the extent to which domestic and foreign interest rate will move together. First, the degree of financial integration of the domestic economy into the world markets moulds the domestic capital market. If there are barriers to international capital flows, the response of the local interest rate to changes in the international rates will be less. This will allow the monetary authorities in countries to maintain different interest rates even under fixed exchange rate regime.

Second, the degree of real international integration influences the co-movement of domestic and foreign interest rates. The movement of the two rates will be close if the business cycles in two countries are highly synchronized and the integration of the capital markets in two countries are near perfect with no restriction on capital mobility.

11.1 Financial Integration and Capital Mobility

Many economists now recognize the relentless trend toward globalization and increasing capital mobility. Empirical studies have shown that since the 1980s there have been a growing degree of capital market integration all over the world and capital mobility has increased tremendously. Many experts believe that these trends are largely inevitable and irreversible too. Because, these are partly driven by new innovations of information technology and better communications, and partly because policy makers are increasingly convinced about many benefits of regulatory changes that foster financial integration. So capital mobility is irreversible.

The changed world scenario has some important implications. The more openness of the economy and open environment imply that changes in monetary policy involve a somewhat different transmission mechanism than what it used to be in earlier relatively closed regime. For example, the more integrated the economy, the more quickly do divergent policies affect financial markets and capital flows. Also foreign exchange rate may play an increasing important role in transmitting changes in monetary policy to the macro economy. Thus exchange rate movement may contain more useful information about the changes in domestic monetary policies compared to the earlier times when the world did not experience so much financial integration.

11.2 The Policy Trilemma

The changed world situation of increased capital mobility has placed constraints on the implementation of domestic monetary policy and this Obstfeld (1998) describes as follows:

The limitations that open capital market place on exchange rate and monetary policy are summed up by the ideas of the ' inconsistent trinity' or ..... 'the open economy trilemma' ..... that is, a country cannot simultaneously maintain fixed exchange rates and open capital markets while pursuing a monetary policy oriented toward domestic goals. Governments may choose only two of the above.

[Obstfeld, 1998: pp. 14-15]

We see the consensus above about unrestricted capital mobility, and if that is irreversible and given, the policy choices circumscribed by the above trilemma are limited. For the governments of the developing countries the policy choices are now between flexible exchange rate/domestic monetary policy goal (say, inflation targeting) regimes and fixed exchange rate/

no domestic goal regimes. If policy makers go for fixed exchange rate, they lose control of the exchange rate. If they peg the interest rate, they cannot control the exchange rate. Some economists suggest that the choice in recent time has moved in favour of flexible exchange rate/domestic monetary policy alternative, which boils down to a *de facto* informal inflation targeting regime (Eichengreen, 1996). This also goes well with the contemporary political economy of many developing countries as the authority can exercise control on the domestic monetary policies.

11.3 US Dollar as International Currency

There has been another trend in the international arena and it is that US dollar has appeared in a new role apart from its Bretton Woods role of international currency. Many newly emerging market economies and some Latin American countries have started using dollar as the official currency. US dollar has replaced the domestic currency. Also in many countries people are informally holding dollars. Situation is such that foreigners are holding a large percentage of US dollar currency outside the USA and the amount is no less than 50 per cent (Porter and Judson, 1996). This induces Robert Mundell to state:

> *The need for an international unit of account for purposes of international trade and finance was just as great as ever, and the increased uncertainty associated with flexible exchange rates increased, rather than eliminated the need for international reserve assets..... The dollar remained the principal international monetary reserve (in the 1980s and 1990s). The enhanced role of the dollar under flexible exchange rate was reflected in the rapid expansion of dollar reserves which has more than kept pace with the growth of trade.*

> [Mundell, 1994; p.12].

Thus dollar continues to provide the principal function of international money and so remains the dominant international key vehicle and reserve currency. The use of US dollar as international currency suggests that there remains an important demand for the services of international currency, i.e., *continued demand for a money for other monies*. Given this global demand, the suppliers of this global currency, the Federal Reserve of the United States has a responsibility of adjusting the global supply of US dollar as and when demands for dollar changes. This will promote international stability. But it has another implication. When the Federal Reserve of the USA tightens policy and as a result money supply gets restricted even globally, other central banks in countries that are using dollar should follow the Federal Reserve. Also the use of dollar as international reserve boils down to the role of Federal Reserve as the international lender of last resort. All these imply that monetary policy in the developing countries that use dollar as the currency becomes dependent on the policy of the Federal Reserve of America.

A large body of empirical literature suggests that changes in the monetary policy of Federal Reserve can have significant impact on the policy of foreign countries, and on the global economy. There are evidences that international capital flows, recent crisis in the international banking and currency markets and choice of exchange rate regimes may have been influenced by the policy changes of the Federal Reserve (Calvo, 1996).

Recent research on the choice of exchange rate regime has also revealed that US monetary policy has significant impact on the foreign interest rates. This is evident when the developing countries adjust their interest rates in response to the interest rate changes by the Federal Reserve. This has been seen in times of Russian devaluation in 1998, in times of Asian currency crisis and also Mexican crisis.

The evidences indicate that the changes in the US monetary policy affect financial markets in the developing countries through different transmission channels. These further suggest that international financial markets are becoming more integrated, and the interest rates in the developing countries are becoming more sensitive to the interest rate changes in the United States. This is true irrespective of different exchange rate regimes.

Table 11a: Countries and Their Exchange Rate Regimes

Country	Period	Exchange Rate Regime
Argentina	March 1991 onwards	Peg to US dollar
Australia	December 1983 onwards	independently floating
Canada	January 1975 onwards	independently floating
Chile	January 1999 onwards	crawling band
Columbia	January 1999 onwards	crawling band
Denmark***	January 1972 - March 1999	Limited flexibility with respect to a Cooperative arrangement (LFCA)
Ecuador	January 99 onwards	crawling band
Egypt	January 1997 onwards	managed floating
Finland	Oct 1996 - Mar 99	LFCA
Germany	April 1973 - March 99	LFCA
Greece	March 98 - March 99	LFCA
Hong Kong	December 1990 onwards	Peg to US dollar
India	August 1994 onwards	managed floating
Ireland	Jan 1979 - Mar 99	LFCA
Israel	January 1999 onwards	crawling band
Italy	Oct 1996 - March 99	LFCA
Japan	January 1973 onwards	independently floating
South Korea	December 1997 onwards	independently floating
Mexico	December 1997 onwards	independently floating
Netherlands	Jan 1972 - Dec 1998	LFCA
New Zealand	March 1985 onwards	independently floating
Norway	May 1994 onwards	managed floating
Portugal	April 1992 - Mar 99	LFCA
Singapore	July 1987 onwards	managed floating
Spain	June 89 - March 99	LFCA
Sweden	Nov 1992 - Mar 99	independently floating
Thailand	July 1998 onwards	independently floating
United Kingdom	July 1992 onwards	independently floating
Venezuela	January 1999 onwards	crawling band

Note: *** means countries against which LFCA are written are countries who have joined the European Union, and at present their currency is Euro, and it is independently floating.

As seen in the table over leaf for many developing countries US dollar has become a reference currency. Not only that, there has been a high degree of volatility among the three principal currencies of the world - US dollar, yen and Euro. The exchange rate of both yen and Euro *vis-à-vis* dollar has become volatile and that has created problem for the stability of exchange rate of many developing countries. The question now is whether the three monetary area—USA, Japan and European Union — should initiate policies to stabilize the exchange rates as mentioned. A recent study cautions that in case the three currencies are stabilized, that is not a sure guarantee for the stability of the developing countries (Reinhart & Reinhart, 2002).

For the newly emerging market economies US dollar has been the *de jure* or at least *de facto* medium of exchange. This type of dollarization has other implications that we have covered in other chapters. What is relevant here is that the central banks in these countries can not exercise an independent monetary policy. Also the monetary policy followed by the Federal Reserve has various transmission channels that affect the interest rate policy of not only the new market economies but other developing countries as well who have pegged their currencies to US dollar.

It has been enquired in the literature whether the transmission of international interest rate affecting the changes of the local rates are influenced by the type of exchange rate regimes (Frankel *et al*, 2001). In this debate the issue of monetary independence has played an important role. Supporters of independent-floating exchange rate regime argue that countries adopting free float would be able to pursue their own monetary policy goals. This strategy has been questioned by the proponents of the fixed exchange rate regime (hard peg) regarding its feasibility in face of high international capital mobility. This refers to the policy trilemma as we discussed in the beginning of this chapter.

Empirical evidence suggests that in the 1990s all types of exchange rate regimes showed high degree of sensitivity of local interest rates to the change in the international interest rate. This is particularly true with full transmission in case of smaller countries. The big industrial countries like Canada and Australia have experienced less than one transmission rate (Frankel *et al*, 2001). Only major exception is the countries belonging to European Union, as this group in the 1990s has shown interest rate convergence to the German interest rate. The EU countries have shifted from the US monetary area to the DM-EU monetary area. But here also the convergence of the two principal rates may not be far away.

Option Contracts

"It is not that pearls fetch a high price because men have dived for them; but on the contrary, men dive for them because they fetch a high price."

[Richard Whitely in *Introductory Lectures on Political Economy*]

"Everything should be made as simple as possible, but not more so."

[Albert Einstein]

An option contract has been defined as an agreement between two parties in which one grants to the other the right to buy ('call' option) or sell ('put' option) an asset under specified conditions (price, time), and assumes the obligation to sell or buy it. The party who has the right, but not an obligation, is the buyer of the option, and pays a fee, or premium, to the 'writer' or seller of the option. The 'asset' could be a currency, bond, share, commodity or a futures contract.

When the owner of a call option decides to use the right to buy the underlying asset, he is basically exercising the option. The owner has the choice of deciding whether or not to exercise the right, but counterpart has the obligation to sell the underlying instrument. Thus the structure of the payoffs that an option provides to its owner and to its seller are not same as the former bears a right while the latter has the obligation to buy or sell the underlying asset. Since the option writer provides an important financial instrument and bears all the risk, he is compensated by a price, called the premium of the option. The option premium represents a fair compensation to the seller of the option (also called writer).

An option, say a call, are of two types — an American call, that can be exercised at any time during the time profile, and a European call, that can be exercised at the expiry time only. The underlying instrument may be a common stock. A call or a put option written on a stock has the following properties:

(i)   The size of the contract is the number of shares of stock a single option contract allows the holder to buy or sell.

(ii) The exercise price or the strike price represents the fixed price the owner of the call will have to pay for one share of stock when he exercises his option.

(iii) The time to maturity of an option contract is a standardized one. It is seen that each stock has options with three different maturities (at Chicago Exchange) that trade at the same time and generally belong to any one of the trade cycles:

January / April / July / October
February / May / August / November
March / June / September / December

Thus at any time options are available with the nearest three terms to the present and their time to maturity will never exceed nine months. Also the standardized option contract has a last trading date that is the third Friday of the option month.

(iv) The underlying stock is identified through its name and must satisfy some requirements in order to serve as the underlying instrument of listed option contracts.

The dynamic aspects of an option contract can be seen from the daily transaction report of the option as traded in an Exchange. The quotes are available in leading business papers and information available are of closing price of the underlying asset, with same strike price and different expiry dates like May–June–September–December and the like.

12.1 Basic Properties of an Option Contract

There are four basic strategies associated with the trading of an option contact:

(i) When an individual buys a call or a put, it is then common to say that the individual enters into an *opening long position* in the call or in the put. The buyer acquires the right to buy or sell the underlying stock at a future date in exchange for the price that he pays.

(ii) When the individual sells a call or a put, it amounts to say that the individual enters into *an opening short position* in the call or in the put.

(iii) An individual can exercise his option at any time (American option), or at its expiry date (European option) to buy of a certain number of a financial instrument of the underlying asset at the strike price.

(iv) An individual may face another possibility that is doing nothing and thereby letting his right expire at expiration as the value of the option becomes zero.

12.2 The Need for Options

One essential feature of the forward or futures market is that once you have locked into a rate through either market, you cannot benefit from a movement of the market in your favour. For example, if a US importer has bought forward pounds at say $1.5870 to hedge the exchange risk, and on maturity finds that the spot rate is $1.50, he still has to pay the contracted rate. In a forward contract the risk is kept at a minimum and the holder of the contract gets the certainty of the liability involved.

When the amount of the contract is rather large and the firm bases the calculation on that basis, any loss of potential contract may land the firm in huge loss. Suppose an Indian firm has signed a contract of exports with an invoice amount of US $ 50 million. To avoid the potential loss due to the appreciation of rupee the whole amount is sold in forward market at a rate $ 1 = Rs. 49.45. Suppose on the day of maturity the spot rate goes in favour of the firm and it is $1= Rs. 49.50. But the firm is to get at the contractual rate and it means a loss of Rs.[49.50 – 49.45] x 50 million or, Rs. 2.5 million.

The above example shows that the firm should go for the option contract and a put option in the above case could have saved the firm huge amount of money. The asset price is higher than the exercise price, and the option is out of the money. The firm will sell the dollar in spot market.

12.3 Payoff of a Call Option

Because the holder of such a call option must pay the issuer a premium to purchase the option, he stands to lose that premium should the option expire worthless. However, that is all the purchaser stands to lose. His potential profit from purchasing the option is unlimited because there is (in theory) no limit to how much the underlying stock might appreciate during the life of the option. The profit or loss from purchasing a call option is illustrated in **Exhibit 1**.

Purchasing a Call Option
Exhibit 1

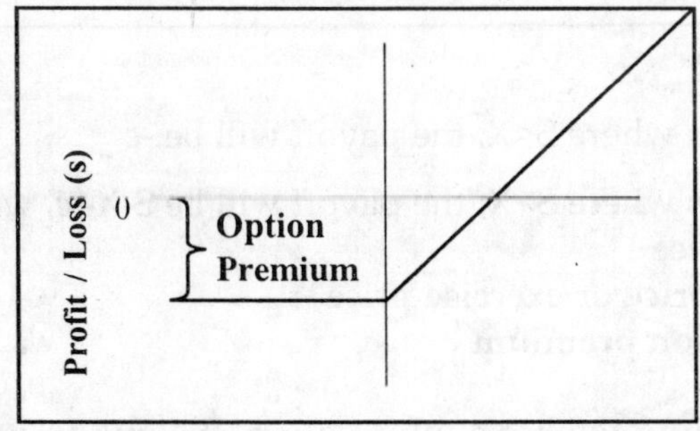

Exhibit 2 provides a similar illustration for the profit or loss from purchasing a put option.

For explaining the basic mechanism underlying an option's price, we assume that the exercise price is X, the asset price (the spot price of the stock that changes day after day) S, and the premium or price of the option C. The taxonomy is as shown below.

CALL OPTIONS

In the case of a call option buyer's profit can be defined as follows:

Purchasing a Put Option : Payoff
Exhibit 2

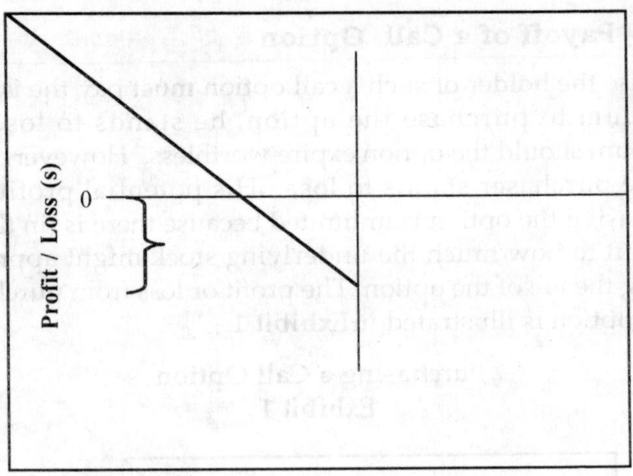

At all points where S<X, the payoff will be -c

At all points where S>X, the payoff will be S-X- c, where
S = Spot price
X = Strike price or exercise price
c = call option premium

But corresponding to above information, the option writer's profit will be as follows:

At all points where S<X, the payoff will be c
At all points where S>X, the payoff will be -(S-X- c)

Buy a call option:

(A call option is: a right to buy an underlying stock for a specific price and time period)

The above graph shows the profit or loss of buying a call option for a range of projected underlying prices at expiration day for the call option. We see below that the loss is limited to the price of the call option if the underlying price at options expiration is LOWER than the current underlying price.

Payoffs From Buying A Call Option

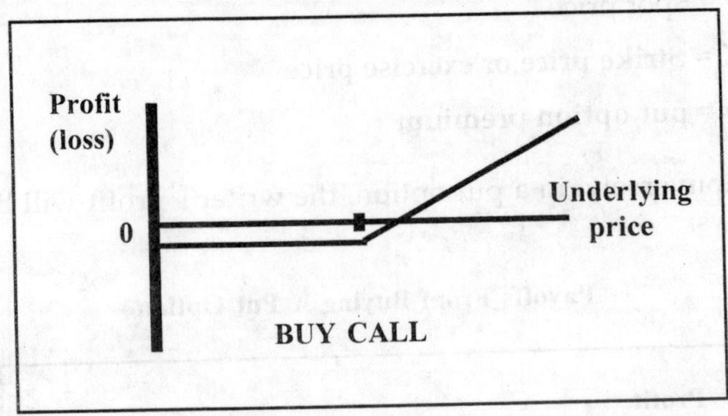

As we see in the diagram, profit and loss moves incrementally (45 degree angle as shown in the diagram) if the underlying price at options expiration day is greater than the underlying price today.

PUT OPTION

In a put option buyer's profit can be defined as follows:
At all points where S<X, the payoff will be X-S-p

Limited Losses

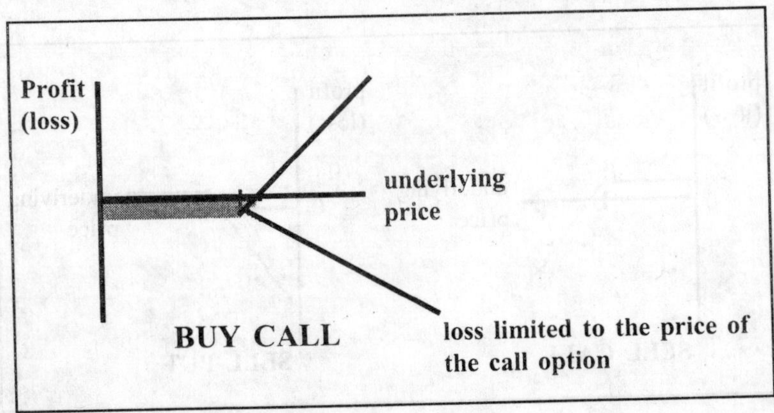

At all points where S>X, the payoff will be -p, where

S = Spot price,

X = Strike price or exercise price

p = put option premium

Conversely, in a put option, the writer's profit will be as follows:

Payoffs From Buying A Put Option

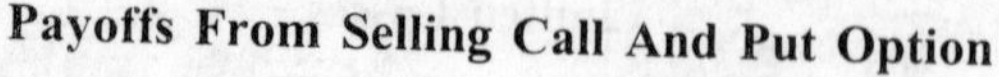

Selling call or put options

Payoffs From Selling Call And Put Option

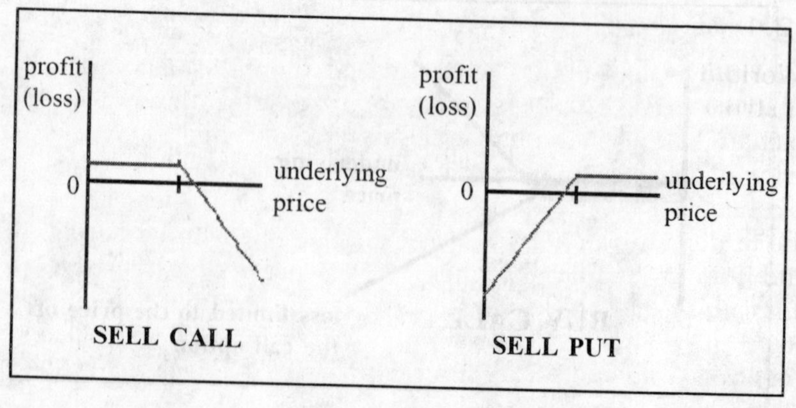

At all points where S<X, the payoff will be -(X-S- p)

At all points where S>X, the payoff will be p

We see in the above graph the profit or loss of buying a put option for a range of projected underlying prices at expiration day for the call option.

It is important to note that while the losses for selling call or put options are virtually without limit, the profit is limited to the price of the option. The option writer must calculate net liability properly while calculating the option premium.

Profits and Losses from Selling Options

12.4 Strike Price of Options

World over options are generally traded on different variety of strike prices. These strike prices are determined by the exchange. For example if a call option is traded at a strike price equal to that of the underlying spot price, then the option is called **At-The-Money** option, if the strike price is lesser than the underlying spot price, it is called **In-The-Money** option and if the strike price is higher than the underlying spot price, it is called as **Out-of-Money** option. In case of put option if the strike price is higher than the underlying spot price it is called **In-The-Money** and when the strike price is lower than the underlying spot price, it is called **Out-of-Money** option. **At-The-Money** option is same for both a call and put on the same underlying stock and the same strike price.

12.5 Option Premium

Option premium consists of two parts: **Intrinsic value** and **Time value.** The intrinsic value of a call option is the difference between the spot price and the strike price, whereas the intrinsic value of a put option is the difference between the strike price and the spot price. In-the-money options have intrinsic value. However, At-The-Money and Out-of-Money options have no intrinsic value. Time value of an option is the price a holder of an option has to pay to the seller of an option because of the risk the seller of an option takes. This is over and above the intrinsic value that an option holder pays. Typically, the premium charged by the seller of an option is equal to the sum of both intrinsic value and the time value.

12.6 The Black–Scholes Option Pricing Model

Fischer Black and Myron Scholes published a paper in 1973 that became the precursor of all option pricing models and later research on risk management (Black & Scholes, 1973). The main result of this paper (to be called B-S model) is an option pricing formula based on simple and reasonable assumptions in a continuous time model.

Given below is the B-S formula for the price of a Call option. The latter gives the owner the right but not the obligation to buy one share of the underlying stock at the strike price X specified in the option contract on or before the maturity date of the option. If the stock price is S and the price of the bond promising to pay the amount of the strike price at the maturity of the option is B, the Black-Scholes price of the option or the premium of the call option C will be

$$C = S \, N(x_1) - B \, N(x_2) \qquad\qquad Equation\ 12.1$$

Where

$$x_1 = \log(S/B) / s + s/2,$$

$$x2 = \log (S/B) / s - s / 2,$$

and s is the standard deviation of the stock price at maturity. The function N(.) is a cumulative Normal distribution. If there is a continuously compounded constant interest rate r and T is the time profile of the option, B is the discounted exercise price of the option, or

$$B = X. \exp(- rT) \qquad\qquad\qquad Equation\ 12.2$$

And if the stock has a variance v per unit of time, we get,

$$s^2 = v\ T$$

is the variance of the stock price.

The important aspect of the result is that it depends on the absence of arbitrage. Also part of the proof is a formula that specifies a trading strategy in the underlying stock and the risk-less bond that replicates the pay-off of the option at the end (Rubinstein and Leland, 1995). When the option is priced differently in the economy, trading the option and following either the trading strategy or the reverse of it will make money.

In the expression of the formula C, the first term is the stock holding in the hedge strategy, and the second term is the bond holding. The principal assumptions of the B–S model are: absence of arbitrage, a constant risk-less rate, continuous stock prices, and a constant variance of returns for the underlying asset. The intuitive idea is that we can replicate the risk of holding the option by holding the right portfolio of risk-free bonds and the underlying stock.

Black and Scholes assumed a frictionless market and a constant risk-free interest rate. Further, they assume that the stock price follows a continuous time lognormal stochastic distribution. In other words, the continuously compounded rate of returns on the stock follow a normal distribution with a constant mean and constant variance per unit of time.

Given the set of assumptions, the authors used the perfect hedge methodology to price the call. They constructed a perfectly hedged position consisting of a non-arbitrary quantity θ of shares held long for every call option written such that the investment is fully protected independent of the direction the stock is moving over the next instant. The gains in the θ shares of stock are exactly offset by the loses on the written call option. Because the position is perfectly risk less over the next point of time, it shall earn the risk-less rate of return to prevent risk less arbitrage opportunities. Based on this no-arbitrage condition and assumed distribution properties of the stock price, the authors derived a partial differential equation that is satisfied by the price of call. The solution of this equation is the Black-Scholes (B-S) formula as shown above.

There are some fundamental characteristics of the B-S formula of option premium as in Equation (12.1) and these are:

First, the theoretical call prices satisfying equation (12.1) are equilibrium prices and these are only with respect to the stock price and the risk-less interest rate. Because the B-S formula originates from a relative pricing approach. The pricing equation is derived by forming a risk-less hedge between the stock and the option. As a result the resulting equilibrium condition involves only the stock, the option and the risk-less interest rate, and there is no concern for the equilibrium prices of other assets.

Second, the B-S formula does not depend on the expected rate of return on the stock that reflect investor's preferences. It is a preference-free pricing formula and it can be derived in any type — risk neutral or risk averse. Because of this characteristic, the B-S formula can be used to compute the theoretical option price in any kind of economic conditions.

Third, the B-S formula is related to its 'continuous time perfect hedge' assumption. The main corollary of this is that a person should be able to continuously rebalance the hedged position in the market till the expiry date of the option contract. This requires an active and liquid market that shall facilitate a continuous rebalancing of the portfolio. In other words, the relevance of the B-S formula will be greater in a perfect market with the features of liquidity.

The Determinants of an Option's Price

From the Equation (12.1) we see that price of option depends on five parameters and these are:

(i) the current stock price level S
(ii) the strike price X
(iii) the continuously compounded risk less interest rate r
(iv) the time to maturity t
(v) the standard deviation of returns s

The parameter that brings uncertainty in the pricing is the standard deviation s, and through this the B-S formula links the risk of the underlying asset and option price. The historical value of s is used to calculate option price with the implicit assumption that it has not changed meanwhile. This is the source of risk for the writer of the option that the standard deviation of the returns changes over time.

The strike price X and option price are inversely related. The higher the strike price, the less valuable a Call option will be as the strike price represents a higher cost of exercising the call and thus purchasing the stock. Mathematically, from the Equation (12.1) it follow:

$$\delta C / \delta X = - e^{-rt} N (x_2) < 0 \qquad \textit{Equation 12.3}$$

Since the derivative is negative, it implies that a small increase in the exercise price will decrease the option price by a proportionality factor equal to the R.H.S. of Equation (12.3).

When stock price (asset price) increases, the option price will increase and this is seen as follows:

$$\delta C / \delta S = N (x_1) > 0 \qquad \textit{Equation 12.4}$$

This derivative is known as 'hedge delta' of call option. Its value is always positive and this 'delta' is an important tool for valuing and hedging option position. Equation (12.4) shows that a Re. 1 change (increase) in the asset price (stock price) will change (increase) the price of option by $N(x_1)$ in money terms. If the theoretical value of hedge delta is 0.75 (say), it implies that the option writer should cover at least 75 per cent of the option contract to keep the position neutral. This is known as *delta neutral position.*

The option price varies directly with the length of time to maturity. As the time profile of an option increases, the risk factor increases and the seller of the option is to bear it. This is compensated by higher price of the option. Similarly, the higher the risk free interest rate, the higher is the price of the option. Moreover, if interest rate changes during the span of the option, that changes the risk profile of the option to the writer. An increase in interest rate will increase the risk of the option contract to the seller, and he seldom finds hedge to safeguard from this type of risk.

This chapter deals with elementary aspects of option pricing model. As an illustration the European call option is taken for discussion. Readers are advised to see more advanced book for a discussion of American option.

12.6 Conclusion

The Black-Scholes option formula has been used in finance literature for portfolio management. The B-S model represents a fundamental contribution to the option pricing theory. It gives a simple pricing formula that depends on observable parameters. It also provides several risk exposure measures to monitor various types of dynamically managed option strategies. The formula has been modified and improved further to accommodate more complex situation and for the solution of more complex problem.

Some experts have raised the question that how accurate are the model's theoretical prices? The answer of this question depends on the empirical evidence regarding the model's pricing performance and the compatibility of the assumptions in light of these empirical evidences. In the same dimension the B-S model has been extended to become more nearer to reality.

Thirteen

International Capital Flow, Currency Crisis and Problems of Contagion

"No matter what problems a country may have, their manifestation as a balance of payments problem is always a consequence of government policy."

[Harry G. Johnson]

"Everything's got a moral if only you can find it."
[Lewis Carroll in *Alice's Adventure in Wonderland*]

13.1 The Background

Since the middle of 1980s some countries in the south Asian region had experienced rapid economic growth in the range of 7-8 percent per annum. Most of these countries have a liberal exchange rate regime and they took advantage of their export expansion and huge inflow of foreign capital. Hong Kong and Singapore became two strong offshore financial centres apart from Tokyo. Over the years this region also had become a centre of 'Geo Finance' holding huge amount of international reserve. By June 1997, international reserve of Japan was USD 222 billion, China had USD 121 billion, while Hong Kong had USD 82 billion. To what extent this economic muscle of these three countries affected the strength of the currencies of countries like Thailand, Malaysia, Philippines and Indonesia remains a matter of conjecture. There is a debate in the literature that the North American free trade bloc NAFTA may have been responsible for the weakness of the Mexican peso, as Mexico is the weakest in the bloc. If it is true, one can draw a parallel in case of the south Asian trade bloc where major economic powers like Japan, China and Hong Kong might have contributed to the weakness of the currencies of the fellow countries. We are to remember that all these countries were pursuing a strategy of economic development that was known as export led growth. Or, they depended heavily on exports.

13.2 The Crisis

In 1997 Thailand experienced heavy pressure on its currency baht as it was perceived to be overvalued. When the pressure became too severe, the government decided not to defend it further and to allow the currency to float in order to avoid defaulting on its obligations to international creditors. This induced a rapid spread of the crisis throughout the region, culminating in the collapse of the currencies of Thailand, Indonesia, Malaysia, the Philippines and South Korea within a matter of weeks. Along with the currency collapse there were steep falls in the stock markets of these countries also. This spread to other economies in the region, particularly Hong Kong and Singapore. This regional turmoil rapidly turned into a major world financial crisis and led to a substantial downturn in world economic growth.

The question that occupied the minds of the academicians was why was this region, previously described by economists and commentators as representing a 'growth miracle', plunged into one of the world's most serious recessions. The traditional explanation of fiscal profligacy and macro-economic instability, which plagued Latin America in the 1980s and 1990s, were not applicable because most of the important macro-economic indicators were generally healthy. The fiscal balance was generally in surplus. Inflation in these countries was low, and domestic saving and investment as a proportion of GDP were among the highest in the world. But these countries were suffering from severe current account deficits. In the two years preceding 1997, the current account deficits as a percentage of GDP were: Thailand (7.9%); Malaysia (7.3%); Philippines (4.7%); Indonesia (3.4%), and South Korea (3.3%)

(McCombie and Thirlwall, 1999). These ratios are very high as from historical experience we see that the maximum sustainable deficit to GDP ratio seems to be of the order of 2-3 percent, beyond which the financial markets start to get nervous for understandable reasons. However, the quick spread of the crisis in the region, known as contagion, has induced the growth of literature to which we now turn.

13.3 Currency Crisis

A currency crisis is defined as speculative attack on the currency of a country. This is brought out by the high volume traders when they attempt to alter their portfolio by selling that particular currency to buy another preferred one, that they perceive to be safe. This may happen for a variety of reasons. One explanation is that sometimes investors fear that the government will finance its high prospective deficits through printing money or it may attempt to reduce its non-indexed debt through devaluation. When the pressure comes on the exchange rate, the central bank must step in and it should buy up its currency with international reserve. When the reserve is not adequate, the central bank allows the currency to float and devaluation follows.

The currency crisis in south Asia had been so severe that it induced academic interest in the literature for proper explanation of the genesis of the crisis and its effects. The series of models tried to explain the phenomenon and that is known as generation models.

13.4 First Generation Models

The models of currency crisis developed by Krugman (1979), Flood and Garber (1984) and Obstfeld (1986) and others depend on government debt and the perceived inability of the government to control the budget as the principal causes for the explanation of the crisis. The argument is that a speculative attack on the currency may result from an insistent current account deficit and also from an expected monetization of the fiscal deficit. When the attack starts in the form of high sale of the domestic currency, the central bank initially tries to defend by the buy back of the domestic currency with foreign reserve, and when it is depleted, it allows the currency to float. The implicit assumption of Krugman's model is that a fixed exchange rate regime with no sound fiscal policy is the inevitable target of attack. The crisis is triggered when the market expects the government to abandon the peg. The potential conflict between the fiscal policy of the government and the fixed exchange rate (peg) regime changes the market perception about the intrinsic worth of the currency, and that creates the environment of attack.

13.5 Second Generation Models

The second generation models of crisis are provided by Obstfeld (1994), Eichengreen, Rose and Wyplosz (ERW) (1997) and others. These models explain self-fulfilling currency crisis that are contagious. Devaluation in one country affects the price level and demand for money of the country, it also affects the current account by a reduction of exports in the partner country, and through trade link the devaluation in the partner country becomes increasing likely. ERW finds that there exists a correlation between the likelihood of default across the countries. They have estimated that a speculative attack on currency somewhere in the world increases the probability of a domestic currency crisis by about 8 percent. The spill-over of the crisis from one country to another are attributed to a number of scenarios and these are: an economic events like oil price hike, a devaluation or default by one country, or collapse of the stock market in a neighbouring country. Any combination of such scenarios can help to explain the international linkages that are responsible for the spread of speculative attacks from one country to another.

13.6 Third Generation Models

The earlier models have not provided a policy recommendation for the central bank when it faces the crisis. The third generation models of Krugman (1999), Aghion, Bacchetta and Banerjee (2000, 2001) and others examine the effects of monetary policy in a currency crisis. These models suggest that a currency crisis is a result of the combination of factors like high debt, low foreign reserves, falling government revenue, increasing expectations of devaluation and domestic borrowing constraints. Firms' access to domestic credit is constrained by assuming they can borrow only a portion of their wealth. In the face of lending constraints in the economy, credit markets do not clear, and though interest rate increases, the increase is not considered enough to compensate the lenders the potential default risk. Thus the rise in the interest rate neither increases the supply of loanable funds nor induces the banks to increase the credit.

These models offer a role of monetary policy through a binding credit constraint when the financial market is imperfect. When the firms' leverage in the domestic market is reduced, they go to the foreign market and in the process accumulate foreign debt. In the domestic market nominal interest rate is important for the amount of available lending and when central bank raises the interest rate in response to typical prescription for a currency crisis; it deepens the crisis by reducing the firms' ability to invest. The lowering of investment reduces productive capacity of the economy and the perceived decline in output exerts additional pressure on the exchange rate.

The models of three generations suggest four factors that can influence the onset and magnitude of the currency crisis of a country and these are: domestic public and private debt, expectations generated in the market, state of the financial markets and pegged exchange rate. These factor either in combination or alone can trigger the currency crisis and after that the course of the crisis and its magnitude may be influenced by the policies pursued by the central bank and the governments. But the differences in the nuances of the three categories of models remain and there emerged a new strand in the theoretical literature emphasized moral hazard as well as contagion as the missing links that could probably explain the differences between the set of models as stated above.

13.7 Contagion: The Definition

The incident of currency crisis that helped the emergence of contagion as a concept has been defined in multiple ways. The

World Bank has used three definitions: one broad, one moderately restrictive and the third very restrictive.

The broad definition defines contagion as the cross-country transmission of shocks – whether real, financial or from exogenous sunspots. So contagion can take place both during the tranquil period and crisis period, though the latter is generally referred. The examples are Asian currency crisis of 1997-98, the EMS crisis of 1992-93.

The moderately restrictive definition of contagion is that it is the transmission of shocks to other countries, and more generally, this happens when significant cross-country correlation exists beyond any fundamental links between countries and beyond common shocks. This is usually referred to excess co-movement and is explained by herding behaviour leading to sunspots.

The most restrictive definition of contagion is that phenomenon when cross-country correlation increases during the crisis period relative to correlation during the tranquil period. This is tested with econometric tools and as such it is very exclusive.

Outside the World Bank study contagion has been defined as a significant increase in cross-country linkages after a shock to an individual country or group of countries (Dornbush, Park and Claessens, 2000). This definition asserts that contagion arises due to a shift in cross-market linkages, and this tendency is sometimes known as 'shift-contagion'.

For the recognition of contagion researchers have applied the following strategies: correlation of asset returns, conditional probability of currency crises, the transmission of volatility changes and co-movements of capital flows and rates of returns. The estimation of correlation coefficients among stock returns is most popular method used in the estimation of contagion effects. Since study based on correlation has obvious limitation, some researchers go for more refined methods like vector auto regression and causality analysis.

The currency crisis in south Asia has been followed by similar crisis in some Latin American countries like Argentina, Russia and some east European countries. Whatever may be the reason(s) that first triggers the crisis, the countries suffered in terms of loss of productivity and employment? The IMF came to the rescue to most of these countries with a package that is basically based on a theoretical structure known as 'Washington Consensus'.

13.8 Washington Consensus

The name Washington Consensus (W-C) was given by John Williamson in 1990 to a package of ten policy recommendations for countries willing to reform their economies and these are:

(i)	Tax reforms	(ii)	Financial liberalization
(iii)	Fiscal discipline	(iv)	Redirect public expenditure
(v)	Adopt a single competitive	(vi)	Trade liberalization exchange rate
(vii)	Eliminate barrier to foreign direct investment	(viii)	Privatize state owned enterprises
(ix)	Deregulate market entry	(x)	Ensure secure property rights

Later on Williamson articulated the concept of W–C in subsequent papers (Williamson, 1993, 1990). But the debate continued about the contents of the so-called consensus. Even important persons within the administration of World Bank expressed doubts about the applicability of the general package.

The general ideas derived from the Washington Consensus had a huge influence on the economic reforms of the countries that were implementing this. Yet, the way these countries interpreted such ideas varied substantially. Moreover, the original ten policy prescriptions of the Washington Consensus reigned unchallenged only for a short time. Changes in the international economic and political environment and new domestic realities in the reforming countries created problems and adjustment and compromises were called for. The newfound answers often complemented the recommendations originally offered by the Washington Consensus, though some were opposed to the original package. The wildly gyrating ideas about controls on foreign capital or about exchange rate regimes that have been offered at different times are good examples of the lack of consensus.

When John Williamson summarized what he saw as the consensus that had emerged among the 'political' Washington of the US Congress, within the IMF, World Bank, and the think tanks, he did not suspect that he was fathering one of the brand names that would come to characterize the decade. He even could not imagine that his basic proposal would draw so many disagreements among the academics and it would generate political controversy.

From the beginning, advocates of the Washington Consensus have been greatly divided about the pace and sequence of the reforms. Even among the specialists of market-friendly reforms serious differences emerged about the need or desirability of what came to be known as the application of a 'shock therapy' approach to policy reforms. This approach implied the implementation of as many reforms as quickly as possible. Some economists argued for a slower, more sequenced pace. This is not a debate just between experts in Washington and others elsewhere. It also rages among insiders.

It would be a mistake, however, to assume that these differences emerged all of a sudden. Early in the decade, Williamson acknowledged that not all of the assertions he included in his original 'ten-best' policy recommendations enjoyed the same degree of consensus. According to his assessment at the time, in five of the ten policy prescriptions "consensus has been established". Thus the existence of consensus had been assumed. But it was perceived that over time agreement could be reached on the remaining items, though two conditions—changing public budget priorities and according the same treatment to foreign and domestic firms— is always controversial in nature due to political overtones.

It is important to stress that Williamson was an innocent victim of the success of his useful summary of the prevailing thought among the persons within the think tank of the IMF. Williamson tried hard to qualify very carefully what he really meant when he framed the Washington Consensus. He sought to correct those who misinterpreted the approach and made repeated attempts at clarifying the nuances of his conceptual framework. Wide use and popularity of W-C had a price and soon it was revealed in the form of distortions of the concepts. Williamson's efforts at clarifying the meaning and implication of W-C were not enough to compensate for the distortions already created. Very soon, even the ten prescriptions were not that well known. The concept Washington Consensus acquired a life of its own, and it became a brand name known worldwide and used quite independently of its original intent.

But every ideology has an evolutionary process and very soon W-C became an ideology with the IMF. May be one can link it to the early Polak model that may give it the theoretical back up. But the evolution of the idea is interesting.

13.9 Evolution of Washington Consensus

Short words are usually bad economics and that was said by Alfred Marshal. By that measure the decade of the 1990s was full of such expressions: international financial contagion, sequencing, bailouts, the tequila effect, moral hazard, crony capitalism to name only a few. None of these terms figured in the original formulation of the Washington Consensus. But slowly with new interpretations by economists new words were coined. New concepts and names, and the realities they tried to encapsulate, gained importance as a result of the many surprise events that impaired the implementation of market reforms. While this jargon-filled list of terms may sound like a cacophony of jumbled words, they help the understanding of the signposts marking the road through which common wisdom about market reforms evolved since 1990. This evolution had a pattern. It usually began with the increase in popularity of a general set of policy recommendations. For sometime these recommendations embodied the views of an influential majority of academics and high level staff of the IMF and the World Bank. But crises came in some countries in the process of implementation of the reforms. New experiences created learning and it was realized the need of new data would the previous crises missed some important element whose critical importance had now been clearly illuminated by the next crisis. Another new explanation is required and another set of jargons are coined.

The Mexican crisis of 1994 explain how the original W-C remained on the path of evolution. The lesson drawn from this crisis was that a low domestic savings rate made Mexico overly vulnerable to the volatility of foreign capital markets by making it too dependent on foreign funds. Therefore, a higher rate of domestic savings along with sound macro-economic fundamentals would serve to inoculate a country from a crash induced by the volatility of short-term international capital flows.

Again the higher saving-income ratio was unable to explain the crisis of south Asia that came in 1997. That crisis came in spite of high savings rate and sound macro-economic fundamentals of the south Asian economies. So another explanation was required. The concept of 'crony capitalism' came and that meant the reliance on a private sector highly distorted by the dominance of a few, large 'economic groups' closely associated with those in government. Sound macro-economics and increasing the savings rate are not discarded as the worthy policy goals. But apart from these necessary conditions something additional was considered necessary and that was the reforms in the domestic industrial sector to encourage competition. The process continues.

13.10 Globalization

It is ironic that the Washington Consensus missed globalization. Because the elimination of obstacles to international trade and investment that fueled much of the economic integration the world has witnessed owes a lot to the influence of the Washington Consensus on many liberalizing countries. But the subsequent financial troubles some of these countries faced had little answer in the package of W-C.

The package in the Washington Consensus did not provide a set of policies that would enable reforming countries to better cope with the consequences of globalization, especially in the financial sphere. In the 1990s a large number of countries experimented with market reforms, and most of them experienced periodic financial crashes that rocked these countries and spread across borders in quick and unpredictable ways. Between 1994 and 1999, some middle-income developing countries like South Korea, Thailand and others had a major financial crisis[1]. These crises wrought havoc in these countries' financial systems, bankrupted their banks, set the economic clock back for several years. But still why these happened and at a massive scale remains unanswered. For better credibility of the W-C new explanations are required.

What are the factors that created the crashes of that magnitude remains still not answered properly and confusion prevails. Some economists having ideology not necessarily toeing the mainstream one raise interesting questions of the following nature:

Was financial opening in a developing country with questionable infrastructure a good idea? Is trade liberalization necessarily good? Should currencies of the developing countries float freely or are countries better off with a currency board or some sort of pegged rate? Should the IMF be abolished or strengthened? These are just a few examples.

The disagreements as stated in the above paragraph can be grouped into three general categories:
- the fix or float debate,
- the capital account liberalization debate, and
- the inflate versus deflate debate

The **fix or float debate** is about the nature of the exchange rate regime a country should have. This area is full of controversy largely because monies are fiduciary issues and

---

1. The countries are Turkey, Venezuela, Argentina, Mexico, Indonesia, South Korea, Malaysia, Philippines, Russia, Brazil and Thailand.

not adequately backed by the issuing authority. Yet, while a certain convergence has emerged in favour of floating exchange rates, the debate is still far from reaching the kind of expert consensus. Faced with currency crisis leaders in Mexico, Asia, Brazil, and Russia received a barrage of contradictory advice.

The debate about exchange rate regimes is closely linked to the debate on the liberalization of a country's capital account. In the words of Alan Binder, "the hard-core Washington Consensus — which holds that international capital mobility is a blessing, full stop — needs to be tempered by a little common sense." On the other hand, proponents of capital controls do not share the same common sense about what kind of measures are the best. Some radical proponents, like Paul Krugman, recognize that "there is virtually unanimous consensus among economists that exchange controls work badly". Yet, imposition of currency control was the only alternative left in Asian crisis because of its magnitude and severity and it is the view of Krugman.

Some economists who have moderate view suggest some mechanism that will slow down the flow of hot money. In this they refer Chile as it is open to foreign banks and allows outflow of capital. But Chile taxes the inflow of short term capital. But there is disagreement on the effectiveness of this measure.

The prescriptions for the solution in the crisis ridden countries have been stringent fiscal and monetary policies. These have become the reasons for severe recession in such countries and the question that haunts the economists is:

Why a financial crash has to be cured with a recession is the crux of the **deflate versus reflate** debate?

Some economists argue that the unequivocal priority after a country suffers a financial crash is to stabilize its exchange rate. Protecting the currency sliding down too much requires some drastic measures like cutting public budgets, raising taxes and hiking interest rates. This combination of measures slows down the economy and boosts unemployment. Also in countries where banks had not been competently supervised and they suffer from moral hazard problems, the recession may also create a costly banking crisis. This is a bitter medicine, but to many experts this is the solution.

In fact, the debate boils down to the issue of increasing the interest rate. While this is thought necessary to save the currency, it also discourages investment and the result may be severe recession and high unemployment. Thus the consensus on the prescriptions of so called 'Washington Consensus' remains elusive.

Fourteen

New Open Economy Models: An Overview

*'Oh, you can't help that,' said the Cat; we're all mad here.
I'm mad. You're mad.'*

. . . .

*Alice didn't think that proved it at all; however, she went on.
'And how do you know that you're mad?'
'To begin with,' said the Cat, 'a dog's not mad. You grant that?
'I suppose so', said Alice.
'Well, then,' the Cat went on, 'you see, a dog growls when it's
angry, and wags its tail when it's pleased. Now I growl when
I'm pleased, and wag my tail when I'm angry. Therefore
I'm mad.'*

*[Alice's Adventure in Wonderland
- Lewis Carroll]*

A series of papers published since late 1980s had changed the main theoretical contours of traditional international economic theories. The latter had largely been built on the solid foundations of Heckscher-Ohlin model, though some extensions had been achieved in some papers published in the 1980s. These were mainly concerned with the inclusion of the assumptions of imperfect competitions, counter trade and to some extent price rigidity. But the basic premise of the H–O model remained intact. While the pure theory of international trade remains tied to H-O framework, the monetary theory, i.e., balance of payments and exchange rate determination had been built upon either the Keynesian framework or the monetarist framework.

In 1995 Maurice Obstfeld and Kenneth Rogoff (henceforth OB-RO) jointly published a paper (Obstfeld and Rogoff, 1995) that started a series of research changing many assumptions of traditional theory of international economics. The basic model of OB-RO is a two-country dynamic general equilibrium model with the provisions of nominal price rigidities, imperfect competition, and a continuum of agents who both produce and consume. Each agent produces a single differentiated good and all of them have identical preferences. The latter are characterized by an intertemporal utility function that depend positively on consumption and real money balances but negatively on work efforts. The work efforts are positively related to output. While two countries are home and foreign, exchange rate is the price of foreign currency in terms of home currency. The exchange rate works as the bridge between the domestic price and the foreign price.

The OB–OR model assumes that there are no restrictions on international movements of commodities. This implies that law of one price (LOP) holds for individual commodity and internationally identical commodity basket is governed by Purchasing Power Parity (PPP), i.e., each traded commodity attracts the same price when converted to a single international currency. Strict version of PPP implies a fixed real exchange rate, as the later is defined as the nominal exchange rate adjusted for relative national price levels, or,

$$RER = NER \times (CPI^*/CPI)$$

Where CPI and CPI* are price levels of home and foreign respectively. Thus twin assumption of LOP and continuous PPP imply a fixed RER for the home country. When PPP holds only in the long run and not on continuous basis, RER may have fluctuations over time.

OB-OR model assumes that two countries can borrow and lend in the integrated capital market of the world. The only asset traded internationally is the risk free real bond denominated in consumption good. Agents maximize their lifetime utility subject to budget constraint.

Each agent decides his optimal choice of consumption, money holding, labour supply and also determine the price of his output. Nominal rigidity is introduced into the model by fixing prices one period in advance. The system is first solved for the steady state of the model. A log-linear approximation is made of the steady state to study the effects of a monetary shock. Since prices are sticky for one period , the solution distinguishes between the impact effects of a shock and the long run steady state effects. The welfare effects of a shock are the sum of the short run change of utility and the long run change in steady state utility.

The model also considers the experiment of an unanticipated permanent increase in domestic money supply (a la Dornbusch). The effects of a monetary shock is an increase in output and consumption. The real interest rate of the world declines and a nominal depreciation of domestic currency boils down to a decline to domestic terms of trade. Both these factors lead to an increase in foreign consumption. Since the increase in aggregate consumption and the shift in relative prices work in opposite dimension, the effects on foreign output are ambiguous. The current account of the home country moves to a surplus. This implies a permanent improvement in net foreign assets. When the latter is translated to positive net investment income inflow, this increases consumption permanently above domestic output and that leads to a domestic trade deficits. Again the wealth effects of an increase in net foreign assets reduces domestic labour supply, as leisure consumption increases, domestic output declines and this leads to a permanent improvement in the home country's terms of trade. Thus money is not neutral in this model.

In the model the monetary shock's impact on home and foreign welfare can be calculated. For that the different effects of the money shocks on consumption both in short run and in long run , real balances and leisure can be aggregated adjusting to the respective weights implicit in the utility function. It follows from the model that home and foreign welfare increase in the same proportion, though the output effects of the shock are asymmetric. This is because the first order effects of the monetary shocks are the initial increase in world demand. But the distortions will be there because of imperfect competition, and that initial levels of output will be too low compared to world total, a demand- driven increase in world output increases welfare to the equal benefits of both countries.

14.1 Extension of OB-RO Model

The OB-RO model has been extended by later research works. Nominal rigidity is one particular assumption. Harald Hau has generalized the model in three ways with the objective of investigating the role of factor price rigidities and nontradables for the international transmission mechanism (Hau, 2000). First, the model allows for factor markets and also for nominal rigidity originating from sticky factor prices. Second, Hau's paper also allows for nontraded goods.

Third, it is assumed that there is no international goods arbitrage and there is flexible price setting in local currency. Because of optimal monopolistic price fixation, law of one price still holds, though nontradables in the consumer price index will create deviations from Purchasing Power Parity.

The main result of the Hau's paper is that factor price rigidities have similar implications to rigid domestic producer prices. In the context of a market structure with factor price rigidities, the conclusion of OB-RO model is confirmed here also. However, a large share of nontradable goods in consumer's budget implies that exchange rate movements are magnified, because money market equilibrium depends on a short run price adjustment that are associated with fewer tradable commodities. This is important as this effect may explain the high volatility of the nominal exchange rate relative to price fluctuations as observed in the market.

14.2 The Steady State Again

In OB-RO framework, current account plays an important role in the transmission of shocks across the countries. But the steady state is indeterminate and both the consumption differential between countries and the net foreign assets of a country are non-stationary in character. After a monetary shock the economy will move to a new steady state, and continue there till another shock arrives. Later formulations of OB-RO have not emphasized the role of net foreign assets accumulations as a channel of macro-economic transmissions between countries. This is achieved with two assumptions:

(i) the elasticity of substitution between domestic and foreign goods is unity, and,

(ii) financial markets are complete in the sense that international capital market is complete with perfect capital mobility.

Under complete financial markets and law of one price, full risk-sharing means that there will be no shift in wealth between countries arising out of monetary shocks. This makes the persistence channel non-functional, and there is no longer a shift in relative wealth having a permanent effect on relative labour supplies, that causes permanent effects on relative prices and outputs. Because of these, the assumption of complete markets helps to simplify the analysis by denying both the current account and net foreign assets the role of dynamic propagation mechanism.

The two assumptions (i) and (ii), by denying the current account to generate dynamic persistent effects have helped for the achievement of the determinacy of the steady state. The assumption may be strong, but the role of current account dynamics in the generation of persistent effects of transitory shocks have also been found to be quantitatively not important in the literature (Kollman, 1996).

14.3 Uncertainty and Stochastic Nature

OB-RO (1998) has introduced the effects of an unanticipated monetary shock in a sticky price general equilibrium model with a stochastic setting. Thus monetary uncertainty is introduced by assuming home and foreign money stocks follow log-normal stochastic process. Since uncertainty affects equilibrium prices, it has effects on expected consumption levels, the terms of trade and also relative output levels. For example, if the home country faces monetary uncertainty, the corporate of this country will add a risk premium in the prices of commodities. This will reduce production, but will improve terms of trade. Thus uncertainty has first order effects on equilibrium welfare levels. These effects are symmetric on welfare levels of both countries, home and foreign, despite *ex-ante* differences in price setting and *ex-post* differences in relative output levels. This induces both the countries to design an optimum global exchange rate system, and this will hold irrespective of the relative size of home and foreign countries.

The model as developed in OB-RO (1998) has another interesting implication. Regarding its predictions for asset pricing, the risk premium on a volatile currency may be negative if exchange rate movement hedges consumption volatility. This again explains a puzzle related to forward premium: a high inflation country may have a relative volatile and unstable currency that hedges consumption risk, and thus it simultaneously generates a positive expected depreciation and a negative forward premium. Also monetary uncertainty has magnified effects on the level of exchange rate relative to the forward premium. When the latter is volatile, the analysis then provides an explanation for the high volatility of the level of exchange rate. This also explains that not only high interest rate leads to potential depreciation of the currency, but the expectation of a depreciation of the home currency due to monetary shock may increase the interest rate.

The results obtained above in the extended OB-RO model are based on the assumptions specific to the model along with the micro foundations. This aspect has been questioned in subsequent literature and some papers have attempted to relax some strong assumptions (Sarno, 2001).

14.4 Equilibrium Exchange Rate and Pass-through

Empirical evidence in the literature indicates that changes in the nominal exchange rates are not fully passed through to the prices of commodities. It seems that consumer prices are not very responsive to nominal exchange rate changes. One implication of this is that the *'expenditure switching'* effects of exchange rate changes might be very small, which means that a change in the nominal exchange rate might not lead to much substitution between domestically produced commodities and internationally produced commodities, as the relative prices of the commodities do not change much for the consumers.

When the exchange rate changes have small effects on the behaviour of final users of commodities, it will require large change in the exchange rates to achieve equilibrium after some initial shock to fundamentals. Suppose there is a shock that reduces the supply of imported commodities, that implies that a very large home depreciation might be required in order to increase the relative prices of imported commodities enough to reduce demand for that sufficiently. This shows that low pass-through of exchange rates may imply high exchange rate volatility in equilibrium.

The central issue is market segmentation and practice of local-currency pricing of traded commodities. This practice of local-currency pricing impedes the linkages of commodity prices across the countries that again cause the deviations from Purchasing Power Parity (PPP) doctrine and also high exchange rate volatility. But there are some caveats to this conclusion and these are as follows.

First, international finance markets often allow for complete risk sharing across countries. This means that exchange rate will be determined by risk sharing condition, in spite of the fact that local currency prices are independent of exchange rate movements.

Second, even in situation of limited risk sharing in the sense as above, the linkage of asset prices through bond markets will impose a very narrow limit of exchange rate movements, and that rules out high volatility.

Apart from local-currency pricing, two other factors are added in the literature to explain high volatility of exchange rates—heterogeneity in the distribution of internationally traded commodities and the existence of 'noise traders' in the foreign exchange markets. The first comes through the way commodities are sold and prices are set in the international markets. Some firms market their products directly, while others have foreign distributors. In the latter case the exporters set the price in home currency, and the distributors translate that in the currency of the importing country. The second one, i.e., traders adjusts changes in the exchange rate changes by the information of interest rate differentials. The expectations of these traders regarding the interest rate changes are said to be conditionally biased as reported in empirical literature (Devereux, 2002). All these cause high volatility in the exchange rate while the economy reaches equilibrium.

14.5 More on Microstructure of Exchange Rate

There has been further research to explain the short run volatility of the exchange rate. It is argued that dispersed information is rapidly summarized in the public quote of macro variables. This contention is challenged in recent literature (Lyons, 2002). The argument is as follows. The market information of important macro variable like exchange rates gives a set of information in *abstract* form and the argument in favour of this abstraction is not tenable as it lacks empirical support, while dispersed information approach (Payne, 1999, Evans and Lyons, 2002) has better credibility so far as empirical support is concerned.

The difference between the public information approach and the dispersed information approach is the importance of the variable *order flow* in the latter. Order flow is a concept borrowed from microstructure finance. The latter has two main strands — market design and information processing. The latter is important for dispersed information approach as it borrows heavily from it. Order flow concept also belongs to it, i.e., information processing.

Order flow is transaction volume that is signed according to whether the transaction is initiated from the buy side (+) or the sell side (-). Over time order flow is measured as the sum of signed buyer-initiated and seller-initiated orders. A positive sum means that net buying over the period. Order flow as a concept has some similarity with *excess demand*, but with a difference. Excess demand will be zero in equilibrium, but this is not the case with order flow. In foreign exchange market, orders are initiated against a market maker, who stands ready to absorb imbalances between buyers and sellers. These *uninitiated trades* of the market maker make the difference between the two concepts — excess demand and order flow.

Order flows convey information about dispersed fundamentals because these contain the trades of those who analyze those fundamentals. It is a transmission mechanism. The dispersed information approach (DPA) may speak to longer horizon exchange rates in the same way that microscopes speak to pathologies with micro impact. This helps solve the puzzles in exchange rate movements like why the latter are virtually unrelated to macro-economic fundamentals or, why exchange rates are excessively volatile. The DPA links these puzzles with another important phenomenon—how market participants form their expectations of future fundamentals—and this DPA does through expectation formation. The focus is on information types and how information maps into expectations. The issue of information type and mapping to expectations are the important tools of analysis of the microstructure finance to resolve the puzzles as said earlier.

14.6 Stabilization Programme in Crisis Economies: Monetarist Approach and Polak Model

Money supply is recognized as one of the determinants of aggregate demand of the economy. When we treat money supply as a policy variable, we implicitly assume that the monetary consequences of payments imbalances are sterilized. It is recognized that when devaluation of exchange rate increases price level, it reduces the real money balances and so it reduces real demand. Therefore, money is important, and the monetarist approach starts with placing money at the core of the argument.

The monetary approach to balance of payments was developed by two schools. The first was based at University of Chicago under the leadership of Robert Mundell and Harry Johnson. The second was initiated by J.J. Polak at IMF and the justification of the new approach as stated was that it would try to develop models that would be usable to monitor macro-economic management when only rudimentary statistical information is available. We develop the Polak model briefly in the following paragraphs.

The objective of the model was to study the effects on both income formation and the balance of payments of the two important exogenous variables – autonomous changes in exports and the creation of domestic credit. A model that requires to reveal the effects of these two variables needs a demand for money function.

In a simplified banking system of a country the consolidated balance sheet will reveal the identity:

Money supply = Reserve + Domestic Credit, or,

$$H = R + D \qquad\qquad Equation\ 14.1$$

When there is a deficit in the balance of payments, it implies a loss of international reserve. It follows then from Equation (13.1) that there must a counterpart to a deficit in balance of payments in the form of either credit creation (sterilization) or dehoarding (which implies a fall in H). Since dehoarding is a disequilibrium phenomenon (and a temporary thing), a payments deficit can persist *only if it is accompanied by credit creation*. In other words, any additional credit creation will ultimately leak out abroad. This is the central theorem of monetary approach to balance of payments. In this category the Polak model is a model of payments adjustments under a fixed exchange rate regime.

The Polak model is based on a number of assumptions. First, the country is having a fixed exchange rate regime and capital mobility is not allowed. Second, exports are treated as exogenous and so is the domestic credit creation. So the latter can be treated as a policy variable. Third, velocity of circulation of money is constant. This enables one to normalize velocity as unity, and then one can write without no loss to generality:

$$Y(t) = H (t) \qquad\qquad Equation\ 14.2$$

Fourth, imports are always a fixed proportion (m) of the value of nominal income with one period lag, or,

$$M(t) = m. Y (t-1) \qquad \text{Equation 14.3}$$

This is rather a simplifying assumption, as it means that the propensity to import is independent of whether a given nominal income is the result of high price level and low output, or high real output and low price level.

The model is completed by the money supply and balance of payments identities:

$$\Delta H(t) = \Delta R (t) + \Delta D(t) \qquad \text{Equation 14.4}$$

$$\Delta R(t) = X(t) - M(t) \qquad \text{Equation 14.5}$$

And the symbols are:

$$
\begin{aligned}
H &= \text{Money supply} \\
R &= \text{Monetary reserve} \\
D &= \text{Domestic credit} \\
X &= \text{exports} \\
M &= \text{Imports} \\
\Delta &= \text{a change operator}
\end{aligned}
$$

A substitution of equations (14.3) and (14.4) into equation (14.2) gives,

$$
\begin{aligned}
Y(t) &= H (t) \\
&= H (t-1) + \Delta H (t) \\
&= Y (t-1) + \Delta R (t) + \Delta D (t) \qquad \text{Equation 14.6}
\end{aligned}
$$

Equation (14.6) gives the basic monetary theorem. Since in equilibrium,

$$Y (t) = Y (t-1),$$

A payments deficit (that is $\Delta R < 0$) can persists only when domestic credit creation is positive or, $\Delta D > 0$.

The dynamic nature of the model derives from the fact that it contains both income and the change in income. The solution of the model gives the endogenously determined values of income, changes in the reserve and change in the domestic credit of the banking sector.

The model is simple but robust. The message is clear that any expansion of domestic credit will create disequilibrium in the domestic money market and the spill over in the external sector will make the balance of payments worse. Based on this conclusion IMF has traditionally given to limiting domestic credit expansion as an important element of programme of the adjustment in balance of payments. The implicit assumption is that the fall in nominal income (a result of limiting domestic credit) will come through fall in price level and *not through a fall in real output*. But the critics argue that the contraction of domestic credit may lead to a fall in output.

Critics of the IMF stabilization programme argue that IMF uses same programme for all countries without realizing that conditions may differ. Recent experience of the stabilization programme in countries like Russia, Argentina, and even in some countries in south Asia has not been good. Some countries have suffered severe contraction in GDP that have caused huge unemployment.

As if in response to the critics' arguments, Polak (1997) in a recent paper has argued that the model addressed the persistent problems of the late sixties and early seventies of the 20th century. But though world financial system has undergone some fundamental changes during the last two decades. For this IMF should consider some modifications in its policies while applying the model. Polak suggests three changes and these are:

First, the flexibility of international capital movements imply that variable can no longer be treated as exogenous as in the original model. Capital movements depend on domestic interest rates and exchange rate expectations. The required modification is a challenge to IMF.

Second, in the present scenario domestic interest rate depends strongly on the size of the government deficit irrespective of the mode of financing of it, that is, whether that deficit is financed from the banking system or in a domestic capital market. The interest rate is not in the model, but that should be accommodated.

Third, the exchange rate is to be incorporated in the model, as it is important in its effects on the trade flows and also on inflation expectations.

Though Polak argues for the extension of his original model on lines suggested by him, he has not done the necessary extension. In the absence of that he rather suggests that IMF should take into account some other macro-economic conditions of the country before setting forth the conditionality.[1]

14.7 G-3 Exchange Rate Volatility

In recent times the exchange rates of US dollar, yen and Euro are going through large fluctuations and this volatility has caused huge problems in the stabilization programme of developing countries. This is because the latter have tied their currency to US dollar and the volatility in dollar/yen and dollar/Euro rates are creating stability problems in their exchange rates.

In an important paper Reinhart and Reinhart (2002) have tried to address this issue with the hypothesis whether there is a trade off between the exchange rate and interest rate volatility. The paper reviews the traditional North- South links through trade, commodity markets and capital flows. It also adds transmission channels in the form of interest rate and exchange rate volatility. The empirical part of the paper finds no clear support for the hypothesis that limiting G-3 exchange rate volatility is desirable from the perspective of the emerging market economies.

Ricardian Equivalence

Ricardian Equivalence (RE) implies that government budget imbalance is irrelevant to resource allocation. If in a particular year the government goes for higher expenditure based on huge deficit, the citizens understand that the resulting debt

---

1. In the absence of a theoretically sound model, the IMF has recently tended to adopt an "all risk" policy regarding its approach to CIS countries with a triple set of conditions: a ceiling on domestic credit, a floor under net international assets, and an indicative target for base money.

accumulation would require future tax increase for servicing the debt. Thus the effects on the consumption will be minimum. But history contains few Ricardian experiments in which taxes are changed independently of other events which may simultaneously influence consumption and savings.[2] Further, many of the empirical tests one might conduct require strong assumptions about the nature of consumption function, interest rate and income expectations, and other features of economic parameters.

But literature reveals that both time-series and cross-section data indicate a generally positive correlation between consumption and measures of government deficits. The government deficits capture the intergenerational impact of tax policy imperfectly. Nonetheless, some research studies suggest that current accounts might be negatively related to government deficits that is similar to the results of overlapping generation model, and these two are not completely unrelated as claimed in Ricardian equivalence.

---

2.   Although David Ricardo explained the theoretical arguments for equivalence in his book *Principles of Political Economy and Taxation (1817)*, he did not believe that the results would be applied in practice. He warned against the dangers of high public debt levels as he feared that labour and capital might migrate abroad to avoid the tax needed for servicing the national debt (Ricardo, 1951; pp 247-249).

Fifteen

Foreign Direct Investment in India[1]

"Before we can feel much for others, we must in some measure be at ease ourselves. If our own misery pinches us very severely, we have no leisure to attend to that of our neighbour; and all savages are too much occupied with their own wants and necessities, to give much attention to those of another person."

[Adam Smith in Theory of Moral Sentiments]

15.1 Introduction

Since 1991-92 India has been trying to attract foreign capital to bridge the gap between intended investment and actual saving of the country. To increase the rate of growth of GDP in the range of 7 per cent, the rate of net capital formation should be increased in the vicinity of 28 to 30%. The savings of the country have been hanging around 24%. There is a gap and this gap is to be bridged by (a) Portfolio investment by foreign financial institutions (b) lending by foreign banks and other institutions and (c) Foreign Direct Investment. Of these three routes, developing countries prefer the third that is Foreign Direct Investment, as this gives certain advantages to the host country. The advantages of foreign direct investment (FDI) are:

(i) It increases capital for investment automatically. If we compare this with the acquisition route, we see that foreign capital replaces the domestic capital by a take over or purchase. The released domestic capital may be

---

1. This chapter is written jointly by Dr. Biswajit Nag and Dr. Soma Mukhopadhyay, both of them are Assistant Professors of Indian Institute of Foreign Trade, New Delhi.

invested in some other sectors of the economy.

(ii) FDI in green field ventures brings new technology and modern management technique. In these areas, developing countries are lagging behind.

(iii) Foreign capital inflow through FDI route creates a permanent stake of foreign capital in the domestic economy. This may be beneficial for the host country in the sense that it brings a stabilizing force in the economy.

The world investment report 2000 reveals that in the line of countries receiving foreign direct investment, India ranks 17th that means that 16 countries are ahead of India regarding their ability to attract FDI. Countries like Vietnam are also ahead of India. India's share of total FDI inflow into developing countries for the period 1997 to 2000 is 1.4% only. There is no point of comparison with China and this is for two reasons.

(1) China could attract about 25% of total FDI inflow into the developing countries. The next country in the line, that is, Brazil could attract only 10%. The predominant position of China in attracting FDI from 1995 onwards cannot be explained by normal economic parameters.

(2) Second, some economists point out huge amount of capital flight from China that is very high compared to countries of the similar situations. This reminds one of the revolving door situations of some countries suffering from capital flight.

15.2 Objective

The objective of the present chapter is to give a fair account of the status of FDI in India during the recent period. The study focuses attention at three levels:

(i)   At the level of the states
(ii) At the level of the sectors
(iii) At the level of the industry

This is the usage side of FDI. We are to see also the source side. So far FDI inflow into India is concerned, the USA and the European Indian provides the lion's share of FDI to India. Japan comes next in importance of source. For some years Mauritius became important and the role of Non-Residents Indians (NRI) is a bit complex. Some people argue that many NRI's are taking advantage of the Mauritius route regarding the supply side of FDI. There is another problem and this is the widening gap between the approval and actual inflow of FDI. If we see the international situation, we find that there is normally a gap of 30% between the approval and the actual inflow. But, in India the gap is much wider and sometimes it becomes difficult to find explanation for that gap.

There have been some studies on the determinants of FDI inflow into the host countries in the literature. The economic parameters often mentioned as explanatory variables are: Growth rate of GDP, state of infrastructure, exchange rate stability, equitable value of the exchange rate, openness of the economy, legal structure of the host country and the attitude of the Government. The models, which are implicit in the study of these variables, are based on a market economy framework. In India the paradigm shift occurred from 1991-92, that is, the Indian think-tank became accustomed to explore the role of market mechanism in explaining the movement of economic variables. This happened from 1991-92 onwards. A broad section of people — executives in the corporate, officials of foreign Embassies, academicians, independent consultants and industrialists — often express the opinion that India has a great problem regarding the mind set, that is, a popular belief is that foreign capital inflow leads to the exploitation of the domestic economy by the owners of foreign capital. There is another popular belief that India suffers from "too much government Syndrome". The latter means that the role of government in India is spread everywhere, but ironically the governance is weak in areas where it is called for. The latter are areas of external security, the safeguards of the downtrodden people, preservation of the environment and a true reform in the financial sector. The perception is partly qualitative in nature.

The extent to which this perception exists can be measured only by a survey method, and this is beyond the scope of this chapter.

15.3 Approach Towards FDI in India

The exact position of FDI in India will be put up first at three levels; at the level of the State, at the level of the sector and at the level of the industry. The objective of doing this is to examine several hypotheses like the role of infrastructure in attracting FDI, the role of labour situation, the role of law and order etc. We are to see also whether the inflow of FDI in India has certain favourable destination—region wise or sector wise.

A broad explanation of the above will enable us to zero in to certain areas that could be explored further to ascertain the causes of a slow inflow of FDI. It can facilitate the drawing of our conclusion.

15.4 Role of Infrastructure

There is a popular perception that Foreign Direct Investment flows to the region where infrastructure is better. But state of infrastructure in a particular region covers many aspects. Broadly infrastructure can be placed under two categories:

(a) Physical infrastructure, which may be called as social capital. This category includes roads, railways and other communication system, the availability of power and other viable inputs.

(b) The second category includes those aspects which are non-physical in nature like law and order system, availability of efficient work force, education system, work culture and a common growth oriented human psychology. In many developing countries the work culture may be not conducive to modern age industrial society. Also the over all impression regarding the work culture on the mind of the potential investors is important.

The role of Government in the development of the economy is an important factor in the second category of infrastructure. While Government as a facilitator is appreciated everywhere as it helps rapid economic development, too much Government control, and particularly bureaucratic red-tapism is not liked by foreign investors.

In spite of planned economic development in India during the last five decades, the development of infrastructure has not been uniform in 28 States/Regions of the country. One study places the situation of infrastructure in the form of an index. Taking the average India situation as a hundred, the study shows the index of Delhi 730, Kerala 162, Punjab 172, Tamil Nadu 195, while Gujarat is 105 and West Bengal 102. States like Rajasthan, Meghalaya, Manipur are lagging behind as their index is far below 100. When we place the flow of FDI in different states in contrast to the indices of infrastructure of different states, we find that while the states successfully attracting FDI are generally the states that have good infrastructure, but the converse is not true. The states having good infrastructure index have not been able to attract FDI.

15.5 Hypothesis of the Study as Pursued in the Chapter

We are trying to test the following hypotheses:

(1) Foreign Direct Investment flows to the region where returns on capital are higher. This is true both in the case of inter-country comparison and intra-country regions. One important factor in this study is the rate of growth of Gross Domestic Product. The latter has another important role and this is that a higher growth rate of GDP ensures higher absorption capacity of the economy. It implies that the necessary condition for attracting higher volume of FDI is the higher growth rate of gross domestic product in the region.

(2) While the first hypothesis shows the necessary condition for inflow of FDI in a region, this may not be sufficient. The sufficient condition is the existence of both infrastructure in the region that can facilitate the profitable investment and a long term sustenance of the investment procedure. By infrastructure we put

emphasis on the way we have defined infrastructure in a qualitative way. It implies that while the existence of good physical infrastructure is important, the other aspects of non-physical infrastructure as explained before are also important.

We will test the above two hypotheses with the help of analysis through tables, diagrams and also with some rigorous analysis in the form of testing of models.

15.6 Data and Methodology

This study is based on secondary level data collected from the Ministry of Commerce and Industry and also Reserve Bank of India. While traditional method of analysis will be followed, a small model also will be tested with the help of simple method of econometrics. Charts and diagrams will supplement this.

In the following pages we try to test these two hypotheses both qualitatively and quantitatively on the basis of available data. The examples of other countries will be used as supplements, and the major focus will remain on India.

15.7 FDI: A Model in the Making

Foreign Direct Investment is one aspect of foreign capital flow in the domestic economy. In the open economy set-up, capital funds flow will maintain equilibrium by adjustment in the real variables in the external sectors.

In an open economy aggregate demand [AD] will be

$AD = C + I + G + X + T^*$, where, C, I, G, and X are consumption, investment, government expenditure and export respectively. T^* is transfer of funds abroad.

The aggregate supply [AS] will be

$AS = C + S + T + M + Tr^*$, where, C, S, M and T are consumption, savings, import and taxation respectively. Tr^* is the funds transfer inflow in the country.

Using traditional macro-economic assumptions that government budget is balanced, which means G=T, and consumption plan is always satisfied, that means we can eliminate C from both sides we can write after *imposing equilibrium in the economy,*

$$I + X + T^* = S + M + Tr^*,$$

Or, $$T^* - Tr^* = (S - I) + (M - X)$$

Or, $$Tr^* - T^* = (I - S) + (X - M)$$ *Equation 15.1*

In our scheme of things, $Tr^* - T^*$ is the excess funds inflow into the country that can be taken as the foreign direct investment [FDI]. Both S and I are functions of income Y and rate of interest r. Again, X and M are functions of domestic price P, foreign price P* and exchange rate e. Also,

$$P = e \cdot P^*$$ *Equation 15.2*

From [1] we can write using functions,

$$FDI = \{I(Y, r) - S(Y, r)\} + \{X(P, e) - M(P, e)\}$$

Or, $$FDI = f(Y, r, e, P)$$ *Equation 15.3*

Since nominal exchange rate and price level move in the same direction [e is the price of foreign currency in terms of domestic currency], and nominal interest rate includes inflation expectations, keeping all the three — nominal interest rate, exchange rate and price level — may lead to multi-collinearity, a particular problem in econometrics when some of the independent variables are correlated among themselves. So we drop price level for the purpose of econometric estimation. So equation [15.3] in estimable form looks ~~like~~ [through logarithmic transformation],

$$Log\ FDI = a_0 + a_1 \log Y + a_2 \log e + a_3 r + u$$ *Equation 15.4*

Theoretical value will be $a_1 > 0,\ a_2 < 0,\ a_3 > 0$

The estimation can be made in level form also. That shows the relative strength of different determinants of FDI in a developing country.

The variable Y will capture the importance of the absorption capacity of the economy. It is expected that a faster growth can absorb larger amount of capital, domestic or foreign, into the economy. The exchange rate takes care both the potential return and opportunity cost of investment. Again, the interest rate reveals the reference rate of the feasible return on capital and also the cost of domestic capital.

15.8 Empirical Exercise

The data on FDI in India can be had only from 1991 onwards and as such the data base is weak. We have taken the time series 1991 to 1997 for the econometric estimation of the model (Equation 15.4). The results for India and Malaysia are placed below. We find that the coefficient of log e gives wrong sign though the t-value is not satisfactory. Other coefficients are of correct signs.

Indian case of regression results

Dependent Variable: FDI				
Method: Least Squares				
Date: 07/06/00 Time: 17:10				
Sample: 1991 1997				
Included observations: 7				
Variable	Coefficient	Std. Error	t-Statistic	Prob.
C	-9973.503	5568.279	-1.791128	0.1712
GDP	0.00696	0.008616	0.807765	0.4783
LR	143.4031	206.9004	0.693102	0.5382
ER	212.8466	130.8458	1.626697	0.2023
R-squared	0.943273	Mean dependent var		1431.571
Adjusted R-squared	0.886545	S.D. dependent var		1307.848
S.E. of regression	440.5233	Akaike info criterion		15.30936
Sum squared resid	582182.2	Schwarz criterion		15.27845
Log likelihood	-49.58277	F-statistic		16.62815
Durbin-Watson stat	1.708655	Prob(F-statistic)		0.022543

The same analysis is applied in case of Malaysia and the results are as follows:

15.9 Technology Transfer, Capital Formation and International Trade

Foreign Trade Investment is associated with large multinational corporations (MNCs). Economic theory explains how Foreign Direct Investment (FDI) induces the firms for international operations. For this, the relationship between FDI and MNCs is very strong. In the context of FDI, the overseas expansion of a firm is determined by three factors and these are—ownership advantages, location advantages and internalization of incentives. A firm wishing to operate abroad should possess adequate advantages so that it can offset the handicap of working in an alien atmosphere and also cover for higher risk. The advantages mentioned come from the ownership of proprietary intangible assets possessed by the firm and this can be employed abroad in an efficient manner. These intangible assets include brand goodwill, technology

Table 1: Malaysia

Year	Direct Investment Million USD	GDP Million USD	Lending Rate	Exchange Rate
1984	6510	32737	11.35	2.43
1985	7388	31912	11.54	2.43
1986	6111	27536	10.69	2.6
1987	6806	31978	8.19	2.49
1988	7054	33405	7.25	2.72
1989	8096	37945	7	2.7
1990	10318	42852	7.17	2.7
1991	12440	48669	8.13	2.72
1992	16860	56911	9.31	2.61
1993	20591	61187	9.05	2.7
1994	22916	74326	7.61	2.56
1995	—	86091	7.63	2.54
1996	—	98618	8.89	2.53
1997	—	70788	9.53	3.89
1998	—	—	10.61	3.8

Dependent Variable: FDI				
Method: Least Squares				
Date: 07/17/00 Time: 12:01				
Sample(adjusted): 1986, 1994				
Included observations: 9 after adjusting endpoints				
Variable	Coefficient	Std. Error	t-Statistic	Prob.
C	-11709.42	10544.32	-1.110495	0.3173
GDP	0.378765	0.028102	13.47845	0
LR	303.9656	223.4611	1.360262	0.2319
ER	1375.409	3515.937	0.391193	0.7118
R-squared	0.977099	Mean dependent variable		9064.778
Adjusted R-squared	0.963358	S.D. dependent variable		3568.531
S.E. of regression	683.0949	Akaike info criterion		16.19225
Sum squared resid	2333093	Schwarz criterion		16.2799
Log likelihood	-68.86511	F-statistic		71.10889
Durbin-Watson stat	1.429221	Prob (F-statistic)		0.00016

management skills, access to cheaper sources of raw materials and capital etc. The firm may exploit these advantages through exports from the home base in the initial stage. Later production facility is created abroad to cater to the foreign market. This practice is to exploit other advantages like tariffs and quantitative restrictions imposed by host countries, transport and communication cost and cheaper input prices.

Many factors like imperfect market, licensing of intangible assets and also internalization of incentives available on local production led to the inflow of FDI in 1970s. The nature of FDI flows changed with the improvement of communication and advancement of information technology. Whenever cost of market transactions of intangible assets become very high, firms tend to avoid these costs by internalizing the transactions of the intangible assets. This is done through Foreign Direct Investment also.

Literature also reveals that exporting commodities directly from the home base and production of the same in foreign countries to serve the foreign markets either through licensing or Foreign Direct Investment are two alternative modes of overseas operations. From this angle it becomes obvious that if trade liberalization becomes extreme, the locational advantage of the country for the local market may be lost.

15.10 Inter-Industry Variation in FDI

The hypothesis that some industries in the host country could contract more FDI than others has been tested empirically in the literature. These studies have ignored the possibility of discrimination in licensing and have concentrated on behaviour of FDI regarding its destination to particular industries. The common elements of the study include FDI intensity to vary positively with the intensity of advertisement, skill intensity, R&D expenditure, capital output ratio and certain other factors. Also in the absence of any particular strong policy factor, the choice between FDI and licensing will be determined by the transaction cost. Since transaction cost are quite high for branded consumer goods, there a pronounced tendency that FDI will concentrate in those industries. This finding has one implication and this is as follows:

A developing country with the desire to contract more FDI should follow a liberalization policy in such a way that it makes the effects of intangible asset and internalization incentives to be more pronounced.

FDI and Economic Growth: There is a common hypothesis in the literature that higher rate of Gross Domestic Product leads to a higher inflow of FDI. The literature also compares the relative productivity of FDI *vis-à-vis* domestic capital. So far as FDI increases the availability of capital, this should increase the rate of growth of GDP. Thus we have a circularity and it is whether higher growth rate leads to higher inflow of FDI, or higher inflow FDI leads to higher growth rate. This is a standard causality problem in econometrics literature. Many studies have empirically tried to see the direction of causality and result is a mixed one.

15.11 Indian Economy and Foreign Capital

The domination of foreign capital in the Indian industrial scene just before independence was the result of history. Foreign capital in general and British capital in particular, played a crucial role in the development of jute textiles and engineering industries in the Indian sub-continent. The philosophy of economic development to be pursued in post independent India had changed radically and it was thought that least importance should be attached to the role of foreign capital in India's economic growth. The result was a socialist pattern of industrial development based on self-sufficiency.

The import-substitution and inward looking industrialization led to minimum role of foreign capital and the paucity of foreign exchange induced the authority to enact the stringent law like Foreign Exchange Regulation Act (FERA), 1973. The strictness of this piece of legislation had been responsible for much of capital flight from India in the seventies and eighties. Indian planners were so much immersed with self-delusion that they could not believe the reality of capital flight until the national coffer became almost empty in 1990. The gravity of the situation changed the whole perspective and the paradigm shift happened. This led to the attempt of economic reforms.

15.12 Foreign Direct Investment and Development

The political economy of the role of FDI in the development process of an economy is full of controversy. The arguments are on both sides. Those who advocate a more liberal regime claim that FDI will provide the much-needed resources and foreign exchange for reviving Indian industry, improve the crumbling infrastructure, and allow India to modernize its technological base. Also greater competition in Indian manufacturing will benefit the Indian consumer. On the other hand, critics point to the poor record of multinational corporations in India, their excessive profitability. Also they argue about the adverse impact of profit remittances on India's balance of payments.

Does foreign investment contribute to growth? Empirical investigation does not offer any clear answer. Countries like China have experienced large FDI inflows and high growth in recent years, while Korea grew rapidly without significant levels of foreign capital. In Latin America, many countries have periods of slow growth despite openness to foreign capital. Even if we did find some positive correlation between FDI and growth, the issue of causality remains unresolved.

15.13 Technology: Policy and Reality

Host country governments often encourage foreign investment in the hope of improving the productivity of domestic firms. Foreign Direct Investment potentially brings new technologies to the host economy. Technology inflows can also improve the productivity of domestic firms through 'spillovers', as better production and management techniques diffuse in the host economy. In some situations foreign investment can be a catalyst for growth. The literature isolates two channels for this spillover process. The more disembodies aspects of superior technologies used by foreign firms can spread to domestic firms through the mobility of trained workers and managers, and through technical guidance provided.

15.14 FDI: A Segmented Analysis

In the following paragraphs we will explain the current position of FDI in India in different parts. This method of analysis will help us to have an in depth analysis of dynamics of the flow of FDI in different sectors of the economy.

A Macro View

The source countries from which FDI flows into Indian economy are large in number but the major partners are the USA, the European Union countries and couple of countries in Asia like Japan, South Korea, Singapore, Hong Kong and Mauritius. An interesting phenomenon is that even after the accession of Hong Kong to mainland China, capital has followed from Hong Kong into India. All the European Union countries, particularly countries like UK, Germany, France and Netherlands are important source countries of FDI. As a single country outside EU block, Japan is very important as a source country.

Table 1 reveals that though the number of countries from which FDI flows into India is impressive, only a handful of countries are important as the source of FDI inflow. Some countries are reluctant to make investment in India, Taiwan is an example. Non-resident Indians (NRI) is a category in Table 1 and the fact revealed in the Table is that the contribution of NRI in the FDI investment in India is not impressive.

15.15 Sectorwise Inflow

The flow of FDI in different sectors of Indian economy is not uniform and some sectors have been able to attract large volume of FDI. From this angle the important sectors are: metallurgical industries, electrical instrument, telecommunication, chemicals, drugs and textiles, pharmaceuticals, textiles, paper and paper pulp and food processing industries. In Tables 2 & 3, sector wise approvals and actual incomes are revealed. Table 4 keeps sector wise inflow as a percentage of approval. Table 5 is derived from Table 4 in an aggregate form for the period 1991 to 1998. One interesting aspect of Table 5 is that in some particular sectors the inflow as a percent of approval are pretty large like drugs and pharmaceuticals (93%), mechanical engineering (61%) trading (46%). But in most other areas the percentage is low like telecommunication, fuel, metallurgical industry, photographic films and other materials, soaps and cosmetics, consultancy services etc. A very low percentage in these sectors require further research and case studies to understand the nature of the problem in the implementation stage of the project.

15.16 Nature of FDI Inflow

As indicated earlier the nature of FDI inflow into India is not uniform of the two routes of FDI inflow, automatic route and Government route. There has been a steady rise from 1991–1997, but after that there has been a perspective decline of inflow to FDI into India. This aspect revealed in Exhibit 1 should be investigated for the factors responsible for the deceleration of FDI inflows into India from 1997. The same picture in a different format is presented in Exhibit 3.

Between the two routes of FDI inflow into India the Government route is predominant as the percentage of volume through the Government route is much higher compared to the automatic route. This aspect is revealed in Exhibit 2.

Though the number of source countries from which FDI inflows into India happens is impressive, the principal sources are; USA, UK, Japan, Germany, France, South Korea, Mauritius and NRI. This aspect has been revealed in Exhibit 4.

Actual inflow of FDI as a percentage of total approval for the period 1991-1999 is not uniform country wise and this interesting aspect is revealed in Exhibit 5. We note that the percentage is quite high for countries like Russia, Netherlands, Mauritius and Hong Kong. But countries like UK, USA,

Exhibit 1: FDI Inflows into India

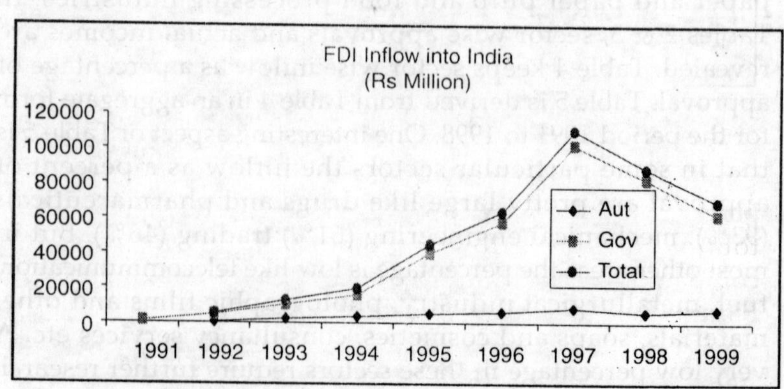

Exhibit 2: Shares of Automatic Route and Government Route in the Total Inflow of FDI

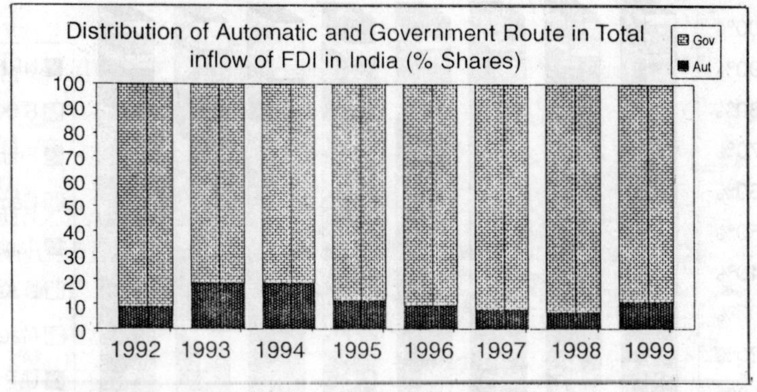

Exhibit 3: FDI in India — Approved to Actual

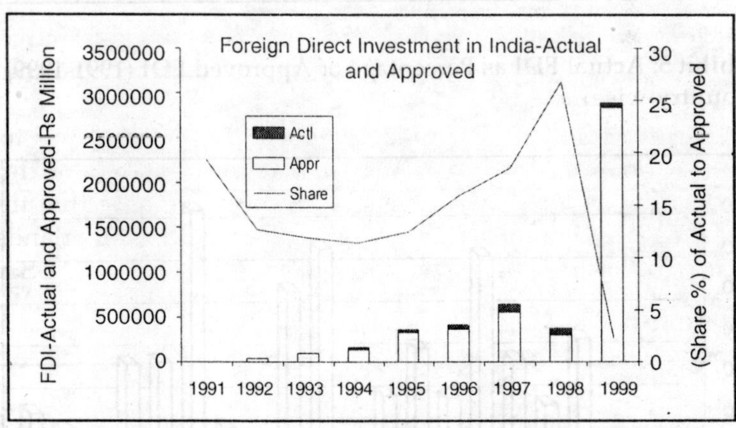

Canada depict very low percentage of actual inflow as a percentage of the total approval. One explanation may be that total volume of inflow from these countries is very high compared to other countries that register higher percentage, but this fails to give the total explanation.

We have seen earlier that FDI inflows in major sectors in India during the period 1991–1999 is not uniform and the dis-

Exhibit 4: FDI Inflow into India from Select Company

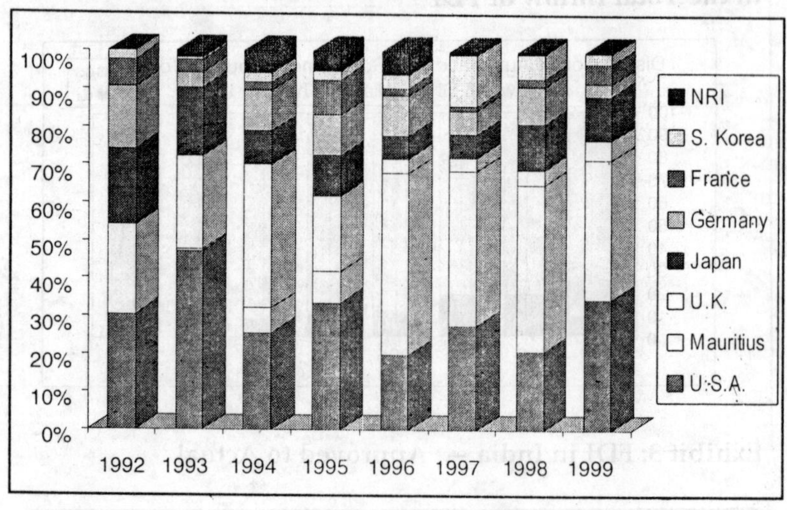

Exhibit 5: Actual FDI as Percentage of Approved FDI (1991-1999) (Country-wise)

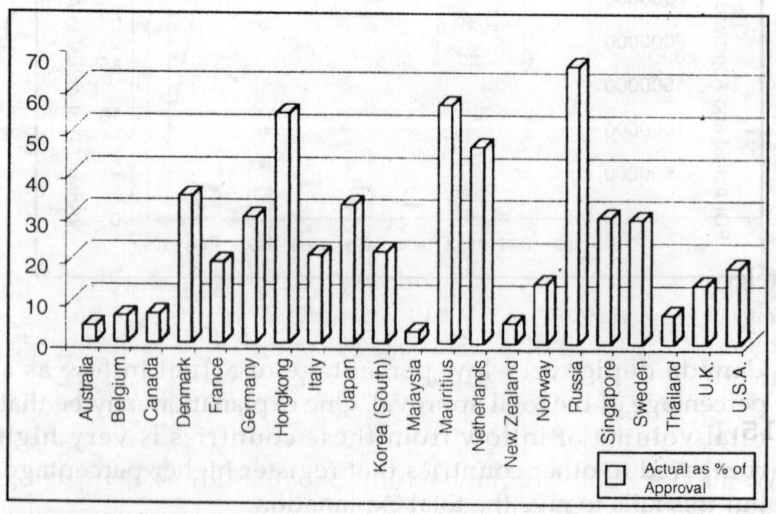

tribution is very skewed. This is revealed in Exhibit 6. We see that while transportation industry 7.3%, computes to

Exhibit 6: FDI Inflows (1991-1999) in Major Sectors

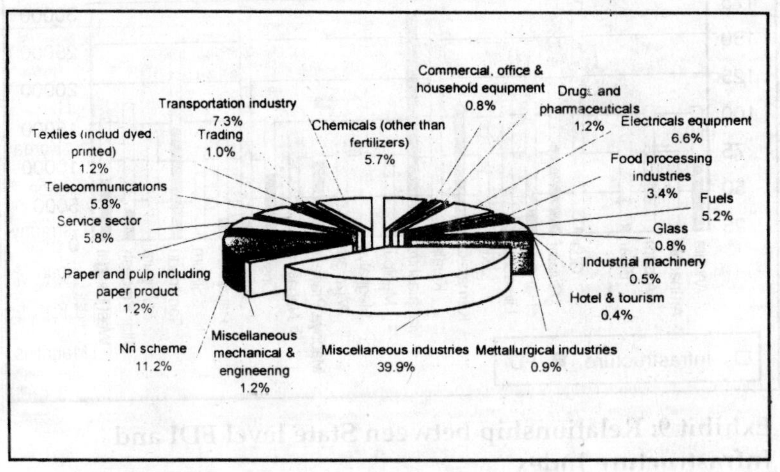

Exhibit 7: FDI (Approved and Inflow)

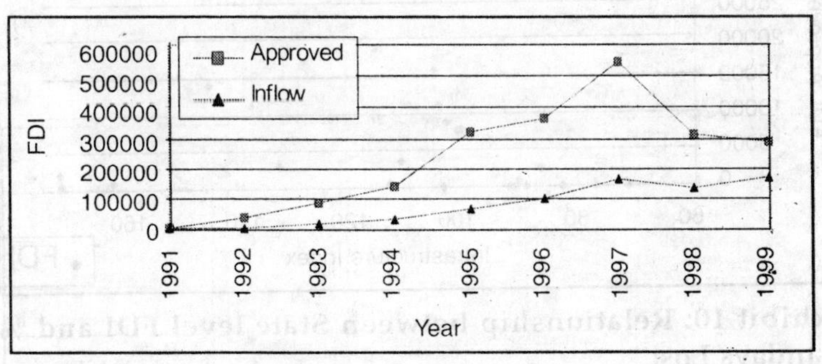

telecommunication 5.8%, service sector 5.8%, chemicals 5.7%, electrical equipment 6.7% and fuels 5.2%, other things like hotel and tourism, trading, industry machinery etc., have failed to attract sizeable FDI inflow.

15.17 Infrastructure and FDI Inflow

We have mentioned in the hypothesis that infrastructure is a condition for FDI inflow. We have bifurcated infrastructure into two parts; physical infrastructure and subjective

Exhibit 8:

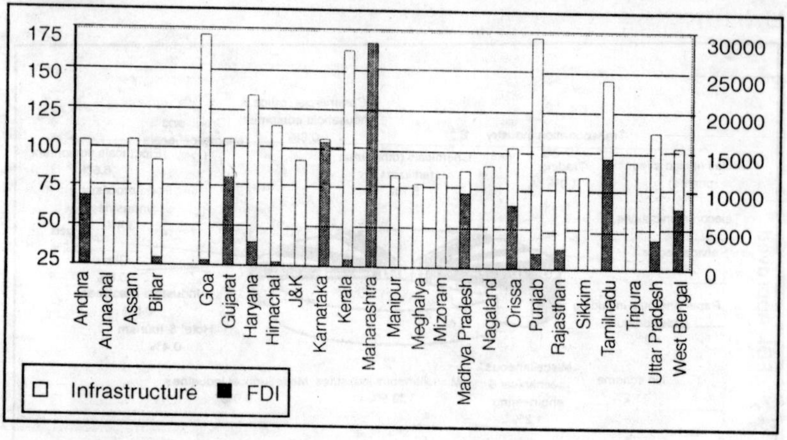

Exhibit 9: Relationship between State level FDI and Infrastructure Index

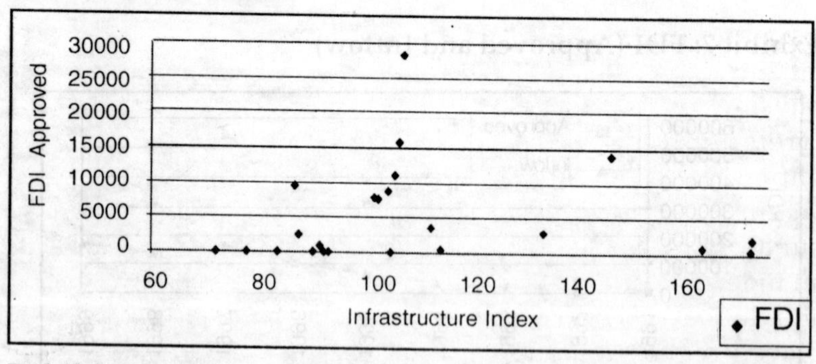

Exhibit 10: Relationship between State level FDI and % mandays Lost

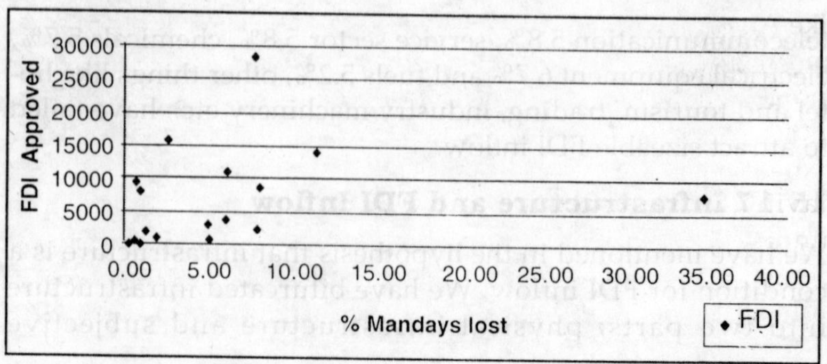

Exhibit 11: Relationship between State level FDI and Urbanisation Growth

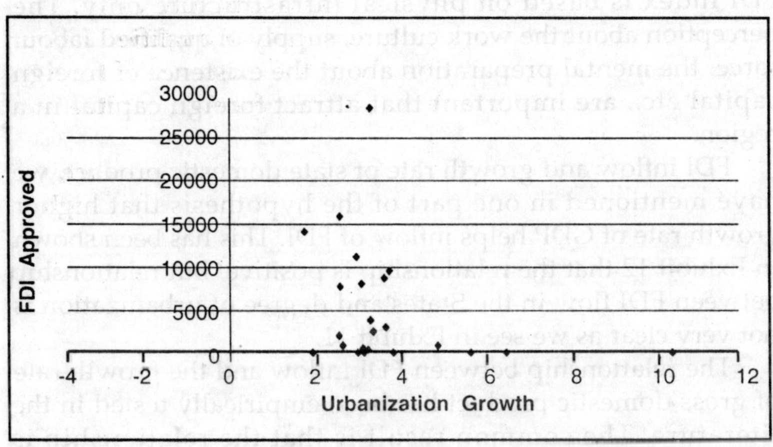

infrastructure. We maintained that while the existence of both physical and subjective infrastructure is necessary to attract foreign direct investment, it may not be sufficient if the important elements of qualitative aspect of infrastructure are lagging. This interesting proposition has been confirmed by our analysis of data taking from the States. CMIE has compiled an index of infrastructure for all the States. The average is 100 and the States whose indices are above 100 are termed as better placed regarding the existence of physical infrastructure. Following this criteria the States are: Goa, Haryana, Himachal Pradesh, Kerala, Maharashtra, Punjab, Tamil Nadu. The States like Andhra, Assam, Gujarat, Karnataka, Orissa, Uttar Pradesh and West Bengal are just above 100 so far as the infrastructure indices are concerned, it is important to mention that CMIE indices are based on physical infrastructure only. We find from Exhibit 8 that the States like Goa, Haryana, Kerala and Punjab having good infrastructure have failed to attract sufficient amount of FDI. But States like Andhra, Orissa and West Bengal, though relatively weak in infrastructure have been able to attract sizeable amount of FDI. The relationship between infrastructure index and State level FDI is also shown in exhibit 9. The lack of clear trend is due to the fact that the FDI index is based on physical infrastructure only. The perception about the work culture, supply of qualified labour force, the mental preparation about the existence of foreign capital etc., are important that attract foreign capital in a region.

FDI inflow and growth rate of state domestic product, we have mentioned in one part of the hypothesis that higher growth rate of GDP helps inflow of FDI. This has been shown in Exhibit 12 that the relationship is positive. But relationship between FDI flow in the States and degree of urbanization is not very clear as we see in Exhibit 11.

The relationship between FDI inflow and the growth rate of gross domestic product has been empirically tested in the literature. The common result is that the relationship is positive. But the issue whether higher growth of GDP causes higher inflow of FDI, or higher inflow of FDI causes higher growth of GDP, is a question of causality. The answer to this complex question requires sophisticated treatment of empirical data that has not been done here. We have tested the simple model to determine the empirical influence of the growth rate of State domestic product and the infrastructure index. The

Exhibit 12: Relation between State level FDI and SDP Growth rate

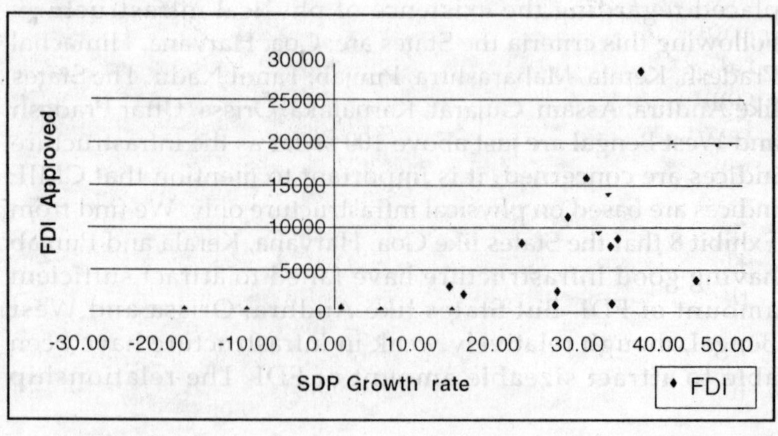

result is reported and we find that the effects are positive. This proves our initial hypothesis to be correct.

15.18 A Quantitative Exercise to Ascertain the Role of Infrastructure

In earlier section we have estimated a model to determine the quantitative effects of some macro variables on the inflow of FDI in India and other countries. That was basically a time series study. Since in the second section we are more concerned about the role of infrastructure in the inflow of FDI in different states of India, we use here a different model and test the model on cross section data.

We have developed a model for the quantitative estimation of the effects of some economic variables like GDP, infrastructure, exchange rate and interest rate. We have estimated the model both at the level terms and by logarithmic terms. The latter enables us to get the elasticities of the relevant variables as the effects on the inflow of FDI. This is a cross-section data and so the problem of auto-correlation is not relevant. Also we have checked the potential problem of heteroskedasticity and this problem does not exist.

The following two tables show the results of regressions. These are based on the cross-section data of 26 states in India that are shown in Exhibit 8. We see that both infrastructure and growth rates of state level domestic products have coefficients that are statistically significant. Also adjusted R^2 0.447 approximately. Thus both infrastructure and GDP growth rates can explain the inflow of FDI in the regions. Our comment on heteroskedasticity is based on the figure in Table E2 that shows the plot of residuals against the infrastructure indices.

15.19 Conclusion

The developing countries will need FDI inflow to supplement the inadequate domestic savings in face of growing requirement of capital to maintain a crucial rate of economic growth so that the people below the poverty line can be lifted within a reasonable time. We have seen that the share of FDI

Table E1. Regression: Level Terms

Dependent Variable: FDI

Method: Least Squares

Sample: 1 26

Included observations: 23

Excluded observations: 3

Variable	Coefficient	Std. Error	t-Statistic	Prob.
C	-671.7450	2098.041	-0.320177	0.7522
INFRASTR	40.58214	10.48555	3.870290	0.0010
SDPGR	114.1215	45.86812	2.488036	0.0218

R-squared	0.497407	Mean dependent var	6397.589
Adjusted R-squared	0.447148	S.D. dependent var	8733.885
S.E. of regression	6493.995	Akaike info criterion	20.51625
Sum squared resid	8.43E+08	Schwarz criterion	20.66436
Log likelihood	-232.9369	F-statistic	9.896823
Durbin-Watson stat	2.834082	Prob (F-statistic)	0.001028

inflow in the developing countries is very much high, with some countries like China have been able to attract huge amount on foreign capital. Though the comparison with China regarding the inflow of FDI is not truly justified, India should have been able to attract the relatively larger volume of Foreign Capital than what she has done so far. In the earlier paragraphs attempts have been made to point out the factors which are responsible for the inflow of FDI. In certain quarters studies have been made to analyze the nature of FDI inflow in developing countries particularly in South Asian and Latin American countries. Filtering down the studies available in the literature help us to identify certain factors, which are also relevant in Indian situation. We should be clear that some of these variables are qualitative in nature and those are mentioned often in academic literature to Thailand. But China

Table E2: Regression: Residual Plot

obs	Actual	Fitted	Residual	Residual Plot
1	8685.40	7501.23	1184.17	| . |* . |
2	11.0600	142.445	-131.385	| . * . |
3	1.49000	5210.26	-5208.77	| .* | . |
4	831.180	6907.09	-6075.91	| .* | . |
5	30267.6	29967.8	299.821	| . * . |
6	502.260	-5121.22	5623.48	| . |* . |
7	11083.5	6871.21	4212.25	| . |* . |
8	2938.81	6337.38	-3398.57	| . * | . |
9	360.310	4035.34	-3675.03	| . * | . |
10	8.41000	3719.23	-3710.82	| . * | . |
11	15820.2	7165.75	8654.43	| . | . * |
12	808.020	9005.45	-8197.43	| *. | . |
13	28467.8	7939.63	20528.1	| . | . *|
14	3.19000	1641.84	-1638.65	| . *| . |
15	52.9600	1255.19	-1202.23	| . *| . |
17	9491.51	6539.22	2952.29	| . | * . |
19	7986.74	6063.26	1923.48	| . |* . |
20	1926.62	8111.68	-6185.06	| * | . |
21	2441.15	5991.08	-3549.93	| . *| . |
23	14059.9	9066.60	4993.32	| . |* . |
24	0.68000	2525.70	-2525.02	| . *| . |
25	3707.99	8937.51	-5229.52	| .* | . |
26	7687.81	7330.87	356.935	| . * . |

is an example how export orientation can be properly utilized to attract foreign capital and also to maximize the growth process. Not only that China has been able to use FDI on a selective basis to maximize the rate of growth, but China has one unique advantage, which India is lacking and this should be mentioned to keep the comparison straight.

China is lucky to have two highly developed regions like Hong Kong and Taiwan. The first it has obtained from the United Kingdom in 1997 and a large chunk of FDI in China is

Table E3. Regression: Log Transformation

Dependent Variable: LOG(FDI)
Method: Least Squares
Sample: 1 26
Included observations: 18
Excluded observations: 8

Variable	Coefficient	Std. Error	t-Statistic	Prob.
C	-5.995820	6.406615	-0.935879	0.3642
LOG(INFRASTR)	1.999758	1.199575	1.667055	0.1162
LOG(SDPGR)	1.377390	0.597440	2.305488	0.0358
R-squared	0.311402	Mean dependent var		7.703807
Adjusted R-squared	0.219589	S.D. dependent var		2.662105
S.E. of regression	2.351727	Akaike info criterion		4.699189
Sum squared resid	82.95928	Schwarz criterion		4.847584
Log likelihood	-39.29270	F-statistic		3.391699
Durbin-Watson stat	2.421010	Prob(F-statistic)		0.060918

from Hong Kong. Taiwan is a breakaway province of China and in spite of political row, Taiwan invests huge amount of capital in China. Apart from these two highly developed regions and a large supplier of foreign capital China has a large ethnic Diaspora in South Asian countries. This group is financially very rich and they invest huge amount in the mainland.

These two factors i.e. the existence of Hong Kong and Taiwan and a large Chinese Diaspora having strong economic linkage make China unique among the developing countries regarding the inflow of FDI. This is true in spite of a political regime which is totally opposite of the capitalist system. This aspect is interesting. China has become a capitalist economic system with a totalitarian political set-up as only Chinese Communist Party is the legitimate political party there.

The inflow of FDI is sometimes associated with the level of technological development in the country. In this case again the China example should be mentioned. So long as foreign capital is flowing in and particularly in areas where China is lacking, the Chinese authority is not bothered about the type of technology the foreign investor is bringing. The system is regimented and it has ruled out a debate in political circles which are very common in a democratic set up in India. This type of system has been found to be very suitable for the foreign investors. South Korea also has been able to import modern technology in crucial industries so that it can maintain competitive edge in the export front.

Sometimes the export performance requirements are tagged with the inflow of FDI and authority of developing countries puts emphasis on this aspect. On this point several questions are important.

1. How well do international markets work in apportioning FDI in line with comparative advantage?

2. What investment diverting actions are being taken by other countries to set a location of international manufacturing production in their own directions?

3. What obstacles inhibit international markets from functioning more effectively?

These questions are crucial to understand the nature of FDI inflow in developing countries. It is a fact that the developing countries are competing among themselves to attract foreign capital.

Sometimes the location issue also becomes important for the inflow of FDI and the nature of industry becomes related to that. Some particular industries like automobile, petrochemical and electronics are mentioned for the initial phase of investment. The sources of inputs and location of cheap labour becomes important sometimes in the determination of location of particular industries.

Another important issue has surfaced in a study related to the dynamism of FDI in developing countries. While the host government tries to convince the international investor to commit capital to develop a new production side, a country would have to spend more resources to build up a infrastructure so that foreign firm's commitment remains. But the concern of the host country does not end here. Literature in this particular areas has identified five broad categories of concern in developing countries which are in the process of transition:

1. Cultural Factors (worker's motivation, cultural preparation)
2. Labour regulations (Flexibility in hiring and laying off of workers)
3. Responsiveness of the surrounding economy in providing supporting goods and services
4. Institutional base of commercial law to give guidance when dispute arises
5. The credibility of public sector commitments about taxes, infrastructure and other regulatory issues.

Literature also reveals the concern of foreign investors regarding the credibility of promises of the host government and the institutional factors like the judicial systems of security. These are the pattern of information gap which the foreign companies desire to bridge in order to evaluate the returns associated with the investment opportunity. The MNCs are most often oligopolies and the countries where they are having head quarters behave also as oligopolies. They introduce entry barriers and transfer knowledge only when it becomes a public good. In most cases technological knowledge is strictly kept under control. This practice prevents dissemination of latest technology in the host country. In this case experience of all the countries is not the same.

Annexures

Table 1: Total FDI (Approvals and Inflows)

(Value in Rs. Million)

Country Name	App. 1991	Inflow 1991	App. 1992	Inflow 1992	App. 1993	Inflow 1993	App. 1994	Inflow 1994	App. 1995	Inflow 1995	App. 1996	Inflow 1996	App. 1997	Inflow 1997	App. 1998	Inflow 1998	App. 1999	Inflow 1999	App. Total	Inflow Total
Argentina	0	0	0	0	0	0	0	0	0	0	183.8	0	0.2	0.38	0	0	0	0	184	0.38
Australia	26.1	0	776.2	0.19	295.6	23.98	3885	18.81	15042.2	327.27	8344.32	515.89	4316.72	213.18	26377.2	593.78	6489.62	870.52	65552.46	2563.64
Austria	15.9	0	61.4	34.57	155.7	15.06	249.7	8.04	296.1	41.14	828.08	310.66	258.94	157.77	554.79	133.68	326.77	3.1	2747.37	704.03
Bahrain	0	0	4	0	4.1	0	48.4	17.53	0	8.95	530.2	2.95	6	2.47	633	26.5	641.97	673.05	1867.67	731.44
Belgium	16.1	0	237	20.23	60	7.32	76.6	102.26	1659	76.82	1947.14	11.4	2163.27	1648.81	32887.7	116.82	139.96	496.87	39186.8	2480.52
Belorussia	0	0	0	0	0.5	0	0	23.77	0	0	0	0	0	0	0	0	0	0	0.5	23.77
Bermuda	0	0	33.2	42.67	0	12.52	260.3	14.2	207.2	190.15	1765.2	0	237.31	300	2660.5	402.5	158.54	57.43	5322.25	1019.47
Brazil	0.1	0	1.1	0	0	0	0	0.11	0	22.97	0	0	0	0	5.1	0	0	0	6.3	23.09
Canada	48.6	0	7.8	0	272.8	14.37	420.8	0.5	13735.6	141.76	1965.42	257 38	3842.64	395.92	3156.79	395.63	368.42	450.46	23818.87	1656.02
Cayman Isld	0	0	0	0	33	0	35	30	0	0	86.9	0	36058.8	0	5	0	108.4	0	36327.1	30
Channel isld	0	0	0	20	0	0	12.5	0	20	0	0.7	1.56	67.5	0	20	0	0	0	120.7	21.56
China	7.5	0	0	1.35	616.6	0	272.5	0	5810.6	0.18	139.73	0	3.6	15.4	68	2	210.85	0.04	7129.38	18.98
Cyprus	0	0	0	0	0	0	0.3	2.59	4.5	4.09	0	166.71	60.69	196.89	70	434.34	68.36	169.96	203.85	974.59
Czech Rep.	0	0	0	0	4.4	0	0	4.2	20.7	0.7	0	0	70	5.75	450	35.28	2352	124.85	2897.1	170.77
Denmark	111.7	12.2	252.3	8.81	319.9	36.01	533	49.4	1224.7	751.86	729.01	436.77	1067.15	200.49	295.41	66.46	761.65	271.63	5294.84	1833.64
Egypt	0	0	0	0	0	0	0	0	0	0	12.03	3.15	0	0	3.15	0	0	0	3.15	15.18
Estonia	0	0	0	0	70	0	0	0	3.1	31	0	0	0	0	0	3.1	0	0	73.1	34.1
Finland	25.3	0	105	105.8	20.7	23.91	103.7	14.82	131.9	111.87	539.62	100.13	1186.97	200.38	495	0.07	2.92	99.47	2611.12	656.45

(Contd.)

Annexures

Table 1 (Contd.): Total FDI (Approvals and Inflows)

(Value in Rs. Million)

Country Name	App. 1991	Inflow 1991	App. 1992	Inflow 1992	App 1993	Inflow 1993	App. 1994	Inflow 1994	App. 1995	Inflow 1995	App. 1996	Inflow 1996	App. 1997	Inflow 1997	App. 1998	Inflow 1998	App. 1999	Inflow 1999	App. Total	Inflow Total
France	193.3	60.6	296.4	267.0	1290.9	314.3	897.3	292.98	4203.6	2405.24	16716.9	961.96	7134.12	1123.14	5135.57	1588.24	14486.17	2624.94	50354.3	9638.43
Germany	418	65.4	862.7	612.5	1759.3	401.5	5694	1396.53	13394.9	2370.8	15378.9	4726.48	21558.14	5686.84	8537.58	6269.21	11429.46	1981.54	79032.6	23510.8
Gibraltar	0	0	0	0	0	0	0	0	0	0	0	0	0	0	0	0	7	7	7	7
Greece	0	0	0	0	0	0	0	0	6	0	0	0	0	80.08	0	15.4	14.4	0	20.4	95.48
Hong Kong	211.5	12.7	570.8	124.3	879.5	252.9	1648	687.79	4071.7	3348.26	5078.81	1669.31	2585.7	1509.06	2380.25	1909.19	441.36	159.85	17867.42	9673.31
Hungary	0	0	0	0	22.7	0	1.6	0	0	1.78	0	4.25	0	0	10	0	0	0	34.3	6.03
Ice Land	0	0	0	0	0	0	0	0	0	0	3.41	0	10.05	0	0	9.73	0	0	13.46	9.73
Indonesia	0	0	19	0	3.8	0	0	0	3133	0	375	32.46	105	80	294	79.89	0	40.11	3929.8	232.46
Iran	0	0	0	240.6	0	35.4	0	0	0	70	109.8	0	0	0	600	278.6	1.5	0	711.3	624.6
Ireland	0	0	0.1	0.89	1656.4	8.68	64.1	75.52	312.6	41.3	63.57	35.7	228.3	13.44	42.7	15.36	64.11	26.7	2431.88	217.59
Isle Of Man	0	0	0	0	0	0	0	4.5	7.3	0	2.42	9.28	0	0	1560	0	0	7.2	1569.72	20.98
Israel	0	0	12.7	0	14.6	6.51	85.2	6.26	41372.2	14.18	150.49	55.5	514.16	1220.72	120.8	42.65	77.33	31.81	42347.48	1377.62
Italy	178.1	24.0	893.9	46.48	1173.5	53.98	3909	69.47	4603.4	320.48	1388.76	698.44	11949.96	1134.05	2783.53	4291.33	17594.76	2582.38	44475.3	9220.65
Japan	527.1	55.8	6102	716.5	2574.3	810.0	4009	2758.14	15142.6	2271.66	14882.5	3008.28	19063.5	5911.39	12828.2	7805.56	15947.28	6356.38	91076.81	29693.65
Jordon	0	0	0	0	0	0	0	0	0	0	0.06	0	0	0.09	20	0	2.5	0	22.56	0.09
Korea(S)	61.5	0	394	83.89	293.3	64.75	1069	336.13	3141.9	522.24	32209.2	1587.41	19559.76	12279.58	3683.54	4389.06	36489.3	1657.79	96901.01	20920.85
Kuwait	0	0	0.9	0	0.5	0.44	345.9	2.47	1500	0	2600	0.3	1393.54	35.74	2	40.14	0.77	0.19	5843.6	79.28
Liechtenstei	0	1.48	0	0	0	0	0	2.96	0	1.24	0	4.75	308.74	43.42	0	0.08	0	0	308.74	53.93

(Contd.)

Annexures

Table 1 (Contd.): Total FDI (Approvals and Inflows)

(Value in Rs. Million)

Country Name	App. 1991	Inflow 1991	App. 1992	Inflow 1992	App. 1993	Inflow 1993	App. 1994	Inflow 1994	App. 1995	Inflow 1995	App. 1996	Inflow 1996	App. 1997	Inflow 1997	App. 1998	Inflow 1998	App. 1999	Inflow 1999	App. Total	Inflow Total
Luxmbourg	0	0	0	46.46	29	0	0	0	531.4	109.91	93.26	42.23	1737.22	19.05	6.4	192.53	65.55	13.16	2462.84	423.33
Malaysia	1.8	0	744.3	0	84.8	5.1	252.2	94.75	13860.9	209.4	423.31	120.23	21046.41	513.24	18031.0	380.12	1161.46	195.46	55606.2	1518.3
Maldives	0	0	0	0	0	0	6	0	0	0	0	0	0	0	3.7	0	3.07	1.54	12.77	1.54
Malta	0	0	1.3	0	0	0	0	1.25	0	0	0	0	0	0	0	0	0	0	1.3	1.25
Mauritius	0	0	0	0	1242.4	37.5	5347	903.22	18084.9	16380.1	23340.2	22768.3	104278.9	36643.22	31659.1	29020.2	38030.48	18906.4	221983.3	124659
Mexico	0	0	52.8	0	2389.8	0	0.1	0.06	81.6	0	0	0	0	0	0	0	0	0	2524.3	0.06
Nepal	0	0	0	0	0	0	0.2	0	0	0	30.1	0	0	5.04	0	0	0	0	30.3	5.04
Netherlands	559.2	15.0	967.9	148.4	3216.5	1611	2070	1489.12	9664.6	1237.6	10487.1	4693.9	8705.43	5236.78	4962.56	3719.89	6322.14	3591.58	46955.07	21743.34
New Zealand	0	0	3.2	0	0.5	0	0	0	503.3	133.35	371.35	0	0.51	0	1908.82	70	0	63.35	2787.68	133.35
Norway	3.8	0	9.2	2.03	26.7	1.91	3.2	35.62	48.1	3.61	68.77	41.68	91.73	21.91	246.41	26.15	452.68	1.64	950.59	134.54
NRI	197	0	4391.3	0	10433.2	175.71	4908.8	760.34	7097.1	1190.49	21906.97	2181.69	18171.79	658.41	7503.39	296.66	4548.08	103.46	79157.63	5366.76
Oman	0	0	0	0	5429.8	0.05	173.8	40	58.5	33.6	7.5	0	27.64	5.5	18.32	10.45	71.58	6	5787.14	95.59
Panama	0	0.01	0	54.93	25.5	6.5	0	4.8	0	0	0.5	0	6188.4	4.07	0	36.99	191.05	24.05	6405.45	131.34
Philippines	0	0	50	27.5	132.42	39.5	41	146.4	729.5	111.91	2836.84	0	49	929.42	0	610.14	0	0	3838.76	1864.88
Poland	0.4	0.4	0	0	1.5	0	0	3.1	16	0	32.98	0	0.75	0	100	0	0	1.91	151.63	5.41
Portugal	1.6	0	12	0	140	0	0	0	1735.6	0	0	0	42.3	0	0	12.56	7.53	7.5	1939.03	20.06
Qatar	0	0	45.3	0	0	0	0	0	0	0	0	0	270	0.03	0	0	0	0	315.3	0.03
Romania	0	0	0	0	0	0	0	0	0	0	20	0	0	0.71	0	0	0	0	20	0.71

(Contd.)

Annexures

Table 1 (Contd.): Total FDI (Approvals and Inflows)

(Value in Rs. Million)

Country Name	App. 1991	Inflow 1991	App. 1992	Inflow 1992	App. 1993	Inflow 1993	App. 1994	Inflow 1994	App. 1995	Inflow 1995	App. 1996	Inflow 1996	App. 1997	Inflow 1997	App. 1998	Inflow 1998	App. 1999	Inflow 1999	App. Total	Inflow Total
Russia	86.1	24.74	115.9	0.8	19.5	62.74	1056.9	65.93	1161.3	2.5	2.99	7.98	0.48	0	145.48	11	87.58	1572.93	2676.23	1748.63
Saudi Arabia	0	0	3.1	20	108.7	0.1	0	5.01	1.2	0	6094	0	61.79	0	584.68	396.35	1265.3	0.75	8118.77	422.21
Singapore	13.7	0	602.1	114.97	667.4	223.78	2655	172.71	9910.4	2431.72	3197.72	2220.16	8619.01	1346.99	7673.39	4071.82	8258.94	1811.04	41597.66	12393.18
Slovakia	0	0	0	0	0.5	0	0	0.25	0	0	0	0	0	0	0.8	0.8	0.25	0	1.55	1.05
South Africa	0	0.01	0	0	0	0	2.5	0	157.8	0	567.5	21	925.97	0	17077	0	250.86	0	18981.63	21.01
Spain	3.3	0	19.2	0	98	22.05	20.2	10.02	227.1	0.44	91.7	110.72	593.25	14.2	627.22	25.97	1810.35	66.93	3490.32	250.34
Sudan	0	0	0	0	0	0	0	0	0	0	0.25	0	0.05	0	0	0.25	0	0	0.3	0.25
Sweden	69.8	0	484.1	59.92	6.2	422.91	116.4	150.96	5022.5	536.26	5330.19	2087.13	1089.99	630.55	2154.25	388.02	2739.34	701	17012.77	4976.75
Switzerland	355	1.87	6897.6	544.43	4268	1073.58	483	930.59	3094.8	263.49	1597.53	2378.52	4936.63	942.35	2850.48	646.57	2912.14	1169.84	27395.18	7951.23
Syria	0	0	0	0	0	0	0	0	0	0	0	0	0	0	1.2	0	0	0.22	1.2	0.22
Taiwan	4.5	2.4	180	3	100.1	9.15	102	115.65	38.8	91.89	778.63	21.15	13.23	39.97	35.74	6.98	74.49	19.65	1327.49	309.84
Thailand	0	0	25.2	0	3684.2	0	99.8	17.94	19680.9	166.79	765.22	881.67	259.44	523.91	3.45	100.75	70	8	24588.21	1699.05
U.A.E.	2.2	0	64.5	7.5	4044.9	7.24	512.3	56.21	143.6	34.44	526.14	40.83	935.56	20.7	162.92	124.79	101.2	75.76	6493.33	367.47
U.K.	321	479.12	1176.7	871.78	6227.3	2422.7	12991.5	4967.58	17258.6	2236.82	15245.99	1809.37	44907.19	3323.18	32008.44	2208.52	29630.47	3959.95	159767.18	22279.01
U.S.A.	1858.5	277.67	12315	1148.28	34618.5	4527.72	34880.9	3731.16	70543.7	6769.51	100558.7	9484.26	135698.2	25780.72	35619.6	13710.95	35751.7	18112.05	461844.82	83542.33
Ukraine	0	0	8.4	0	2.8	0	4.5	0	0	4.02	40.15	0	33.57	0	0	0	0.42	0.86	89.85	4.88
West Indies	0	0	3	0	0	0	0.5	1.02	0	7.39	16	0	999.8	15.9	4185	22.12	1270	0	6474.3	46.43

Table 2: Sectorwise Approval of FDI

(Rs. Million)

Sectorwise Approvals	1991	1992	1993	1994	1995	1996	1997	1998	1999	Total
Metallurgical Industries	8.3	777.8	12565.3	9173.9	18442.3	23163.3	25167.2	22198.4	14001.5	125498.5
Fuels	23	15073.1	28225.4	38090.5	35614.7	57525.9	264326.1	138917.7	56734.7	634531.1
Boilers and Steam Generating Plants	7.2	1.2	538.3	34.7	384.5	134	66.5	13.8	286.4	1466.6
Prime Movers Other Than Electrical	0	0	0	22.5	153	358.9	128.9	250	4	917.3
Electricals Equipment	878.3	3689.8	6113.5	6922.5	10124.9	31221.9	21929.9	14274.9	25498.5	120654.2
Telecommunications	133.9	1190.7	469.8	164.4	178230.3	44362.1	71856	31001.3	39017.8	366426.3
Transportation Industry	201.1	1511	3046.7	12090.9	12897.3	28790.4	37900.7	15628.8	62207	174273.9
Industrial Machinery	450.8	634	868.4	6581.2	5810.8	1976.2	2181.8	1080.9	2694.2	22278.3
Machine Tools	43.9	67.3	107.3	188.9	213.6	740.8	1280.1	143.6	972.2	3757.7
Agricultural Machinery	0	55.5	0	1558	0.5	563.8	0	2163.4	7.3	4348.5
Earth-Moving Machinery	0.8	5.6	6	117.3	0	0	699.8	3.9	18.5	851.9
Miscellaneous Mechanical & Engineering	4.8	371.8	303.7	696.7	1140.6	2956.6	3833.2	1892.7	2753	13953.1
Commercial, Office & Household Equipment	0	637.7	90.8	87.1	2096.1	1575	2523.1	2808	853.3	10671.1
Medical and Surgical Appliances	2.8	36.3	81.5	64.3	1521.6	28.6	424.7	258.5	38.4	2456.7

(Contd.)

Table 2 (Contd.): Sectorwise Approval of FDI

(Rs. Million)

Sectorwise Approvals	1991	1992	1993	1994	1995	1996	1997	1998	1999	Total
Industrial Instruments	19	148.1	16.9	8.4	421.2	425.1	118	9.1	49.4	1215.2
Scientific Instruments	15.4	327.7	1.9	3.4	119.1	17.8	117.7	11.4	3	617.4
Mathematical, Surveying and Drawing	0	0	0	0	1.2	0	2.5	380	0	383.7
Fertilizers	10	0	16.6	9.9	0	2420.4	12	0	0	2468.9
Chemicals (Other Than Fertilizers)	1358.2	4292.6	3701.2	14486.9	11754.9	30298.9	28271.8	18137.3	8104.1	120405.9
Photographic Raw Film and Paper	0	79	107.3	20	42.5	3	1962.7	0	83.3	2297.8
Dye-Stuffs	0	0.8	21.7	37	197.8	45.1	28.9	735.9	45	1112.2
Drugs and Pharmaceuticals	8	291.1	299.1	1629.6	1869.7	1182.1	1828.9	911.4	797.8	8817.7
Textiles (Includ Dyed, Printed)	141.3	962.6	787.6	9742.1	4002.4	4154.3	5953.2	2325.5	3227.6	31296.6
Paper and Pulp Including Pap Product	0	201.5	1135.7	2587.2	618.6	10626.6	6846.8	1071.2	6857.7	29945.3
Sugar	0	0	535	0	0	132.5	9340	0	0	10007.5
Fermentation Industries	0	119.4	1724.5	235	5801.5	833	2536.7	5.1	22.2	11277.4
Food Processing Industries	1104.3	3246.8	9524.6	6856	3231.9	33847.7	19269.3	6325.4	1414.2	84820.2
Vegetable Oils and Vanaspati	13.2	51.8	107	116.8	149.1	40	1452.9	8.5	483	2422.3

(Contd.)

Table 2 (Contd.): Sectorwise Approval of FDI

(Rs. Million)

Sectorwise Approvals	1991	1992	1993	1994	1995	1996	1997	1998	1999	Total
Soaps, Cosmetics and Toilet Preparations	0	184.6	4.7	250.3	580.4	286	1450.3	605.5	12.4	3374.2
Rubber Goods	10.9	23.7	602.7	324.8	210.5	3431.6	458.3	5512.5	1237.1	11812.1
Leather, Leather Goods and Pickers	7.9	284.5	164.4	252.5	662.7	291.3	590.6	488.3	265.6	3007.8
Glue and Gelatin	0	0	0	0	0	0	0	0	12	12
Glass	7.5	437.4	505.8	857.6	1986.3	3029.5	4663.4	1929.3	4253.3	17670.1
Ceramics	98.3	193.8	285.8	2099.1	1099.3	1945.6	1245.9	935.8	680.9	8584.5
Cement And Gypsum Products	120	67.9	267	3354.9	167.8	1561.5	591.3	895.9	6810.6	13836.9
Timber Products	0	0	1.1	0	62.6	25	67.2	7.3	0	163.2
Defence Industries	0	0	0	0	0	0	34.7	0	0	34.7
Consultancy Services	72.8	85.7	84.1	163.8	1375.1	5244.9	3693.7	6362.2	2536.2	19618.5
Service Sector	3.8	608.1	11258.5	12117.3	7670.7	52697.1	14369	16971.2	22879	138574.7
Hotel & Tourism	160	1990.7	3794.9	4381.3	8002.2	4490.9	7281.1	4805.2	7844.9	42751.2
Trading	0	56.3	351.5	345.3	537.9	2852.6	1193.6	6851.1	2382.8	14571.1
Miscellaneous Industries	143.6	473.2	901.7	6184.6	3520.8	8218.1	3215	2214	8576.3	33447.3
Total	5049.1	38179.1	88618	141856.7	320716.4	361498.6	548913.5	308135	283665.2	2096632

Table 3: Sectoral Inflows

(Rs. Million)

Sectorwise Inflows	1991	1992	1993	1994	1995	1996	1997	1998	1999	Total
Mettallurgical Industries	1.6	249.2	140.18	169.99	581.37	1275.84	1014.39	1258.96	1641.81	6333.34
Fuels	16.68	97.36	539.91	884.96	3121.58	3493.26	15245.9	5635.55	7484.58	36519.77
Boilers and Steam Generating Plants	0	1.26	0	28.82	14.02	26.01	21.5	62.9	2.87	157.38
Prime Movers Other Than Electrical	0	0	0	13.69	277.9	443.25	161.33	94.49	62.6	1053.25
Electricals Equipment	72.16	910.54	1589.72	2917.37	5050.15	7670.49	13312.38	7865.89	7036.06	46424.75
Telecommunications	0	0	16.63	140.19	1274.47	7529.76	11850	17410.18	2155.58	40376.82
Transportation Industry	40.13	1081.53	579.62	1308.66	2307.37	4993.91	15138.31	14769.16	11301.98	51520.67
Industrial Machinery	6.97	74.81	129.79	372.4	575.6	296.16	1039.63	139.19	993.35	3627.9
Machine Tools	3.2	6.08	8.13	62.68	62.9	746.39	369.54	256.01	99.87	1614.8
Agricultural Machinery	0	0	1.5	8.15	1362.63	0.51	0	0	510.69	1883.49
Earth-Moving Machinery	0	0	0	0	8.97	0	11.52	256.39	1.02	277.9
Miscellaneous Mechanical & Engineering	199.31	561.11	628.38	700.49	1585.05	884.14	2142.5	1181.14	629.07	8511.2
Commercial, Office & Household Equipment	0	4.97	534.75	202.8	3181.84	544.15	81.51	179.49	677.69	5407.19
Medical and Surgical Appliances	0	2.13	23.59	24.89	14.7	72.34	245.95	391.15	91.67	866.42
Industrial Instruments	0	35.41	10.65	141.35	28.78	116.81	57.34	1.31	6.35	397.99
Scientific Instruments	0	0.75	3.3	5.08	40.04	24.5	38.62	0.39	31.38	144.06
Fertilizers	0	240.61	35.4	2.46	86.78	10.98	320.4	0	0	696.63
Chemicals (Other Than Fertilizers)	373.12	714.45	2299.27	4258.48	2726.35	5880.76	8212.65	10640.01	4756.19	39861.28
Photographic Raw Film and Paper	0	0	0	0	0	0	287.08	0	2.45	289.53
Dye-Stuffs	0	0	20.88	0	9.8	198.9	177.74	56.82	0	464.14
Drugs and Pharmaceuticals	112.26	60.45	1326.99	391.28	426.74	2426.87	1881.48	838.36	757.34	8221.75

(Contd.)

Table 3 (Contd.): Sectoral Inflows

(Rs. Million)

Sectorwise Inflows	1991	1992	1993	1994	1995	1996	1997	1998	1999	Total
Textiles (Includ Dyed, Printed)	2.85	186.51	354.18	1407.72	1478.83	1520 72	1590.32	503.53	1248.83	8293.49
Paper and Pulp Including Paper Product	0	0.21	0	136.97	1114.34	3080.8	1471.66	2341.71	513.65	8659.35
Sugar	0	0	0	0	15.31	0.75	244	0	0	260.06
Fermentation Industries	0	0	0	291.95	67.25	125.31	320.17	0	0	804.69
Food Processing Industries	21.16	580.91	1428.06	2094.83	1547.27	6411.5	5177.4	2368.8	4046.97	23676.92
Vegetable Oils and Vanaspati	0	3.75	0	371.36	8.32	0	0	0	86	469.43
Soaps, Cosmetics and Toilet Preparations	0	0	0	0	0	0	0	0	24.17	24.17
Rubber Goods	0	99.26	36.24	241.09	40.64	476.58	1625.49	362	177.59	3058.89
Leather, Leather Goods And Pickers	1.3	0	294.34	53.54	80.8	32	554.24	53.25	1.53	1120.98
Glue and Gelatin	0	0	0	0	0	0	0	1180	0	1180
Glass	0	0	575	2.55	1056.64	198.17	646.13	1454.85	1718.08	5651.42
Ceramics	1.45	19.25	102.56	350.62	80.11	594.38	464.37	69.25	37.46	1719.45
Cement and Gypsum Products	0	6.82	146	354.88	562.71	102.27	118.16	279.35	93.36	1663.54
Consultancy Services	0	0	0	0	0	0	0	5.82	214.19	220.02
Service Sector	0.3	48.3	1214.87	943.08	11014.94	10106.94	5411.44	7679.8	4023.82	40443.49
Hotel & Tourism	0	7.42	2.92	532.97	219.07	444.29	1031.94	399.49	405.38	3043.49
Trading	0	1.93	55	240.86	3320.06	650.73	945.1	519.98	980.55	6714.21
Miscellaneous Industries	180.88	386.99	727.57	4087.82	6129.73	22920.07	62651.83	51548.61	113375.7	262009.2
NRI Scheme	1622.96	1529.97	5794.15	11452.59	19878.38	20620.63	10396.19	3594.8	3488.3	78377.98
Total	2656.31	6911.99	18619.57	34196.62	69351.43	103970.2	164258.2	133398.6	168678.2	702041.1

Table 4: Sectorwise Inflows as a Percentage of Approvals

	1991	1992	1993	1994	1995	1996	1997	1998	1999	Total
Metallurgical Industries	19.27711	32.03908	1.115612	1.852974	3.152373	5.507905	4.030603	5.6714	11.72596	5.046546
Fuels	72.52174	0.645919	1.912852	2.323309	8.764864	6.0725	5.767838	4.056754	13.19224	5.755395
Boilers and Steam Generating Plants	0	105	0	83.05476	3.646294	19.41045	32.33083	455.7971	1.002095	10.73094
Prime Movers Other Than Electrical	Na	Na	Na	60.84444	181.634	123.5024	125.159	37.796	1565	114.8207
Electricals Equipment	8.215872	24.67722	26.00344	42.1433	49.87852	24.56766	60.70424	55.10294	27.59402	38.47753
Telecommunications	0	0	3.539804	85.27372	0.715069	16.97341	16.49132	56.15952	5.524607	11.01908
Transportation Industry	19.95525	71.5771	19.02452	10.82351	17.89033	17.34575	39.94203	94.49964	18.16834	29.56304
Industrial Machinery	1.54614	11.79968	14.94588	5.658543	9.905693	14.98634	47.65011	12.87723	36.86994	16.28446
Machine Tools	7.289294	9.034175	7.576887	33.18158	29.44757	100.7546	28.86806	178.2799	10.27258	42.9731
Agricultural Machinery	Na	0	Na	0.523107	272526	0.090458	Na	0	6995.753	43.31356
Earth-Moving Machinery	0	0	0	0	Na	Na	1.646185	6574.103	5.513514	32.6212
Miscellaneous Mechanical & Engineering	4152.292	150.9172	206.9081	100.544	138.9663	29.90394	55.89325	62.40503	22.85035	60.99863
Commercial, Office & Household Equipment	Na	0.779363	588.9317	232.8358	151.7981	34.54921	3.23055	6.392094	79.4199	50.67135
Medical and Surgical Appliances	0	5.867769	28.94479	38.70918	0.966088	252.9371	57.91147	151.3153	238.724	35.26764
Industrial Instruments	0	23.90952	63.01775	1682.738	6.832858	27.47824	48.59322	14.3956	12.85425	32.75099
Scientific Instruments	0	0.228868	173.6842	149.4118	33.61881	137.6404	32.81223	3.421053	1046	23.33333
Mathematical, Surveying and Drawing Fertilizers	0	Na	213.253	24.84848	Na	0.453644	2670	Na	Na	28.21621
Chemicals (Other Than Fertilizers)	27.47165	16.64376	62.12228	29.39538	23.19331	19.40915	29.04891	58.66369	58.68869	33.10575

(Contd.)

Table 4 (Contd.): Sectorwise Inflows as a Percentage of Approvals

	1991	1992	1993	1994	1995	1996	1997	1998	1999	Total
Photographic Raw Film and Paper	Na	0	0	0	0	0	14.62679	Na	2.941176	12.60031
Dye-Stuffs	Na	0	96.2212	0	4.954499	441.02	615.0173	7.721158	0	41.7317
Drugs and Pharmaceuticals	1403.25	20.76606	443.661	24.0108	22.82398	205.3016	102.875	91.98596	94.92855	93.24143
Textiles (Includ Dyed, Printed)	2.016985	19.37565	44.96953	14.44986	36.94858	36.60593	26.7137	21.65255	38.69222	26.49965
Paper and Pulp Including Paper Product	Na	0.104218	0	5.29414	180.139	28.9914	21.49413	218.6062	7.490121	28.91723
Sugar	Na	Na	0	Na	Na	0.566038	2.61242	Na	Na	2.598651
Fermentation Industries	Na	0	0	124.234	1.159183	15.04322	12.62152	0	0	7.135421
Food Processing Industries	1.916146	17.89177	14.99339	30.5547	47.87493	18.9422	26.86865	37.44902	286.1667	27.91425
Vegetable Oils and Vanaspati	0	7.239382	0	317.9452	5.580148	0	0	0	17.80538	19.37952
Soaps, Cosmetics and Toilet Preparations	Na	0	0	0	0	0	0	0	194.9194	0.716318
Rubber Goods	0	418.8186	6.012942	74.22722	19.30641	13.88798	354.6782	6.566893	14.35535	25.89624
Leather, Leather Goods And Pickers	16.4557	0	179.0389	21.20396	12.19255	28.14967	93.84355	10.90518	0.576054	37.2691
Glue and Gelatin	Na	Na	Na	Na	Na	Na	Na	Na	0	9833.333
Glass	0	0	113.6813	0.297341	53.1964	6.541343	13.85534	75.40818	40.39405	31.98295
Ceramics	1.475076	9.932921	35.88523	16.70335	7.287365	30.54996	37.27185	7.400085	5.501542	20.0297
Cement and Gypsum Products	0	10.04418	54.68165	10.57796	335.3456	6.549472	19.98309	31.18094	1.370804	12.02249
Timber Products										
Consultancy Services	0	0	0	0	0	0	0	0.091478	8.445312	1.121492
Service Sector	7.894737	7.942773	10.79069	7.782922	143.5976	19.17931	37.66052	45.25196	17.58739	29.18533
Hotel & Tourism	0	0.372733	0.076945	12.16465	2.737622	9.893117	14.17286	8.313702	5.167434	7.119075
Trading	Na	3.428064	15.64723	69.75384	617.2253	22.81182	79.18063	7.58973	41.15117	46.07895
Miscellaneous Industries	125.961	81.78149	80.6887	66.09676	174.1035	278.3974	1948.735	2328.302	1321.965	783.3494

Table 5: Sectorwise FDI Inflows as a percentage of FDI Approved from 1991 to 1998

Metallurgical Industries	5.05
Fuels	5.76
Boilers and Steam Generating Plants	10.73
Electricals Equipment	38.48
Telecommunications	11.02
Transportation Industry	29.56
Industrial Machinery	16.28
Machine Tools	42.97
Agricultural Machinery	43.31
Earth-Moving Machinery	32.62
Miscellaneous Mechanical & Engineering	61.00
Commercial, Office & Household Equipment	50.67
Medical and Surgical Appliances	35.27
Industrial Instruments	32.75
Scientific Instruments	23.33
Fertilizers	28.22
Chemicals (Other Than Fertilizers)	33.11
Photographic Raw Film and Paper	12.60
Dye-Stuffs	41.73
Drugs and Pharmaceuticals	93.24
Textiles (Includ Dyed, Printed)	26.50
Paper and Pulp Including Paper Product	28.92
Sugar	2.60
Fermentation Industries	7.14
Food Processing Industries	27.91
Vegetable Oils and Vanaspati	19.38
Soaps, Cosmetics and Toilet Preparations	0.72
Rubber Goods	25.90
Leather, Leather Goods and Pickers	37.27
Glass	31.98
Ceramics	20.03
Cement and Gypsum Products	12.02
Consultancy Services	1.12
Service Sector	29.19
Hotel & Tourism	7.12
Trading	46.08

Appendix

A : Demise of a Hedge Fund, Long Term Capital Management (LTCM)

The development of mutual funds in the financial markets has been a new phenomenon in the early part of 1980s and people started investing money in these funds for higher returns. Most of these funds were invested in corporate equities and in the process the future income expectations of the savers class became intertwined with the growth of equity markets. But initial scepticism about this phenomenon[1] became true after couple of years when some mutual funds failed to keep the promise of high returns.

Several events had shaken the financial world in early part of 1990s and these became standard cases in global macroeconomics. Some of these are: Barings fall, the Russian meltdown, Procter & Gamble problem, LTCM and some others. These are all events in the financial markets which have become standard stories to show us where the market went wrong, in the hope that the market would not allow the same thing to happen again.

Long Term Capital Management, L.P. (LTCM) was formed in 1993 with headquarter at Greenwich, Connecticut, USA. LTCM also used to manage Long Term Capital Portfolio L.P., a Cayman Island partnership and a variety of investment vehicles. The driving force behind LTCM was John Meriwether, who built a reputation as a fixed income trader at Salomon Brothers. Meriwether was joined by a distinguished group of partners. Two of the group — Myron Scholes and Robert Merton, shared the 1998 Noble Prize for economics for

---

1. Sometimes this has been called as casino capitalism or pongi capitalism by some economists.

their contribution in the areas of risk management in financial economics. Also former regulator David Mullins joined LTCM, and the latter achieved credibility compared to an average broker operating on Wall Street.

LTCM is a hedge fund, and hedge funds often describe themselves as market neutral. But there were several things that distinguished LTCM from other hedge funds and these were as follows:

(i)   Its managers proposed to carry out trading strategies that would be time consuming to deliver profits. For this the investors were not allowed to withdraw fund quarterly or annually.

(ii) LTCM was more scrupulous about secrecy than other hedge funds. It never disclosed the nature of its trades, even after it had made money in these.

(iii) It used to charge higher management fees compared to other funds.

As LTCM managed the portfolio, a very special relationship between the Fund's partners and the investment banking community became important. Since some powerful persons on Wall Street backed LTCM, the investment banking community treated LTCM as another investment bank when it borrowed money, and as a result LTCM used to get much liberal treatment regarding collateral. But that could not save the fund in the long run.

The LTCM fiasco is full of lessons about the following factors:

1. Model risk (assumptions too abstract away from reality)

2. Unexpected correlation or the breakdown of historical correlations

3. The need for stress-testing of model results by simulations

4. The value of disclosure and transparency

5. The danger of over-generous extension of trading credit

6. The woes of investing in star quality instruments

LTCM was largely unregulated and free to operate in any market, without capital charges and only light reporting requirements to the US Securities & Exchange Commission (SEC). It traded on the basis of its goodwill with many respectable counterparties as if it was a member of the same club. This enabled the firm to put on interest rate swaps at the market rate for no initial margin - an essential part of its strategy. It boils down to borrowing 100% of the value of any top-grade collateral, and with that cash to buy more securities and post them as collateral for further borrowing. In this money spinning game it could leverage itself to infinity, at least in theory. No wonder that in first two years of operation LTCM earned 43% and 41% return on equity. This helped the firm to attract more high value deposits and the investment capital became a staggering $7 billion (Dunbar, 1998).

To make 40% return on capital any firm has to leverage its position. In standard theory, market risk is not increased by stepping up volume, provided the firm sticks to liquid instruments only and keep the size of the deal within some optimum bounds. Once that limit is crossed, potential problems attain higher probability of becoming real and wait on the horizon to manifest at opportune moment. Some of the big macro hedge funds had encountered this problem and reduced their size by giving money back to their investors. In the last quarter of 1997 LTCM also returned $2.7 billion to investors.

LTCM had made the credit spread between mortgage-backed securities and the government bond markets. It also ventured into equity trades and started selling index options with big premium in 1997. It also got into new emerging markets, including Russia. One report revealed that the exposure to Russia was "8% of its book" which would come to $10 billion.

Some of LTCM's biggest competitors, the investment banks, had been trying to buy into the fund. But Meriwether applied a formula which brought in new investment, as well as providing him and his partners with a virtual put option on the performance of the fund. During 1997, under this formula UBS put in $800 million in the form of a loan and $266 million in straight equity. Again, another firm, Credit Suisse Financial Products, put in a $100 million loan and $33 million in equity. Investors in LTCM were pledged to keep in their money for at least two years. In 1998 the capital of LTCM was reduced to $4.8 billion.

According to a New York *Sunday Times* article the trouble for LTCM started on July 17 when Salomon Smith Barney announced it was liquidating its dollar interest arbitrage positions. On August 17, 1998 Russia declared a moratorium on its rouble debt and domestic dollar debt. The result was that hot money fled into high quality instruments. Top preference was for the most liquid US and G-10 government bonds.

Most of LTCM's bets had been variations on the same theme, which is convergence between liquid treasuries and more complex instruments that commanded a credit or liquidity premium. Unfortunately the theoretical positions could not be realized and the convergence turned into dramatic divergence.

The counterparties of LTCM, marking their exposure to market at least once a day and also sensing trouble with LTCM liquidity, began to call for more collateral to cover the divergence. On one single day, August 21, the LTCM portfolio lost $550 million. Meriwether and his team, still convinced of the logic behind their trades, believed strongly that all they needed was more capital to see them through a distorted market.

Perhaps the group running LTCM was right. But several exogenous factors went against LTCM and these were:

1. It became increasingly difficult to predict the time-frame within which rates would converge again.
2. The counterparties had lost confidence in LTCM.
3. Many counterparties had put on the same convergence trades following closely LTCM.

On September 2, 1998 Meriwether sent a letter to his investors saying that the fund had lost $2.5 billion and its capital base had shrunk to $2.3 billion.

Meriwether was looking for fresh investment of around $1.5 billion to carry the fund through. He approached those known to have big investible capital, including George Soros. But offers of new capital weren't forthcoming. May be, these big players were waiting for the price of an equity stake in LTCM to fall further, or even they were making money just trading against LTCM's positions. Under these circumstances it was felt that it was dangerous for LTCM to show potential buyers more details of its portfolio.

LTCM management realised that the loss suffered is irreversible and that was correct. Even till date they could not recover from the loss of the portfolio. A bail out package was affected to save LTCM by further infusion of capital to increase liquidity to the required level. The consortium of lenders that agreed to bail out LTCM included Barclays, Bankers Trust, Chase Manhattan, Credit Suisse First Boston, Deutsche Bank, Dean Witter, Goldman Sachs, J.P. Morgan, Lehman Brothers, Merrill Lynch, Morgan Stanley, Paribas, Societe General, the Travellers Group and Union Bank of Switzerland. The group is really a Who's Who of the leading investment banks of the world (Edwards, 1999).

B. The Debt Crises and OPEC Recycling

Two oil price hikes, in 1973 and 1978, gave the greatest life to the Eurodollar markets. . OPEC countries received large dollar inflows. What they could do with the dollars? One option was domestic absorption, but the "Ayatollah effect" in Iran put limits on the amount of absorption, in the form of fast-paced investment and modernization, in many OPEC countries. Another option was direct foreign investment. Again, however, there were limits. The news of large-scale takeovers of firms, hotels, and property in many Western countries by the ruling oligarchy in OPEC countries would bring on resentment and heighten international tension.

Given the limited option available, the only other alternative was to put the money in a bank. But where to keep the money? US banks at the time were still heavily regulated, so the OPEC finance ministers brought the "petrodollars" to the Eurodollar banks.

On the other spectrum the petroleum importing developing countries needed cash to finance their oil bills, but where could they go? The International Bank for Reconstruction and Development (IBRD), also known as the World Bank, was set up for long-term development lending, such as building dams, and others forms of developmental infrastructure. The International Monetary Fund, on the other hand, only provided short-term lending to avoid balance-of-payments crises. Oil bills simply fell between the institutional cracks of the two major international lending institutions.

The situation called for concrete actions on the part of world institutions.While the World Bank and IMF were quietly debating what to do about the oil crisis, the Eurodollar markets did the job of recycling the OPEC surplus funds to the LDC oil-deficit countries. The LDC countries went directly to the Eurodollar markets and borrowed the funds to pay the OPEC countries for their oil bills. Thus, the banks were receiving petrodollar deposits, lending the money to the LDC oil-deficit countries, which in turn paid the OPEC countries. The latter in turn deposited the money in the Eurodollar system.

Such recycling is not new in history. After World War I, the Allies imposed large debts on defeated Germany. In turn, the Allies owed large amounts of money to US firms and banks. The Dawes-Young act created the Bank for International Settlements in Basel, Switzerland. Through the BIS, the US provided funds to lend to Germany, which in turn paid the Allies, and which in turn paid the US. This was an attempt to resolve the "German transfer problem", about which John Maynard Keynes warned in *Economic Consequences of the Peace*. Unfortunately, the Dawes-Young solution offered too little, too late. An embattled Germany, after the hyperinflation, turned to Hitler, who abrogated the debts, and the offer of aid from the BIS, and began the militarization of the country.

The Eurodollar recycling continued on through the 1970's

and 1980's. It should be noted that this recycling was not the result of any government or inter-governmental planning agency. It was the response of the market to the needs of the system. Ultimately the market resolution crashed. In 1982 LIBOR rates nearly doubled. The value of the US dollar against major currencies appreciated by more than 30 per cent, and the world economy went into a recession. For many less developed countries (LDC's), commodity prices also fell. Such a multi-dimensional shock could not be sustained. Ultimately many countries, starting with Mexico in 1982, defaulted on their payments to the Eurodollars system.

When large scale default threatened, the IMF and World Bank woke up from their slumber. They started a system of "program lending", with attempts to coordinate structural adjustment loans from the World Bank, and "stand-by agreements" from the IMF. Such agreements with the World Bank and the IMF not only provided cash to less developed countries (LDC) in the 1980's, but also acted as a "seal of approval" for aid from other governments and organizations.

International Debt Crisis of the 1980's: Macro-economic Indicators: Before and After
The decade of the 1980's has been called the "lost decade" of growth, especially for Latin America. To understand the magnitude of the problem of the debt, it is useful to look at several macro-economic indicators, during the periods 1970 - 1984 . The indicators are the LIBOR rate, inflation in industrial goods, inflation in commodities, and the OECD growth rate. During the period 1970-79, many Latin American countries accumulated large-scale debt, and this was mainly from capital inflows from the Eurodollar banks in London, Germany, and Japan.

During this period, the LIBOR rate, in nominal terms was about 7 per cent, but inflation in commodity prices was about 14 per cent, and inflation in industrial goods was lower. So real interest rates were actually negative. Again, the terms of trade, taken as the price of export goods relative to the price of imports goods, were moving in favour of the developing countries.

After Paul Volcker came to power, in October 1979, as Chairman of the Board of Governors of the Federal Reserve System in the United States, interest rates almost doubled. With the contraction of the export markets, the initial advantage of terms of trade was neutralized. Also the burden of debt increased in real sense as dollar appreciated against major currencies. The situation of the borrower countries became very bad.

How the lending banks would recover the loans became the important issue. Here the institutional problem comes. International debts are essentially unenforceable claims. In a domestic situation if one party does not meet debt-servicing obligations, there are bankruptcy proceedings. No such thing is possible in the international arena. There is no mechanism, short of international conflict, which can arbitrate different claims on international debt obligations. It all depends on the willingness of the parties.

C. World Currencies
Currencies of the World Countries: a selective list

Country	Currency name	Symbol	Subdivision-unit	Ex-Regime
Afghanistan	afghani	Af	100 puls	float
Albania	lek	L	100 qindarka	float
Algeria	dinar	DA	100 centimes	composite
Angola	kwanza	Kz	100 lwei	(replaced)
Angola	kwanza	Kz	100 lwei	m.float
Angola	kwanza (new kwanza, 2001-)	Kz,100 lwei		m.float
Anguilla	dollar	EC$	100 cents	US-$ (2.7)
Antigua and Barbuda	dollar	EC$	100 cents	US-$ (2.7)
Argentina	austral (-1991)	double dashed A (replaced)	100 Centavos	100
Argentina	peso (1991-)	$	100 centavos	US-$ (1.0)
Armenia	dram		100 luma	
Aruba	guilder	Af.	100 cents	US-$ (1.79)
Australia	dollar	A$	100 cents	float
Austria (-1998)	schilling	S	100 groschen	euro-13.7603
Austria (1999-)				
Azerbaijan	manat		100 gopik	
Bahamas	dollar	B$	100 cents	US-$ (1.0)
Bahrain	dinar	BD	1,000 fils	US-$ (lim.flex.)
Bangladesh	taka	Tk	100 paisa (poisha)	composite
Barbados	dollar	Bds$	100 cents	US-$ (2.0)
Belarus (-1999)	rouble	BR	replaced, 1000	BYB = 1 BYR
Belarus (2000-)	rouble	BR		m.float
Belgium (-1998)	franc	BF	100 centimes	euro-40.3399
Belgium (1999-)	See European Union			
Belize	dollar	BZ$	100 cents	US-$ (2.0)
Benin	franc	CFAF	100 centimes	French Franc (100.0)
Bermuda	dollar	Bd$	100 cents	US-$ (1.0)
Bhutan	ngultrum	Nu	100 chetrum	Indian Rupee (1.0)

(Contd.)

Currencies of the World Countries: a selective list (Contd.)

Country	Currency name	Symbol	Subdivision-unit	Ex-Regime
Bolivia	boliviano	Bs	100 centavos	float
Bosnia-Herzegovina (-1999)		B.H. dinar		100 para
Bosnia-Herzegovina (1999+) convertible mark		KM	100 fennig	DM (1.0)
Botswana	pula	P	100 thebe	composite
Brazil	cruzeiro (-1993)		100 centavos	(replaced)
Brazil	cruzeiro (1993-94)		100 centavos	(replaced)
Brazil	real (1994-)	R$	100 centavos	float
Brunei	ringgit (a.k.a. B.dollar)	B$	100 sen (a.k.a. 100 cents)	S$ (1.0)
Bulgaria	leva	Lv	100 stotinki	German Mark (1.0)
Burkina Faso	franc	CFAF	100 centimes (100.0)	F. Franc
Burundi	franc	FBu	100 centimes	composite
Cambodia	new riel	CR	100 sen	m.float
Cameroon	franc	CFAF	100 centimes	F. Franc (100.0)
Canada	dollar	Can$	100 cents	float
Cape Verde Island	escudo	C.V.Esc.	100 centavos	composite
Cayman Islands	dollar	CI$	100 cents	US-$ (0.85)
Central African Republic	franc	CFAF	100 centimes	F Franc (100.0)
Chad	franc	CFAF	100 centimes	F Franc (100.0)
Chile	peso	Ch$	100 centavos	indicators
China	yuan renminbi	Y	10 jiao = 100 fen	m.float
Colombia	peso	Col$	100 centavos	m.float
Comoros	franc	CF	-	F. Franc (75.0)
Congo	franc	CFAF	100 centimes	F.Franc (100.0)
Congo, Dem. Rep. (former Zaire)	franc		100 centimes	US-$ (2.50)
Congo, Dem. Rep. (2001-)	franc		100 centimes	float
Costa Rica	colon	slashed C	100 centimos	float
Côte d'Ivoire	franc	CFAF	100 centimes	F. Franc (100.0)
Croatia	kuna	HRK	100 lipas	float

(Contd.)

Currencies of the World Countries: a selective list (Contd.)

Country	Currency name	Symbol	Subdivision-unit	Ex-Regime
Cuba	peso	Cu$	100 centavos	US-$ (1.0)
Cyprus	pound £C	100 cents	1.7086	EUR/CYP +/- 2.25%
Czech Republic	koruna	Kc (with hacek on c)	100 haleru	float
Denmark	krone (pl. kroner) Dkr		100 øre	EMS-II
Djibouti	franc	DF	100 centimes	US-$ (177.72)
Dominica	dollar	EC$	100 cents	US-$ (2.7)
Dominican Rep.	peso	RD$	100 centavos	m.float
Ecuador	sucre	S/	100 centavos	m.float
Ecuador (15-Sep-2000 -)	country has adopted US dollar			
Egypt	pound	£E	100 piasters	m.float
El Salvador	colon	¢	100 centavos	float
Equatorial Guinea	franc	CFAF	100 centimos	F Franc (100.0)
Eritrea	nakfa	Nfa	100 cents	
Estonia	kroon (pl. krooni)	KR	100 senti	German Mark (8.0)
Ethiopia	birr	Br	100 cents	float
European Union (-1998)	European Currency	Unit	ecu	
European Union (1999-)	Euro		100 euro-cents	
Falkland Islands	pound	£F	100 pence	British Pound (1.0)
Fiji	dollar	F$	100 cents	composite
Finland (-1998)	markka	mk	100 penniä (sg. penni)	euro-5.94573
Finland (1999-)	see European Union			
France (-1998)	franc	F	100 centimes	euro-6.55957
France (1999-)	European Union			
French Polynesia	franc	CFPF	100 centimes	FFr (18.18)
Gabon	franc	CFAF	100 centimes	F Franc (100.0)
Gambia	dalasi	D	100 butut	float
Georgia	lari		100 tetri	float
Germany (-1998)	deutsche mark	DM	100 pfennig	euro-1.95583
Germany (1999-)				

(Contd.)

Currencies of the World Countries: a selective list (Contd.)

Country	Currency name	Symbol	Subdivision-unit	Ex-Regime
Ghana	new cedi	¢	100 psewas	float
Gibraltar	pound	£G	100 pence	B. Pound (1.0)
Greece (-2000)	drachma	Dr	100 lepta	euro-340.750
Greece (2001-)	see European Union			
Grenada	dollar	EC$	100 cents	US-$ (2.7)
Guadeloupe				
Guam				
Guatemala	quetzal	Q	100 centavos	float
Guernsey				
Guinea-Bissau (-Apr1997)	peso	PG	100 centavos	m.float
Guinea-Bissau (May1997-)	franc	CFAF	100 centimes	FFranc (100.0)
Guinea	syli	FG	10 francs	m.float
Guyana	dollar	G$	100 cents	float
Haiti	gourde	G	100 centimes	float
Honduras	lempira	L	100 centavos	m.float
Hong Kong	dollar	HK$	100 cents	US-$ (7.73 central parity)
Hungary	forint	Ft	-none-	composite
Iceland	króna	IKr	100 aurar (sg. aur)	composite
India	rupee	Rs	100 paise	float
Indonesia	rupiah	Rp	100 sen	m.float
International Monetary Fund	SDR Special Drawing Rights			
Iran	rial	Rls	10 rials = 1 toman	US-$ (4750)
Iraq	dinar	ID	1,000 fils	US-$ (0.3109)
Ireland (-1998)	punt or pound	IR£	100 pingin or pence	euro-0.787564
Ireland (1999-)	European Union			
Israel	new shekel	NIS	100 new agorot	m.float
Italy (-1998)	lira (pl. lire)	Lit	unit	euro-1936.27
Italy (1999-)	European Union			

(Contd.)

Currencies of the World Countries: a selective list (Contd.)

Country	Currency name	Symbol	Subdivision-unit	Ex-Regime
Jamaica	dollar	J$	100 cents	float
Japan	yen	¥	100 sen (not used)	float
Jordan	dinar	JD	1,000 fils	composite
Kazakhstan	tenge		100 tiyn	float
Kenya	shilling	K Sh	100 cents	float
Korea, North	won	Wn	100 chon	
Korea, South	won	W	100 chon	float
Kuwait	dinar	KD	1,000 fils	composite
Kyrgyzstan	som		100 tyyn	float
Laos	new kip	KN	100 at	m.float
Latvia	lat	Ls	100 santims	SDR
Lebanon	pound (livre)	L.L.	100 piastres	float
Lesotho	loti, pl., maloti	L, pl., M	100 lisente	S.African Rand (1.0)
Liberia	dollar	$	100 cents	US-$ (1.0)
Libya	dinar	LD	1,000 dirhams	SDR (8.5085)
Liechtenstein	see Switzerland			
Lithuania	litas, pl., litai		100 centu	US-$ (4.0)
Luxembourg (-1998)	franc	LuxF	100 centimes	euro-40.3399
Luxembourg (1999-)		see European Union		
Macao (Macau)	pataca	P	100 avos	HK-$ (1.03)
Macedonia (Former Yug. Rep.)	denar	MKD	100 deni	composite
Madagascar	ariayry = 5 francs	FMG	1 francs = 100 centimes	float
Malawi	kwacha	MK	100 tambala	float
Malaysia	ringgit	RM	100 sen	m.float
Maldives	rufiyaa	Rf	100 lari	m.float
Mali	franc	CFAF	100 centimes	F.Franc (100.0)
Malta	lira, pl., liri	Lm	100 cents	composite
Mauritania	ouguiya	UM	5 khoums	composite
Mauritius	rupee	Mau Rs	100 cents	composite

(Contd.)

Currencies of the World Countries: a selective list (Contd.)

Country	Currency name	Symbol	Subdivision-unit	Ex-Regime
Mexico	peso	Mex$	100 centavos	float
Mongolia	tugrik	Tug	100 mongos	float
Montserrat	dollar	EC$	100 cents	US-$ (2.7)
Morocco	dirham	DH	100 centimes	composite
Mozambique	metical	Mt	100 centavos	float
Myanmar	kyat	K	100 pyas	US-$ (5.86 of, 200-300bm)
Namibia	dollar	N$	100 cents	S. African Rand (1.0)
Nepal	rupee	NRs	100 paise	composite
Netherlands Antilles	guilder (a.k.a. florin or gulden)	Ant.f. or NAf.	100 cents	US-$ (1.79)
Netherlands (-1998)	guilder (a.k.a. florin or gulden) f.		100 cents,	euro-2.20371
Netherlands(1999-)	See European Union			
New Caledonia	franc	CFPF	100 centimes	FFr (18.18)
New Zealand	dollar	NZ$	100 cents	float
Nicaragua	gold cordoba	C$	100 centavos	indicators
Niger	franc	CFAF	100 centimes	French Franc (100.0)
Nigeria	naira	double-dashed N	100 kobo	US-$ ((82.0))
Norway	krone (pl. kroner)	NKr	100 øre	float
Oman	rial	RO	1,000 baizas	US-$ (1/2.6)
Pakistan	rupee	Rs	100 paisa	m.float
Panama	balboa	B	100 centesimos	US-$ (1.0)
Papua New Guinea	kina	K	100 toeas	composite
Paraguay	guarani	slashed G	100 centimos	float
Peru	inti		100 centimos	(replaced)
Peru	new sol	S/.	100 centimos	float
Philippines	peso	dashed P	100 centavos	float
Poland	zloty	z dashed l	100 groszy	m.float

(Contd.)

Currencies of the World Countries: a selective list (Contd.)

Country	Currency name	Symbol	Subdivision-unit	Ex-Regime
Portugal (-1998)	escudo	Esc	100 centavos	euro-200.482
Portugal (1999-)	European Union			
Puerto Rico	See United States			
Qatar	riyal	QR	100 dirhams	US-$ (lim.flex.)
Romania	leu (pl. lei)	L	100 bani	float
Russia (-1997)	rouble	R	100 kopecks	(replaced, 1000/1)
Russia (1998-)	rouble	R	100 kopecks	float
Rwanda	franc	RF	100 centimes	SDR (201.8?)
Samoa (America)	See United States			
Sao Tome & Principe	dobra	Db	100 centimos	m.float
Saudi Arabia	riyal	SRls	100 halalat	US-$ (lim.flex.)
Senegal	franc	CFAF	100 centimes	French Franc (100)
Serbia	See Yugoslavia			
Seychelles	rupee	SR	100 cents	SDR (7.2345)
Sierra Leone	leone	Le	100 cents	float
Singapore	dollar	S$	100 cents	m.float
Slovakia	koruna	Sk	100 haliers	composite
Slovenia	tolar	SIT	100 stotinov (stotins)	m.float
Solomon Island	dollar	SI$	100 cents	composite
Somalia	shilling	So. Sh.	100 centesimi	float
South Africa	rand	R	100 cents	float
Spain (-1998)	peseta	Ptas	100 centimos	euro-166.386
Spain (1999-)	see European Union			
Sri Lanka	rupee	SLRs	100 cents	m.float
St. Helena	pound	£S	100 new pence	GBP (1.0)

(Contd.)

Currencies of the World Countries: a selective list (Contd.)

Country	Currency name	Symbol	Subdivision-unit	Ex-Regime
St. Kitts and Nevis	dollar	EC$	100 cents	US-$ (2.7)
St. Lucia	dollar	EC$	100 cents	US-$ (2.7)
St. Vincent and the Grenadines	dollar		EC$ 100 cents,	US-$ (2.7)
Sudan (-1992)	pound		100 piastres	m.float
Sudan (1992-)	dinar		100 piastres	m.float
Swaziland	lilangeni, pl., emalangeni	L, pl., E		100 cents
South African rand (1.0)				
Sweden	krona (pl. kronor)Sk		100 öre	m.float
Switzerland	franc	SwF	100 rappen/centimes	float
Syria	pound	£S	100 piasters	US-$ (11.225)
Taiwan	new dollar	NT$	100 cents	
Tajikistan (- 5-Nov-2000) rouble		replaced,	1000 TJR = 1 TJS	
Tajikistan (6-Nov-2000 -)		somoni	100 dirams	
Tanzania	shilling	TSh	100 cents	float
Thailand	baht	Bht or Bt	100 stang	float
Togo	franc	CFAF	100 centimes	F Franc (100.0)
Tonga	pa'anga	PT or T$	100 seniti	composite
Trinidad and Tobago	dollar	TT$	100 cents	float
Tunisia	dinar	TD	1,000 millimes	m.float (1.0)
Turkey	lira	TL	100 kurus	m.float
Turkmenistan	manat		100 tenga	US-$ (10.0;230.0)
Tuvalu				
Uganda	shilling	USh	100 cents	(replaced)
Uganda	shilling	USh	100 cents	float
Ukraine	Hryvnia		100 kopiykas	float
United Arab Emirates	dirham	Dh	100 fils	US-$ (lim.flex.)
United Kingdom	pound	£	100 pence	float
United States of America	dollar	$	100 cents	float

(Contd.)

Currencies of the World Countries: a selective list (Contd.)

Country	Currency name	Symbol	Subdivision-unit	Ex-Regime
Uruguay (-1975)	peso	Ur$	100 centésimos	(replaced)
Uruguay (1975-93)	new peso	NUr$	100 centésimos	(replaced)
Uruguay (1993-)	peso uruguayo	$U	100 centésimos	m.float
Uzbekistan	som		100 tiyin	
Vanuatu	vatu	VT	100 centimes	composite
Vatican				
Venezuela	bolivar	Bs	100 centimos	float
VietNam	new dong	D	10 hao or 100 xu	m.float
Virgin Islands				
Wallis and Futuna Islands	franc	CFPF 100 centimes		FFr (18.18)
Western Samoa	tala	WS$	100 sene	composite
Yemen	rial	YRls	100 fils	float
Yugoslavia	dinar	Din	100 paras	
Zaïre (-Nov 1994)	zaire	Z	100 makuta	(replaced)
Zaïre (-1997)	new zaire	NZ	100 new makuta	float
Zaïre	Zambia	kwacha	ZK 100 ngwee	float
Zimbabwe	dollar	Z$	100 cents	float

Note: When pegged to a currency, the figure immediately after that currency denotes the number of units per the denoted currency. The 11 currencies that Euro has replaced have the number per unit of Euro written.

m. float = managed float currency

lim. Flex. = limited flexibility over a narrow band

References

- World Currency Yearbook, 27th edition. Currency Data & Intelligence, Inc. (Continues Pick's currency yearbook.)

- Pick, Albert: Standard catalog of world paper money. München: Krause, 1975 (1st edition) ISBN: 0873410025. 7th ed. edited by Neil Shafer and Colin R. Bruce II. Iola, WI: Krause Publications, 1994

- PACIFIC Exchange Rate Service

- IMF, International Financial Statistics, various issues

D. Exchange Rate Behaviour of some important currencies including Indian rupee

(1) Nominal and effective exchange rate of Chinese renminbi yuan

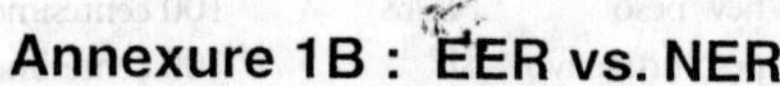

Annexure 1B : EER vs. NER

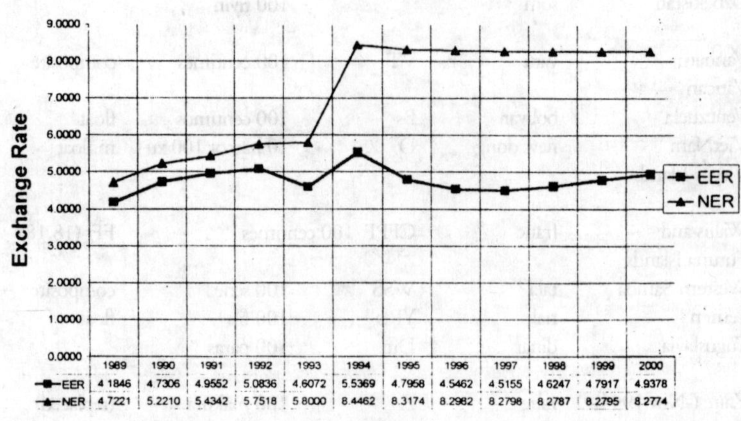

Time	1989	1990	1991	1992	1993	1994	1995	1996	1997	1998	1999	2000
EER	4.1846	4.7306	4.9552	5.0836	4.6072	5.5369	4.7958	4.5462	4.5155	4.6247	4.7917	4.9378
NER	4.7221	5.2210	5.4342	5.7518	5.8000	8.4462	8.3174	8.2982	8.2798	8.2787	8.2795	8.2774

Annexure 1C: NER vs. Current Account

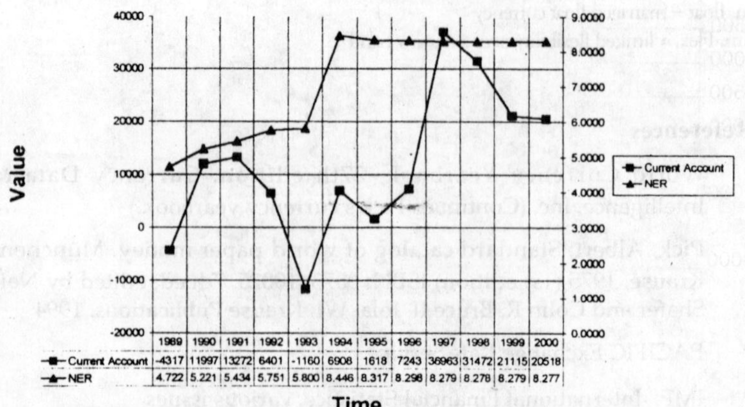

Time	1989	1990	1991	1992	1993	1994	1995	1996	1997	1998	1999	2000
Current Account	-4317	11997	13272	6401	-1160	6908	1618	7243	36963	31472	21115	20518
NER	4.722	5.221	5.434	5.751	5.800	8.446	8.317	8.298	8.279	8.278	8.279	8.277

(2)   The following is the diagram of German Deutchmark *vis-à-vis* US dollar for the period as shown in the figure:

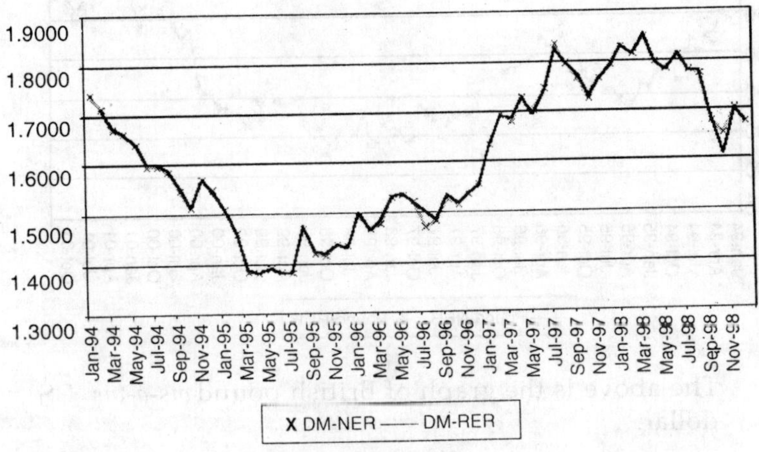

(3)   The following is the graph of Euro in recent years.

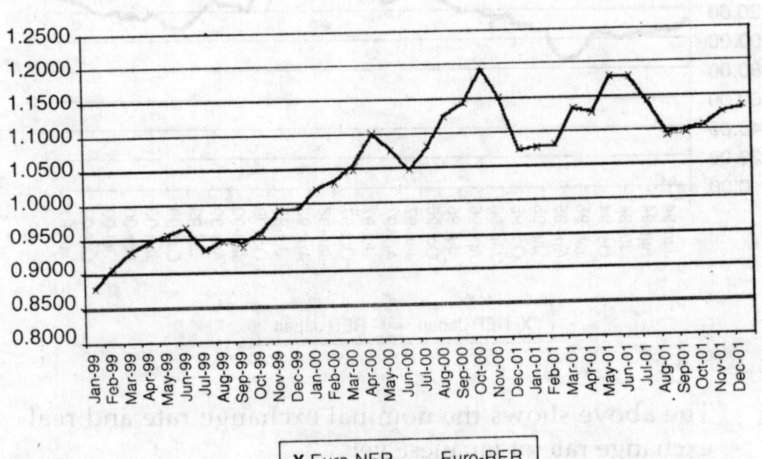

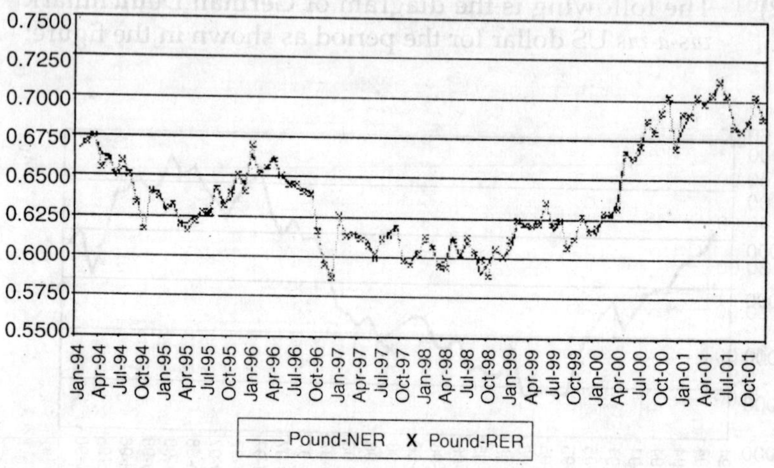

(4)   The above is the graph of British pound *vis-à-vis* US dollar.

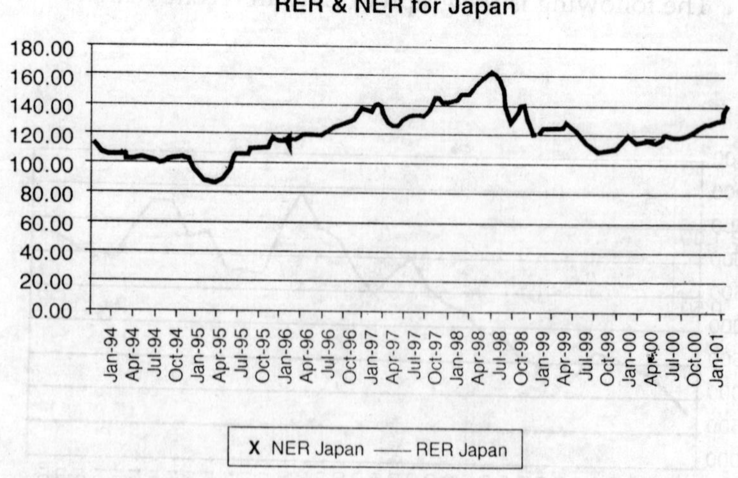

(5)   The above shows the nominal exchange rate and real exchange rate of Japanese yen.

(6)   The figure below shows NER and RER of Thailand baht.

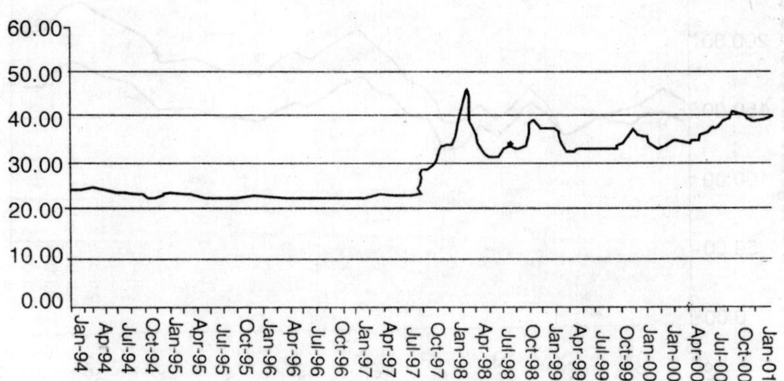

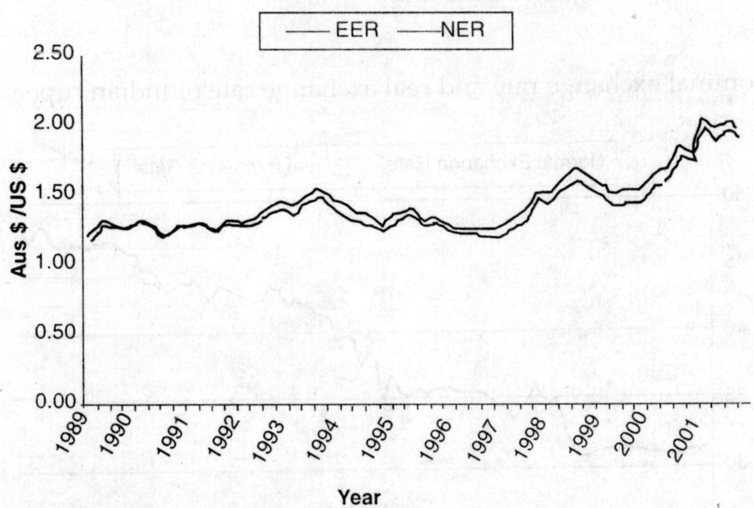

(7)   The above diagram shows movement of Australian
dollar against US dollar.

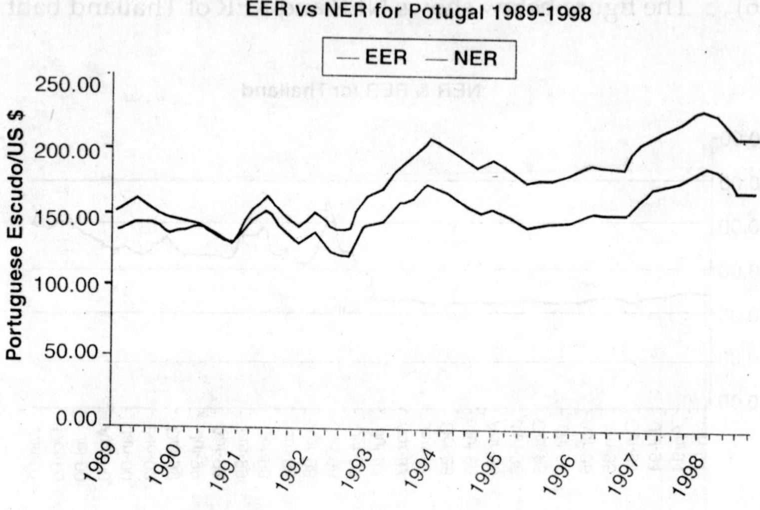

(8) The above diagram shows the movements of Portugal's escudo against US dollar.

Nominal exchange rate and real exchange rate of Indian rupee

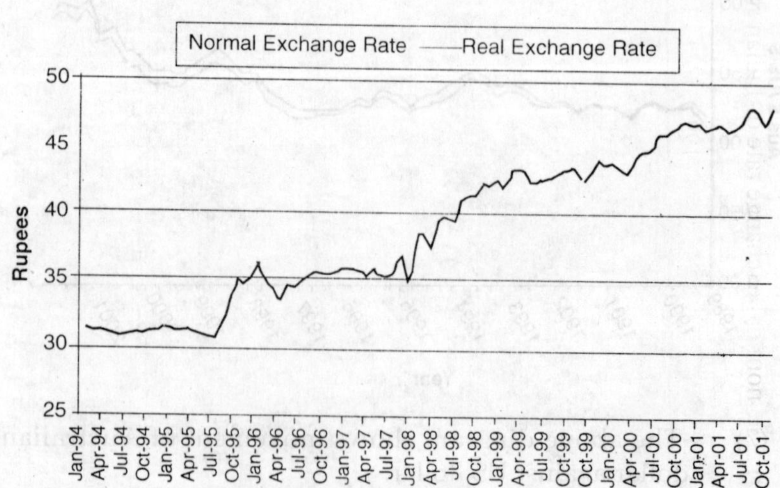

(9) The nominal exchange rate of Indian rupee

	1994	1995	1996	1997	1998	1999	2000	2001
January	31.37	31.37	36.49	35.88	38.92	42.5	43.64	46.41
February	31.37	31.43	35.03	35.89	39.3	42.49	43.61	46.61
March	31.37	31.5	34.33	35.91	39.5	42.43	43.62	46.64
April	31.37	31.39	34.52	35.78	39.73	42.82	43.66	46.86
May	31.37	31.42	35.09	35.79	41.5	42.84	44.58	46.99
June	31.37	31.42	35.06	35.82	42.47	43.36	44.68	47.04
July	31.38	31.4	35.68	35.71	42.56	43.29	44.99	47.16
August	31.37	31.84	35.68	36.36	42.545	43.48	45.8	47.15
September	31.37	34.01	35.76	36.18	42.49	43.61	46.07	47.86
October	31.37	34.62	35.68	36.4	42.37	43.42	46.8	47.97
November	31.39	34.94	35.76	38.57	42.63	43.41	46.84	47.99
December	31.38	35.18	35.93	39.28	42.48	43.49	46.75	48.18

The real exchange rate of Indian rupee calculated as NER x (CPI*/CPI) where CPI is domestic consumer price index and CPI* is the foreign one (of USA)

	1994	1995	1996	1997	1998	1999	2000	2001
January	31.4766	31.47949	36.61994	35.99822	37.75417	43.47965	43.75859	46.79088
February	31.23877	31.36456	35.04418	36.00787	39.57466	43.19901	43.97954	47.03945
March	31.24024	31.38805	34.42191	35.88358	39.7771	42.42226	43.56899	46.49575
April	31.1804	31.2796	33.60074	35.50782	39.51611	42.72639	43.30162	46.77297
May	31.05372	30.94653	34.75852	35.96894	40.91009	42.74626	44.43323	46.87177
June	30.90953	30.86094	34.53057	35.5773	41.48564	42.95272	44.70039	46.48904
July	31.00438	30.69018	35.14036	35.44159	41.33963	43.40904	44.79888	46.44738
August	31.15017	31.73308	35.31251	36.3354	42.42092	43.37983	46.02172	46.84001
September	31.02532	33.87684	35.78168	37.09551	42.25712	43.52714	46.21787	48.1604
October	31.27606	35.14214	35.58621	35.09225	42.602	42.67577	46.33845	48.02747
November	31.24357	34.81573	35.51319	38.44076	42.12321	43.31893	46.78528	46.97502
December	31.58219	35.40191	35.83439	38.61931	43.39029	44.20092	47.12614	48.32805

The nominal exchange rate and 5-point moving average of Indian rupee.

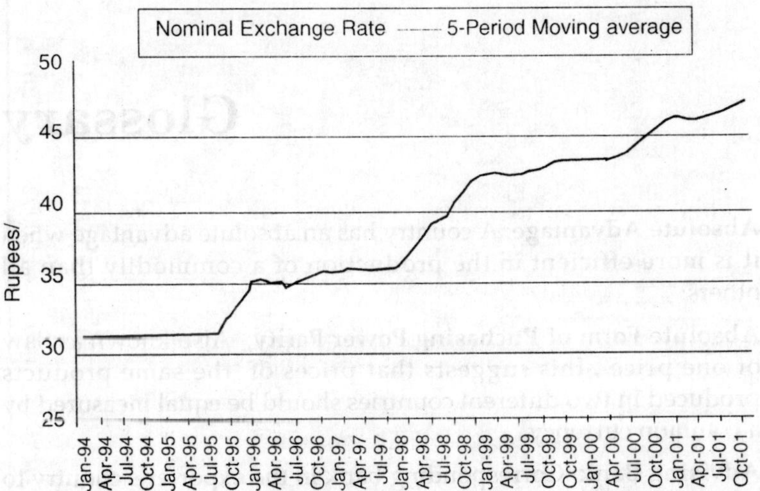

(10) The nominal exchange rate and real exchange rate of Indonesian rupiah.

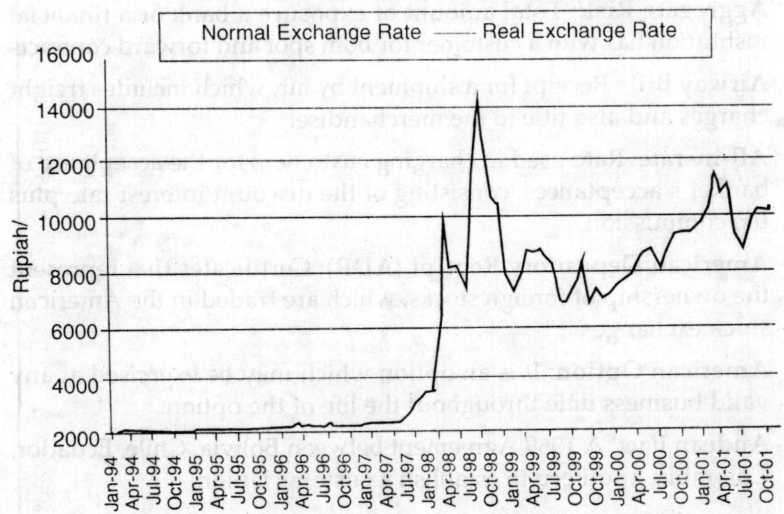

Glossary

Absolute Advantage: A country has an absolute advantage when it is more efficient in the production of a commodity than all others.

Absolute Form of Puchasing Power Parity: Also known as 'law of one price', this suggests that prices of the same products produced in two different countries should be equal measured by a common currency.

Advising Bank: Corresponding bank in the exporter's country to which the issuing bank sends the letter of credit.

Adjustable Peg: It is an exchange rate system where a country's exchange rate is 'pegged' (i.e. fixed) in relation to another currency. The official rate may be changed from time to time.

Aggregate Risk: Total amount of exposure a bank or a financial institution has with a customer for both spot and forward contracts

Airway Bill: Receipt for a shipment by air, which includes freight charges and also title to the merchandise.

All-in-rate: Rate used in charging customers for the acceptance of banker's acceptances, consisting of the discount interest rate plus the commission.

American Depository Receipt (ADR): Certificates that represent the ownership of foreign stocks, which are traded in the American stock exchanges.

American Option: It is an option which may be exercised at any valid business date throughout the life of the option.

Andean Pact: A 1969 Agreement between Bolivia, Chile, Ecuador, Colombia, and Peru to establish a customs Union.

Appreciation: Increase in the value of a currency in terms of the currency of partner country.

Arbitrage: A risk-free type of trading where the same instrument is bought and sold simultaneously in two different markets in order to cash in on the difference in these markets.

Around: It is often used in quoting forward 'premium/discount'. 'Five-five around' would mean five points on either side of the present spot value.

Ask Price: The price at which the currency or instrument is offered.

Assignment of Proceeds: Arrangement which allows the original beneficiary of a letter of credit to pledge or assign proceeds to an end supplier.

Association-Cambiste-Internationale: The international society of foreign exchange dealers consisting of national 'Forex clubs' affiliated on a worldwide basis.

ASEAN: Association of South East Asian Nations; formed in 1967 it is an attempt to establish a free trade area between Brunei, Indonesia, Malaysia, Philippines, Singapore and Thailand.

At Best: An instruction given to a dealer to buy or sell at the best rate that is currently available in the market.

At Par Forward Spread: When the forward price is equivalent to the spot price.

At the Price Stop-Loss Order: A stop-loss order that must be executed at the requested level regardless of market conditions.

Average Rate Option: A contract where the exercise price is based on the difference between the strike price and the average spot rate over the contract period. Sometimes it is called an 'Asian option'.

Back office: Settlement and related processes are taken care of by staff.

Balance-of-Payments: System of recording a country's economic transactions associated with international trade.

Bank for International Settlement (BIS): Institution that facilitates cooperation among countries involved in international transactions and also provides assistance to countries experiencing international payments problems.

Banker's Acceptance: Bill of exchange drawn on and accepted by a banking institution. It is generally used to guarantee exporters that they will receive payments on goods delivered to importers.

Bar Chart: A charting method which consists of four significant points: the high and the low prices, which form the vertical bar, the opening price, which is marked with a horizontal line to the left of the bar, and the closing price, which is marked with a little horizontal line to the right of the bar.

Barter: Exchange of goods between two parties without the use of any currency as a medium of exchange.

Base Currency: The currency in which the operating results of the bank or institution are reported.

Base Price: It is one hundredth of a percentage point. 50 basis points [50bp] is half a percentage point.

Basel Accord: Agreement among country representatives in 1998 to establish standardized risk-based capital requirements for banks across countries.

Bear Call Spread: A spread designed to exploit falling exchange rates by purchasing a call option with a high exercise price and selling one with a low exercise price.

Bear Put Spread: A spread designed to exploit falling exchange rates by purchasing a put option with a high exercise price and selling one with a low exercise price.

Bid-Offer Spread: The difference between the buy (bid) and sell (offer) price of a currency or financial instrument.

Bilateral Grid: It is an exchange rate system which links all of the central rates of the EMS currencies in terms of the ECU.

Bilateral Netting System: Netting method used for transactions between two units. Settlement in which the amount one subsidiary owes another can be cancelled by the debt the second subsidiary owes the first.

Bill of Exchange: Promisory note drawn by one party (an exporter) to pay a specified amount to another party at a specified future date, or on the presentation of the draft.

Bill of Lading: Document serving as a receipt for shipment and a summary of freight charges and conveying title to the merchandise.

Bollinger Bands: A quantitative method which combines a moving average with the instrument's volatility. The bands were designed to gauge whether the prices are high or low on relative basis. They are plotted two standard deviations above and below a simple moving average. The bands look like an expanding and contracting envelope model.

Breakaway Gap: A price gap which occurs in the beginning of a new trend, many times at the end of a long consolidation period. It may also appear after the completion of major chart formations.

Break-Even Point: The price of a financial instrument at which the option buyer recovers the premium.

Bretton Woods: The place is in the state of New Hampshire, USA. The site of the conference which in 1944 led to the establishment of the post war foreign exchange system that remained intact until the early 1970s. The conference resulted in the formation of the IMF. The system fixed currencies in a fixed exchange rate system with 1% fluctuations of the currency to gold or the dollar.

Broken Dates: Deals that are undertaken for value dates that are not standard periods e.g. 1 month. The standard periods are 1 week, 2 weeks, 1,2,3,6, and 12 months. Terms also used are odd dates, or cock dates, or broken period.

Broker: An agent, who executes orders to buy and sell currencies and related instruments either for a commission or on a spread. Brokers are agents working on commission and not principals. They do not act on their own account. In the foreign exchange market brokers tend to act as intermediaries between banks for a commission paid by the initiator or by both parties.

Buying Rate: Rate at which a bank is prepared to buy foreign exchange. Also known as the Bid Rate.

Buying Selling FX: Buying and selling in the foreign exchange market always happens in the currency which is quoted first. 'Buy dollar/mark' means buy the dollar/sell the mark. Traders buy when they expect a currency's value to rise and sell when they expect a currency to fall.

Cable/Sterling: A term used in the foreign exchange market for the US Dollar/British Pound rate.

Call Option: (1) An option that gives the holder the right to buy the underlying instrument at a specified price during a fixed period. (2) The right of a bond issuer to pre-pay debt and demand the surrender of its bonds.

Calendar Spread: An option position comprised of purchase and sale of two option contracts of the same type with different expiration dates at the same exercise price.

Calendar Combination: A compound option strategy which consists of simultaneous buying of a longer-term straddle and near term straddle with a common strike price.

Candlestick Chart: A type of chart which consists of four major prices: high, low, open, close. The body of the candlestick bar is formed by the opening and closing prices. To indicate that the opening was lower than the closing, the body of the bar is left blank. If the currency closes below its opening , the body is filled. The rest of the range is marked by two 'shadows': the upper shadow and the lower shadow.

Capital Account: Account reflecting changes in country ownership of the long term and short term financial assets.

Carry: The interest cost of financing securities or other financial instruments held.

Carry-Over Charge: A finance charge associated with the storing of commodities (or foreign exchange contracts) from one delivery date to another.

Cash Settlement: A procedure for settling futures contract where the cash difference between the future and the market price is paid instead of physical delivery.

Central Bank: A central bank provides financial and banking services for a country's government and commercial banks. It implements the government's monetary policy, as well, by changing interest rates.

Central Rate: Exchange rates against the ECU adopted for each currency within the EMS. Currencies have limited movement from the central rate according to the relevant band.

CHIPS: (Clearing House Inter-bank Payment System) A computerized system used for foreign exchange dollar settlements among participating banks.

CHAPS: Clearing House Automated Payment System.

Chartist: An individual who studies graphs and charts of historic data to find trends and predict trend reversals which include the observance of certain patterns.

Closed Position: A transaction which leaves the trade with a zero net commitment to the market with respect to a particular currency.

Closing Purchase Transaction: The purchase of an option identical to one already sold to liquidate a position.

Comparative Advantage: Theory suggesting that specialization by countries can increase worldwide production and welfare.

Compensatory Financing Facility: Facility that attempts to reduce the impact of export instability on country economies.

Consignment: Arrangement in which the exporter ships goods to the importer while still retaining title to the merchandise.

Contingency Graph: Graph showing the net profit to a speculator in currency options under different exchange rate scenario.

Correlation: A statistical measure referring to the relationship between two or more variables (events, occurrences etc.). A correlation between two variables suggests some degree of association.

Cost of Carry: The interest rate parity, where the forward price is determined by the cost of borrowing money in order to hold the position.

Counter-Purchase: Exchange of goods between two parties under two distinct contracts expressed in money terms.

Counter Trade: Sale of goods to one country which is linked to the purchase of goods from the same country.

Country Risk: Characteristics of the host country that can affect the MNC's cash flows.

Covered Interest Rate Arbitrage: An arbitrage approach which consists of borrowing currency A, exchanging it for currency B, investing currency B for the duration of the loan, and, after taking off the forward cover on maturity, showing a profit on the entire set of deals.

Cross-Rate: The exchange rate between currency A and currency B, given the values of both with respect to a third currency.

Cross-Hedging: Hedging an open position in one currency with a hedge on another currency that is highly correlated with the first currency.

Currency Board: System of maintaining the value of local currency with respect to some other specified currency.

Day Trader: Speculators who take positions in commodities which are then liquidated prior to the close of the same trading day.

Deal Ticket/Deal Slip: The primary method of recording the basic information relating to a transaction.

Dealer: An individual or firm acting as a principal, rather than as an agent, in the purchase and/or sale of securities. Dealers trade for their own account and risk.

Dealing Systems: On-line computers which link the contributing banks around the world on a one-on-one basis.

Declaration Date: The latest day or time by which the buyer of an option must indicate to the seller his intention to the option.

Delivery Date: The date of maturity of the contract, when the exchange of the currencies is made. This date is more commonly known as the value date in the FX or Money markets.

Delivery Month: The calendar month in which a futures contract comes to maturity and becomes deliverable.

Delivery Points: Those locations designated by futures exchanges at which the currency represented by a futures contract may be delivered in fulfilment of the contract.

Delivery Risk: A term to describe when a counterparty will not be able to complete his side of the deal, although willing to do so.

Delivery: The settlement of a futures contract by receipt or tender of a financial instrument or currency.

Delphi Technique: Collection of independent opinion without group discussion by the assessors who provide the opinion. This is used for various types of assessment, e.g., country risk.

Devaluation: A downward adjustment of a currency against its fixed parities or bands, normally by formal announcement by the central bank.

Delta: The change in the value of the option premium made fully paid by the capitalization of reserves and given relative to the instantaneous change in the value of the underlying instrument, expressed as a coefficient.

Direct Quotation: Quoting in fixed units of foreign currency against variable amounts of the domestic currency.

Discount Rate: The interest rate at which eligible depository institutions may borrow funds directly from the Federal Reserve Banks. This rate is controlled by the Federal Reserve and is not subject to trading.

Double: An option either to buy or sell an instrument or currency at a specified price. The exercise of the right to sell causes the right to buy to expire and vice versa.

Durable Goods Order: An economic indicator which measures the changes in sales of products with a life span in excess of three years.

Dynamic Hedging: Strategy of hedging in those periods when existing currency positions are expected to be adversely affected, and remaining non-hedged in other periods when currency positions are expected to remain favourable.

Economic Exposure: Reflects the impact of foreign exchange changes on the future competitive position of a company.

Elliot Wave Principle: A system of empirically derived rules for interpreting action in the markets. It refers to a five-wave/three-wave pattern which forms one complete bull market/bear market cycle of eight waves.

Economic and Monetary Union (EMU): The irrevocable fixing of exchange rates between member currencies and their replacement by a single European currency, the Euro. The Euro is to be issued by a future European central bank, to be independent of political control and federal in nature. All countries which fulfil the five convergence criteria in 1998 will proceed to EMU in 2000. The UK and Denmark have secured opt-outs from EMU. Sweden's joining is subject to ratification by parliament.

European Currency Unit: A basket of the member currencies. As a composite unit, the ECU consists of all the European Community currencies, which are individually weighted. It was created by the European Monetary System with the eventual goal of replacing the individual European member currencies.

Euro: The currency of the European Union (EU) that has replaced ECU, and it is the legal tender of 11 countries within EU. Originally 1 unit of Euro was constituted with 0.6242 unit of Deutsche mark, 1.332 unit of French franc, 0.08784 unit of British pound, 151.8 of lira, 0.2198 Dutch guilder, 3.301 Belgian franc, 6.885 peseta, 0.1976 Danish krone, 0.00855 Irish punt, 1.393 Portuguese escudo, 1.44 Greek drachma and 0.13 Luxembourg franc.

Euro Banks: Commercial banks that participate as financial intermediaries in the Euro currency market.

Eurobonds: Bonds sold in countries other than the country represented by the currency in which these are denominated.

Euro-Clear: Telecommunications network that informs all traders about outstanding issues of Eurobonds for sale.

European Monetary System: A EU system designed to create a zone of monetary stability in Europe, control inflation and coordinate exchange rate policy of member countries with single currency Euro.

European Union: An economic group of 15 European nations — Austria, Belgium, Denmark, Finland, France, Germany, Great Britain, Greece, the Netherlands, Ireland, Italy, Luxembourg, Portugal, Spain and Sweden. Except Great Britain, Sweden and Denmark, 12 countries have now common currency Euro.

Exercise Notice: A formal notification that the holder of an option wishes to exercise it by buying or selling the underlying stock at the exercise price.

Exercise Price (Strike Price): The price at which an option may be exercised.

Expiry Date: The last day on which the holder of an option can exercise his right to buy or sell the underlying security.

Exposure: The total amount of money loaned to a borrower or country. Banks set rules to prevent overexposure to any single borrower. In trading operations, it is the potential for running a profit or loss from fluctuations in market prices.

FASB #8 (Financial Accounting Standards Board's Statement Number 8): The original accounting rules regarding foreign exchange were standardized in 1975, which set the procedures for foreign currency translations into US Dollars in the consolidated balance sheets of US multinational corporations.

Fed Wire: An automated communications and settlement system linking the Federal Reserve banks with other banks and with depository institutions.

Fill or Kill: An order which must be entered for trading, normally in a pit three times, if not filled is immediately cancelled.

Finex: A currency market part of the New York Cotton Exchange (NYCE), the oldest futures exchange in New York. Futures on the European Currency Unit and the USDX a basket of 10 currencies are listed in the exchange.

Flat Rate: When both the spot rate and the forward rate of a currency are the same in the market, this term is used.

Foreign Exchange Centres: London is the largest centre of foreign exchange trading. New York, Tokyo, Singapore, Zurich and Hong Kong are also important.

Foreign Exchange-Market: Market where currencies are traded internationally. About a trillion dollars-worth of foreign exchange is traded globally every day, making forex larger than all bond markets put together. Currency markets exist in the form of spot, forward, futures and options markets.

Forward Forward: A forward / forward deal is one where both legs of the deal have value dates greater than the current spot value date.

Forward Outright: Foreign exchange deal which matures on any day past the spot delivery date.

Forward Rate: Forward rates are quoted in terms of forward points, which represents the difference between the forward and spot rates. In order to obtain the forward rate from the actual exchange rate the forward points are either added or subtracted from the exchange rate.

Forward Spread (forward points or forward pips): Forward price used to adjust a spot price to calculate a forward price. It is based on the current spot exchange rate, interest rate differential and the number of days to delivery.

Futures: Exchange-traded contracts. They are firm agreements to deliver (or take delivery of) a standardized amount of something on a certain date at a predetermined price. Futures exist in currencies, money market deposits, bonds, shares and commodities.

G-7 (Group of Seven): The seven leading industrial countries: The United States, Germany, Japan, France, United Kingdom, Canada, and Italy.

Gap: The price gap between consecutive trading ranges (i.e. the low of the current range is higher than the high of the previous range)

Globex: A system for global after hours electronic trading in futures and options developed by Reuters for CME and CBOT for use in conjunction with various exchanges around the world.

Gold Standard: The original system for supporting the value of currency issued. The way that where the price of gold is fixed against the currency it means that the increased supply of gold does not lower the price of gold but increases the money supply.

Gold Tranche: Part of the country quota for IMF members that had to be paid in gold. This was normally 25% of the quota, the remainder being in domestic currency. The Gold Tranche was automatically available to members without condition.

Golden Cross: It is an intersection of two consecutive moving averages which move in the same direction and suggest that the currency will move in the same direction.

Good Until Cancelled: An instruction to a broker that unlike normal practice the order does not expire at the end of the trading day, although normally terminates at the end of the trading month.

Gross Settlement: A process where full payment of each transaction is made rather than clearing a group of transactions as currently occurs in the FX market. A method designed to eliminate capital risk.

Gross Domestic Product: Total value of a country's output, income or expenditure produced within the country's physical borders.

Gross National Product: Gross domestic product plus 'factor income from abroad' — income earned from investment or work abroad.

Hard Currency: It is a currency whose value is expected to remain stable or increase in terms of other currencies.

Head and Shoulders: A pattern in price trends which chartist consider indicates a price trend reversal. The price rises for some time, at the peak of the left shoulder, profit taking has caused the price to drop. After that price rises steeply again to the head before more profit taking causes the price to drop to around the same level as the shoulder.

Hedging: A strategy used to offset market risk, whereby one position protects another.

Hedge Ratio: The number of futures or options required to hedge a given exposure in the cash market.

ICCH: International Commodities Clearing House Limited, a clearing house based in London operating world wide for many futures markets.

IFEMA: International Foreign Exchange Master Agreement.

IMF (International Monetary Fund): It is established in 1946 to provide international liquidity on a short and medium term and encourage liberalization of exchange rates. The IMF supports countries with balance of payments problems with the provision of loans.

IMM: International Monetary Market part of the Chicago Mercantile Exchange that lists a number of currency and financial futures.

Implied Volatility: A measurement of the market's expected price range of the underlying currency futures based on the traded option premiums.

Implied Volatility Skews: The implied volatility varies for different strikes of an option.

Implied Rates: The interest rate determined by calculating the difference between spot and forward rates.

In-the-Money: A call option is in-the-money if the price of the underlying instrument is higher than the exercise/strike price. A put option is in-the-money if the price of the underlying instrument is below the exercise/strike price.

Inconvertible Currency: This is currency which cannot be exchanged for other currencies, because this is forbidden by the foreign exchange regulations.

Index Linking: The process of linking wages, social benefits payments, prices, interest rates or loan values to an economic index, usually of prices.

Indicative Quote: A market-maker's price which is not firm.

Industrial Production Index: A coincident indicator measuring physical output of manufacturing, mining and utilities giving a comparative position over the years.

Inflation: Continued rise in the general price level in conjunction with a related drop in purchasing power.

Initial Margin: The margin is a returnable deposit required to be lodged by buyers and sellers with the clearing house to secure a new futures or options position.

Instruction: The specification of the banks at which funds shall be paid upon settlement.

Inter-bank Rates: The bid and offer rates at which international banks place deposits with each other. This is the basis of the Inter-bank market.

Inter-dealer Broker: A specialist broker who acts as an intermediary between market-makers who wish to buy or sell securities to improve their book positions, without revealing their identities to other market-makers.

Interest Arbitrage: Switching into another currency by buying spot and selling forward, and investing proceeds in order to obtain a higher interest yield. Interest arbitrage can be inward, i.e. from foreign currency into the local one or outward, i.e. from the local currency to the foreign one.

Interest Parity: One currency is in interest parity with another when the difference in the interest rates is equalized by the forward exchange margins. For instance, if the operative interest rate in Japan is 3% and in the UK 6%, a forward premium of 3% for the Japanese yen against sterling would bring about interest parity.

Interest Rate Options: An agreement permitting a party to obtain a particular interest rate, issued both by OTC and by exchanges.

Interest Rate Cap: An agreement that provides the buyer of a cap with a maximum interest rate for future borrowing requirements.

Interest Rate Collar: A combination of a cap and a floor to provide maximum and minimum interest rates for borrowing or lending.

Interest Rate Floor: An agreement which provides the buyer of the floor with a minimum interest rate for future lending requirements.

Interest Rate Swap: An agreement to swap interest rate exposures from floating to fixed or vice versa. There is no swap of the principal. It is the interest cash flows be they payments or receipts that are exchanged.

Intervention: Action by a central bank to effect the value of its currency by entering the market. Concerted intervention refers to action by a number of central banks to control exchange rates.

Intra-Day limit: Limit set by bank management on the size of each dealer's Intra Day Position.

Intra-Day Position: Open positions run by a dealer within the day. Usually this is squared by the close of the market.

Intrinsic Value: The amount by which an option is in-the-money. The intrinsic value is the difference between the exercise/strike price and the price of the underlying security.

Inverted Market: Where short term instruments are trading at premiums to long term instruments.

J Curve: A term describing the expected effect of a devaluation on a country's trade balance. It is anticipated that import bills rise before export orders and receipts increase. The result is an initial worsening of balance of trade position, and then it improves. This creates a time path that looks like the alphabet "J".

Jawbone: Announcements and statements by politicians or monetary authorities to influence decisions by business, consumer, or trade union sectors, often associated with forecasts and policy implications.

Jurisdiction Risk: (1) The risk inherent in placing funds in the Centre where they will be under the jurisdiction of a foreign legal authority, or, (2) The risk in making a loan subject to the laws of another country.

Kappa: A measure of the sensitivity of the price of an option to a change in its implied volatility (k).

Key Currency: Small countries, which are highly dependent on exports, orientate their currencies to their major trading partners, the constituents of a currency basket.

Kiwi: Slang for the New Zealand dollar.

Knock In: A process where a barrier option (European) becomes active as the underlying spot price is in the money. Knock out has a corresponding meaning although the option may permanently cease to exist.

Ladder: Dealers analysis of the forward book or deposit book showing every existing deal by maturity date, and the net position at each future date arising.

Lagging Indicator: A measure of economic activity which tends to change after change has occurred in the overall economy e.g. CPI.

Lapsed Rights: Rights for which call payments have not been made by the acceptance date.

Last Trading Day: The day on which trading ceases for an expiring contract.

Lay Off: To carry out a transaction in the market to offset a previous transaction and return to a square position.

Leading Indicators: Statistic that are considered to precede changes in economic growth rates and total business activity, e.g. factory orders.

Leads and Lags: The effect on foreign trade payments of an anticipated move in the exchange rate, normally a devaluation. Then payment of imports is faster and export receipts is slowed down.

Left-hand Side: Taking the left hand side of a two way quote i.e. selling the quoted currency.

Letter of Credit (LC): Agreement by a bank to make payments on behalf of a specified party under specified conditions, everything explicit on the contract.

Leverage: In options terminology, this expresses the disproportionately large change in the premium in terms of the relative price movement of the underlying instrument.

Liability: In terms of foreign exchange, the obligation to deliver to a counterparty an amount of currency either in respect of a balance sheet holding at a specified future date or in respect of an unmatured forward or spot transaction.

LIBOR: The London Inter-bank Offered Rate, the rate charged by one bank to another for lending money.

Life of Contract: The period between the beginning of trading in a particular future and the expiration of trading.

LIFFE: London International Financial Futures Exchange.

Limit Down: The maximum price decline from the previous trading day's settlement price permitted in one trading session.

Limit Move: A price that has advanced or declined the permissible limit permitted during one trading session.

Limit Order: An order to buy or sell a specified amount of a security at a specified price or better.

Limit Up: The maximum price advance from the previous trading day's settlement price permitted in one trading session.

Limit: (1) The maximum price fluctuation permitted by an exchange from the previous session's settlement price for a given contract. (2) In international banking the limit a bank is willing to lend in a country. (3) The amount that one bank is prepared to trade with another. (4) The amount that a dealer is permitted to trade in a given currency.

Limited Convertibility: When residents of a country are prohibited from buying other currencies even though non-residents may be completely free to buy or sell the national currency.

Lines: An arrangement by which a bank agrees to lend to the line holder during some specified period any amount up to the full amount of the line.

Liquidation: Any transaction that offsets or closes out a previously established position.

Liquidity: The ability of a market to accept large transactions.

Local: A futures trader who normally trades on an exchange on his/her own account.

Locked Market: A market is locked when the bid price equals the asked price.

Long Dated Shorts: A forward purchase and sale with a brief uncovered position between them. This may also be referred to as long short dates.

Long Position: The holding of an excess of a particular currency.

Long Hedge: The purchase of futures contracts for price protection purposes, as a defensive position against an increase in cash prices, or falling interest rates.

Louvre Accord: The 1987 Agreement between countries to attempt to stabilize the value of US dollar.

Maintenance Margin: The minimum margin which an investor must keep on deposit in a margin account at all times in respect of each open contract.

Make a Market: A dealer is said to make a market when he or she quotes bid and offer prices at which he or she stands ready to buy and sell.

Managed Float: When the monetary authorities intervene regularly in the market to stabilize the rates or to aim the exchange rate in a required direction.

Margin: (1) Difference between the buying and selling rates, also used to indicate the discount or premium between spot or forward. (2) For options the sum required as collateral from the writer of an option. (3) For futures a deposit made to the clearing house on establishing a futures position account. (4) The percentage reserve required by the US Federal Reserve to make an initial credit transaction.

Margin Call: A demand for additional funds to be deposited in a margin account to meet margin requirements because of adverse future price movements.

Marginal Risk: The risk that a customer goes bankrupt after entering into a forward contract. In such an event the issuer must close the commitment running the risk of having to pay the marginal movement on the contract.

Mark to Market: The daily adjustment of an account to reflect accrued profits and losses often required to calculate variations of margins.

Market Amount: The minimum amount conventionally dealt for between banks.

Market Maker: A market maker is a person or firm authorized to create and maintain a market in an instrument.

Market Order: An order to buy or sell a financial instrument immediately at the best possible price.

Marshall–Lerner Condition: A model that states that if the sum of the elasticity of demand for a country's exports and that of the imports exceed one, then devaluation will have a positive effect upon the trade balance.

Marry: Where a dealer is able to match two customer deals which offset one another.

Matched Book: If the distribution of the maturities of a banks liabilities equal that of its assets, it is said to be running a matched book.

Matching: The process of ensuring that purchases and sales in each currency and deposits given and taken in each currency are in balance, by amount and maturity.

Matching Systems: Electronic Systems duplicating the traditional brokers market. A price shown by a bank is available to all trades.

Maturity Date: (1) The last trading day of a futures contract. (2) Date on which a bond matures, at which time the face value will be returned to the purchaser. Sometimes the maturity date is not one specified date but a range of dates during which the bond may be repaid.

Mid-price or Middle Rate: The price half-way between the two prices, or the average of both buying and selling prices offered by the market makers.

Minimum Price Fluctuation: The smallest increment of market price movement possible in a given futures contract.

Minimum Reserve: Reserves required to be deposited at central banks by commercial banks and other financial institutions. Sometimes it is referred to as Registered Reserves.

Mismatch: (1) A mismatch between the interest rate maturities of a banks assets and liabilities. (2) Forward purchases differ in the value date from the forward sales in a given currency.

MITI: Japanese ministry of International Trade & Industry.

Monetarism: A school of economics which believes that strict control of money supply is the principal tool for implementing monetary policy, especially against inflation. Main proponent comes from University of Chicago.

Monetary Base: Currency in circulation plus banks' required and excess deposits at the central bank.

Monetary Easing: A modest loosening of monetary constraint by changing interest rate, money supply, deposit ratios.

Monetary Policy: A central bank's management of a country's money supply. Economic theory underlying monetary policy suggests that controlling the growth of the amount of money in the economy is the key to controlling prices and therefore inflation.

Monetary Union: An agreement between countries to maintain a fixed exchange rate between their currencies. It is a process which the EMS is intended to lead to, especially after the Maastricht Treaty.

Money Market: A market consisting of financial institutions and dealers in money or credit who wish to either borrow or lend.

Money Market Operations: Comprises the acceptance and re-lending of deposits on the money market.

Money Supply: The amount of money in the economy, which can be measured in a number of ways. Standard measures are M1, M2, M3. While M1 includes currency with public and demand deposits in banks, M3 includes M1 plus term deposits. Of course there are small variations in other countries.

Most Favoured Nation (MFN) status: An undertaking to give the rate of tariff concession offered to members of the GATT. More concessionaire rates can exist.

Moving Average: A way of smoothing a set of data, widely used in price time series.

Naked Intervention: A central bank type of intervention in the foreign exchange market which consist solely of the foreign exchange activity. This has a monetary effect on the money supply and a long term effect on foreign exchange.

Narrow Money: Limited definition of money to include cash or near cash, i.e. M1.

Nearby Contracts: The closest active futures contracts, i.e. those that expire the soonest.

Negative Sloping Yield Curve: A yield curve where interest rates in the shorter dates are above those in the longer dates.

Netting: A process which enables institutions to settle only the net positions with one another at the end of the day, in a single transaction, not trade by trade.

Net Position: The number of futures contracts bought or sold which have not yet been offset by opposite transactions.

Next Best Price Stop-loss Order: A stop-loss order which must be executed after the request level was reached.

Nominal Quotation: Used in Futures markets to refer to the estimated price for a future month or date for which there is no bid, ask or trade price.

Nostro Account: A foreign currency current account maintained with another bank. The account is used to receive and pay currency assets and liabilities denominated in the currency of the country in which the bank is resident.

Note: A financial instrument consisting of a promise to pay rather than an order to pay or a certificate of indebtedness.

Notice Day: Any day on which notices of intent to deliver on futures contracts may be issued.

Odd Lot: A non standard amount for a transaction.

OECD: Organization of Economic Cooperation and Development- a club of rich nations like USA, Japan, Canada, Australia, New Zealand and all west European countries.

Offered Market: Temporary situation where offers exceed bid.

Offset: The closing-out or liquidation of a futures position.

Official Settlements Account: A US balance of payments measure based on movement of dollars in foreign official holdings and US reserves. Also referred to as reserve transaction account.

Omnibus Account: An account maintained by one broker with another in which all of the accounts of the former are combined and carried only in its name, rather than designated separately.

Open Interest: The total number of outstanding option or futures contracts that have not been closed out by offset or fulfilled by delivery.

Open Outcry: A public auction method of trading conducted by calling out bids and offers across a trading ring or pit and having them accepted.

Open Market Operations: Central Bank operations in the markets to influence exchange and interest rates.

Open Position: The difference between assets and liabilities in a particular currency. This may be measured on a per currency basis or the position of all currencies when calculated in base currency.

Option: A contract conferring the right but not the obligation to buy (call) or to sell (put) a specified amount of an instrument at a specified price within a predetermined time period.

Option Class: All options of the same type — calls or puts — listed on the same underlying instrument.

Option Series: All options of the same class having the same exercise/strike price and expiration date.

OTC: A market conducted directly between dealers and principals via a telephone and computer network rather than a regulated exchange trading floor. These markets have not been very popular.

Out-of-the-Money: A put option is out-of-the-money if the exercise/strike price is below the price of the underlying instrument. A call option is out-of-the money if the exercise/strike price is higher than the price of the underlying instrument.

Outright Deal: A forward deal that is not part of a swap operation.

Overhang: A holding of foreign exchange that is temporarily unable to be converted from the reserve currency into other reserve assets.

Overheated (Economy): Is an economy where high-growth rates placing pressure on production capacity resulting in increased inflationary pressures and higher interest rates.

Overnight Limit: Net long or short position in one or more currencies that a dealer can carry over into the next dealing day. Passing the book to other bank dealing rooms in the next trading time zone reduces the need for dealers to maintain these unmonitored exposures.

Overnight: A deal from today until the next business day.

Oscillators: Quantitative methods designed to provide signals regarding the overbought and oversold conditions.

Package Deal: When a number of exchange and/or deposit orders have to be fulfilled simultaneously.

Par: (1) The nominal value of a security or instrument. (2) The official value of a currency.

Paris: A term for USD / FRF Spot Rate.

Parity: (1) Foreign exchange dealer's slang for your price is the correct market price. (2) Official rates in terms of SDR or other pegging currency.

Parities: The value of one currency in terms of another.

Parity Grid: A term used in the context of the European Monetary System which consists of the upper, central and lower intervention points between member currencies.

Pegged: The date on which a dividend or bond interest payment is scheduled to be paid.

Payment Date: A system where a currency moves in line with another currency, some pegs are strict while others have bands of movement.

Petro-dollars: Foreign exchange reserves of oil producing nations arising from oil sales.

Philadelphia Stock Exchange (PHLX): The oldest US securities exchange which offers currency futures and options on currency futures.

Point (pip): (1) 100th part of a per cent, normally 10,000 of any spot rate. Movement of exchange rates are usually in terms of points. (2) One percent on an interest rate e.g. from 8%-9%. (3) Minimum fluctuation or smallest increment of price movement.

Portfolio Insurance: An option hedging strategy to protect long cash market positions.

Position: The netted total commitments in a given currency. A position can be either flat or square (no exposure), long, (more currency bought than sold), or short (more currency sold than bought).

Position Clerk: A clerk who assist the dealer in recording a dealers position and ensures that all deal tickets are completed and transferred to the back office or input into the books in a position keeping system.

Position Limit: The maximum position, either net long or net short, in one future or in all futures of one currency or instrument combined which may be held or controlled by one person.

Pre-Spot Dates: Quoted standard periods that fall between the transaction date and the current spot value date.

Premium: (1) The amount by which a forward rate exceeds a spot rate. (2) The amount by which the market price of a bond exceeds its par value. (3) Options, the price a put or call buyer must pay to a put or call seller for an option contract. (4) The margin paid above the normal price level.

Primary Reserves: Gold related monetary reserves, being gold, SDR, etc.

Prime Rate: (1) The rate from which lending rates by banks are calculated in the US. (2) The rate of discount of prime bank bills in the UK.

Principal: A dealer who buys or sells stock for his/her own account.

Producer Price Index: An economic indicator which gauges the average changes on prices received by domestic producers for their output at all stages of processing.

Profit Graph: A graphical representation of the profits to a given options strategy for different underlying asset prices.

Profit Taking: The unwinding of a position to realize profits.

Proxy Hedge: A term to describe when it is necessary to hedge against a currency where there is no market but it follows a major currency, the hedge is entered against the major currency.

Purchasing Power Parity: Model of exchange rate determination stating that the price of a good in one country should equal the price of the same good in another country, exchanged at the current rate. It is also known as the law of one price.

Put Option: A put option confers the right but not the obligation to sell currencies, instruments or futures at the option exercise price within a predetermined time period.

Put Call Parity: The equilibrium relationship between premiums of call and put options of the same strike and expiry.

Pyramiding: The use of cash generated by positive variation margins on a futures position to increase the size of the position, each reinvestment in successively smaller increments.

Quota: (1)A limit on imports or exports. (2) A country's subscription to the IMF.

Quote: An indicative price. The price quoted for information purposes but not to deal.

Random Walk Theory. An efficient market hypothesis, stating that prices move randomly versus their intrinsic value.

Rally: A recovery in price after a period of decline.

Range: The difference between the highest and lowest price of a future recorded during a given trading session.

Rate: (1) The price of one currency in terms of another, normally against USD (2) Assessment of the credit worthiness of an institution.

Ratio Spread: Buying a specific quantity of options and selling a larger quantity of out-of-the money options.

Ratio Calendar Spread: Selling more near-term options than longer maturity options at the same strike price.

Reaction: A decline in prices following an advance.

Realignment: Simultaneous and mutually coordinated re- and devaluation of the currencies of several countries. An activity that mostly refers to EMS activity.

Reciprocal Currency: A currency that is normally quoted as dollars per unit of currency rather than the normal quote method of units of currency per dollar. Sterling is the most common example.

Reinvestment Rate: The rate at which interest earned on a loan can be reinvested. The rate may not attract the same level of interest as the principal amount.

Repurchase Agreement (Repo Rate): Agreements by a borrower where they sell securities with a commitment to repurchase them at the same rate with a specified interest rate.

Reserve Currency: A currency held by a central bank on a permanent basis as a store of international liquidity, these are normally dollar, deutschemark, and sterling.

Reserves: Funds held against future contingencies, normally a combination of convertible foreign currency, gold, and SDRs. Official reserves are to ensure that a government can meet near term obligations. They are an asset in the balance of payments.

Reserve Requirement: The ratio of reserves to deposits, expressed as a fraction prescribed by national banking authorities, including the United States.

Reserve Tranche: The 25% of its quota to which a member of the IMF has unconditional access, and for which there is no obligation to repay.

Resistance Point or Level: A price recognized by technical analysts as a price which is likely to result in a rebound but if broken through is likely to result in a significant price movement.

Rescheduling: The renegotiation of the terms of existing debts. The term is usually used with reference to LDC debt. The term rescheduling is considered to be refinancing to avoid any implication of default. Major sovereign debt rescheduling for Brazil, and Mexico have been undertaken in recent years.

Reversal: It is process of changing a call into a put.

Revaluation: Increase in the exchange rate of a currency as a result of official action.

Revaluation Rate: The rate for any period or currency which is used to revalue a position or book.

Right-hand Side: To do a deal on the right hand side of a two way quote, normally to buy the currency and sell dollars.

Ring: An area on a trading floor where futures or equities are traded.

Risk/Return: The relationship between the risk and return on an investment. Usually, the more risk you are prepared to take, the higher the return you can expect. Depositing your money in a bank is safe and therefore a low return is regarded as sufficient. Investing in stock market exposes you to more risk (from capital losses) and so investors will expect a higher return.

Risk Factor: The risk factor (delta) indicates the risk of an option position relative to that of the related futures contract.

Risk Management: The identification and acceptance or offsetting of the risks threatening the profitability or existence of an organization. With respect to foreign exchange involves among others consideration of market, sovereign, country, transfer, delivery, credit, and counterparty risk.

Risk Position: An asset or liability, which is exposed to fluctuations in value through changes in exchange rates or interest rates.

Risk Premium: Additional sum payable or return to compensate a party for adopting a particular risk.

Risk Reversal: A combination of purchasing put options with the sale of call options.

Rollover: An overnight swap, specifically the next business day against the following business day (also called Tomorrow Next, abbreviated to Tom-Next).

Rollover Credit: Medium term credit with a variable interest rate, which is governed by the currently prevailing rates on the Euro market.

Round Trip: Buying and selling of a futures or options contract.

Running a Position: Keeping open positions in the hope of a speculative gain.

Scalping: A strategy of buying at the bid and selling at the offer as soon as possible.

SDR: Special Drawing Right. A standard basket of five major currencies in fixed amounts as defined by the IMF.

SEBI: Security and Exchange Board of India — it is a regulatory body for monitoring the activities of the stock exchanges.

Selling Rate: Rate at which a bank is willing to sell foreign currency.

Serial Expiration: Options on the same underlying futures being contract which expire in more than one month.

Series: All options of the same class which share a common strike price and expiration date.

Settlement Date: The date by which an executed order must be settled by the transference of instruments or currencies and funds between buyer and seller.

Settlement Price: The official closing price for a future set by the clearing house at the end of each trading day.

Settlement Risk: Risk associated with the non settlement of the transaction by the counter party.

Short/Short Position: A shortage of assets in a particular currency.

Short Contracts: Contracts with up to six months to delivery.

Short Covering: Buying to unwind a shortage of a particular currency or asset.

Short Forward Date/Rate: The term short forward refers to period up to two months, although it is more commonly used with respect to maturities of less than one month.

Short Sale: The sale of a currency futures not owned by the seller at the time of the trade. Short sales are usually made in expectation of a decline in the price.

Short-Term Interest Rates: Normally the 90 day rate.

Sidelined: A major currency that is lightly traded due to major market interest being in another currency pair.

SIMEX: Singapore International Monetary Exchange

SITC: Standard International Trade Classification. A system for reporting trade statistics in a common manner.

SOFFEX: Swiss Options and Financial Futures Exchange, a fully automated and integrated trading and clearing system.

Soft Market: More potential sellers than buyers, which creates an environment where rapid price falls are likely.

Sovereign Immunity: Legal doctrine which means that the state cannot be sued or have its assets seized.

Sovereign Risk: (1) Risk of default on a sovereign loan (2) Risk of appropriation of assets held in a foreign country. Split Date See <u>Broken Date</u>.

Spot: (1) The most common foreign exchange transaction (2) Spot or Spot date refers to the spot transaction value date that requires settlement within two business days, subject to value date calculation.

Spot Next: The overnight swap from the spot date to the next business day.

Spot Month: The contract month closest to delivery or settlement.

Spot Price/Rate: The price at which the currency is currently trading in the spot market.

Spot Week: A standard period of one week swap measured from the current value date of the currency spot rate.

Spread: (1)The difference between the bid and ask price of a currency. (2) The difference between the price of two related futures contracts. (3) For options, transactions involving two or more option series on the same underlying currency.

Square: Purchase and sales are in balance and thus the dealer has no open position.

Squawk Box: A speaker connected to a phone often used in broker trading desks.

Squeeze: Action by a central bank to reduce supply in order to increase the price of money.

Stable Market: An active market which can absorb large sale or purchases of currency without major moves.

Standard: It is a term sometimes used referring to certain normal amounts and maturities for dealing.

Stand by Credit: An arrangement with the IMF for draw downs on a 'need' basis. The term is sometimes more generally used.

Sterilization: It is a standard central bank activity in the domestic money market to reduce the impact on money supply for its intervention activities in the foreign exchange market.

Sterling Index: An index based on the movement of sterling against the major currency.

Sterling: British pound, otherwise known as cable.

Stocky: Market slang for Swedish Krona.

Stop Loss Order: Order given to ensure that , should a currency weaken by a certain percentage, a short position will be covered even though this involves taking a loss. Realize profit orders are less common.

Stop Out Price: US term for the lowest accepted price for Treasury Bills at auction.

Straddle: The simultaneous purchase/sale of both call and put options for the same share, exercise/strike price and expiry date.

Stagflation: Recession or low growth in conjunction with high inflation rates.

Strap: A combination of two calls and one put.

Strike Price: Also called exercise price. This refers to a price at which an options holder can buy or sell the underlying instrument.

Strip: A combination of two puts and one call.

Supply Side Economics: The concept is that tax cuts will boost investment leading to an increase in the supply of goods in the economy. To be compared with demand led Keynesian economics.

Support Levels: When an exchange rate depreciates or appreciates to a level where (1) Technical analysis techniques suggest that the currency will rebound, or not go below; (2) the monetary authorities intervene to stop any further downward movement.

Swap: The simultaneous purchase and sale of the same amount of a given currency for two different dates, against the sale and purchase of another. A swap can be a swap against a forward.

Swap Price: A price as a differential between two dates of the swap.

Swaption: An option to enter into a swap contract.

SWIFT: Society for World-wide Inter-bank Telecommunications is Belgian based company that provides the global electronic network for settlement of most foreign exchange transactions.

Swissy: Market slang for Swiss Franc.

Synthetics: Options or futures that create a position that is able to be achieved directly but is generated by a combination of options and futures in the relevant market. In foreign exchange a SAFE combines two forward contracts into a single transaction where settlement only involves the difference in values.

Technical Analysis: It is concerned with past price and volume trends and often with the help of chart analysis in a market in order to be able to make forecasts about future price developments of the commodity being traded.

Technical Correction: An adjustment to price not based on market sentiment but technical factors such as volume and charting.

Temporal Accounting: Method of determining accounting exposure which translates all balance sheet items at the current rate of exchange, not the one at the time the cost was incurred.

Tender: (1) A formal offer to supply or purchase goods or services. (2) In the UK the term for the weekly Treasury Bill issue.

Tenor: Maturity or number of days to maturity normally on bills of exchange.

Terms of Trade: The ratio between export and import price indices.

Theory of Elasticity: A model of exchange rate determination stating that the exchange rate is simply the price of the foreign exchange which maintains the BOP in equilibrium.

Threshold of Divergence: A safety feature for the EMS which creates an emergency exit for currencies which become the singular focus of various adverse forces. The threshold of divergence indicates that the specific country with the currency under pressure should take additional steps for stability.

Theta: A measure of the sensitivity of the price of an option to a change in its time to expiry.

Thin Market: A market in which trading volume is low and in which consequently bid and ask quotes are wide and the liquidity of the instrument traded is low.

Thursday/Friday Dollars: A US foreign exchange technicality. If the bank leaves the funds overnight and transfers them on Friday by means of a clearing house cheque then clearance is not until Monday, the next working day. Higher interest rates for this period are thus available.

Tick: A minimum change in price, up or down.

Tier One: A measure of a banks financial strength used by the BIS being the shareholders' equity available to cover actual or potential irredeemable and non-cumulative preference shares. It excludes, hybrid forms of capital such as fixed term stock, goodwill, and revaluation reserves. BIS has a minimum requirement of 4 percent on risk-weighted assets.

Tight Money: A condition where there is a shortage of credit as a result of monetary policy restricting the supply of credit normally through raising interest rates.

TIFFE: Tokyo International Financial Futures Exchange.

Time Decay: The decline in the time value of an option as the expiry approaches.

Time Value: That part of an option premium which reflects the length of time remaining in the option prior to expiration. The longer the time remaining until expiration, the higher the time value.

Today/Tomorrow: Simultaneous buying of a currency for delivery the following day and selling for the spot day, or vice versa. Also referred to as overnight.

Tombstone: Colloquial term for announcement in a publication that a loan or bond has been arranged.

Tomorrow Next (Tom Next): Simultaneous buying of a currency for delivery the following day and selling for the spot day or vice versa.

Trade-weighted Exchange Rate: The changes in the exchange rate against a trade weighted basket including the currencies of the county's principal trading partners.

Traded Options: Transferable options with the right to buy and sell a standardized amount of a currency at a fixed price within a specified period.

Transaction Date: The date on which a trade occurs.

Tranche: A portion of, specifically used for borrowings from the IMF.

Transaction: The buying or selling of securities resulting from the execution of an order.

Transaction Exposure: Potential profit and loss generated by current foreign exchange transactions.

Translation Exposure: The calculation of loss or profit resulting from the valuation of foreign assets and liabilities for balance sheet purposes, when consolidating into the base currency.

Treasury Bills: Short-term obligations of a Government issued for periods of one year or less. Treasury bills do not carry a rate of interest and are issued at a discount on the par value.

Turnover: The total money value of currency contracts traded is calculated by multiplying size by the number of contracts traded.

Two-Tier Market: A dual exchange rate system where normally only one rate is open to market pressure, e.g. South Africa.

Two-Way Quotation: When a dealer quotes both buying and selling rates for foreign exchange transactions.

Uncovered: Another term for an open position.

Under Reference (Order): Before finalizing a transaction all the details should be submitted for approval to the order giver, who has the right to turn down the proposal.

Under-Valuation: An exchange rate is normally considered to be undervalued when it is below its purchasing power parity.

Unload: Term for sale of assets or unwinding positions either to limit loss or to undermine other market participant's positions.

Unmatched Book: If the average maturity of a bank's liabilities is less than that of its assets, it is said to be running an unmatched book.

Unwind: Selling of assets and or instruments to square a position.

Up-Tick: A transaction executed at a price greater than the previous transaction.

USDX: Currency index which consist of the weighted average of the prices of ten foreign currencies against the U.S. Dollar: These are — Deutsche mark, Japanese yen, French franc, British pound, Canadian dollar, Italian lira, Dutch guilder, Belgian franc, Swedish krona, and Swiss franc.

U.S. Quote: Exchange rate quotation on a reciprocal basis. Also known as an American Quote.

Value at Risk: The expected loss from an adverse market movement.

Value-date: For exchange contracts it is the day on which the two contracting parties exchange the currencies. In the case of a spot transaction it is two business banking days forward in the country of the bank providing quotations which determine the spot value date.

Value Spot: Normally settlement for two working days from today.

Value Today: Transaction executed for same day settlement; sometimes also referred to as 'cash transaction.'

Vanilla: A simple option whose terms and conditions do not include any provisions other than exercise style, expiry and strike. To compare with exotic options which have additional terms.

Variation Margin: Profits or losses on open positions in futures and options contracts which are paid or collected daily.

Vega: Expresses the price change of an option for a one per cent change in the implied volatility.

Velocity of Money: The speed with which money circulates or turnover in the economy. It is calculated as the annual national income: average money stock in the period.

Vertical (bear or bull) Spread: The sale of an option with a high exercise price and the purchase (in the case of a bull) or the sale (in the case of a bear) of an option with a lower exercise price. Both options will have the same expiration date.

Visible Trade: Trade in merchandise goods as compared with capital flows and invisible trade.

Volatility: A measure of the amount by which an asset price is expected to fluctuate over a given period and it is normally measured by the annual standard deviation of daily price changes (historic). Can be implied from futures pricing, implied volatility.

Vostro Account: A local currency account maintained with a bank by another bank. The term is normally applied to the counterparty's account from which funds may be paid into or withdrawn, as a result of a transaction.

Weak–form Efficient: Description of foreign Exchange markets, implying that all historical and current exchange rates information is already reflected in the quote of prevailing exchange rate.

Whipsaw: Term for where a trader takes a position, then has to move against it, triggering stop-loss limits and liquidation of positions, then having to move in the original direction. Normally occurs in volatile markets.

Wholesale Money: Money borrowed in large amounts from banks and institutions rather than from small investors.

Wholesale Price Index: It measures changes in prices in the manufacturing and distribution sector of the economy and tends to lead the consumer price index by 60 to 90 days. The index is often quoted separately for food and industrial products.

Window-dressing: Where financial institutions or companies raise funds for specific reporting dates such as year ends to give the appearance of high liquidity.

Working Balance: Discretionary element in the monetary reserves of a central bank.

Working Day: A day on which the banks in a currency's principal financial centre are open for business. For FX transactions, a working day only occurs if the bank in both (all relevant currency centres in the case of a cross) are open.

Writer: The seller of a call or put option in connection with an opening position who receives a premium and who is required to perform if it is exercised.

WTO (World Trade Organization): Organization established to provide a forum for multilateral trade negotiations and to settle trade disputes related to the GATT accord.

Yield Curve: The graph showing changes in yield on instruments depending on time to maturity. This shows the relation between the short term interest rate and the long term one.

References

Aghion, P., Bacchetta, P. and A. Banerjee, Currency Crisis and Monetary policy in an economy with credit constraints, *European Economic Review*, June 2001, 45(7), 1121–50.

Aghion, P., Bacchetta, P. and A. Banerjee , A Simple Model of Monetary Policy and Currency Crisis, *European Economic Review*, May, 2000, 44 (4-6), pp 728-38.

Akelis, Stephen B., *Technical Analysis from A to Z*, Moscow, Diagramma, 1999.

Alexander, S. S., Effects of Devaluation on the Trade Balance, *IMF Staff Papers*, 2, April, 1952.

Argy, V., The Mundell-Fleming Model : Its Strength and Limitations, in V. Argy, *International Macroeconomics: Theory and Policy*, NY., Routledge, 1994.

Balassa, Bela, The Purchasing Power Parity doctrine: A Reappraisal, *Journal of Political Economy*, 72, December, 1964, 584-596 .

Bank for International Settlement (BIS), *International Banking and Financial Market Development*, Basle, November, 1991.

Bergin, Paul, and Robert Feenstra, Pricing-to-Market, Staggered Contracts, and Real Exchange rate Persistence, *Journal of International Economics*, 54, August, 2001, 333-59.

Betts, Caroline, and Michael B. Devereux, Exchange Rate Dynamics in a Model of Pricing–to- Market, *Journal of International Economics*, 50, February, 2000, 215-44.

Bhagawati, J. N. (ed), *Illegal transactions in Foreign Trade*, Asterdam, North Holland, 1974.

Bhagawati, J.N. *Anatomy and Consequences of Exchange Control Regimes* , Cambridge, MIT Press, 1978.

Black, S., "Seignorage", in J. Eatwell, M. Milgate and P. Newman (eds), *The New Palgrave Money* , New York, Norton, 1989.

Black, S. W., Exchange Policies for Less developed Countries in a World of Floating Rates, in D. M. Leipzig (ed), *The International Monetary System and the Developing Nation*, Washington D.C., 1976.

Black, F. and M. Scholes, The Pricing of Options and Corporate Liabilities, *Journal of Political Economy*, 81, May-June, 1973.

Blejer, M., Exchange Restriction and the Monetary Approach to the Exchange Ratio, in Frenkel and Johnson (1978).

Blejer, M. and A. Cheasty, The Measurement of Fiscal Deficits: Analytical and Methodological Issues, *Journal of Economic Literature*, 29 (4), December, 1991.

Branson, W.H., Asset Markets and Reserve Prices in Exchange Rate Determination, Institute of International Economic Studies, *Reprint Series No. 98*, 1977.

Bresman, H., Birkinshaw, J. and R. Nobel, Knowledge Transfer in International Acquisitions, *Journal of International Business studies*, 30(3), 1999, 439-462.

Buckley, P. and M. Casson, Analysing Foreign Market Entry Strategies: extending the internalization Approach, *Journal of International Business Studies*, 1998, 29 (2).

Cagan, P., "Hyperinflation" in J. Eatwell *et al* (eds.) , 1989, *op. cit.*

Calvo, G, L. Leiderman, and Carmen Reinhart, Inflows of Capital to developing Countries in the 1990s, *Journal of Economic Perspective*, 10(2), Spring, 1996, 126-36.

Calvo, G. and Carmen Reinhart, *Fixing for your Life*, Brookings Trade Forum 2000, 2001, 1-39.

————— , Fear of Floating, *Quarterly Journal of Economics*, 117, (2), 2002.

Cassel, G., Abnormal Deviations in International Exchange, *Economic Journal*, 28, December, 1918, 413–15.

Caves, R. E., *Multinational Enterprises and Economic Analysis*, Second Edition, 1996.

Chang, R., Financial Integration with and without International Policy Coordination, *International Economic Review*, 38 (3), 1997, 547-64.

Colbie, Robert V. and Thomas A. *Meyers, Encyclopaedia of Technical market Indicators*, Alpina Publishers, 1998.

Corsetti, G., and P Pesenti, Welfare and Macroeconomic Interdependence, *Quarterly Journal of Economics*, August, 2001.

Devereux, M. B., Exchange Rate Pass-Through, Exchange Rate Volatility, and Exchange Rate Disconnect, *NBER working Paper No. 8858*, NBER, April, 2002.

————— , Real Exchange Rates and Macroeconomics : Evidence and Theory, *Canadian Journal of Economics*, 30, 1997, 773- 808.

Dollar, D., Outward Oriented Developing Countries Really Do Grow More Rapidly: Evidence from 95 LDCs, 1976-85, *Economic Development and Cultural Change*, April, 1992.

Dooley, M.P. and P. Isard, The Portfolio Balance Model of Exchange Rates and Some Structural Estimates of the Risk Premium, *IMF Staff Papers, 30*, 1983, 683-92.

Dooley, M. P., A Survey of Literature on Controls over International Capital Transactions, *IMF Staff papers*, 43 (4), December, 1996, 639-687.

Dornbusch, R., Expectations and Exchange Rate Dynamics, *Journal of Political Economy*, 84, 1976, 1161-76.

Dornbusch, R., Special Exchange Rates for Capital Account Transactions, *NBER Working paper, No. 1659*, NBER, 1985.

Dornbusch, R. and S. Fischer, Exchange Rates and Current Account, *American Economic Review*, 70, 1980, 960-71.

Dornbusch, R. and J.A. Frankel, The Flexible Exchange Rate System: Experience and Alternatives, *NBER Working Paper, No. 2464*.

Dornbusch, R., Y.C. park and S. Claessens, Contagion: How it Spreads and How it can be stopped, Proceedings of the World Bank Conference on International financial Contagion, Washington D.C., Feb 3-4, 2001.

Duarte, Margarida, International Pricing in New Open- Economy Models, *Federal Reserve Bank of Richmond Economic Quarterly*, 87, Fall, 2001, 53-70.

Dunbar, Nicholas, Meriwether's Meltdown, *Risk*, October, 1998.

Edison, H. and J.T. Klovland, A Quantitative Reassessment of the Purchasing Power Hypothesis: Evidence from Norway and the United Kingdom, *Journal of Applied Econometrics*, 2, 1987, 209-33.

Edwards, F. R., Hedge Funds and the Collapse of Long-Term Capital Management, *Journal of Economic Perspectives*, 13(2), spring, 1999, 198-210.

Eichengreen, Barry, *Towards a New International Financial Architecture*, Institute for International Economics, Washington D.C. 1999.

Eichengreen, B., A. Rose, and C. Wyplosz, Contagious Currency Crisis, *Scandinavian Journal of Economics*, December 1996, 98(4).

Engel, Charles, real exchange Rates and Relative Prices: An Empirical Investigation, *Journal of Monetary Economics*, 32, August, 1993, 35-50.

Evans, M. and R. Lyons, Order Flow and Exchange Rate Dynamics, *Journal of Political Economy*, 110, 2002, 170-180.

Fischer , S. and W. Easterly, The Economics of the Government Budget Constraint, *World Bank Research Observer*, 5 (2), July, 1990.

Fischer, S., Seignorage and the Case for a National Money, *The Journal of Political Economy*, 90 (2), 1982, 295-313.

Fleming, J.M., Domestic Financial Policies under Fixed and under Floating Exchange Rates, *IMF Staff Papers*, 9 (3), November, 1962, 369-379.

Flood, Robert and P. Garber, Collapsing Exchange Rate Regimes: Some Linear Examples, *Journal of International Economics*, 17(1-2), 1984, 1-13.

Frankel, J. A., International Nominal Targeting (INT): A Proposal for Monetary Policy Coordination in the 1990s, *The World Economy*, 13(20, 1990, 263-73.

Frankel, J., S. Schmukler and L. Serven, Verifiability and the vanishing Intermediate Exchange Rate Regime, *Journal of Development Economics*, 66 (2), 2001, 351-386.

Frenkel, J. A., Flexible Exchange Rates, Prices and the Role of news: Lessons from the 1970s, *Journal of Political Economy*, 89, 1981, 665–705.

——————— , Global Transmission of Interest Rates: Monetary Independence and Currency Regime, *NBER Working Paper series*, Paper No. 8828, March 2002.

Frenkel, J and H. Johnson (eds.), *The Economics of Exchange Rates : Selected Studies*, Reading, Mass., Addison Wesley Publishing Co. 1978.

Fry, M. J., Money, *Interest and Banking in Economic Development*, Baltimore, John Hopkins University Press, 1988.

Gandolfo, Giancarlo, *International Finance and Open Economy Macroeconomics*, Heidelberg, Springer–Verlag, 2001.

Ganesh, S., Who is Afraid of Foreign Firms ? Current Trends in FDI, *Economic and Political Weekly*, March, 1997.

Gibson, Rajna, *Option Valuation: Analyzing and Pricing Standardized Option Contracts*, McGraw- Hill, New York, 1999.

Giovannetti, G., A Survey of recent Empirical Test of the Purchasing Power Parity Hypothesis, *Banca Nazionzle del Lavaro Quarterly Review*, 180, march, 1992, 81-101.

Goldberg, Pinelopi, and Michael Knetter, Goods Prices and Exchange Rates : What have we Learned? *Journal of Economic Literature*, 35, September, 1997, 1243-72.

Goldstein, M and Phillip Turner, *Banking Crises in Emerging Economies: Origin and Policy Options*, B.I.S. Economic Papers, No. 46, October, 1996.

Hamada, K., *The Political Economy of International Monetary Independence*, Cambridge, Mass, USA., MIT Press, 1985.

Hanke, S. H. and K. Schuler, *Currency Boards for Developing Countries*, San Francisco, ICG press, No. 9 in ICG Sector Study Series, 1994.

Hartmann, Phillip, *Currency Competition and Foreign Exchange Markets; the Dollar, the Yen and the Euro*, Cambridge University Press, Cambridge, 1998.

Hau, Harald, Exchange rate Determination: The Role of Factor Price Rigidities and Nontradables, *Journal of International Economics*, April, 2000, 50 (20, 421- 47.

Hausmann, R., Ugo Panniza, and Ernesto Stein, Why Do Countries Float the way They Float?, *Journal of Development Economics*, 66 (2), 2001, 387-414.

Hayek, F. A. Von, *Denationalisation of Money: An Analysis of the Theory and Practice of Concurrent Currencies*, London, Institute of Economic Affairs, 1976.

————, The Use of Knowledge in Society, *American Economic Review*, September, 1945.

Heller, H.R. and R. R. Rhomberg (eds.), *The Monetary Approach to Balance of Payments*, Washington, International Monetary Fund, 1977.

Hoover, Kevin D., *Causality in Macroeconomics*, Cambridge, Cambridge University Press, 2001.

Hume, David, (1739), *A Treatise of Human Nature*, Oxford, Clarendon Press, 1888.

————, (1754), *Essays: Moral, Political, and Literary*, Indianapolis, Liberty Classics, 1985.

Isard, P., *Exchange Rate Economics*, New York, Cambridge University Press, 1995.

Johnson, H., Tariffs and Economic Development: Some Theoretical Issues, *Journal of Development Studies*, Vol. 1, 1964.

Kaldor, N., The Effects of Devaluation on Trade in Manufactures, in *Further Essays on Applied Economics*, London, Duckworth, 1978.

Kenen, P. B., (ed), *Understanding Interdependence: The Macroeconomics of the Open Economy*, Princeton, Princeton University Press, 1995.

Keynes, J. M., Social Consequences of Changes in the Value of Money, in J. M. Keynes, *Essays in Persuasion*, New York, W. W. Norton, 1963.

Kindleberger, C., International Public Goods without International Government, *American Economic Review*, 76 (1), 1986, 1-13.

Kokko, A., Technology, market Characteristics and spillovers, *Journal of Development Economics*, 43, 1994.

Kumar, N., *Multinational enterprises and Industrial Organisation, The case of India*, Sage Publications, Delhi, 1994.

Kollmann, Robert, Incomplete Asset Markets and the Cross-Country Consumption Correlation Puzzle, *Journal of Economic Dynamics and Control*, May, 1996, 20 (5), 945-61.

Krugman, Paul, a Model of Balance of Payments crisis, *Journal of Money Credit and Banking*, August, 1979, 11(3), 311-25.

Krugman, P., Balance Sheets, the Transfer problem, and Financial Crisis, *International tax and Public Finance*, November, 1999, 6(4), 459-72.

Laidler, David, The Quantity Theory is Always and Everywhere Controversial–Why?, *Economic Record*, 67, December, 1991, 289-306.

Lincoln, A., *Many Free countries Have Lost Their Liberty, a Speech on the Sub treasury*, Springfield, Illinois, December 26, 1839.

Lucas, Robert E., Interest Rates and Currency Prices in a Two –Country World, *Journal of Monetary Economics*, November, 1982, 10 (3),

335-59.

Lyons, R. K. , Foreign Exchange: Macro Puzzles, Micro Tools, *Economic Review* , (Federal Reserve bank of San Francisco), 2002.

MacDonald, R., *Floating Exchange Rates: Theories and Evidence*, London, Unwin Hyman, 1988.

Marshal, A., *Money, Credit and Commerce*, London, Macmillan, 1924.

McCombie, J. and A. P. Thirlwall, East Asian Financial Crisis: Retrospect and Prospect, *Asia and Australasia: Regional Overview*, 3rd. Quarter, 1999, Economist Intelligence Unit.

McKinnon, R.I. , Mundell, the Euro, and the World Dollar Standard, *American Economic Review*, May, 2000.

————— , *Money in International Exchange*, New York, Oxford University Press, 1979.

————— , The Exchange Rate and Macroeconomic Policy: Changing Post war perceptions, *Journal of Economic Literature*, 19, June, 1981, 531–557.

Meese, R A. and K. Rogoff, Empirical Exchange Rate Models of the Seventies: Do they fit out of sample? *Journal of International Economics*, 14, 1983, 3-29.

Misselden, E., *The Centre of the Circle of Commerce*, London, J. Dawson for N. Bowne, 1623.

Mundell, R.A., *International Economics*, Macmillan, 1967.

————— , Capital Mobility and Stabilization Policy under Fixed and Flexible exchange Rates, *The Canadian Journal of Economics and Political Science*, 29 (4), 1963, 487-99.

————— , The Future of the Exchange Rate System, *Paper prepared for the Rocca de Salimbeni Conference*, Siena, Italy, November, 1994.

————— , What the Euro Means for the Dollar and the International Monetary System?, *Atlantic Economic Journal*, 26(3), September, 1998.

Murphy, John J., *Technical Analysis of Future Market: Theory and Practice*, Sokol, 1996.

Nandi, Sukumar, *International Money and Finance*, Samskriti, New Delhi, 2001.

————— , *International Money and Capital*, Business Publications Inc., Mumbai, 1999.

Nandi, Sukumar, *Growth , Financial Cycles and Bank Efficiency: An Analysis of Indian Money Market*, Business Publications Inc., Mumbai, 1998.

————— , *Essays on International Finance: The Indian Perspective*, National Institute of Bank Management, Pune, 1996.

Nandi, Sukumar, Exchange Rate Behaviour of Indian Rupee: A Cointegration Approach, *Journal of Indian School of Political Economy*, January-March, 1994.

————— , An Empirical Study of Demand for International Reserve, *Journal of Foreign Exchange and International Finance* (JFEIF), April-June, 1996.

————— , Exchange Rate of Indian Rupee and Price Level Behaviour in India, in D. K. Das (ed), *Trade ad Development: Experiences and Challenges*, New Delhi, Deep and Deep Publications, 1999.

————— , Hong Kong Dollar and Chinese Renminbi (RMB), Two Currencies in One country, JFEIF, July-September, 1998.

Nayyar, D., Transnational Corporations and Manufacturing exports from Poor Countries, *Economic Journal*, 88, 1978.

Neumann, M.J.M. , Seignorage in the United States: How Much Does the U. S. Government Make from Money Production?, *Federal Reserve Bank of St. Louis REVIEW*, 74 (2), March-April, 1992, 29-40.

Obstfeld, Maurice, The Global Capital market: Benefactor of Menace? *Journal of Economic Perspective*, 12 (4), Fall, 1998, 9-30.

————— , Rational and Self-Fulfilling Balance of Payments Crises, *American Economic Review*, March, 1986, 76, 72-81.

————— , The Logic of Currency Crises, *cahiers Economiques et Monetaires 43*, Bank of France, 1994, 189-213.

Obstfeld, Maurice, International Capital Mobility in the 1990s, in Peter Kenen (ed.), *Understanding Interdependence*, Princeton University Press, 1995.

Obstfeld, Maurice, and Kenneth Rogoff, New Directions for Stochastic Open economy Models, *Journal of International Economics*, 50, February, 2000, 117–53.

————— , Exchange Rate Dynamics Redux, *Journal of Political Economy*, 103, 1995a, 624-660.

Obstfeld, Maurice, and Kenneth Rogoff, The Intertemporal Approach to the Current Account, in, G. Grossman and K. Rogoff, (eds.), *Handbook of International Economics, vol. 3*, Amsterdam, North-Holland, 1995b.

————— , *Foundations of International Macroeconomics*, Cambridge, Mass., MIT Press, 1996.

————— , Risk and Exchange Rates, *Working Paper No. 6694*, National Bureau of Economic Research, August, 1998.

————— , New Directions for Stochastic Open Economy Models, *Journal of International Economics*, 50, 2000, 117- 153.

Officer, L.H., The Purchasing Power Parity Theory of Exchange Rates: A Review Article, *IMF Staff Papers*, 83, 1976, 1-60.

Pick, F., *Pick's Currency Yearbook*, Pick Publishing Corporation, New York, 1960, 1968.

Polak, J. J. , Monetary Analysis of Income Formation, *IMF Staff Papers*, 4, 1957.

Polak, J. J., The IMF Monetary Model : A Hardy Perennial, *Finance and Development*, December, 1997, 16-19.

————— , The IMF Monetary Model at Forty, *IMF Working Paper No. 97 / 49*, Washington D.C., April, 1997.

Porter, R.D. and R.A. Judson, The Location of the US Currency: How

Much is Abroad?, *Federal Reserve Bulletin*, October, 1996, 883—903.

Payne, R. , *Informed Trade in Spot Foreign Exchange market markets: An Empirical Investigation*, London School of Economics, (Typescript), 1999.

Reinhart, C. and V. Reinhart, What Hurts Most? G-3 Exchange Rate or Interest rate Volatility, *NBER working Paper No. 8535*, 2002.

Ricardo, David, *On the Principles of Political Economy and Taxation*, edited by Piero Sraffa, Cambridge, UK, Cambridge University Press, 1951.

Rogoff, Kenneth, The Purchasing Power Parity Puzzle, *Journal of Economic Literature*, 34, June, 1996, 647- 68.

Sachs, J. D., A. Tornell and A. Velasco, The Collapse of the Mexican peso: what have we learned? *Economic Policy*, 22, April, 1996, 15-63.

Sachs, J. D. and F. Larrain B., *Macroeconomics in the Global Economy*, Englewood Cliffs, Prentice Hall, 1993.

Samuelson, Paul, Theoretical Note on Trade Problems, *Review of Economics and Statistics*, 46, May 1964, 145-154.

Sargent, T., *Dynamic Macroeconomic Theory*, Cambridge, Harvard University Press, 1987.

Sarno, Lucio, Towards a New Paradigm in Open Economy Modeling: Where Do We Stand?, *Federal Reserve Bank of St. Louis Review*, 83 (3), May- June, 2001.

Stern, R., *Balance of Payments Theory and Economic Policy*, London, Macmillan, 1973.

Taylor, Alan, Potential Pitfalls for the Purchasing- Power–Parity Puzzle? Sampling and Specification Biases in Mean- Reversion tests of the Law of One Price, *Econometrica*, 69, March, 2001, 473-98.

Tobin, J., Agenda for International Coordination of Macroeconomic Policies, in *International Monetary Cooperation : Essays in honor of Henry C. Wallich*, Essays on International Finance, No. 169, Princeton, Princeton University Press, 1987, 61-69.

Triffin, R., *Gold and the Dollar Crisis: Yesterday and Tomorrow*, Essaays in International Finance, No. 132, Princeton University, December, 1978.

Ugur, Mehmet, Extensions on the Mundell–Fleming Model; Perfect capital mobility and Flexible Prices, in Ugur, M. (ed), *An Open Economy Macroeconomics Reader*, New York, Routledge, 2002, 42-50.

UNCTAD, *World Investment Report 1998: Trend and Determinants*, Geneva, UNCTAD, 1998.

UNCTAD, *World Investment Report 1999: Foreign Direct Investment and the Challenge of Development*, Geneva, 1999.

Wacziard, R., Measuring the Dynamic Gains From Trade, *World Bank Economic Review*, 15(3), 2001.

Wallich, H. C., Institutional Cooperation in the World Economy, in J. A. Frenkel and M. L. Mussa (eds), *The World Economic System :*

Performance and Prospects, Dover, MA., Auburn House, 1984.

Wang, J. Y. and M. Blomstrom, Foreign Investment and Technology Transfer: A Simple Model, *European Economic Review*, 36, 1992.

Williamson, J., A Survey of the Literature on the Optimal Peg, *Journal of Development Economics*, 11, 1982, 39-61.

Williamson, J., Democracy and the Washington Consensus, *World Development*, 21(8), 1993.

Williamson, J (ed), *Latin American Adjustment: How Much Has happened*, Washington D.C., Institute of International economics, 1990.

Williamson, J. and M. H. Miller, Targets and Indicators: A Blueprint for International Coordination of Economic Policy, *Policy Analysis in International Economics*, 22., Washington D.C. Institute for International Economics, 1987.

World Bank, *The East Asia miracle: Economic Growth and Public Policies*, Washington DC. World Bank, 1993.

Index

A

Absorption approach, 63–65
American option, 242
Arbitrage
    on interest, 90–91
Arbitrage incentive, 166
Asian crisis, 256–257
Asset stripping, 277

B

Balance of payments, 63
Balance of payments adjustment
    Absorption approach, 63–65
    Elasticity approach, 62–63
    Monetary approach, 64 65
    Price-specie-flow mechanism, 53
Balassa–Samuelson theory, 111
Basle Committee, 29
Basket currency, 213–215
Basis point, 81
Beggar-thy-neighbour policy, 13
Bid-offer spread, 80–81
Black–Scholes Option pricing model, 250–52
Bretton woods agreement
    System, 12–22
    Recent changes, 28–31
    Par value system, 14

C

CAR (Capital Adequacy Ratio), 29
Capital mobility, 95–96
Chicago Board of Trade (CBOT), 158

Chicago Mercantile Exchange (CME), 158
Covered Interest Parity (CIP), 91–92
Contagion , 2–4, 260–61
Convertibility, 10
Crawling peg, 129
Currency basket, 213–215
Currency crises, 256–257
    And IMF plans, 261–265
    Contagion, 260–261
    First generation models, 258
    Second generation models, 258–259
    Third generation models, 259–260
Currency derivatives
    Future and forwards, 169–172
    Options, 249
    Swaps, 172–173
Currency Union, 128–129

D

Debt crisis, 326–329
Demonetization of gold, 25–26
Derivative and risk, 163
Disequilibrium models, 125–126
Dollarization, 148
    Effects on income, 151–155
    On monetary policy, 150
    And central bank independence, 149–150

E

Economic exposure, 162–163
European Central Bank(ECB), 46
European Union (EU), 43–44
ESCB (European System of Central banks), 49
Equilibrium exchange rate, 206
Euro, 44, 48–49
Eurodollar markets, 146–147
Exchange Rate
 Arrangement, 34–35
 Blackmarket, 217–221
Exchange rate determination
 Empirical studies, 205–213
 Micro structural approach, 120–122 , 275–76
 Overshooting model, 114–115
 Portfolio approach, 118–120
 Purchasing power parity, 108–111
 Interest parity model, 111–112
 Micro-structure model, 275–276
 Monetary approach, 112–114
Exchange rate dynamics
 And overshooting, 114–115

F

Feldstein–Horioka model, 95–96
Fischer effects, 92–93
Fixed exchange rate, 127
Foreign exchange market, 76–78
 Monetary intervention, 122–124
Forward contract, 168–169
 Covering, 168
 Discount, 168–169
 Premium, 169
Futures and forwards, 174–75

G

Globalization, 265–267
Global monetary objective, 266–267

Gold exchange standard, 11–12
Gold pool, 25
Gold standard, 9–12, 106–108
 Gold points, 9
 Mint parity, 107
Gold
 Demonetization of, 25–26
 Price-specie-flow mechanism, 53
Gresham's law, 193
Greenfield investment, 226–227
Group of Seven (G-7) countries, 38–39

H

Hedge
 Of currency risk, 90
Hedge Fund (LTCM), 322–3
Hedgers, 165
Horioka puzzle, 95–96
Hume's price-specie-flow mechanism, 53

I

International Monetary Fund (IMF), 16–37
 New changes, 35–38
 Measures for developing countries, 39–40
 Conditionalities for loan, 38
 Second Amendment, 29
Inconvertibility, 105
Interest rate differential, 92–93, 168-69
IBRD (International Bank for Reconstruction and Development), 14
International banking transactions, 136–139
International capital flows, 31–32
International Fisher effects, 92–93
International liquidity, 20–22
International monetary system
 Current nonsystem, 32–34, 41–42